THE
BOOK OF
SALSA

A book in the series

Latin America in Translation /

en Traducción / em Tradução

Sponsored by the

Consortium in Latin American Studies

at the University of North Carolina at Chapel Hill

and Duke University

THE
BOOK OF
SALSA

A CHRONICLE
OF URBAN MUSIC
FROM THE
CARIBBEAN TO
NEW YORK CITY

CÉSAR MIGUEL RONDÓN

TRANSLATED BY
FRANCES R. APARICIO
WITH JACKIE WHITE

The

University of

North Carolina

Press

Chapel Hill

Set in Arnhem and Spontan types by Tseng Information Systems, Inc.
Manufactured in the United States of America
Originally published in Spanish with the title *El libro de la salsa:
Crónica de la música del Caribe urbano*, © 1980 Editorial Arte,
Caracas, Venezuela

Translation of the books in the series Latin America in Translation /
en raducción / em Tradução, a collaboration between the Consortium in
Latin American Studies at the University of North Carolina at Chapel Hill
and Duke University and the university presses of the University of North
Carolina and Duke, is supported by a grant from the Andrew W. Mellon
Foundation.

The paper in this book meets the guidelines for permanence and durability
of the Committee on Production Guidelines for Book Longevity of the
Council on Library Resources.

Library of Congress Cataloging-in-Publication Data
Rondón, César Miguel.
[Libro de salsa. English]
The book of salsa : a chronicle of urban music from the Caribbean to New
York City / by César Miguel Rondón ; translated by Frances R. Aparicio with
Jackie White.
p. cm. — (Latin America in translation/en traducción/em tradução)
Originally published in Spanish: Caracas : Editorial Arte, 1980.
Includes discography (p.) and index.
ISBN 978-0-8078-3129-8 (cloth : alk. paper) —
ISBN 978-0-8078-5859-2 (pbk. : alk. paper)
1. Salsa (Music)—History and criticism. 2. Salsa musicians—Caribbean
Area. I. Aparicio, Frances R. II. White, Jackie. III. Title.
ML3475.R6613 2008
781.64—DC22   2007030141

A Caravan book. For more information, visit www.caravanbooks.org.

cloth   12 11 10 09 08   5 4 3 2 1
paper   12 11 10 09 08   5 4 3 2 1

CONTENTS

TRANSLATOR'S NOTE

César Miguel Rondón's *The Book of Salsa*, published here in English for the first time, is a transnational and pan-Caribbean history of the production, reception, and circulation of salsa music from the 1950s through the late 1970s. For this edition, Rondón, a Venezuelan journalist, writer, media personality, and salsa fan, has added a new chapter that brings the story up to the present. It is the only book-length and systematic study of the production, performances, styles, movements, and musicians within salsa music, not only in New York but also in Puerto Rico, Cuba, the Dominican Republic, and Venezuela.

While reggaeton and other fusion musics may have replaced and displaced salsa music as the central sonorous expression of many Latino Caribbean communities in the United States, salsa remains a symbolic popular discourse that is still profoundly meaningful for many U.S. Latinos. More interestingly, salsa music, now globalized, has become an exotic discourse that triggers new intercultural spaces on the dance floors of studios, ethnic festivals, parks, and nightclubs. It is time to introduce this foundational book to the United States and to the wider English-speaking world.

Salsa has been resignified and globalized and has struggled to keep its connections to the local Latino communities from where it emerged. Of course, there is a sense of loss because so many of the "big" salsa stars that Rondón examines in this book have died: Tito Puente, Ray Barretto, and Celia Cruz, among others. The musical and cultural losses embodied in the deaths of these musicians are considered in the new section written by Rondón for this translation. Of course, we can still enjoy the recordings of these figures, and in this sense, their music is immortal. However, it is also true that their physical absence from the stage creates new spaces for the younger generations who will, naturally, forge their own styles and their own musical identities.

The Book of Salsa reminds us how far we have come in the study and understanding of salsa music, particularly in the United States, where salsa music continues to trigger the intellectual curiosity of many scholars and aficionados. As a Venezuelan, however, Rondón offers his readers a unique Caribbean vantage point. First, he discusses the role of Cuba in the production and diffusion of salsa and Caribbean music overall, and he provides a critical look at the common Cuba-centric view of Caribbean music held in the United States. Rondón suggests that Cuba is often seen as the center of Caribbean music not only because so many cultural and artistic expressions found a common origin in Cuba but also because Cuba historically had the appropriate infrastructure for Cuban music to develop more fully. He argues that Venezuela likewise became an important site for salsa production and for musicians in the late 1970s, given its national resources and strong oil economy. In the new chapter, Rondón speaks to the importance of the Buena Vista Social Club phenomenon of recent years and the need for musicians of an older generation to be visible on stages all over the world. Rondón criticizes the policies of the Cuban government that impeded the dissemination of the old Cuban traditional music, such as the *son*. At the same time, he explains why Cuban music has been historically central to the development of salsa music in New York, without undervaluing the national meanings of other musical genres of the region, including the Dominican Republic, which is so typically ignored in discussions of Caribbean music.

Second, Rondón addresses the question, much debated in the United States, of whether salsa music is more than just old Cuban music. Rondón, for instance, courageously and riskily situates Celia Cruz outside the salsa style. He lucidly shows how her musical style and repertoire were truly a return to the Sonora Matancera performance style in Cuba. Yes, she brought this repertoire and style to the U.S. musical industry and inserted herself into the Fania salsa circuit, but this does not mean that she herself performed the new New York style of salsa; rather, Rondón says, she continued to reproduce and reinvent the old Cuban classics she knew so well. This agrees with Celia's own past public statements to the effect that salsa music did not really exist, but that it was old Cuban music recycled by the U.S. industry. In her case this truly was the case, but Celia was not the only singer and performer who represented salsa in the United States.

Third, Rondón strongly argues that salsa was created in New York, was characterized by the use of trombones (as in Eddie Palmieri's orchestra and influenced by Mon Rivera), and evolved in the 1960s from the Cuban big-band music and sound to the smaller ensembles that performed barrio salsa. Rondón discerns a meaningful and important shift from a Cuban music of entertainment to a music rooted in the ethnic and working-class experiences of Puerto Ricans and other Latinos in the New York barrios. Thus, Rondón defines salsa:

This novel music had three chief characteristics: (1) the use of the son as the main basis for its development (especially in the long and aggressive *montunos*); (2) arrangements that were modest in terms of harmonies and innovations but markedly bitter and violent; and (3) the imprint of the marginalized barrio. This was music produced not for the luxurious ballroom but for hard life on the street. Music no longer aimed to reach a general audience. Now its only world was the barrio, the same barrio where salsa music would be conceived, nurtured, and developed. That is where it all started.

This barrio life, according to Rondón, was truly transnational. His descriptions of how the challenges and difficulties of barrio life were shared by Latinos in New York as well as by poor Venezuelans in Caracas or by Puerto Ricans in San Juan explains the transnational circulation and successful reception of this music that was working-class in its origins.

Because *The Book of Salsa* was originally published in 1980, some historical contextualization may be helpful. While the book's very palpable critique of the music industry reflects a Latin American political stance that was typical of the 1970s, Rondón's assessment continues to carry weight today. Rondón's strong anti-imperial critique of the United States as a political presence in the Caribbean, whether through military intervention in the Dominican Republic or through the presence of pop music on television and radio, also reflects the ideologies of many Latin American intellectuals and cultural workers that were prevalent in the 1970s. Rondón accordingly views the authenticity of salsa music as a true expression of the spirit of a people, particularly of an oppressed minority in the United States. While nowadays a number of writers have demonstrated the complexities and contradictions of progressive popular music—which, in order to be distributed successfully, does have to be integrated into the industry's capital circuits of power and distribution—Rondón's passion for establishing the authenticity of salsa versus the industry's capitalist agendas is extremely pertinent today. While the complexity of the relationship between musicians and the industry that produces, records, and distributes their music is well known today, the sense that a specific musical style or trend does speak to a particular community of listeners is not effaced by that knowledge. That salsa was a popular music created by, listened to, danced to, and enjoyed by most Caribbean peoples speaks to the urgency that salsa embedded in its early years during the 1970s and even through today.

That salsa music was produced, as Rondón points out, by musicians who were perhaps not formally trained but who played by ear indicates the lack of access and resources that Puerto Rican working-class musicians in the United States, for example, faced and surely still face in today's world. The roughness, lack of sophistication, and unpolished sound of the salsa of Willie Colón, Ray Barretto, Héctor Lavoe, and others is measured, then, not as a deficiency—that is, against the more bourgeois values and standards of elite music—but as an outcome of the socioeconomic marginalization experienced by that community. At the same time, obviously, the music spoke to listeners in the larger urban community in New York as well as to larger Caribbean cohorts in other barrios throughout the region. Rondón's strong criticism of the industry, and particularly of the entrepreneurs and producers who sat behind their desks without studying or taking into consideration what listeners identify with, are still valid in today's music world. Rondón provides numerous examples of the failures of many recordings that were produced with only capital gain in mind rather than the authentic musical, social, and cultural values of the music or the musicians who produced it. In this sense, Rondón's use of the term "authentic," or "true," cannot be easily dismissed as a nostalgic return to the 1970s. It should, rather, be valued as a central criterion for assessing the impact of popular music throughout the various historical periods of its development. Salsa emerged and became national and transnational in a musical world now different from what it was in the 1970s, so while salsa may no longer be "authentic" in the way it was, it has now shifted to become a global music, one mediated mostly by the industry's dictates and by a fusion of diverse musical styles and genres. Andy Montañez's *Salsaron*, for example, illustrates new experimentation by older salseros with reggaeton interpreters.

Other significant topics that Rondón discusses in this book include the historical emergence of salsa music in New York City; gender issues in salsa addressing lyrics and individual female singers, including Celia Cruz and La Lupe; the importance of the *sonero*; the circulation of musicians and music between New York and Puerto Rico and other Caribbean countries; the *matancerization* trend; and the tensions between the traditional or "typical" (mostly older Cuban music) and modern or avant-garde forms. Also documented are the numerous groups, singers, and styles of salsa music that developed in the 1960s and 1970s, with a focus on the diverse instrumentations, arrangements, lyrics, and performance styles that emerged. Ultimately, to be sure, Rondón writes about all of the salsas, for he embraces the heterogeneous styles and performances of the myriad groups categorized within salsa, from New York to Venezuela, from Cuba to Puerto Rico, and even from the Dominican Republic to California.

Regarding the work of translating the book, all of the inevitable editing and adjustments that a translator must make were undertaken with the goal of not jeopardizing the style or content of the book. To honor the importance and consistency of the Spanish musical terms, including those for instruments and musical forms, such as *son*, *tumbadora*, *charanga*, rumba, and others, those terms were left in the original Spanish. When necessary, we noted and defined certain terms at their first appearance in the book in order to clarify for the reader their technical meanings. In addition to musical terms, cultural and social terms such as "barrio" and "sabor" were also left in Spanish. Neither "neighborhood" nor "ghetto" does justice to the semantic importance of the term "barrio" in Spanish for the working-class and poor Caribbean Latino communities.

I am pleased to offer readers *The Book of Salsa*. For helping to make it possible, I thank, first of all, Jackie White, who spent countless hours during the last two years working with me on the translation. Her passion for and commitment to the specificity of each phrase and the clarity of the expression were a true inspiration to me. Many thanks also to editor Elaine Maisner and the staff at the University of North Carolina Press for their interest in the original proposal and for their sustained support and hard work. I am also of course indebted to César Miguel Rondón himself and to his wife and agent, Floralicia de Rondón, for their generous assistance, for prompt answers to questions and queries, and for their enthusiasm throughout. My appreciation also to Marisol Berrios Miranda, who helped clarify musical terms and definitions in Spanish. Finally, my profound love and appreciation to John, my husband, and to Gaby and Camila, our daughters, for the patience, love, and understanding they have shown to me throughout the years, and to our new son, Alejandro, for the gift of life once more.

ONE :
SALSA ZERO
THE 1950S

Though located on Broadway and Fifty-third Street, an area famous for music and theater, the Palladium, an immense ballroom capable of holding a thousand couples on its dance floor, was in decline by 1947. It seldom filled to capacity as fewer and fewer white couples went there to dance the fox-trot, tango, and some of the old swing, the popular swaying rhythm that was easy on the feet and ears of its audience. At that time the Palladium's manager, a man named Moore, faced the challenge of turning the situation around and attracting dancers back to the ballroom. He contacted Federico Pagani, one of the city's most important promoters of Caribbean music, who was then the director of his own band, the Conjunto Ritmo. Moore felt that the solution was to be found in drawing in the Latino community, even though he feared a different problem could result: the blacks also would come down to Broadway with, in his mind, all of their bad habits, knives, and unbridled impulses.

By 1947, only one black Latin orchestra—Machito and his Afro-Cubans—had made its way into those venues of Broadway populated by white and predominantly Jewish dance audiences, and it did so with comfort and prestige. This orchestra had performed for several seasons at the Concord Hotel in the Catskills, and it had been able to please all audiences. In the midst of the bebop boom, Machito and his Afro-Cubans had had the luxury of merging Cuban rhythms with the harmonies and phrasings of avant-garde jazz. The result was the famous, and misnamed, "Latin jazz," a direct creation of Mario Bauzá, musical director of the Afro-Cubans and, as he himself put it, "father of the newborn."

Moore talked with Pagani and Bauzá. They agreed that Machito was the ideal alternative, the perfect solution for bringing the Caribbean to Broadway. But the risks were still high: the "lowlife," no matter what, would be the dancing audience. Believing that this could jeopardize a great opportunity for Latin music, Pagani suggested proceeding carefully and taking serious precautions. Their idea was to open a club, a special club that would offer Sunday afternoon dance concerts for the Hispanic community. Mario Bauzá christened it the Blen Blen Club.

"Blen blen" was the name of a successful musical composition by Chano Pozo, an extraordinary Cuban percussionist who, while playing with Dizzie Gillespie's band, had revolutionized the rhythmic and percussive concepts of the jazz trends of bebop. Pozo had been close friends with Bauzá ever since Miguelito Valdez had introduced the two of them in New

York, and it was Bauzá who then connected Pozo and Gillespie. Pozo had no objection to giving the new dance club the name of his composition, and so this meaningful name brought together, albeit briefly, the best of jazz with the best music of Cuba. Given that the New York community was basically Puerto Rican, it was somewhat odd that Cuba was the one country to impose its dance rhythms and dominate the scene.

The first dance matinee succeeded beyond anyone's expectations. The Palladium once again filled to capacity. For the first time ever, Latin orchestras were the stars, not the uncomfortable warm-up acts they had been reduced to by U.S. promoters of that era. The essence of the music was no longer hidden; the dancers perfectly deciphered the hidden codes of the authentic Caribbean dance, and the musicians, finally, could let themselves go. It took only a couple of weeks for the promoters to realize that the Sunday dances were not enough. They extended the Blen Blen Club hours to include Wednesday nights, and within a year, the Palladium was devoted exclusively to Afro-Cuban music.

Machito's orchestra, founded by Mario Bauzá in 1941, set the standards. It represented a perfectly fluid convergence of all the qualities that enlivened the city. Leader of the Cuban musicians in New York, Bauzá had arrived in 1930 as a member of the Azpiazu Orchestra, the same band with which the very famous Antonio Machín had performed. For ten years, Bauzá had worked with the most diverse and important jazz orchestras, developing his own styles and trends. In 1941, after leaving Cab Calloway's band, he started one of his own. Now Bauzá called on his childhood friend, Frank Grillo—known as "Machito"—and asked him to fuel the project and serve as its public image. It was "the most beautiful marriage ever," as Bauzá recalled, "each one had his own place, one on top and one on the bottom." From its first recordings, his orchestra influenced others, not only in the United States, but also in Cuba with such hits as "Sopa de pichón," "La paila," and "El ninche."

In 1943, Machito's sister, Graciela, a former member of the Anacaona all-female orchestra that had achieved success in Havana, joined Machito's band. Following their lead, all the bands in and outside New York that performed Afro-Cuban rhythms attempted to wed jazz with Caribbean music, a synthesis that would reach its heights during the 1950s in those same ballrooms of the already all-important Palladium.

Once the Palladium became wildly popular, it had to find orchestras that could match the sound and quality of Machito's Afro-Cubans. An audience was already in place and, more importantly, so was a venue where good music could be developed. The first orchestra to share the stage with Machito during the Blen Blen Club dances was the Picadilly Boys, a small

2

band led by Tito Puente, who was also playing timbales for Brazilian Fred Martin at the Club Copacabana. Puente, a graduate of the prestigious Juilliard School, added other musicians to the ensemble soon after it began playing the Palladium. The Picadilly Boys quickly became Tito Puente's Orchestra, a band of such renown that it established its own standards and following. In the mid-1950s, Puente was already known as the King of the Timbales, a recognition not only of his very special style of playing the instrument but also of his unique and effective way of bringing Afro-Cuban music into his arrangements.

The Palladium thus became a musical empire thanks to three orchestras—Puente's, Machito's, and the other Tito's, Tito Rodríguez's. Rodríguez was an extraordinary Cuban vocalist who broke with the modes and influences of Cuban singing and went on to become the most famous singer in the Caribbean. He began singing in a trio founded by his brother Johnny. He then worked his way through the diverse styles popular in the 1930s and 1940s. His first important gig in the United States was with the extraordinary band of Noro Morales, a virtuoso pianist who formerly had played with the orchestra of Chiquito Socarrás.

Singing in Morales's orchestra, Rodríguez began to polish his style with phrasings that eventually became classics in the articulation of the *son*[1] and the *guaracha*. By the end of 1946, when La Conga cabaret reopened on Broadway and Fifty-second Street (where the Casablanca would later be located), a musical duel between Machito's and José Curbelo's orchestras was announced. Curbelo, an experienced Cuban pianist who came from a long line of distinguished musicians, understood the importance of this challenge and bolstered his band with the two Titos, Puente and Rodríguez. This was the first and only time those two performed together, and soon after they took off in different directions.

Tito Rodríguez decided that it was time for him to form his own band. He began a small septet that subsisted in the modest and seedy clubs along and above Harlem's 110th Street, in what was already called the Latino barrio. As with the Picadilly Boys, once the Blen Blen Club had taken over the Palladium, Rodríguez's septet had the wonderful opportunity to play there. Rodríguez began playing short sets, insignificant fillers. His voice, however, already had something subtle and probing, an allure that was

---

1. The *son* is Cuba's most popular and traditional syncretic music and dance form. It emerged as improvised verses accompanied by the *tres* (a six-stringed guitarlike instrument), and it brings together Spanish and African musical elements. Later, it developed two sections: one song by the solo singer and the second sung by a chorus. During the 1920s, the son was performed by ensembles called *conjuntos* (sextets or septets) that gave it greater visibility and popularity.

bound to captivate any audience. While he had less formal knowledge of musical theory, especially in comparison with Bauzá or Puente, Rodríguez was obsessed with perfectionism—everything had to be in its place, in tune, on the beat, and above all, performed with sufficient *sabor*,[2] a special musical nuance or flavor. Because of this, when his septet became a full orchestra, a so-called Latin big band, Rodríguez considered himself an equal to Puente and Machito and was ready to challenge them. His band had the necessary power, and his voice was an unstoppable driving force. During this golden age, the Palladium became the site of many live recordings, and Rodríguez was the star of most of them. These recordings are still in circulation, and there is not a single one that does not deserve the praise of the most demanding music lovers.

In the 1950s, with its sophisticated jazz fusions, the New York sound had already diverged a little from its early Cuban influence. Although Cuba remained the center of Caribbean music, Puerto Rico and Venezuela, two countries with their own unique musical traditions, began to provide powerful alternatives that struck a further blow to Cuba's dominance. The sole aim of the New York musicians had been first to emulate and then to surpass the Cuban sound. This ambitious goal was achievable because in the Cuba of the 1950s, Fulgencio Batista's own extravagant administration encouraged the cultivation of the most diverse musical forms and styles. The influence of the Cuban *charangas*[3] of the previous decade—as performed by Melodía del 40, La Ideal, Belisario López, and, primarily, Antonio Arcaño and his Maravillas—was still evident in the euphoria that had been unleashed by Enrique Jorrín, violinist and director of Orquesta América. His new cha cha chá rhythm had been fully developed by José Fajardo and his Stars and even more so by the very important and extraordinary Orquesta Aragón from Cienfuegos. Meanwhile, the bland and weak rumba, written especially for elite white audiences, continued to be performed by the Havana Cuban Boys, under the direction of Armando Oréfiche, and by the less sophisticated but more effective Casino de la Playa, which succeeded due to the extraordinary voice of Miguelito Valdez.

2. *Sabor* literally means "flavor" or "taste" in Spanish, but in the context of Latino popular music it is an untranslatable term that refers to an undefinable quality in a musical performance, a unique sense of style and rhythm, an edge and passion that allows listeners to identify with the music.

3. The Cuban *charanga* was an ensemble that emerged in the early twentieth century as a derivation of the traditional wind orchestra. It included the flute, violin, piano, bass, timbal, and guiro; later it added the congas, more violins, and singers. It usually performed *danzones* and the *cha cha chá* after the 1950s.

Moreover, these jazzlike styles had been perfectly Cubanized, mostly because they had been primarily influenced by Pérez Prado, who achieved his glory in Mexico during the 1940s, and not by Machito, who was performing during that same period for mostly Jewish audiences in New York. Jazzlike styles were also heard in the orchestras of Armando Romeu and Bebo Valdez, and it was Valdez who created the *batanga* rhythm that later was attributed to Benny (or Beny) Moré. Meanwhile, the bolero had gained considerable prominence through a new style known as "feeling," widely developed by such composers as César Portillo de la Luz, José Antonio Méndez, Luis Yánez, and the duet of Piloto and Vera. The basic structure of all these styles was the son, and twenty years later it would inform the best of Caribbean salsa music. During the 1950s the son was widely disseminated by such orchestras as the Sonora Matancera, in the reigning voice of the always impressive Celia Cruz; by Chapotín, with the great Miguelito Cuní, who extended the best innovations and trends of Arsenio Rodríguez; and by the famous Tribu ensemble, which served as a foundation for Benny Moré's vocal and stylistic expressions.

The Cuban influence also hovered around Venezuelan music. Cuba's La Casino Orchestra, for example, was perfectly mirrored in Billo's Caracas Boys, directed by the Dominican Luis María "Billo" Frómeta. Since the end of the 1930s, Frómeta had set the dance standards for the Venezuelan middle class. On the other hand, Luis Alfonzo Larrain's avant-garde approaches, richly experimental in rhythm and melody, were taken up by two young musicians, Jesús "Chucho" Sanoja and Aldemaro Romero. Romero can be credited with exporting his influence back to Cuba and also to the jazz syntheses of New York. Likewise, Venezuela developed the Cuban son through its various performative styles in the more traditional ensembles, such as the *conjunto*, *septeto*, and *sonora*, as in the Sonora Caracas founded by Carlos Emilio Landaeta, also known as "Pan con Queso" (bread and cheese). Since the bolero singers used the same inflections characteristic of the performers of "feeling," the Venezuelan flavor was detectable only in the songs of Alfredo Sadel and in the *joropos* of Adelia Castillo, a well-established international star at the time. For instance, Sadel's version of "El cumaco de San Juan," an extraordinary merengue from Caracas composed by Francisco Delfín Pacheco, became an unequaled hit in Havana. When Caracas held its Carnivals, so highly reputed throughout the Caribbean, only the Cuban rhythms, performed by local bands or by bands specifically hired for the Carnival, provoked any noticeable enthusiasm among the dancing audience.

Yet, during this period so completely dominated by the Cuban influence, one modest but rousing Puerto Rican band managed to assert elements of a distinct sonority: the Combo of Rafael Cortijo. That combo, with a singer named Ismael Rivera, was not at all seduced by jazz, and its music, therefore, was in no way open to Americanization. Likewise, though they had great respect for the Cuban son, they kept its influence at a distance. Their main focus was the *bomba* and the *plena*, rhythms they used with confidence and flair when they performed at the Palladium for the first time. The rest of the music in Puerto Rico, however, absorbed the diverse influences of Cuba and the United States without any resistance. The principal music of local quality focused on the old, traditional bolero through which Pedro Flores, Rafael Hernández, and Bobby Capó continued to display their mastery. Otherwise, Puerto Rican music consisted of jazz-band orchestras, son conjunto ensembles, and combos that continued to pay a profound and deserved debt to Ignacio Piñeiro and his classic Septeto Nacional.

Clearly, Cuba was the beginning and the end of Caribbean popular music, even though the musical expressions that emerged from Cuba were later enriched by New York, Caracas, and Puerto Rico. Mexico also contributed, since we cannot forget that Pérez Prado, Mariano Mercerón, and Benny Moré himself achieved their grandeur in the Aztec capital. This is not to affirm that Cuba alone possessed the most valuable and interesting rhythms among the various Caribbean countries, but simply to acknowledge that Cuba successfully combined all the necessary conditions to make itself the musical center of the Caribbean.

Given the overwhelming reception of the son in the 1920s—a son that by the 1930s was already considered legitimately Caribbean and not exclusively Cuban—it would have been very difficult to develop and impose globally rhythms that were not identified with the son. Previously I highlighted Cortijo as the notable exception that confirms the rule, and even he always finished off the bombas with *montunos* through which Ismael Rivera distinguished himself with his very popular style of improvisation. Because of the popularity of the son, the Colombian *cumbia* was relegated to the status of folk music, like many of the black rhythms of the Venezuelan coast. For example, the *gaita marabina* was listened to only during Christmastime in Zulia, and the dazzling merengue from Caracas similarly was condemned to a virtual, early death after the arrival of the splendorous and lavish jazz bands. The presence of the Cuban sound was, therefore, clearly inescapable.

Years later the definition and meaning of the Cuban influence would provoke a range of opinions that, in most cases, served to rally political interests. For example, in the name of a misunderstood nationalism, salsa was accused of being a foreign influence, because it was basically Cuban.

In its place, musical expressions emerged that, although authentic and folkloric, met the conditions necessary to make them fully popular, that is, representative of the tastes and tendencies of the people. Pop and folk music are not necessarily the same thing; each follows distinct, perhaps parallel lines, but they are not identical ones. The Cuban influence that began virtually with the onset of the twentieth century—with the first recordings and with the influence of radio distribution—affected only pop music, not folk music. For many generations Venezuelans had identified with the southern tango, and now, for example, they turned to it to a greater degree than the joropo or *galerón* in order to sing about the circumstances of their everyday lives.

From a shortsighted and egotistical perspective, all of this was considered cultural treason. Yet, this identification with other musical traditions occurred, of course, because the popular culture of the continent, and especially that of the Caribbean, has so many common elements that an important and highly noticeable similarity surfaces among them. If the son rapidly overstepped Cuba's Oriente province to take over Havana and, within no time, the whole Caribbean region, it did so because it possessed characteristics that could absorb and represent those shared elements. A similar case would occur with salsa fifty years later. Since the people that inhabit the region are basically the same, each of the musical forms that they identify with, that sing to their realities, has to be similar to the others.

I do not know of any authentic, popular music that has *not* crossed national boundaries in Latin America. Therefore, in the case of Caribbean music, it does not make sense to speak about "transculturation" because this term implies a relationship between two or more cultures that are different from each other. This is not at all the case on our continent: our popular culture has a common origin, and it has been maintained and developed under the same conditions in all of our countries. In one way or another, it continually flows into common, albeit unique currents. It is true that there is a "Cubanness," just as there is a "Venezuelanness" and a "Mexicanness," but each scarcely overshadows the deeper bond that unites us. On the contrary, far from separating or unsettling us, these particular identities have become the extraordinary instruments through which our shared expressions are enriched. Simply put, this is the fundamental virtue that characterizes the fabulous music of the Caribbean, and we consider any of its music legitimately our own.

The Latin jazz band, then, as its name suggests, was dedicated to performing Caribbean rhythms. It was made up of a rhythm section, in which the piano and the bass were central, and the traditional sections of saxophones, trumpets, and trombone, although Tito Rodríguez, for instance, eliminated the trombones. The only variation was in the percussion, where a trio made up of tumbas (or congas, as they are better known in the United States), bongos, and the timbaleta (a set of timbales) replaced the conventional U.S. drum kit.

The bongo had been indispensable since the early septets, since in them the bongo alone, strengthened by the beats of the clave, constituted the only rhythmic base. The tumba, an instrument originally unrelated to the son, was incorporated into the conjunto ensemble by the blind *tres* player Arsenio Rodríguez. In the late 1930s he invented this structure of the conjunto that revolutionized the future development of the son. Chano Pozo, who was not only a master musician but also an authentic composer with multiple talents, also brought the tumba into jazz styles in a unique and direct way. Once Tito Puente established his orchestra, the third element, the timbal, was used as a simple instrument to join the isolated section of the tumba and the bongo to the rest of the band. The purely Cuban timbal, which used to be relied on more extensively for performing the *danzón*, became merely an addition to the conventional drum kit in this new, Americanized musical expression. In Mexico, Pérez Prado had assigned one musician to move seamlessly from the timbal to the drum set, while the conga player also was responsible for keeping the beat. Even in Cuba, when jam sessions integrated the improvisational elements of jazz, musicians such as Guillermo Barreto began to use the timbales according to U.S. jazz methods, rather than those of the Cuban danzón. Yet it was in New York, where the jazz band acquired its true configuration, that the timbal was definitively modified. This was the direct result of Puente's pioneering work, which made him known throughout the entire Caribbean and, undoubtedly, the most influential of all timbaleros for decades to come.

The son conjunto, whether configured as septet or a sonora, still disregarded the timbal, a tendency that lasted without major changes well into the salsa of the 1970s. The timbal was basically used in the charanga or traditional orchestras, where the combination of tumba and *paila* remained unchanged. In the face of the new tendencies imposed by jazz bands, the charanga was the only ensemble that managed to retain the traditional role of the Cuban timbal, partly because of its reinvigoration through the cha cha chá. Orquesta Aragón, with its vocalists perfectly in tune and always in unison and its delicate but captivating, melodious style, remained an irreplaceable favorite. Farther north, in New York, Gilberto Valdez had already founded his own charanga orchestra, the first ever to originate inside the

United States. This orchestra exerted a profound influence on Dominican Johnny Pacheco and on Puerto Rican Charlie Palmieri, two musical personalities who led the charanga fever that took over the city just a few years later.

In November 1958, José Fajardo and his Stars (among them, Ulpiano Díaz, timbal; Tata Güines, tumba; Pedro Hernández, violin; Elio Valdez, violin; and Alfredo "Chocolate" Armenteros, trumpet) traveled to New York City. Fajardo had been hired to play at a private dance at the Waldorf Astoria: then-senator John F. Kennedy was running his political campaign, and the colorful and exotic music of flute and violins was considered quite an attraction for his guests. But Fajardo's visit, as one would expect, stirred much more interest in the Hispanic community than among the Democratic politicians. The Palladium's manager at the time was Catalino Rolón, a very skilled promoter since the days of the mediocre Catalan musician Xavier Cugat. Rolón had also worked with the great comedian but less talented singer Desi Arnaz. He approached Fajardo and offered him an informal session in Broadway's famous ballroom. The Cuban flutist agreed and performed with his star musicians the night before their return to Cuba. Aníbal Vásquez, a first-rate music lover and superb dancer, recorded part of that night's performance, and I consider my copy of that tape as one of the most valued treasures in my collection.

The whole musical community was together that night at the Palladium, and the music had nothing to do with the jazz of the big orchestras. Fajardo performed sones, but they barely resembled the ones usually played by the conjuntos of the city. Even the charanga style was radically different from Palmieri's and Pacheco's renditions of "Duboney" and from the earlier antecedents played by Gilberto Valdez. Fajardo performed danzones (a magisterial version of "Fefita") and the cha cha chá (the classic "Bodeguero" of Orquesta Aragón, composed by Richard Egües, Fajardo's longtime rival on the flute). To close, he performed the "Bilongo" by Rodríguez Fiffe, a composition that ever since that night has become a "must" in the repertoire of all orchestras, including those that lived through the salsa years of the 1970s.

According to witnesses, Fajardo's performance that evening set off the New York fever for the Cuban charanga, the same musical style that led to the *pachanga* a few years later. The pachanga, in turn, dominated the first years of the next decade. Curiously, that decade began scarcely two months after this famous New York dance concert, when, on January 1, 1959, Fidel Castro, having defeated Fulgencio Batista's dictatorship in the Movement of July Twenty-sixth, entered Havana with his guerrillas. Castro established the first Communist government in the hemisphere, a political fact that radically divided the global situation of Latin America. Music, which like any art reflects social conditions, would manifest the fullness and significance of this event. Musically speaking, things would never be the same.

TWO : THE 1960S

Two important factors of the Cuban revolution shaped the development of Caribbean popular music. First, the blockade imposed by the United States and the Organization of American States closed the doors to an island that had long served as an ideal site for the convergence of all of the region's musical tendencies. From then on, this music had to function outside Cuba. Secondly, the migrations of many Cuban musicians, especially to New York, considerably changed the way that musical forms had been handled. The Sonora Matancera left with Celia Cruz, and the same happened with Fajardo, although most of his original stars remained on the island. Arsenio Rodríguez also reestablished himself in New York, along with Vicentico Valdez, Rolando Valdez, and Miguelito Valdez. During the first half of the 1960s, this list of relocated musicians grew considerably.

With all the big bands at the height of their popularity, New York easily absorbed this new avalanche of musicians and influences from Cuba. The pachanga style, created by Eduardo Davison, was wisely adopted by the big bands, and the music that developed between 1960 and 1963 bore the imprint of that beat, the last rhythm to leave Cuba. During a time full of confusion, anticipation, and fear, with thousands of Cuban musicians leaving the island and with Venezuelan, Puerto Rican, and Dominican music lagging, Tito Rodríguez established himself as the reigning musician. No one else was able to take up the baton. More than Machito's or Tito Puente's, Rodríguez's orchestra dominated the fusion of jazz and Caribbean rhythms, while, with ample eloquence and skill, he went on to become the best singer of the pachanga and the absolute leader of the entire Caribbean expression. Using the popularity of the pachanga to draw in larger audiences, he significantly enriched his music and reinforced his repertoire with notable Cuban classics that had acquired important sentimental value after the embargo. Through an interesting modification based on the stellar format established by Pérez Prado, the mambo, likewise, became one of his fortes. To top it all off, Rodríguez's voice was suave enough to sound new, but it also had the vigor and mischief needed to get even the young "tough guys" to dance. In this transitional period, the musical scene needed an icon, and Tito Rodríguez was the only one fully capable of playing that role.

Nineteen sixty-four may be the year that best marks the decline of the pachanga and, with it, the big bands that performed it. The powerful Palladium, which had served as the springboard for all trends and successes, suffered a blow so devastating that it led to its demise in just a few years: the ballroom's liquor license had been suspended. But this was only one of the factors that led to the pachanga's undoing, for the lack of a stage does not always imply the disappearance of the performance. Worse, then, Machito and his Afro-Cubans, the pioneers of this movement, decided to retreat to a safer place, the world of U.S. jazz that had always guaranteed them economic survival. And even Tito Puente, who had never been much of a jazz musician, decided to take the middle road and mold his orchestra to the new tastes that were being imposed.

Confronted with the loss of the big clubs, the public had to return to the modest, local clubs, where a band with more than twelve musicians was not only uncomfortable but considerably unwieldy. This cleared the way for the charanga orchestras—smaller bands that did not require as much sound equipment or space as the big bands—and a great proliferation of charangas followed. These groups managed to take on the stylistic diversity initiated by Fajardo, yet they rarely achieved the vitality and quality of his original stars. Lasting only two years, this charanga fever barely caught on enough to sustain the splendor and spectacle of the city's Latin music. Nineteen sixty-six saw the culmination of the crisis, and we can begin to speak of the emergence of the new sounds that led to the fullness of salsa. Before going ahead with that fundamental object and theme of this book, it would be wise to examine some of the elements, musical and otherwise, that were decisive factors in this rupture.

In 1964 the Beatles arrived in New York. In less than a year, this British quartet had totally revolutionized the world of international pop music. Incorporating black rock from the 1950s, the Beatles developed a musical expression that superseded its models and was incredibly attractive. The importance of the Beatles in 1964, however, went beyond the music itself. Financed by the most astute and ambitious publicity campaign ever known, the Beatles were the representatives of a new, international movement—a youth movement that formed a powerful and influential counterculture in Europe and the United States.

President Kennedy had been assassinated the year before, Lyndon Johnson was beginning to increase the U.S. military presence in Vietnam, and the beatnik movement on the California coast was already characterized by protest and rebellion. On the opposite side of the country, in the Southeast, blacks, inspired by Malcolm X, were forming protest groups. Their willingness to make their rights known, even through violence, gave rise to the feared and admired Black Power Movement. Meanwhile, the U.S. Latino community was increasing in number, an increase that in some ways would make Latinos an equally important factor in social and politi-

12

cal decision-making. In the Southwest, César Chávez organized the farm-workers, and in the Northeast, Puerto Rican youth organized themselves into the Young Lords, a group that was remarkably similar to the Black Panthers. In the Caribbean, U.S. marines invaded the Dominican Repub-lic, and Venezuela was instituting democracy while still fighting both left-wing guerrillas and economic sabotages from the right.

During this period of instability and change, music gave way to the over-whelming influence of international pop. On the radio, the Beatles dis-placed guarachas, and some Latino youth abandoned Spanish in order to babble in an English that no one understood. The turbulence of this de-cade came at a very high cost. The great Venezuelan orchestras dissolved, and in Puerto Rico, Rafael Cortijo's important band was forced to leave the musical scene. New York, which had replaced Havana as the center for the cultivation of all Caribbean music, found itself undergoing thousands of abrupt changes until, finally, the sounds of the past had lost all of their relevance. If the 1950s had been a time of splendor and bounty, the 1960s were the complete opposite: confusion reigned and there was no place left for nostalgia.

The major U.S. record companies, which are generally part of even larger communications monopolies that include news agencies, film studios, and television networks, decided abruptly to cut all ties that would suggest any connections with the old Cuban presence. Remember that under Ba-tista, Cuba had been the ideal paradise for U.S. tourists who traveled to the island to do as they pleased, and this required the communications em-pire to create a certain image of Cuba, one that would breathe life into that Antillean paradise. Cuba was a marvel, Ricky Ricardo (Desi Arnaz) used to say in the very popular television series *I Love Lucy*. That same spirit extended to the ballrooms where the U.S. middle class danced to cheap imitations of rumbas performed by orchestras with questionable skills. People in the United States have been consistently characterized as seeing the world outside their borders the way they want to see it, not the way it really is. To them, Cuba was nothing more than a palm tree under which a most beautiful mulatta offered rum to a white, U.S. male who was enjoying life and also—why not?—the mulatta herself. Cuba was the Tropicana and casinos and that was that.

When the Cuban revolution declared itself Communist and Kennedy, after the Bay of Pigs, considered it the foremost enemy of the United States, the image of Cuba as a tourist's paradise had to be radically revised. To replace Cuba and its music, the United States turned to Brazil, a country that was then shifting its samba into the bossa nova, a palatable beat that allowed U.S. singers to perform in the same old ways. Why hadn't the U.S.

industry previously targeted Brazilian music? Why did it wait until Cuba was closed off? The answers are neither in the music nor in the artists that produced it. The only possible answer lies in that huge machinery that controls popular taste, a machine that functions like an octopus pointing to both paradise and hell. Once Cuban music was banned, Caribbean musicians in New York and in the other countries of the region had no other option but to surrender to playing the mixed forms that allowed them to survive. With the world demanding pop and with the old Caribbean sound prohibited, it was as if music were thrown over a cliff and left to tumble to a slow death, as decreed by the magnates of mass culture.

In 1963 Tito Rodríguez traveled to Venezuela with his orchestra, and once again they took over the Carnivals. They next released a record titled *En puerto azul*, which included a wonderful version of "La pollera colorá." Months later, they returned to Venezuela to play for the last time with an orchestra that brought together such musicians as Israel "Cachao" López on bass, Marcelino Valdez on tumba, René Hernández on piano, Bobby Porcelli and Mario Rivera on saxophones, and Tony Cofresí and the Panamanian master Víctor Paz on trumpets. After playing a couple of dances in Caracas (probably at the Hotel Tamanaco, the most important venue of Rodríguez's local successes), the orchestra dissolved. Tito understood perfectly well that, given its aspirations and characteristics, his band would not continue to find the necessary backing in an environment battered by so many outside forces.

Once in New York, Rodríguez decided to sing boleros exclusively, and so he put together a violin orchestra and recorded *Inolvidable*, the album that would become his biggest recording hit. For an audience that had surrendered to the invasion of European and U.S. music, Rodríguez offered the only acceptable outlet for those particular, tender love songs that can only be rendered in Spanish. Young people alternated between records of the Beatles and those of Tito, and the latter were always the better choice for Saturday night parties. But this Tito, whose boleros provided further evidence of his extensive musical abilities, was different. He was now a figure who hardly evoked the old glory of the Palladium, those golden days of New York music in which he had been a performer of the first rank. Tito the bolero singer was able to penetrate the closed sectors of the Latin American middle class, a sector that never identified with Caribbean rhythms because of its hang-ups and ridiculous sense of sophistication. But the Tito who achieved a truly long-lasting significance and became a factor in shaping popular taste was the Tito of the dance and the pachanga, of "Mamagüela" and the mambo, the very Tito who would never compromise. Rodríguez's shift in direction, then, confirmed the crisis. He knew how to move with the times; since the pachanga form was already dead, there was nothing else for him to do.

The Alegre label, an arm of a very modest Latin recording company, had been able to publish some of the music that was still floating around New York. It primarily recorded charangas, especially those of Johnny Pacheco and one band or another that tried pitifully to jump on the bandwagon of fusing jazz and Caribbean beats. Despite some successes, these bands never measured up to those of earlier years, when everything seemed so much easier. Now, with the breath nearly knocked out of the charanga and the big bands attacked by incessant changes, Alegre released a rather strange album by La Perfecta, a modest band directed by Eddie Palmieri and made up of two trombones, piano and bass, and tumba and bongo. Eddie's older brother, Charlie, was the pianist and in charge of composing and arranging most of their repertoire.

For the first time the trombones, as a distinct and self-contained section, became a key sound in the Latin world of New York. Eddie Palmieri, however, did not initiate this style; he only adapted it. In Puerto Rico, Mon Rivera, singing the bomba with comic, roguish twists full of social irony, had already established the trombones as the only fitting accompaniment to such rhythms. Even so, the Palmieri variation would come to define the sound of salsa music from then on. Eddie made the trombone sound bitter, with a peculiarly aggressive hoarseness. Ignoring the conventional roles established by jazz bands, Palmieri used a skeletal section, a maximum of two trombones that under no circumstances echoed the sound structures built by the great orchestras of the mambo period. This difference shockingly altered the ears and expectations of music lovers. Music stopped being glamorous and became feisty. Where once there was pomp, now there was violence. Things had definitely changed.

Eddie Palmieri was a musician raised in New York, specifically in the Bronx where Puerto Ricans had formed numerous enclaves. His early influences are more jazz-related than Caribbean, and the latter, in any case, came through Bauzá's Afro-Cuban jazz. Indeed, Palmieri's North American elements continued to be more pronounced and more important. Since the big band was a useless dream by now, the initial possibilities for Palmieri were reduced to two particular formats: the son ensemble (in which the distinct nuance is delivered by the trumpets, not the trombones) or the flute-and-violin-based charangas. Eddie rejected both possibilities, since both were weak imitations of past sounds rather than compelling formats for sounds of the future.

Besides, the Latino community in New York was now motivated by very different interests. The entertaining spirit of the Palladium was replaced by the social and political violence of the Young Lords, and music, in one way or another, had to reflect that change. There was no longer a Cuban model to be followed. The rest of Caribbean music was diluted by bland Spanish versions of the powerful U.S.-English pop, and it would take a few more years for salsa to be officially launched. Despite all of this, Eddie Palmieri was already playing the role of a lone pioneer by mapping out the territory.

Even before the 1960s ended, the Caribbean region and the Caribbean communities in New York were filled with trombones. They were also being filled with a still-nascent but urgent sound. This novel music had three chief characteristics: (1) the use of the son as the main basis for its development (especially in the long and aggressive montunos); (2) arrangements that were modest in terms of harmonies and innovations but markedly bitter and violent; and (3) the imprint of the marginalized barrio. This was music produced not for the luxurious ballroom but for hard life on the street. Music no longer aimed to reach a general audience. Now its only world was the barrio, the same barrio where salsa music would be conceived, nurtured, and developed. That is where it all started.

THREE :
SALSA'S
THE THING

For most of the renowned and prestigious Caribbean musicians of the 1950s there was no such thing as salsa. To them, it was merely old Cuban music played with some innovative touches. To the Cubans particularly, who by the second half of the 1970s had reestablished contact with the larger Caribbean community, the onslaught of salsa was seen at the least as a gimmick and at the worst an outright attack. To them, salsa was a sham. But the ultimate insult to salsa was that many of the musicians who depended on it for their survival denied its value as an authentic cultural expression. Some argued that salsa was only a commercial label created merely to bolster sales. Added to this was the view of salsa's gratuitous enemies who considered it an *imported* style and, thus, a passing fad. Meanwhile this label, so harshly debated on all sides, was racking up sales, spawning musical performances that filled the most unlikely venues, and triggering the most diverse reactions. Clearly, something important was happening: the fantastic frenzy of salsa was invading the Caribbean, and its invasion was forceful, persuasive, and undeniable.

Popular music, produced and disseminated by the record industry, always gets put into commercial boxes that never do the music justice. Backed by advertising strategies, the industry routinely sets out to manufacture tastes, styles, or fads that, in turn, will support a steady stream of records. Because of this, a twentieth-century history of Latin American popular music becomes little more than a list of never-ending trends: the tango of the 1930s, the mambo and bolero of the 1940s, the cha cha chá of the 1950s, the twist and bossa nova of the 1960s, the rock and romantic pop ballads of the 1970s, then disco music, and on and on. The industry depends on these pop trends. Popular music, in turn, depends on the industry, since the music cannot survive if it does not keep up with technological advances. But let us be honest: the one does not suppose the other. The record album is only a tool, never the ultimate object. Therefore, even if a history of popular music were documented through record production rates, let us not confuse those record albums, which are products of the industry, with the music they contain. In other words, trends affect the industry but not the music itself, because truly popular music is always beyond categories and labels.

Furthermore, since popular music has a natural tendency to change, it (unlike folk music) is continuously evolving, and its changes are inevitable and necessary. Of course, if that same music is developed and distributed through recordings that follow the dictates of the industry, then any innovation becomes a trend, part of the hype used to increase sales. A consumer society has to maintain demand, and this is where marketing comes in. While all pairs of shoes have the same features, if new styles were not created to justify new models, there would not be enough demand to sustain an industry that depends on mass consumption. Something similar happens with the recording industry, except that it works with artistic forms, and this fundamental difference has significant implications.

In the case of salsa, then, it is crucial to distinguish between the trends created by the industry and the more intrinsic values and meanings that the music holds. While the trends are clearly powerful, it is the music that deserves to be studied and discussed. Is salsa truly an evolutionary stage in the development of Caribbean popular music, or is it nothing more than an advertising gimmick? If it is true that salsa is only old Cuban music slightly altered through particular arrangements, then its artistic value is inconsequential. If salsa is nothing more than a commercial label, then it has little importance and does not constitute authentic popular music. While this book does deal with the central role of the recording industry, it attempts to emphasize more the social and cultural values of salsa. I am convinced that there *is* something of intrinsic cultural importance at the core of salsa beyond the trends and the marketing. It *is* more than old Cuban music, more than a mere label, and much more than an expendable style of arranging music.

Salsa was born in the Latino barrios of New York where the youth began to use it as the only music capable of expressing their everyday lives. They lived the ups and downs of international pop culture, listening to rock music and absorbing the values disseminated by U.S. advertising, while desperately straddling authenticity and assimilation. The New York barrio, enclosed in the cultural center of our times, was a secluded world full of local codes and behaviors that somehow withstood the onslaught of the outside world. New York Latinos came from the Caribbean, primarily from Puerto Rico, although the 1960s already had seen an increase in Dominican, Panamanian, Colombian, and Cuban immigrants. Together they formed one community with shared cultural roots. The music produced by that community was, simply put, Caribbean, and the son, which had characterized the region from the first decades of the century, became its principal form of expression.

While all of the popular music developed and known in the Caribbean during the first half of the twentieth century emerged from the barrios, there are some significant differences between those earlier barrios and the particular one that produced salsa in the 1960s. The former were part of smaller cities where, without the economic and social vertigo that now characterizes our major urban centers, life still followed the rhythms of the country. There was a minimal, nearly insignificant distance between those placid cities and the small country towns. The music played in those barrios was equally capable of representing both urban and rural worlds. In Caracas, for instance, the people who danced to the Billo's also danced to the rhythms of a song such as "La burrita de Petare," whose lyrics were much more rural than urban. A similar example comes from Havana, where the Trío Matamoros had a hit singing, "al que siembra su maíz, que se coma su pinol" (the one who sows the grain, gets to eat the flour).

During the 1940s, the first expressions of an exclusively urban sound were beginning to be heard, but only here and there. This sound was heavily indebted to U.S. jazz orchestrations of the time, which came from outside the barrio. The first audiences for Pérez Prado, who had been so successful in Mexico, were members of the middle class who found his music sufficiently sophisticated and *lofty*, and in Cuba, the leading orchestras never performed for the barrios. The Casino de la Playa, for example, a considerably "Americanized" orchestra, always played at the parties and dances of the "blanquitos" (the white upper class), delighting them with all the propriety such venues required.

Even Mario Bauzá commented on the embarrassing tendency that ruled the orchestras of the time: bandleaders felt they had to hire "white and pretty" musicians rather than "black, ugly" ones. Bauzá noted, for example, that the bongo player of the Casino de la Playa orchestra always sat behind the rest of the band in order to make himself less conspicuous to the audience. (All of this occurred despite the fact that Miguelito Valdez was forever arguing that he could not imagine a dance band without a strong rhythmic presence). In New York, Machito's Afro-Cubans played predominantly for white Jewish audiences, as did the renowned Noro Morales, and this contributed to their being so highly regarded. While the barrio could give them authenticity and power, it could never accord them such prestige.

Our popular music has yet to be studied as well as and in the depth that it deserves. For the most part, its critics have been journalists from the entertainment world more interested in the love lives of singers than in the real value of their music. While jazz and other U.S. musical expressions are seen as the epitome of music in the twentieth century, Caribbean popular music has been relegated continually to second or third place. It is assumed that value resides only in the United States, and so Latin American music becomes important only if and when it resembles the music of the North. Journalists are responsible for this skewed standard. Critics praised Tito Rodríguez because, unlike most of the other Caribbean singers, he was "serious and elegant"—"he knew how to speak and how to behave on stage"—but also, and chiefly, because he was accepted by U.S. audiences. He had been on television, and his name appeared alongside those of other great figures in international music. Yet, these facts do not amount to much when we assess the real value of Tito Rodríguez as a popular singer. That he had been the first singer wholly accepted by the Venezuelan middle class (a privilege that Rubén Blades would share twenty years later) is a minor fact compared with his popularity among the people. But those who write about music have been interested only in Tito Rodríguez's social class, not the popular attributes of his style.

On the other side of the spectrum, trained musicologists have disdained popular music. To them only "art" or "highbrow" music has any value, while folk music, with its imperfections, is interesting only because it preserves a supposed purity. In the case of Venezuela, for instance, a relationship has been established between the "Cantata criolla" by Antonio Esteves and the songs sung on the open plains during the milking of cows, songs recorded by some zealous anthropologist. At the same time, the *gaita zuliana* is dismissed as vulgar and superficial and is considered to have scant musical value because it is performed for ordinary people drinking beer in the discos of Maracaibo.

Highbrow or art music, by definition, has little or nothing to do with popular sentiments. Granted, since folk music represents the most ancestral traditions of a particular people, it hardly can be expected to reflect contemporary feelings. If it did this, it would risk denying its own nature and negating its own value. Nor can a musician become, by will or decree, a creator of folklore. While folk music is open to those who may or may not become authentic interpreters of it, it can never be created by individual or random composers. A popular musician or an art musician can start with folkloric elements, but the value of the finished work will be measured by its success as popular or art music exclusively, not as folk music. The transformation of any folklore is a slow process that requires the test of several generations and the development of particular customs and circumstances. Popular music, by contrast, responds to urgent social pressures and is tested over a matter of days. Although it may be nurtured by folklore, it will always take place on a different plane and follow a fundamentally different rhythm of change.

Popular music drifts amid the flux of ever-shifting criteria. It eddies about, from the comments of a chronicler who is worried about the types of roses that José "Cheo" Feliciano gave away at a concert, to the opinions of experts who suggest Ismael Rivera is more authentic than Tito Puente because Rivera is darker, and since drumming is black music, the darker the musician, the better. All of this is cloaked in a pitiful discourse that compares our music to that of the United States. By these standards Machito is better than Cortijo, because Machito uses richer and more interesting arrangements, because he uses some jazz and Cortijo does not, and because Machito is, to be blunt, less of a hick.

Meanwhile nobody writes about why Felipe Pirela had a larger following than José Luis Rodríguez. Or why Aldemaro Romero's orchestra, which was musically outstanding and a wonderful representative of the best avant-garde of its time, could not compete for popularity with Eddie Palmieri's paltry trombones coming out of the back alleyways of the South Bronx. Rather than seeing popular music from such a narrow perspective, we must analyze it in its global context and by taking into account the community that produces and enjoys it. In the long run, this community is what really matters. The music itself can be of extraordinary quality, but if the public who receives it does not wholly identify with it, then the music will not ring true.

Therefore, to understand salsa requires an understanding of the cultural and social milieu in and for which it was created. Ignoring this aspect leads to a very weak analysis that can be dismissed easily. If we do not take into account the barrio that musically exploded during the 1960s, we will not understand the gap between Tito Rodríguez and Willie Colón. We will be unable to explain why Colón acquired so much cachet when his music, examined through a strict musical lens, is of noticeably lesser quality than that produced earlier by Rodríguez. Salsa implies the barrio, and that accounts for the difference. The barrio defines its value; everything else is peripheral.

The music produced during the 1950s was basically defined by spectacle. During those years, Havana was a city of carefree parties, full of clubs and cabarets where U.S. tourists freely spent their dollars. The music, of course, had popular roots, yet the frenetic nature of a city that lived only to party meant that the music would not end up where it started. It was paid for by foreigners, and the singers sang just for them. The lyrics were safe, infused with a "blackness" made palatable for the tourist, as in the style of "Juancito Trucupey." At the Tropicana everything revolved around glamour, and the authentic barrio could never make itself felt there. The prestigious Palladium in New York followed suit and, to a lesser degree, so did the Casablanca in Caracas, as it filled with well-dressed dancers during Carnival. There was good music, true, but the popular element was clearly mediated.

This glamorous air disappeared in the 1960s once the great orchestras began to decline and the great cabaret called Havana was closed to the wider public. The ostentation and extravagance of that period were replaced by the violence and bitterness of a particular type of life—that of the barrio. Modest orchestras emerged, full of young, inexperienced musicians who had not been formally trained; the musical quality declined; and the rousing sounds of the previous decade were lost. The singing, however, was much more authentic, and the urgent and piercing sounds of the barrio were expressed through dissonant trombones and the violent stomp of montunos. It could not have been otherwise. It no longer made sense to sing a mellow Cuban cha cha chá. Life in that part of the city was not smooth, nor could its music be. There was simply no way music could go on being "delicate," elegant, or refined.

During the period from 1965 to 1970, a confusing time of musical trial and error, the presence of the barrio was glaringly obvious. In the next chapter we will see how the influence of international pop music led to hybrids such as the boogaloo and how the old jazz fusions became jam sessions full of unruly sounds that frantically grasped at new forms of expression. We will also see how all of these experiments gradually transformed the Cuban son until it became the form par excellence of the new music. Throughout this process, the barrio was the unifying thread. The lyrics recovered an authenticity that had been lost at the expense of glamour. The arrangements, far from being aesthetic displays, tried more and more to reproduce the sounds of the street and the boisterous noises of everyday life. Musicians, who were no longer artists or stars, emerged as ordinary but popular figures who went from the street to the stage, without posturing or fanfare. They were not always outstanding, but they never failed to represent fully everyone who shared with them life in the barrio.

Of course, this process was messy and, like any period of transition, subject to myriad variables. Salsa was not yet defined as such, and according to most experts, it was but the final step into the decadence that followed the glory of the big bands and the splendor of the cabarets. During these years, however, a very interesting and important phenomenon took place: the rudimentary musical expression born in New York was quickly embraced by the barrios of large Caribbean cities. It happened quite spontaneously and outside the control of the media and its publicity. This occurred because the Latino barrio of New York resembled the barrios of the Caribbean. Both had their share of misery and marginalization, and in both violence and cynicism were constants. The Latinos from New York felt the need to identify with their culture as a way of contesting the pressures from the outside. Those in the barrios of Caracas felt the same need.

With the radio playing the Rolling Stones and the television broadcasting U.S. programs, they lacked a cultural expression that represented them. As their situations were the same, so was the solution. It did not matter, then, if the music was not of the highest quality, as long as it spoke to their everyday life.

This is why Willie Colón is better than Machito, and why Los Dementes are better than the Billo's. It is surprising to see how the unassuming music of a twenty-year-old pianist called Ricardo "Richie" Ray spread through the most diverse barrios in the Caribbean. It is equally surprising that it did so without the backing of any major advertising firms at a time when the media insisted on a rigid definition of styles and tastes, particularly those imposed by international pop. This example of a countercurrent against the media empire of our time reveals the definite value of salsa. While the singer Sandro needed a publicity machine to popularize his spastic movements and the droning serenade of his voice, Joe Cuba had only to play "La calle está durísima" ("The Street Is Bad") to become highly praised and respected throughout the barrio. This is all the more striking since at the time he was considered *un tumbador de mal gusto* (a crass tumba player), and he never received the attention of the major media much less that of the entertainment press.

Obviously this newly emerging musical expression, not yet officially called salsa, was much more than the old Cuban music. The Cuban son that unified the Caribbean was its basic tool, but this proved to be a virtue, not a defect, and fortunately, the music was no longer fueled by pretentious egos. The barrio that unified and reflected the Caribbean people became salsa's stage, and in the barrio unfounded insults came at a cost.

At the beginning of the 1970s, the musical expression born in New York reached its first level of maturity. All of the experiences of the preceding five years converged into a perfectly defined form with unique sounds and characteristics. At this point, the record industry that produced Caribbean music in New York had been relatively efficient. It had moved on from its first, amateurish recordings to ones that were more sophisticated and more clearly professional. This influenced the development of salsa, because now there was an industry of some importance that could impose conditions on the music.

By 1975, salsa music was recognized as "salsa," and the musical trend that developed around it led to phenomenal record sales. The famous salsa boom took off, and while this meant that the music was widely disseminated, it also created confusion that detracted considerably from the value of the music. The first condition that the boom imposed on this music was the use of the term, "salsa." The product needed to sell, and one of the first rules in marketing is to deploy a concise and effective term with which the product can be identified. The term itself was the least important part of the music, and, in this, the detractors of salsa were partially right: the term is just another label. It is a mistake, however, to fall into the trap of advertising and identify the content of the music with the name that arbitrarily represents it.

As the Venezuelan scholar Eleazar López Contreras aptly stated,

One has to take into account how helpful it was for the waltz or for jazz to have a name, although we recognize that these and other rhythms or musical styles would exist on their own, without the need for a label to identify them. The name is purely a convenience (although today it has become a commercial necessity). As to the use of *salsa* as a name for that expression, we can say that it is like any other term—like *fire*, *flavor*, *sugar*—and just like the *olé* in flamenco, since these terms represent something animate, alive, this music easily could have been called by any of those other terms.

Nevertheless, the publicity that created fads and took over trends won the battle, at least for the moment; the word "salsa" became more prominent than the music; and (although we could have done without it) a discussion about the origin of the term ensued. The Cubans, who had mistakenly interpreted the expression as a passing fad that robbed them of their musical patrimony, alleged that Ignacio Piñeiro long ago had coined the word "salsa" in his classic tune "Echale salsita," released at the end of the 1920s. In New York, opportunists boasted of having coined the term out of nowhere. Commercially speaking, the term was first used in Venezuela when Federico and his Combo released their record *Llegó la salsa* in June 1966. And Phidias Danilo Escalona, the disc jockey on Radio Venezuela, had popularized salsa and *bembé* for years through *La hora del sabor*, the first radio program exclusively focused on the music that was revolutionizing the Caracas barrio. Back in New York, Félix "Pupi" Legarreta was among the first to use the term on one of his charanga albums, and the ever-trendy Lebrón Brothers had released a record called *Salsa y control*. The term, however, took on even greater importance in 1975 when the Fania Company, the record empire that took over and controlled the commercial boom, released its film, *Salsa*. Still it bears repeating that all of this is significant only if we approach salsa from the perspective of the industry and overlook the value of the music's artistic and cultural meanings. This musical expression came to be called salsa and not bembé, and it is a waste of time to prolong this debate.

Having examined the term and accepted the inevitability of marketing and its hype, everyone moved on to the possible definitions of salsa. I remember many irate Cuban musicians who protested that there was no substance to the salsa beat. Many argued that "in order for a rhythm to exist, it must have a musical notation, and salsa does not." The problem with this was that salsa never pretended to offer itself as a specific rhythm, just the opposite. To fully represent the convergence of the contemporary urban barrio, it fused all of the rhythms that had gathered at those cultural crossroads. Salsa, then, does not have a particular notation, nor does it need to have one. Salsa is not a rhythmic pattern, nor is it a simple style that takes on a defined beat. Salsa is an open form capable of representing all of the musical tendencies that came together in the urban Caribbean experience of the times. That is, again, the barrio was its only defining mark.

In this light, it would be absurd to think that salsa emerged from some scrupulously new music. The barrio implies an amalgam of traditions, a wide spectrum where one easily can find a tango and a Mexican *ranchera*, a gaita or a cumbia, a son or a *guaguancó*, yet each of these forms retained its specificity. José Alfredo Jiménez, the ranchera singer, could never be considered a salsa singer; however, Joc Quijano's salsa version of "Echame a mí la culpa" is markedly salsa. The same can be said about the traditional Argentinian tangos once Ismael Miranda sang them. Likewise, Carlos Gardel never sang salsa, but salsa definitely sang him. One has to keep in mind that we are talking about popular music, an expression that responds to the shared characteristics and demands throughout this region. There, no gaps are unbreachable, the connections are tight, and the bridges are unique, permanent, and, above all, always wide open.

Of course, salsa took on certain Cuban characteristics to the extent that the Cuban son served as the central form behind it. But this represented only one of its facets, not its totality. It is imperative to distinguish between the salsa that emerged spontaneously in the barrios and the salsa-like expression that was later commercialized and made trendy. When that occurred, the musical arena was not equipped to address all of the demands of the industry. More and more music had to sell, and there were not enough orchestras, not enough musicians, not enough arrangers, and ultimately, not enough composers to satisfy those demands. In addition, the radically barriolike character of salsa hindered the superficial and glamorous touch-ups that every commercial trend requires, and when those touch-ups were added, the original expression became devalued.

In order to satisfy the demands, the record entrepreneurs opted for an easy solution: since salsa followed the son, they reached back to the Cuban son that had been so famous in previous decades, especially now that Cuba had been closed by the embargo and nobody would claim copyrights. The old Cuban repertoire was plundered, and, thanks to the industry and consumer demand, the salsa that was being widely sold and distributed limited itself to drawing on Cuban music of the 1940s and 1950s. What developed from this has come to be called the *matancera* style, a variant of salsa that in no way can be confused with the authentic expression that was born in the contemporary barrio with its eyes on the future, not on the past. It was not wrong to record a classic hit now and then, but within the matancera style, only the old music made any sense. While it reaped commercial benefits, the matancera style ended up virtually negating the values of the true salsa. This explains why the Cubans, who never understood the difference between the trend and the music, felt they had been made fools of publicly. And when it comes to the matancera style, they were right.

But let us focus on a very important detail: before the salsa boom, this music moved easily and freely within the barrio. The media did not pay much attention to it, the journalists and experts rejected it, and the rest of the population—that sector that never takes into consideration the concerns of the working class—totally ignored it. At this juncture, salsa was not subject to definitions or classifications: it was not trendy, and therefore it was not worthy of being part of the cultural industry. Performers could sing just as easily a new son or an old bolero or move from one musical extreme to the other, without having to worry about the senseless restrictions that would be imposed later. Authenticity was the defining characteristic of this music, and the name salsa did not even exist. Once the boom arrived, it took that authenticity away. Singers became stars, and the music had to be marketed under particular trends or styles that were invented overnight. The industry, rather than taking care of salsa as an authentic expression, began to busy itself with dressing it up in the trendy forms of the moment. Thus, Tito Puente, Machito, and Celia Cruz became part of salsa, along with Billo, Los Melódicos, and Los Corraleros del Majagual. All Caribbean music was conflated as salsa, and obvious nonsense, such as "Pérez Prado is the old salsa" and "Daniel Santos is the prophet of salsa," circulated. Eddie Palmieri and Oscar D'León were thrown together with Damirón and Leo Marini. This created something like a flea market where, because everything was worth the same price, everything was a bargain.

The commercial boom may have erased a great part of the essence of salsa, but it never destroyed it altogether. The boom did allow for an ex-

26

traordinary diffusion of this music, and so, despite the industry's gimmicks, the true expression of the barrio survived. After the initial vertigo, what remained upright was the strong and permanent music. This book is concerned with that vertigo, but even more so with the wonderful popular music that endured all possible trends.

FOUR : THE NEW YORK SOUND

One of the greatest assets of the Cuban son is its permeability. Its form is open to enrichment and to absorbing diverse types of popular music while remaining solidly well defined. The young New York musicians quickly recognized this. They realized that the invasion of (international) pop music had to be integrated into their own expressive style and that the son was the best tool to make that fusion happen. Thus, from pop to the son, the boogaloo emerged as the first hybrid that marked the difference between the old Caribbean music and the new barrio style. Already by 1966, Pete "El Conde" Rodríguez, a previously unknown pianist, had produced the first successful boogaloo, "Micaela," a son full of new and unusual phrasings. It was noticeably strident and upbeat, with lyrics that moved easily between English and Spanish. In addition to Rodríguez's boogaloo, Ricardo Ray recorded "Jala, jala." Like the orchestra led by Rodríguez, Ray's band was small and unpretentious and also characterized by the sounds of two brilliant trumpets. In the preceding year, Ray Barretto had recorded his famous "Watusi 65," which reached audiences well beyond the conventional Latin market. This son was not labeled as a boogaloo, yet it fully embodied all the rules and traits of that beat. It transformed the rigid, traditional clave (measure) into a new form much closer to rock than to the son, but without losing its essential montuno feel. While the watusi retained the dual rhythms based on a four-beat measure, it lost the sense of hidden malice that characterized the Caribbean clave. In this way, the son became flat and thus acceptable to mainstream U.S. listeners. The two watusis by Barretto are good examples of this. Indeed, "Watusi 65" was nothing more than the reprise of a similar theme Barretto had recorded the year before. Other examples include "Bang, Bang, Bang," by Joe Cuba, which also made it to the U.S. national hit parade, and all of Carlos Santana's Latin rock hits that came out of California two years later.

In this period of transition many felt a desperate need for change. Because musicians also felt compelled to diverge from the traditional paths, every new rhythm sounded equally good. Therefore, we must not overemphasize the role of boogaloo and its later development, Latin rock, in locating the origins of the real salsalike expression. Rather, we should take the boogaloo only as a point of reference, since as a discrete, singular beat, it lacked substance and consequence.

When Pete Rodríguez sang his famous phrase, "I like it like that," in "Micaela," he was building a bridge between the music and the listeners (both Latino and Anglo) who were obsessed with the dominating forms of pop. Record producers eventually used this crossover tendency to tap into diverse and even antagonistic markets. Rodríguez, however, approached it in a more modest way. Coming out of the barrio during those turbulent times, he was more attracted to the new pop style than to Caribbean music. Even so, he wanted to create a barrio music that would draw on the characteristics of pop without sacrificing important nuances of the Caribbean tradition. For this reason, he never gained much popularity among U.S. listeners but only among the Latino barrio youth who made him their most important icon. This was his chief virtue: he never lost sight of the people who really mattered.

Ray Barretto was the opposite. While he was born in a Latino sector of New York, he had become a musician in Germany while serving in the military. There, and in contrast with most of his contemporaries, Barretto began with jazz and then moved on to Caribbean styles. During the early 1960s, Barretto recorded for Latin UA (the Latino subsidiary of the powerful U.S. company United Artists). He recorded Caribbeanized versions of the greatest hits of international music. However, when the charanga fever hit, Barretto decided to ignore the general U.S. audience and to enter fully into the Latino market. He thus achieved his first hit with the Charanga Moderna, which was ten years ahead of the salsa sound. Barretto added the defining pair of trombones to the established mix of violins and flutes, an addition that Mon Rivera and Eddie Palmieri were already developing. Barretto's charanga ensemble also introduced the first son with a New York theme and with a title that even included the word salsa: "Salsa y dulzura."

The watusi was, therefore, a simple variation in the historical development of the "modern charanga," one of those spontaneous but short-lived movements that emerged during this period of musical experimentation. The record executives, however, thought otherwise, and for many years they believed that "Watusi 65" represented the best of Barretto. While many U.S. teenagers partied to the rhythms of this tall, famous Afro-Latino musician, such songs as "Salsa y dulzura" and "La juventud de Borinquen" never made it outside the barrio. Barretto's true importance is that, as a conga player, he gave continuity to the barrio style he had refined in his Charanga Moderna. This was evident by the second half of the 1960s when he began to record under the Fania label, and fortunately at this point the company did not try to merge these two markets. Clearly, the fever for flutes and violins had ended, and the traditional charanga style was no longer viable or pertinent. Therefore, Barretto took on the structures of the Cuban son that Johnny Pacheco had defined with his new *tumbao* technique, added the trumpet sounds that had made Richie Ray and Pete Rodríguez so successful, and transformed his Charanga Moderna ensemble into an orchestra with an amplified sound.

This began a very important period for both Barretto and salsa. Already freed from hybrids such as the boogaloo (inextricably associated with the watusi and later the shingaling), the son began to be played fluidly, without the unnatural tendencies or new fashionable styles that had been forced on it. As a result, all of Ray Barretto's records from this period represent a son that is fully barrio music, and the repertoire is eclectic. It includes both new and old music, both socially angry and traditionally sensual lyrics. Yet, in the midst of this ample repertoire, the son had acquired its unique style—a style marked by marginalization, ghetto roots, and barrio logic.

This same basic analysis of Ray Barretto applies to another conga player who also grew up in the Latino barrios of New York: José Calderón, better known as Joe Cuba. Cuba was the founder and face of the famous sextet that carried his name. Here I want to point out that, unlike the big bands that had an average of fifteen musicians, none of the bands that emerged during this transitional period ever had more than twelve members. Remember that the grand venues—the only ones that could afford to hire big bands—had lost their glory. Now music was performed in small and more modest clubs. Palmieri and Richie Ray did well with eight musicians each, while Joe Cuba used only six. The first two members of his sextet included Jimmy Sabater and Cuba himself, playing a combination of timbales and congas. This combo would become a classic one in the New York sound and in the later sounds of salsa. The other three musicians played the vibraphone (which gave Cuba's sextet its unique sound), piano, and bass, respectively, and the singer was none other than the inimitable José "Cheo" Feliciano.

Of all the groups using English lyrics in order to penetrate the U.S. market, Cuba's was the best. In some cases, and imitating Pete Rodríguez, Cuba mixed both English and Spanish. In his most famous song, "El pito," for example, he combined two refrains: "Así se goza" (this is the way to have fun), alternating with the whistling of the musicians, and "I'll never go back to Georgia, I'll never go back." In other tunes, he was the first to sing exclusively in English, as in his most renowned numbers, "Bang, Bang, Bang," "Yeah, Yeah," and "Push, Push." This approach, coupled with the unique sound of his band, made Joe Cuba one of the most important musicians in the early days of the New York sound. In the long run, however, what secured his popularity was the other music that he recorded alongside his strident and "gringolike" experiments. Together with Eddie

Palmieri, and at a sufficient distance from Ray Barretto, Cuba was one of the first to develop a son that directly addressed the barrio. The small size of his band forced him to use the vernacular, particularly the constant use of *caló*, or barrio slang. As I mentioned previously, his successful "La calle está durísima" became the slogan for that new style, and his original version of "El ratón" became the first great hit of the salsa industry's boom. In addition, his performance of Jimmy Sabater's "Alafia" served as a defining piece for the new, irreverent figure who made music from and for the barrio:

Alafia, alafia, alafia
I feel lucky
Because I was born a chocolate color.

After "Hanging Out," "Bailadores," and "Estamos haciendo algo bien," with the release of his best-selling "Bang, Bang, Bang" in 1967, Joe Cuba and his sextet had reached the height of their most important musical period. Yet in this same year, the group lost Cheo Feliciano and, with him, any clear musical direction. The remaining musicians decided to perform only U.S. music, and this turned out to be a fatal mistake for them. Since pop music in English had served only as a tenuous point of departure once the barrio sound became legitimized, audiences began to dismiss any style that did not come out of the Caribbean context.

Curiously, most of the musicians who had helped to solidify the New York sound during the second half of the 1960s began to lose popularity among the same audience that originally had praised them to the point of fanaticism. Pete Rodríguez shared Joe Cuba's fate. While Rodríguez was justly considered the founding father of the early New York boogaloo sound, after the release of his first four records—*I Like It Like That*, *Ay qué bueno*, *Latin Soul Man*, and *Pete Rodríguez Now*—he found it difficult to maintain his leadership. Richie Ray was luckier. For him, the (Caribbean-pop) fusions were only a necessary stage in this transitional period. In addition to his extraordinary "Jala, jala," he recorded such songs as "Cabo E" and the already classic "Lo atara la araché," which included virtually no U.S. elements. Moreover, Ray's virtuosity and the effective style of his singer, Bobby Cruz, gave his band both the validity and the vitality to outlive the passing trends. By the end of the 1960s, when the salsa sound had proven itself, Ray changed record companies. He left the Alegre label, where he had recorded his first albums with the prestigious producer Pancho Cristal, and moved on to Fania Records, the same label that would establish the first great empire of salsa. In doing so, Richie Ray ensured his own survival.

Barretto also managed to stay afloat after the boogaloo wave subsided. As I noted earlier, his orchestra had embraced the salsa sound well before the boogaloo fever began to die down. Because of this, Barretto was the only one to achieve genuine staying power. The rest of his contemporaries—such as Johnny Colón (who had in fact recorded "Boogaloo Blues"), Joey Pastrana, and the Lebrón Brothers—fell into anonymity once the true salsa took off. Even someone like Tony Pabón, whose La Protesta orchestra had the sound most steeped in the barrio, could not weather the force of this changing tide. After the transition, once salsa's virtues imposed themselves, only the most defined styles survived.

As already stated, since the son had become flat and neutralized, the boogaloo arose as a way of penetrating the international pop scene. It had its heyday to the extent that it was identified as the major trend of the moment, able to capitalize on the sounds already sown by other styles. Having taken over at the end of the decade, it was precisely that opportunism that led the boogaloo to its demise. Again, since this was a period of transition, we need to remember that the boogaloo was a single variant, and not the only one that musicians were exploring. Jazz also made its mark, although it did so in a less pronounced way and with less commercial success, musically speaking, and the influence of jazz proved richer and more fruitful. This was due, first, to its inherent characteristic as a music open to experimentation but assured enough to dominate the diverse trends it encountered. Secondly, Caribbean musicians of the past decade had been borrowing from jazz to develop their traditional cadences. For example, Mario Bauzá's Afro-Cuban jazz and the important achievements of Chano Pozo fed into the work of such diverse figures as Cuban tumba players Mongo Santamaría and Armando Peraza and virtuoso Puerto Rican percussionist José Mangual. Later, Santamaría became more identified as a U.S. musician and lost his Caribbean connections. Nonetheless—allow me to emphasize—the tendency to use jazz elements had little to do with the authentic popular expressions that ultimately led to salsa.

The true influence of jazz on salsa was found elsewhere: not so much in Bauzá's Cuban jazz but in Cachao López's music, and less so in Chano Pozo's showy style than in the rhythms established by Tata Güines. This salsa wanted to remain closer to Cuban music than to the New York sounds being heard around the corner. I state this not to diminish the Cubanness in Bauzá's, Pozo's, or Santamaría's music, but to emphasize that the jazz inflecting the *guajeo* styles of the mambo and the montuno was much closer to the Cuban styles. Younger musicians, therefore, felt free to use the son for jamming in creative and open ways. The "Jam Session Latino" emerged and led to the famous jam sessions of the Tico, Alegre, Cesta, and later, the most important Fania All Stars. All of these ensembles, however, were made up of the same musicians. The idea was to get them together in one venue—generally in the clubs in Greenwich Village—in order to record all of the music that they would create throughout the night. Those recordings documented something very unique: these were not the fine and carefully polished sounds of the big bands of the previous decade, but the new sounds of an irreverent and somewhat piercing, chaotic expression.

While these sessions were very important for the eventual emergence of salsa, their musical experimentations had little impact on the larger public. In most cases, the musicians immersed themselves in musical forms only to satisfy themselves, without considering that the common listener was unfamiliar with their secret codes. In addition, the jam sessions did not encourage dancing, and from a Caribbean perspective, any music that is not danceable is not very meaningful. Though this may sound radical, I mean only to point out that, while the value of music does not exclusively reside in its danceability, popular music can never totally ignore its connection to dancing.

To reiterate, these jazzlike jamming sessions became a kind of closed workshop in which the musicians experimented as they wished, inventing many of the sounds that would later develop into salsa. In other words, these sessions represented an outpouring of very rich music, but to say that they were the most important or ultimate expression of this period of transition would be to undermine one of the true values of authentic popular music: the mutual support of the community. From this perspective, the hybrid form of the boogaloo had a more profound impact on the salsa of the next decade than these jam sessions did. Even for the musicians, the jam sessions were nothing more than exploratory workshops. Indeed, after jamming together, often at small nightclubs, the same musicians would head to the studios to perform and record the music that truly captured the support of the public.

The musicians at the time were thus very versatile, willing and able to experiment on a continuous basis. A clear example is Joe Quijano, a veteran Puerto Rican singer who embodied the spirit of the times. Heavily criticized by the old guard, Quijano was immediately embraced by the young musicians who thought of him as an ideal bridge for any experimentation. With a particularly irreverent style full of phrasings and inflections that lay between the Cuban "feeling" approach and the conventional poses of U.S. balladeers, Quijano's recordings of pop classics already suggested a salsa style. He participated in the jazz-style jam sessions and in small ensembles; he sang boogaloos and boleros; and he performed tra-

ditional guarachas as well as the updated Nuyorican son. That is, Joe Quijano clearly exemplified the current musical scene, when musical traditions were succumbing to the pressures of a spicy, vigorous music that was
continuously on the attack but not always of the highest quality.

Displaced by the boogaloo and jazz-style jamming, the big-band masters struggled to survive and to maintain their past prestige. Most of those
musicians refer to these years with bitterness, defining them as the end of
good music and the beginning of a chaotic sound that treated the son care-
lessly. Indeed, these years were extremely hard and agonizing for them, and
it is painful to listen to their later recordings. For example, the last New
York recordings of Arsenio Rodríguez (the "Marvelous Blindman"), one of
the great geniuses of Caribbean music, have nothing in common with his
earlier works from Cuba. While he was directly responsible for many of the
later innovations used in salsa, he ended up having to record a very mediocre boogaloo. The shift from the fabulous "Me boté de guano" to the flat-
sounding "Hang on Sloopy" is particularly disheartening. Arsenio's case
was not unique, and many of his compatriots were also trying to survive in
exile; yet because of the tres player's important musical capital, his demise
was even more lamentable.

Most of the percussionists, however, rapidly moved into jazz, especially once Chano Pozo and Mongo Santamaría had opened those doors.
Other musicians—trumpeters, violinists, piano players, saxophonists, and
singers—were kept waiting on the sidelines as the new-sounding son took
over. Tito Puente's orchestra was the most important bastion for these
Cuban musicians. "The King of the Timbal" did not dissolve his orchestra,
as did Tito Rodríguez, nor did he migrate into jazz, like Machito. Instead, he
accepted the challenge of trying to stay afloat in these times of shifting and
ill-defined Caribbean cadences. To that end, Puente recorded with Celia
Cruz and with Vicentico Valdez, and he hired veteran Cuban musicians
for his orchestra, all in an attempt to recapture the long-lost image of the
previous decade. It was, however, the figure of La Lupe, a curious Cuban
singer little known on her own island, who enabled Puente to do well despite these disastrous times. Her singing added the irreverent, unruly, and
mischievous style necessary for Puente to rise above the initial chaos of
the new music. In fact, La Lupe was the one woman who reigned supreme
in that unstable and awkward musical period. When Tito Puente's orchestra appeared onstage to accompany La Lupe's singing, they revolutionized
the musical scene. Somehow, they both prolonged the showy and meticulous Cuban tradition and brought in that other element—the piercing and
partly careless song of those on the margins, full of the cunning and gestures that the orthodox Caribbean song would never allow.

With La Lupe, that is, the big-band sound was able to approximate the sound of the barrio. Had she sung the same cuts in the style of ten years earlier, she would have gone unnoticed. Audiences would have branded her as a crazy, screaming, and offensive singer (indeed, some journalists at the time described her in those very terms). However, La Lupe appeared at a time when the refined glamour of the 1950s already had faded and the violent and irreverent style of the barrio was taking over. While not wholly identifying herself as a salsa singer, she was able to adopt many of salsa's characteristics. I am not referring to La Lupe's "show" in itself, with her shoe-throwing and striptease innuendoes. Rather, I call attention to the ways in which she articulated the music—her ability to convey the joyful disorder of guarachas, bombas, sones, and boleros and to create a bridge between one era and the next. After Tito Puente let her go, La Lupe went out on her own, becoming the principal producer of records with such titles as *Reina del soul latino* and *La yiyiyi*, a battle cry that allowed her to imbue the boleros with her own personal dramas. In the 1970s, however, once salsa music was firmly established, La Lupe found herself in a vacuum. The transition that she had effected was complete, and she no longer had a useful role to play. Nonetheless, "Qué te pedí," "La Tirana," "Puro teatro" and her version of "Adiós" have a secure and privileged place in any serious record collection.

In the middle of the 1970s, Caracas was well known for holding the most popular carnivals in the Caribbean. The street celebrations may have paled in comparison with the emotion and spectacle of those in other cities of the region, but in the evenings, the hotels filled their ballrooms with paid mulatta dancers, and the audiences enjoyed the best orchestras of the time—orchestras that came from New York and Puerto Rico. Rafael Cortijo and Ismael Rivera were routinely invited, and Mon Rivera, with his tongue twisters, also frequently appeared. Even Pupi Legarreta, who in exile reinvented a charanga ensemble of high quality and popularity, showed up in the small clubs of the east side, where audiences applauded his skill on the violin. The local orchestras, while smaller than those from abroad, were on par with them in terms of musical qualities. For example, Aldemaro Romero was already recognized as one of the true masters of Caribbean music, and Eduardo Cabrera, the virtuoso Cuban pianist and famous arranger for Benny Moré's orchestra, had lived in Venezuela for some years. Together with Porfi Jiménez, Chucho Sanoja, and the spectacular timbal player Frank Hernández, known as "El pavo," these musicians led dynamic bands that were just as competitive as those from the north.

This situation changed drastically once the big New York bands fully adopted the new musical techniques. Soon, smaller bands—ensembles with as few as eight or ten musicians—started joining the scene. They performed a sound that young Venezuelan music lovers had referred to as salsa long before it had been identified as such by those in New York or the Caribbean. The middle class also succumbed to the invasion of pop culture and abandoned the old orchestras, so much so that even the good Venezuelan orchestras virtually dissolved overnight. The musical field opened up then to the popular sectors and to the youth who clamored to hear Eddie Palmieri, Ray Barretto, Richie Ray, and Joe Cuba. More clearly and precisely than in any other Caribbean country, in Venezuela salsa music truly had become popular music. It was considered a local expression performed for the unique delight of the residents of the barrio.

In 1967, when Caracas celebrated its fourth centenary, the city welcomed the best salsa bands of the time. The popular radio stations embraced them and aired their music widely, but the other stations that catered to the youth with so-called modern music ignored the salsa recordings. In the context of Latin American underdevelopment and the cultural inferiority complexes that it gave rise to, the term "modern" here refers to those products created by or for U.S. and European audiences. Thus, what is "modern" is usually not something recognized as intrinsic to Latin America. That "exquisite" music, sung in English, of course, now was confronted by this other music, one more rooted in the local, more compelling, and more flavorful but dismissed as "the music of monkeys, for monkeys" (vulgar music for the riff-raff). Salsa, then, with all the ups and downs of its beginnings, was already imbued with very important social and cultural meanings: it meant that the barrio had a music of its own.

That same year, Eleazar López Contreras published a news article in the journal *Venezuela Gráfica* in which he defined the musical moment as such: "Caracas is divided into two sectors: the East and the West. This is a musical division, as well. The East likes the 'ye-yé' music of the electric guitar, discos, mini skirts, and long hair. The West is more tropical. Its barrios are more humble and, therefore, closer to what is idiosyncratically 'Latin.'" Months later, Contreras published another article written for a luxurious set of recordings issued to commemorate the 400-year anniversary of Caracas. In Venezuela, pop music was called surf music as a result of the first beatnik movements in California. The title of the article itself, "Surf vs. Salsa," reaffirmed the dichotomy between the foreign culture and the local. While foreign pop music forced the middle and upper classes to falsely assimilate a series of values simply because they were new and foreign, salsa music, by being relevant and spontaneous, became the best representation of the new popular sentiment. The youth from the Catia barrio who fully identified with Eddie Palmieri in "Busca lo tuyo" never adopted any posturing. It was not at all foreign or alien for them to sing the coded lyrics "el niche que facha rumba . . . lo atara la Araché" or those of "The Street Is Bad":

> We're meeting at 6 P.M., don't forget to be there
> I have a lot to tell you
> It's not for nothing, the street is bad.

Fortunately for all who live in those corners of the world, the barrio is the same—each one is identical to the others and yet somehow unique. Barrio unity is real, spontaneous, and natural, and the conditions that shape everyday life there are the same. Anyone from any barrio can walk the streets of the Caribbean with the joy that comes from a sense of belonging; therefore, everyone from the barrio identified with this music. To have dismissed this music as "a thing of monkeys," as vulgar music of the riff-raff, or, more sadly, as "imported music" was an act of cultural uprooting that inevitably undermines the authentic essence of national identity and the trueness of popular sentiment.

On the east side of Caracas, Los Darts were singing the Beatles songs in Spanish, with ridiculous translations of "oh baby" as "oh nena," or "come on, come on!" as "vamos!" which never fit the rock rhythms very well. At the same time on the west side, in the middle of their songs, Perucho Torcat of Los Dementes and Federico and his Combo Latino proudly included the barrios of La Pastora, el 23, Catia, Los Magallanes, and Petare by name. In those neighborhoods the people danced and sang to the music that made them feel good. As I suggested earlier, amid all of this, orchestras like Billo's and Los Melódicos were obviously out of place. Their music *was* Caribbean, but it could scarcely reflect the new scene in the barrios. Their music placated its audiences; it lacked any power or energy. The everyday youth could not identify with music that they labeled *gallega*, or foreign. In fact, while Los Dementes never hosted any gala dances in the luxurious venues on the east side, Billo's was consistently performing in country clubs for the *quinceañera* parties of well-to-do girls. When defining a cultural world is at stake, moving easily from one social situation or locale to another can become a trap or appear to be a trick of demagoguery. Furthermore, it is impossible for the music of the rich to equally speak to the poor. If it does, then it must fail at some level, for it ends up belonging nowhere. The authentic Venezuelan salsa groups were never accused of trying to accommodate the rich, and from my perspective that virtue should be valued highly.

In 1964, while attempting to change the old charanga into a son ensemble, the Dominican musician Johnny Pacheco also established a new label of his own in order to produce and distribute his own albums. "Fania," an old son sung by Reinaldo Bolaños, was among the first songs included in this new repertoire, and one that would become very famous during the height of salsa. Its lyrics were also highly coded:

> Ehhhhh, Pa' goza!!!!!!!
> Aro macaguá
> Faniá.

Pacheco liked the name so much that his first record with his "new tumbao" appeared under this new label, Fania. At first it was difficult to launch a new label, since Tico and Alegre were so firmly established and since United Artists increased the competition with a "Latin" category of its own. The Fania Company was established with the help of Pacheco's lawyer, Jerry Masucci, a well-known U.S. fan of Caribbean music. Even so, people from that time have said that Pacheco initially had to use his own car to deliver records and that he personally made sales calls to record stores. He ran the company virtually from his own home.

Two years later, once Pacheco's own music had made some initial gains for Fania, Pacheco and Masucci, who were now partners, decided to sign new artists, beginning with Larry Harlow and Bobby Valentín. These two figures quickly became stars, not only of Fania but also of salsa. Harlow, a Jewish American pianist with vast experience in rock and jazz, had lived for some years in Cuba, where he had developed a passion for the son. Valentín was a young Puerto Rican trumpet player who incessantly wrote new arrangements for traditional music. Both musicians were swept away by the boogaloo, so their music pales when compared with that of Ray, Rodríguez, and Joe Cuba. Nevertheless, Harlow's music began to move in other directions. Encouraged by Pacheco, who realized early that the son was the only viable alternative, Harlow tried to move back and forth between the new sounds and traditional Cuban music, thus aligning himself with the style of Arsenio Rodríguez. Harlow's first singer was the Cuban Felo Brito, who made his way to New York as a dancer in José Fajardo's orchestra and never returned to the island. With Brito, Harlow remained in second or third place, but the next year, when Ismael Miranda joined Harlow's band, that situation changed. With his unique singing style and baby face, the teenager from the Manhattan barrio known as Hell's Kitchen quickly gained popularity. Miranda sang using the phrasings and gestures typical of the barrio idiom, so that even a mediocre cut, such as the boogaloo "El exigente" made it big because it was part of the trend. However one looks at it, Fania was making headway in the recording world: Pacheco was selling well, Harlow was increasing his popularity, and the recent addition of Ray Barretto and his orchestra to the Fania group injected new life into the company.

Later that same year (1967), Fania signed a fifteen-year-old trombone player who eventually became one of the most important figures in salsa. Born in the South Bronx, in another crowded Latino barrio of New York, Willie Colón was discovered by Pacheco. Pacheco also introduced him to Héctor Pérez, a young singer from Ponce, Puerto Rico. Together they formed an orchestra that, according to everyone at the time, was one of the worst ensembles in the history of Latin music. Still Colón capitalized on the paradigms established by Palmieri, Mon Rivera, and Barretto's Charanga Moderna. Although he was no virtuoso, Colón played first trombone in a combo of two trombones, piano, bass, and full rhythm section. All of the musicians in the combo were young unknowns who had only the most basic musical training or who learned by ear. Following his manager's advice, Pérez changed his last name to Lavoe, and thus the first album they recorded identifies him by his stage name. That album, *Willie Colón: El Malo*, was of terrible quality, riddled with glaring deficiencies, and . . . a total success.

This success caused embarrassment and discomfort among many orthodox Caribbean musicians, yet it is a phenomenon that merits serious analysis. From its initial stages, salsa was characterized as music of the barrio. It was the first full systematic expression that urban Latinos identified with and claimed as their own. Given its collective nature, its musical quality was necessarily uneven and often deficient. Furthermore, the young men who sang the music that they felt belonged to them were not always musicians in the traditional sense of the word. As aforementioned, few of them were formally trained, and most of them played by ear; they were motivated more by their determination and gut than by experience and wisdom. This phenomenon, when seen from the traditional point of view of rigid musical criteria, would not merit any acknowledgment or praise. Yet, as I argued earlier, it is inappropriate or unproductive to judge popular music by rigid, formal standards. Despite Colón's untrained and untuned trombone, he did offer his people a culturally valid music because it was one they could identify with, one that authentically represented them. Willie Colón wrote and sang his "El malo" number for all of those in his generation, for all of those who, like him, had not been raised in the pleasantries of good manners or in a world of finely crafted and polished music:

There's no problem in the barrio
For the one who's called The Bad One
If they say it isn't me
I punch their faces as a gift.

Following the success of Harlow, Valentín, and Colón, the Fania Company decided to sign almost all of the unknown bands emerging from the New York scene. Taking a cue from Pacheco's orchestra, Fania also recorded such veteran Cuban singers as Ramón "Monguito" Sardinas and Justo Betancourt. Fania continued, as well, the now-established tradition of the jam sessions by creating its All Stars, a group that was the best of the best but, granted, because of the musicians it brought in from other labels. It could do this without risk because it was now a well-established company within the industry. Indeed, by the end of the decade, and despite the advantages of Tico and Alegre, Fania had become the only label able to boast a catalog of authentic salsa music. When the 1970s took off, this fact proved significant. Fania would be, par excellence, *the* recording company of salsa music, and the boom that it produced would be both its achievement and its undoing.

FIVE :
OUR (LATIN)
THING

The Cheetah was more like an enormous barn than a ballroom. While it had a great location on Fifty-second Street—the area featuring the most famous clubs of the golden age of jazz in the 1950s—it was set up in the most rudimentary way for dancers and spectators alike. Apparently, the Cheetah had been used previously for a variety of activities, from warehouse to gym, from roller-skating rink to arena for dance marathons and contests. Since the mid-1960s, however, it had become a regular spot for Latin dancing, offering wild parties where, for one small price, the average music lover could hear several orchestras in a single night. More importantly, the Cheetah is significant in the development of salsa because of a single Thursday night—August 21, 1971. It is no exaggeration to say that that evening was historical, for not only was that the night the Fania All Stars performed together for the second time, but in order to celebrate the event, a group of filmmakers recorded the performance.

Two major productions documented that evening: a four-album set that Fania recorded and the film *Nuestra cosa latina* (*Our Latin Thing*), directed by León Gast. Earlier in this book, I argued that as early as 1965 to 1966 a new musical expression with all of the characteristics of salsa already was circulating. After the summer of 1971, however, that expression acquired all the vigor and impetus needed for it to expand into the Caribbean and Latino communities in the United States. Those two documents began that push.

Three years earlier when the company had brought its stars together, it had intended only to offer a super salsa-styled jazz jam session, not to produce music for large-scale consumption by dancers uninspired by jazz. Besides, so many of the guest musicians in the first Fania session had been the foundation for the Alegre and Tico All Stars as well that the first Fania All Stars session produced only two albums of a quality significantly inferior to the jam session recordings that had come before. By the time of this second session, however, the Fania label already had some figures with sufficient capital, in terms of both record sales and popularity. More importantly, some of these musicians were totally new to the scene and had nothing to do with the old Latin expressions that had developed in New York. If we analyze the meaning of this second reunion, then, it is not too much to say that the authentic Fania Stars were born at the Cheetah event.

At the helm of the orchestra was Johnny Pacheco, the co-owner of Fania who already had recorded twelve albums under the label, half of them in the new modality of the conjunto. Next to the Dominican Pacheco, Ray Barretto was the most senior Fania star, and he had abandoned the schemes of the modern charanga completely, producing seven albums in the new style. The third star was Ricardo Ray, a virtuoso Puerto Rican pianist who, along with his singer, Bobby Cruz, had moved to Fania from the Tico-Alegre monopoly. In addition, Fania acquired more power from the presence of two of its best sellers, Larry Harlow and Willie Colón, both born into the world of Fania. The final members capping off the group were two Puerto Rican orchestra leaders, Bobby Valentín and Roberto Roena, who succeeded in developing their own original musical approaches under the wing of this relatively new company.

In this way, the Fania All Stars were formed as a fusion of the best band-leaders and singers from seven orchestras, complemented by some individual veteran musicians from the New York scene. The company executives wisely decided to promote their major record-selling stars on a larger scale. This was the radical difference between the 1971 Fania All Stars session and all other preceding ones. The main objective of those earlier jam sessions was to release musical impulses that could not be explored in commercial recordings, and this produced a music that did not necessarily invite dancing. Thus, the record *Our Latin Thing* is a common item in any salsa lover's collection, while the recordings of the Tico, Alegre, or Cesta Stars are mostly in the hands of collectors or more serious salsa aficionados.

Most importantly, we need to explore the master strategy of Fania, which was to produce a commercially viable record without eliminating the two key components of a jam session—its spontaneity and the freedom of the musicians to play and sing whatever they were enthused about. This is where the quality of these four albums resides, all of which were recorded in a single night.

The mixing of promotion and jam session (commercialism and musical experimentation) succeeded for relatively simple reasons. On one hand, jamming with mambo rhythms—more or less in the earlier style of Cuban musicians during the time of Cachao López, or of the New York musicians under Machito—successfully kept the jazz from taking over, as had happened previously. On the other hand, the performance of pure sones and guarachas allowed the style of the Fania singers to stand out. These jam sessions thus had little to do with the old ones common to the city, and the sones, as a whole, were totally new—they were *salsosa* (salsa-style). In other words, the 1971 jam session had the benefit of combining salsa with jamming in a more balanced way, without the jamming being overly complex or the guarachas rigidly confined to the schemes of son, montuno, mambo, and a closing. This was why a jamming piece like "Ponte duro" aired successfully on many commercial radio stations, and why a savvy music lover could truly enjoy Fania's version of the old Cuban son "Macho cimarrón."

The golden age of salsa music began at this point when the record companies successfully combined what executives thought impossible: a spontaneous, freewheeling, and accessible music of high quality that was also highly profitable. (Unfortunately, this experience occurred only once.) Previously during recording sessions of Caribbean music, the idea of spontaneity and sales had been seen as contradictory. A musician inside the studio recording an easy and commercial record was limited to a couple of simple riffs and not allowed to improvise fully. This explains why so many of these recordings seem mechanical and cold, and why it is commonly believed that "any orchestra sounds better live than in a recording." The other extreme is represented by recordings in which the musicians experiment so much that only other musicians and expert listeners can understand what they were trying to do. The Fania session of 1971 managed to avoid both pitfalls: it created a spontaneous, fresh, and accessible musical sound. It had, one could say, the perfect touch.

The Band

That night at the Cheetah, the Fania All Stars presented an orchestra that both embodied and came to define the basic structure of most salsa bands, past and future. The percussion section, for instance, was heavily indebted to the models set up by Cachao in the Cuba of the 1950s: a fundamental trio of conga, timbal, and bongo, with the occasional addition of maracas, guiros, and claves, played by the singers. But there was a notable difference: keeping the tumba as the base of the rhythm reflected the influence of Arsenio Rodríguez, who had created the inseparable tumba-bongo pair. Also, while the old Cuban players usually alternated between the timbal(es) and the jazz drum set, salsa bands did away with the U.S. drum set almost completely. In the tradition of the old, charanga orchestras, the guiro seemed irreplaceable. In fact, as the roles of Panchito Arbeláez, Gustavo Tamayo, and Rolando Valdez illustrate, those orchestras always included a musician whose only job would be that of scratching the guiro. Given the smaller size of most salsa bands (from eight to ten musicians), the guiro was only occasionally called for, and then the singer would play it. The formerly important clave underwent a similar fate. All of the music that developed from the son revolved around a rigid structure with the clave determining the beat, and the validity of the rhythm was set by its measure. Given a lack of trained musicians and the difficulty of maintaining the beat, the salsa orchestras avoided the use of the claves. Thus, only the maracas maintained a regular presence in salsa bands, not only because they are less demanding, but also because they have been the special instrument of the singer ever since the old tradition of the Cuban septets. Indeed, it has been said that a salsa singer without the maracas is like a man without a leg.

Given its plenitude of singers, the Fania group of 1971 had no problems distributing those three percussion instruments. Even so, its All Star orchestra evinced the very central role of that other percussion trio: the timbal-tumba-bongo. That night at the Cheetah, the orchestra introduced Ray Barretto as the tumba player, Roberto Roena on the bongo, and Orestes Vilató on timbal. Vilató, a veteran Cuban timbal player and the only timbalist as versatile and fast as Tito Puente, had been a regular in Barretto's band. Despite their indisputable talents, these three musicians could hardly be considered the best performers on their respective instruments. Barretto, with an excessively Americanized style, could not match the sound of such Cuban masters as Tata Güines or Carlos "Patato" Valdez. In addition, especially in the New York scene, the tumba playing of Tomás López Sr. was much more popular and captivating. Yet, given the need for name and face recognition, clearly only Barretto could play the tumba in an orchestra as ambitious as Fania's in 1971. With the exception of Mongo Santamaría, who never belonged to salsa, only Barretto could bring that degree of visibility to the stage. Secondly, Barretto's diverse musical experiences, in modern charanga, jazz, and the new styles of the "salsa-son," allowed him to take on the challenges and the possibilities that such an orchestra presented.

The choice for bongo was less evident. Roberto Roena became a member of Fania because he was the only bongo player who was also a bandleader. Although he was considerably less proficient than many of his contemporaries, Roena's talents as a superb dancer made up for his deficiencies on the bongo. He had been a dancer in Cortijo's band, and one day when their regular bongo player did not show up, Roena had to fill in on the bongos in the middle of a set. Roena, however, was one of the most studious and intent musicians in the Latin music scene. Since he had become a bongo player by chance, he was well aware of his own limitations, and his achievements were the result of dedication and effort. Roena always took pride in his instrument; he was meticulous about his performances, corrected his mistakes, and polished his musical skills. On top of this, Roena's true sense of musicality flowed spontaneously and allowed him to lead an innovative and experimental orchestra despite his lack of formal musical training. As a result, Roena's first performance with the Fania All Stars of 1971 contributed to the group's success. His solo in "Ponte duro," while neither spectacular nor classic and worth preserving, fulfilled the All Stars' musical goals and satisfied the most demanding music lover.

Finally, as to the timbales, the reason for the selection of Orestes Vilató is perhaps the least evident of the three. The logical choice was Tito Puente; but Puente was a primary star under the Tico label, so his inclusion was out of the question. Other names, such as Willie Rosario or Orlando Marín or Kako or Jimmy Sabater, surfaced, but a host of musically extraneous factors excluded them as well. Sabater, the most important among them and the only timbal player who, without having led a band, garnered as much popularity as Puente, was also a regular of Joe Cuba's group under the Tico label and likewise rejected. So, the Cuban Vilató appeared to be the best and only choice. Despite having less name recognition, Vilató was a much better timbalist than the others mentioned, and his many years of playing with Ray Barretto made it easy for Vilató to coordinate the percussion section in the Caribbean tradition. Furthermore, because Barretto and Vilató knew each other well, they could more easily incorporate Roena, the less experienced percussionist among them.

The brass section was fully responsible for the creation of what salsa lovers call "the New York sound," that is, the combination of trombones and/or trumpets. Never saxophones. The addition of trombones was the direct result of Mon Rivera's influence and of the unique and compelling sounds created later by Eddie Palmieri and Willie Colón. It would be no exaggeration to say that the trombone is the brass instrument most central to salsa music. In Venezuela, for instance, after the fabulous success of La Dimensión Latina, one of every three bands that emerged depended exclusively on the trombones. By 1977, when many groups were experimenting with more avant-garde sounds, the trombone had become irreplaceable as the foundation of salsa. The overwhelming popularity created by the Conjunto Libre of New York is a good example. In any case, let me now describe the three trombonists in the 1971 Fania All Stars.

Barry Rogers, a U.S.-Anglo musician, played first trombone. Rogers was one of the most spectacular trombone virtuosos ever known. He had learned the tricks to the montuno during the old days of Eddie Palmieri's La Perfecta. He also had long enjoyed prestige in the world of jazz-rock as the star soloist of the exceptional band Dreams. That Rogers can be considered the best U.S. salsa trombonist is significant when we note that other U.S. musicians on the order of Tom Malone, Mike Gibson, Mark Wenstein, Sam Burtis, Keith Oqueen, and Lewis Khan have all played trombone in the salsa scene. Among all of them, this "gringo" trombonist, with his long hair and glasses, ironically became one of the best trombone players in the history of Caribbean music, and he was integral to the primary brass section of the Fania All Stars.

A young Puerto Rican who had recently arrived in New York as a freelance musician played second trombone. His name was Reinaldo Jorge, but little was known about his previous performances. Jorge's superior abilities as an instrumentalist did not take away from the fact that a number of other New York trombonists deserved a shot with the Fania All Stars. For the producers, however, this was not a concern, since the real stars were the singers, and then the percussionists. Even Barry Rogers, the best of the brass players, was never a household name among the dancing audience. Thus, the choice of Reinaldo Jorge did not hurt the band's popularity.

Paradoxically, Willie Colón, the only star in the brass section, played third trombone. As a very young musician (then only 19 years old), his skills were limited. Still, he was both the most famous and the most important idol brought up in the Fania family. Without any major musical aspirations, Colón continually experimented with two or three styles. He recorded more than ten significant solos, and while none of them is particularly exceptional, none disappoints. Simply put, Willie Colón did not undermine the vigor of the brass section; rather, his presence was important and vital for the Fania All Stars of 1971.

As mentioned before, one of the principal traits of salsa bands is their small size. More for economic than musical reasons, the old, spectacular big bands gave way to smaller bands that resembled sextets and octets. So, despite the "super band" or "show orchestra," the Fania All Stars retained the structure of the smaller band. Had Fania of 1971 attempted to reproduce the spectacular style of a Machito or Puente orchestra, it never would have become a valuable example of the predominant band at the time, nor would it have achieved its importance as the salsa group par excellence. This explains why Fania reduced its brass section to six instrumentalists in two trios of trombones and trumpets. By now, saxophones had been officially excluded, and the trombone had become the representative sound of salsa. (Given that, it would be interesting to explore why salsa did not also do away with the trumpets.)

A case in point is Johnny Pacheco. Since the final decades of the 1950s, the Dominican musician had been playing to the popular tastes, with his finger on the pulse of the New York Latino community and their musical preferences. Pacheco was not an outstanding instrumentalist; in fact, while he tried his hand at everything, he never stood out on any one instrument. Yet he was always an excellent bandleader and a complete musician who possessed one of the most important talents in this trade: a sense of sabor. To be honest, Pacheco's albums are rightly open to criticism, but they will always stand out for that particular element—which, contrary to popular thought, is very difficult to achieve—sabor. Given Pacheco's un- wavering sense of sabor, he was able to move easily among all styles and popular tastes, whether as flutist, singer, or conga or timbal player. When the fever for charanga ensembles was sweeping the country, Pacheco put together one of the most popular charangas, and it was precisely his sabor that contributed to its success. In that band, Pacheco played the flute. De- spite his significant limitations as a flutist, his band was not only able to compete with the best charanga groups, but it remained one of the great- est in the New York scene. I stress this because we all know that a charanga band without a great flutist is destined to fail. Nevertheless, even without great technique as a flutist, Pacheco achieved much because of—and only because of—his sabor. Sabor, as we all know, can create miracles.

I am not as interested in analyzing the musical traits of Johnny Pacheco as I am in emphasizing what I have noted above: that he was attuned to the tastes and styles of his dancing audience. In 1964 when Pacheco estab- lished Fania with Jerry Masucci, the former decided to change his style and move from the charanga to a new type of orchestra. His intuition led him to believe that the fever for the Americanized fusions created by other Latinos would not last. The new orchestra would have to have brass instruments, but which ones? He did not know. If he chose the trombones, he would be associated with Mon Rivera and Eddie Palmieri. This was not advanta- geous for someone like him who already had a name in the Latin music scene. Moreover, the "bad boy," Willie Colón, and his trombone orchestra recently had joined Fania, and that was another reason for Pacheco not to include trombones. The second option was to establish a big band in the old style, but that would not be successful now. In other words, he could not set up a band with the combination of trumpets-trombones- saxophones. Instead, he would have to form an orchestra using only one of those sections. Since trombones were out of the question, that left either saxophones or trumpets, but since saxophones were not widely used in the New York music scene, that choice could not guarantee success. Besides, the sound of the sax—whether bass, tenor, soprano, or alto—is too timid and too sweet compared with that of the trombone. Fans were already used to, and demanded, a bitter, vigorous, aggressive sound that could never be produced by saxophones. That point eliminated them as a possibility.

Thus, the trumpets. The Americanized sound of Latin music had brought success to musicians such as Pete Rodríguez and Richie Ray. The latter in particular had combined two trumpets and pushed them to pro- duce their sharpest and most brilliant tones. That was the only way to go.

It was clearly advantageous to make the trumpets the musical base of the orchestra, since, first, their sound would not get lost under the trombones and, second, bands with two trumpets had already established themselves with the public. Third, before it became an exclusive element of the booga-loo sound, the trumpet had historically belonged to the son. This third factor is especially significant when we analyze the presence of trumpets in salsa bands.

When Arsenio Rodríguez transformed the traditional Cuban son en-semble (the septet) and increased its repertoire and size, he added not only the conga but also two or three trumpets as a brass base from which to work. This was totally new, because in the old septets, there had been only one trumpet, and it functioned as a single voice, never as a section, which had been the case also with the modern son arrangements. Pacheco decided to pursue the path that Rodríguez had opened. He was not, how-ever, going to do boogaloos; rather, he performed the music that years later gave a richness and depth to salsa, and that was the son. The Do-minican musician exchanged his old and popular charanga for a new son ensemble similar to that of Arsenio Rodríguez and in the style that had brought so much prestige and popularity to the Sonora Matancera. The trumpets were definitely the way to go.

As everyone knows, during the days of the boogaloo fever, salsa bands used either trombones or trumpets. Here I emphasized the role of Johnny Pacheco because, within the salsa tradition, he was the first to ignore the Americanized styles and delve entirely into the sounds of the son. While the boogaloo had an impact, it did not last long, and when the Fania All Stars emerged in 1971, their musical base was the son. Thus salsa initially possessed the virtues that made it, years later, irresistible as part of the everyday life of the urban Caribbean. Now we can understand why Fania structured its musical base on nothing more than trombones and trum-pets.

To reiterate, although the three instrumentalists who performed with the 1971 Fania All Stars were very good, there were many others in New York who should have performed in that first salsa All Star group. In the minds of the Fania producers, however, the stars were the singers and the percussionists, not those who played brass. Also, at that time, Fania did not have a bandleader who was also a trumpet player, who could maintain the minimal quality of that type of band. They preferred, then, to choose their musicians from the orchestras they already managed. These musi-cians may not have been as famous or renowned as others, but they were very familiar with the current musical styles and with one another. Thus, the three trumpet players chosen for this occasion were the first trumpets of the Pacheco, Harlow, and Barretto orchestras, respectively. The section leader was Roberto Rodríguez, leader of the trumpet section for Ray Barretto's new orchestra and a veteran of the Cuban son who was equally adept with the charanga styles and the jazzy or experimental sounds. Héctor Zarzuela, nicknamed "Bomberito" (little fireman), played second trumpet. This Dominican musician had played for Pacheco's orchestra and was well known for his technique, clean sound, and talent for reaching the high registers, conveying a very unique and effective sabor in his performances. The third trumpet player was Larry Spencer, who, with Barry Rogers, was the other U.S. import to the All Stars. Spencer had been a regular with Harlow's orchestra, but since he had more experience with the pop rock styles than with salsa, he was not up to doing the conventional salsa solo, nor did the arrangers ask him to. He fulfilled a much less ambitious but no less effective role: third trumpet in a section of six brass instruments.

In closing, I would like to mention all of the musicians who, with the percussionists, comprised the rhythm section. The responsibility of pianist should have been given to Richie Ray, the most famous pianist in New York and the greatest virtuoso in the world of salsa. However, Fania hired Larry Harlow because he had directed one of the most interesting orchestras nurtured by the company. That Ray had left New York for Puerto Rico also contributed to Harlow's taking over as a regular in the orchestra. Still, Harlow had earned the post: he was available and ready, he knew the musicians firsthand, and moreover, he was coproducer, with Pacheco and Masucci, of the film and recordings that documented the Cheetah session. Ray, then, became a special guest in the Fania All Stars and played the piano to accompany Bobby Cruz, his colleague. Furthermore, neither the musicians nor the dancers considered Larry Harlow "imported," which was how they felt about Rogers and Spencer, despite Harlow's U.S.-Anglo identity, since he had already been the pianist for the All Stars in their first gathering at the Red Garter in 1968.

The only possible bass player for the 1971 Fania All Stars was Bobby Valentín, who had gained visibility when he switched from the trumpet to the electric bass. He was also the only bass player who had led a band under the Fania label, and he was the arranger of most of the pieces performed at the Cheetah. Finally, at that time there was no other bass player of his caliber.

The closing comment on the rhythm section fittingly goes to Yomo Toro. Toro was a string virtuoso, a veteran of many romantic trios and of numerous typical ensembles of Puerto Rican *aguinaldos* (traditional music). Toro joined Fania as a *cuatro* player. The Puerto Rican cuatro is a guitarlike instrument based on the same principles as the Cuban tres and with a similar sound and function. Once Fania adopted the son as its musical foundation, it had to incorporate the tres as the only guitar capable of creating a strong son. However, Yomo Toro preferred the cuatro to the tres. While this choice, I suspect, was fueled by nationalism, it did not significantly affect the overall sound. What matters here is that traditional Caribbean guitars were being used to create the new music. In New York, and even in the Caribbean, where music was produced outside typical or folkloric traditions, nobody was using traditional guitars in their orchestras. Even in the Cuba of the 1950s, the great son ensembles, such as Benny Moré's, for instance, easily ignored the tres. During the 1960s, when Cuba was isolated by the political and economic blockade and the charanga fever was giving way to international pop, the new orchestras that played Caribbean music found themselves far removed from those curious guitars with metallic strings that had been so intimately tied to the cadences of the son. Therefore, when Fania added a Caribbean guitar to its stellar orchestra, it signaled that the tres was an official part of the salsa sound. It had to be. Since salsa was originally informed by the son, the tres (or the cuatro, for that matter) had to be a very important part of this process.

Before concluding this brief note on the tres in salsa, I need to mention that Arsenio Rodríguez, one of the most influential and important tres players ever, lived his last years in New York. The last, New York recordings of the "Marvelous Blindman," as he was called, were perhaps the less brilliant or the less significant of his stunning and prolific career. Still, Arsenio's presence in New York was significant. His way of conceiving, structuring, and approaching the son was highly influential and determined the overall sound of salsa, particularly for the many musicians just beginning to explore the New York scene. All of this had to do with the choice of the tres in this new musical expression called salsa. The first salsa album where the tres is used in all of its possibilities makes this abundantly clear: *Homenaje a Arsenio*, recorded by Larry Harlow and his orchestra a couple of months after the death of the Cuban master. This recording is also considered one of Harlow's best, and it represents one of the classics of salsa. By then, it was obvious that the new sound of salsa was heavily indebted to Arsenio Rodríguez, and that the tres would be an important presence in the future development of salsa. Not surprisingly, the tres player in Harlow's recording was none other than Yomo Toro, the only guitarist in New York capable of eloquently and appropriately honoring Arsenio's memory. Thus, if Fania "officialized" the presence of the tres in salsa, Yomo Toro had to be the musician playing those metallic chords. No one else would do.

To conclude this summary of the 1971 Fania All Star orchestra, I have to mention, one more time, the thirteenth musician, its director, Johnny Pacheco. He often sang in the chorus, performed as a percussionist, or played his flute during some of the montunos. Here we have the complete band of Fania All Stars, and we can turn to the singers, the members who would become the idols, if they were not so already in that summer of 1971.

The Singers

Characteristically, the Latin music scene in New York always has had plenty of singers. Vocalists from all over the Caribbean came to New York seeking the fame and fortune that, from a distance, seemed so easy to acquire. This migration is easily explained by the fact that the singer is the freest and most independent of musicians, and the one most likely to achieve popularity. An instrumentalist always depends on the band or at least on a small group of others to make music, whereas a guitar or piano is the only accompaniment an outstanding vocalist needs. Thus, the singer can venture out on his or her own. Furthermore, while in most cases the instrumentalists need to adapt to the style and sound of a particular orchestra, the orchestras themselves adapt to the singer. In the Caribbean musical scene, especially, orchestras ultimately depend on and revolve around the singer, adjusting the rhythms to his or her style.

The Pérez Prado, Bebo Valdez, and Tito Puente orchestras, however, never owed their successes to any one singer. But they are the exceptions, not the rule. Even though most orchestras develop a distinctive sound, they do so primarily through the singer identified with them. Examples of this are as numerous as the montunos. Even if we confine ourselves to the world of salsa, we have the example of the crisis of Larry Harlow's and Willie Colón's orchestras when their respective singers, Ismael Miranda and Héctor Lavoe, left to create their own bands. Likewise, Dimensión Latina faced a similar crisis when it lost Oscar D'León. In the same vein, regardless of their overall quality or how distinguished their instrumentalists, repertoire, or arrangements, few orchestras have succeeded without a dominant singer. This was what happened with Roberto Roena, La Sonora Ponceña, Conjunto Libre, La Crítica, and so many others. The combination of a good singer and good musicianship is critically important in the Caribbean musical scene, and this is true whether we refer to salsa or to the old son.

Undoubtedly, one factor that led to the success of the New York salsa was the careful management and marketing of its singers. In the long run, the stars of Fania were its *soneros*—the improvising vocalists—who were so popular that the fans protested if even one or two of them were absent from the stage. Eventually, as Fania depended more and more on the industry and its publicity than on the quality of the music, the public image of its singing stars overshadowed their musical abilities. However, during the summer of 1971, the weaknesses of some of the singers were hardly noticeable or were attributed to their youth, lack of experience, and unfulfilled potential. While most of the Fania singers who performed at the Cheetah never reached their potential, nothing went wrong that evening in 1971, and the singers met everyone's expectations.

The Fania All Stars included seven singers: five were regulars in other Fania recording orchestras, and two were soloists. There were no guest singers—something that had been a "must" in previous all-star groups— and each singer performed his own signature style. The youngest, Ismael Miranda and Héctor Lavoe, already enjoyed great popularity. They exclusively took on the New York sound—that distinctive sound of the barrio, imbued with all of its sights and smells and so radically different from the sounds of the past. Their audiences thought of Lavoe and Miranda as one of their own, like someone they would hang out with down on the corner. They considered Lavoe and Miranda the same as themselves because, basically, they were. Héctor Lavoe had sung on all six of the albums that Wille Colón had recorded with Fania (with the exception of *El crimen paga*, an anthology of previous cuts that had been released months before the Cheetah event). From the outset, Fania had favored Lavoe, and his photo always appeared on the album covers. His singing style was considered new for the times—a style that suggested the scoundrel or troublemaker. He toyed with the streetlike modulations of the vowels, stretching the final phrases in the montunos and playing other vocal tricks that later became the norm. Thus, Héctor Lavoe became an indispensable figure in the salsa scene.

By contrast, Ismael Miranda (better known as "Pretty Boy") had a less innovative style and less natural talent but was already the central attraction around which the sound and popularity of Larry Harlow's orchestra revolved. Miranda, or his singing persona, had grown up with Fania, so he had an indisputable right to a place among the All Stars. Moreover, even before the Cheetah event, Harlow's orchestra had achieved one of its most solid successes with "Abran paso," a son that as composed and interpreted by Miranda exhibited all the traits of the salsa style.

Pete "El Conde" Rodríguez, who sang for Johnny Pacheco, was also in this group of vocalists, along with Adalberto Santiago, from Ray Barretto's band. Unlike Lavoe and Miranda, both Rodríguez and Santiago could be considered veterans. Rodríguez had performed on Pacheco's first Fania album, and Santiago had sung on nearly every album that Barretto had recorded for Fania. Compared to Lavoe and Miranda, El Conde and Adalberto embodied a more Cuban style in their interpretations of the son, and their previous experience allowed them to perform with certain styles and techniques that the younger singers lacked. Indeed, many of the innovations of the younger vocalists resulted from their inexperience.

Rodríguez and Santiago do not really belong in the same camp, however, since they sang with orchestras that represented very different styles. While Pacheco's retained the traditional structure of the old conjunto and was based exclusively on the traditional son, Barretto's did more with jazz-like tendencies, innovations, and experimentation. This meant that, although he lacked the quality or the authenticity associated with Ramón "Monguito" Sardinas or Justo Betancourt, El Conde Rodríguez must be considered the most traditional of the Fania soneros at the Cheetah (but during this moment in salsa history, the traditional sound simply meant more Cuban). Because Adalberto sang with Barretto's band, which encouraged experimentation, he was the more interesting singer. He also had a deeper voice than many others and a true intelligence for improvising with the montuno, but for reasons that had nothing to do with music, he spent less time as a Fania All Star than any of the singers of 1971.

The fifth singer of the Fania orchestras was Bobby Cruz, Richie Ray's longtime musical partner. As popular as anyone else in Ray's band, Cruz can be situated between the veterans and the younger generation, partly because of his age and partly because of his clear mastery in singing salsa. The final two of the seven Fania singers—Santos Colón and Cheo Feliciano—were called soloists because they had no permanent role in any particular orchestra. It is odd that Fania selected these two when it had four other singers under contract. In fact, it is easy to argue that either Justo Betancourt or Monguito should have been an All Star, rather than Santos Colón. Colón, after all, did not sing guarachas, but boleros, a genre that is not central to salsa. Paradoxically known as "Santitos" (a diminutive meaning "the *little* saint"), Santos Colón was a master singer in Fania, and his participation in Tito Puente's orchestra added to his fame. Market limitations, however, made it difficult even for a master bolero singer to survive in New York. Not even in the days when Tito Rodríguez tried to displace the glitzy mambo and find refuge in those love songs did the city of skyscrapers embrace bolero singers. Santitos, therefore, compromised; he improvised with the guaracha and managed to survive. These factors offer some indication of why Fania included Santitos rather than the others we have mentioned. Nevertheless, not even Fania was able to popularize the bolero, and thus Santitos's role in Fania has been ignored.

I close this circle of the 1971 Fania All Stars' singers with a brief discussion of Cheo Feliciano, "the spoiled boy of Puerto Rico," as he was introduced that famous August night. Feliciano was the only singer who had already become a fan idol, having achieved fame by performing with Joe Cuba's sextet. Joe Cuba's group had been the most adept at bridging the Americanizing influences in Caribbean music, and Feliciano benefited from that. At the same time, Cuba's sextet consistently delivered a powerful son true to its most authentic cadences. Undoubtedly this was also to Feliciano's credit and a sign of his versatility. Although personally I have always been amazed by Cheo's skills as a bolero singer, I also recognize his undeniable talent as an interpreter of guarachas and sones. Possibly no other singer who acquired fame during the salsa boom moved as flexibly from one extreme of the Caribbean style to another. That flexibility is a noteworthy skill in the best singers—the truly good ones, the authentic ones. Without meaning to propose false comparisons, I would remind readers of the exceptional facility and mastery that Benny Moré displayed when he sang boleros and sones, or of the talents of Tito Rodríguez, though one has to distinguish his musical identity as a guaracha singer from his abilities as a bolero singer. Likewise, Ismael Rivera stood out for his boleros, although he never focused much on this genre. Among the salsa singers who followed Feliciano, Rubén Blades and Oscar D'León offer high-quality cuts in all of the Caribbean genres. I refer to boleros and guarachas here, not because they are the only or most important genres, but because they are the most distinct from each other. My point, however, is not just about a singer's ability to perform both of them—since many singers have done this—but about the ability to project the particular nuances of each style, something not every singer achieves. A familiar example for Venezuelans is that of Felipe Pirela, who never could interpret a montuno, or that of Cheo García, who never sang a bolero with style or within the proper cadences of the clave. I could mention more examples, but these singers are among the best-known names in Caribbean music.

Given this discussion, it is easy to see one of the fundamental merits of Cheo Feliciano and why he, more than anybody else, had to be at the Cheetah with the Fania All Stars. Other factors also made Cheo an idol during that summer of 1971. First, fans had strong memories of his musical successes and important songs; they were familiar with references to him and Joe Cuba's sextet. Second, in 1971 Cheo was returning to the stage after a forced hiatus due to his drug addiction. He had not been in the hospital, but in prison, as would be the case with many other salsa singers. Before this happened, however, Feliciano had already left Joe Cuba's sextet. Indeed, in the famous recording "Bang, Bang, Bang," Cheo sang only the title song and only as part of the chorus. He then recorded some of the songs that Palmieri included on his excellent album *Champagne*, and after that he disappeared from the scene. His return, however, was considered highly important and had great repercussions. Vaya, a new recording company and subsidiary of Fania, hired him, and he recorded the album *José "Cheo" Feliciano* under the musical direction of Tite Curet Alonso, who had composed most of the cuts. For this album, they strategically included the sextet in order to recall Cheo's collaboration with Joe Cuba. They also virtually brought together what had been the rhythm section of the Fania All Stars: Harlow, Valentín, Vilató, Pacheco, and Louie Ramírez on vibraphone, the instrument most needed to evoke the sounds of Joe Cuba's sextet. This album is now a classic: Cheo is at the height of his singing powers, and Tite showcases some of his best compositions. The album cover portrayed Cheo as nostalgic and youthful, standing alone in Old San Juan with the ocean in the background. It included the original versions of "Anacaona," "Pa'que afinquen," "Esto es el guaguancó," and that compelling bolero titled "Mi triste problema." The rest of the album includes Feliciano singing one of his own boleros and a simple son that he also penned, titled "Si por mí llueve," a masterpiece, effective and well rounded. This album was not only a good follow-up to the previous recordings of the sextet, but it also superseded everyone's expectations at the time. For reasons like these, Cheo became a real idol and the only one who instinctually understood the salsa singing style of the moment. I make this point because neither Tito Rodríguez nor Ismael Rivera represented true salsa in this way.

Of this group of singers who became official All Stars with Fania in 1971, only Héctor Lavoe and Cheo Feliciano enjoyed unconditional popularity in the years that followed. The rest fell victim either to bad management and worse productions or to their own musical weaknesses, which became increasingly apparent to the public as time went on.

The Movie

The world today is like a gigantic tapestry whose complex and individual threads are woven together through an extensive communications network. Thus, we have to evaluate expressions of popular art in two important ways: first, the degree to which that expression is produced in a self-contained context, without regard to its future use and distribution, and, second, how that art is shared with the greatest diversity of peoples and in the most unexpected places as products of the music industry. This leads some people to make a distinction between *pure*, spontaneous, and *truly popular* art, and that other art created by the industry with the express purpose of becoming an international and millions-making enterprise. However, in reality, these two categories are not so drastically opposed — partly because the obsession with pure art is, like a medieval convent, quite archaic, and partly because the commercial nature of a piece of art does not automatically make it false or artificial. As we have observed, authentic popular expressions and simple trends are not necessarily the same thing, despite the recording that tries to bring them together. I bring this up because the recording session of the Fania All Stars in 1971 became meaningful later partly as a result of the music industry's handling of this performance. This does not imply that the music recorded that night was bad, for if that were the case, its commercial success would not have been enough. No, the music was good — as was and is still obvious to the ears of any music lover — but it became a foundational text of salsa chiefly because of its commercial dissemination months and years later.

There is a commonplace that says "a musician's best solo is not the one that was recorded, but the one he performed three days later at a club where he truly made history." This reasserts that while recorded performances are considered a permanent part of a musician's work and are subject to reviews, those that are not recorded are lost, as though they never existed, even if they were superior to the recordings. In the history of jazz — closely affiliated with Caribbean music partly because of the similar conditions of its musicians — one finds numerous examples of this. Some of the best recordings of John Coltrane were issued after his death, and not because of some otherworldly factor. Rather, a few producers researched his recordings and discovered some of his amateur recordings made during performances in some obscure club. In most of these recordings, Coltrane performed at a level he hardly ever reached in the coldness of the recording studio. This makes them much better than his *official* recordings, despite the technical flaws.

Of course, it is impossible to go around with a recorder trying to document all of an important musician's performances. Thus, we resign ourselves to whatever documents are available, despite their imperfections. This is the case with the four albums that Fania recorded that night at the Cheetah: *Fania All Stars: Live at the Cheetah*, published in two volumes, and the double album *Our Latin Thing (Nuestra cosa latina)*. *Our Latin Thing* included some material from the two previous volumes, along with conversations, interviews, and essays from the eponymous documentary film. Marketed as the original soundtrack for the movie, this album wreaked havoc in the music world.

Its songs included the theme of the film, "Cocinando," composed and recorded by Barretto and his orchestra and very much in line with what was already known as Latin jazz. This was followed by some cuts recorded at the Cheetah. Among them, "Quítate tú," a fairly typical son used to introduce the singers, stood out for Yomo Toro's cuatro solo. "Anacaona," Tite Curet's composition, was recorded in two parts—one in the studio and the other at the Cheetah, where Cheo Feliciano came back into his own. Next was "Ponte duro," the only cut from the original repertoire in which Johnny Pacheco smartly inserted a jamming riff by the bongo. "Descarga Fania" followed, a sort of remix of the old and influential "Descarga cubana" that Cachao had published in Havana twenty years before. "Descarga Fania" should be remembered for Santiago's excellent vocal renderings of Barry Rogers's solo and the *pailazos* of Vilató. There was also a cut that featured Ricardo Ray and Bobby Cruz, called "Ahora vengo yo." This number is so fine that, not to take anything away from their other work or from the work of the musicians previously mentioned, one should hold onto the album for it alone. The title and the lyrics deal with Ricardo Ray's decision to move his band to Puerto Rico following the hype stirred up by his albums with the Alegre label. He had started recording under the Vaya label, and his *Sonido bestial* was Fania's inaugural album; but while these recordings included some extraordinary numbers, overall they were quite flat. Rumor had it that Ray had lost his edge, that his move to Puerto Rico had hurt him, that he was not cool anymore, or that he was *gallego*, an outsider. Well aware of the rumors, Ray introduced "Ahora vengo yo" that night at the Cheetah, singing in response:

> When I was in New York, people criticized me,
> And now I'm all mixed up in it . . .
> I'm making a hit, playing my tumba.

"Abran paso," a cut not recorded at the Cheetah, was included on the album with a live performance by Larry Harlow and Ismael Miranda on Thirteenth Street, in the neighborhood known as Devil's Kitchen. Curiously, the filmed version interrupted the montuno part of the son to include a conversation between Miranda and a neighbor from the barrio. The set concluded with two sones: "Estrellas de Fania," structured like "Quítate tú" so that each singer could display his talents fully, and "Tema" ("Theme"), simply titled as such, which became the song played as the Fania All Stars took the stage. This recording paved the way for the salsa boom, but because it was originally a part of the film, we cannot analyze it independently of that context.

A brochure circulating at the time pointed out that León Gast, the director of the film *Nuestra cosa*, was a veteran photographer from New York whose primary experience came from filming television ads. Perhaps this is why the film's images are so dynamic and why, putting aside its musical power for the moment, the film can be read as a ninety-minute commercial. Because this was Gast's first film and one subsidized by his friend Jerry Masucci, it would be inaccurate to consider Gast the creator of the film, since he basically served as the artisan who supervised the six cameramen and wove the sequences together. Clearly, the film's true merits lie in the music and in the script, initially only sketched out and later developed in the process of filming, in response to suggestions from various collaborators, such as Curet Alonso. Those suggestions allowed *Nuestra cosa* to be more than just a film about salsa or, better said, a film with all the elements—the ingredients and spices—of salsa. The film did not limit itself to documenting musical performances. It went further and examined the background of the musicians, the world they represented, and the social and cultural circumstances they addressed through their music. Obviously, the film was never meant to be a sociological documentary, but it came very close. It also came very close to the sabor of salsa, and that was a good thing.

Earlier I indicated that the values and rationales of salsa music have always been framed within the larger community that produces, receives, and enjoys it. Therefore, to micro-analyze a montuno in a dry, structural way is not only ineffective but also counterproductive. If we do not understand what life was like for the marginalized sectors in the major Caribbean cities of the last two decades, then we can hardly understand what salsa represented on a larger scale.

The film begins with a young boy kicking an empty can in an alley lined with overflowing garbage bins. From the outset we know we are in El Barrio, a secluded world that, despite its location in the heart of the Capital of the World, enjoys few of the benefits of progress. In this way, the Latino neighborhoods in New York are identical to those of Caracas or San Juan. The garbage is the same in all of them. The young boy runs, jumping puddles and bumping into *piragüa* (ice cone) vendors until he reaches a platform where a group of children and teenagers are unleashing a street rumba with pots and pans rather than with proper drums. This insistence on maintaining their traditions within an environment that threatens to corrupt and destroy those traditions reoccurs throughout the film. In this context, it is clear that salsa is nothing less than a way to preserve that larger cultural tradition, though now molded and reborn in the confines of a foreign culture. New York is the most obvious and extreme illustration of this, and it is not coincidental that salsa acquires all of its values and meanings in that city. The infamous cultural dependence that has caused Latin America to stagnate has required our countries, little by little, to distort our own values. The desperate desire for sophistication that emerges in underdeveloped nations has led us to dismiss what really belongs to us, in one way or another, and replace it with meaningless and forced styles that come from the culture of the larger metropolis. In New York this situation is even more pronounced, since the metropolis is just around the corner. This extreme situation prompts a much more eloquent and enthusiastic defense of our traditions.

The New York Latino communities then seem like miserable and muddied islands floating clumsily amid the progress of the foreign culture. Despite their odd status as residents of a "free associated state," Puerto Ricans are still considered second- or, worse, third-class citizens in the eyes of U.S. society. They live clustered together, sadly forced into conditions of underdevelopment more egregious than what we find in the Caribbean or the rest of the continent. In response, they cling desperately to their traditions. A brief example of this is the continuous use of the tumbadora (conga drums), ever-present on barrio streets despite changing styles and U.S. fads. In extreme cases the tumbadora adapts itself to foreign musical expressions, yet it reverts to its own musical world whenever possible and has never disappeared.

Granted, from the point of view of the Caribbean, the Nuyoricans are more North American or "gringoish" than they are Latin American. Most of them already constitute a second generation, one born in New York and adapted to its rhythm. They still carry idealized dreams of their beautiful island, an island they belong to but that few of them have ever visited, but this produces a sense of anguish and a strong uprootedness addressed only through the musical domain. Thus, music has become the bastion of an identity that survives despite the effects of transculturation and social marginalization. The large urban centers of the Caribbean reproduce and extend this New York phenomenon, although less intensely. This context allows us to understand the immensity of the salsa movement that unfolded and took root throughout the region from the 1970s on. Caracans, for instance, also felt a sense of displacement, and, accompanied by a spirited and spicy clave beat, they also chose this alternative path to reaffirm their identity.

The film *Nuestra cosa* implicitly revealed the unique bridge that could explain forcefully, once and for all, the phenomenon of salsa. Just as with the so-called commercial (or recording) boom, the film is of interest for how it disseminated, on a large scale, salsa's role as a reaffirmation of cultural identity. Ironically, though salsa music was a response to displacement, its characteristics and extenuating circumstances were similar to those of the artistic productions that led to cultural dependency. Still, it is absurd and rather chauvinistic to claim that salsa is foreign music and just another expression of cultural dependency only because it emerged in New York and was produced and distributed by the same industry that launched pop. The New York that produced salsa was closer to San Agustín del Sur or Petate than to the Empire State Building or the Statue of Liberty. In other words, to call, among ourselves, some Latin Americans foreigners, especially when we all belong to a region of the continent (the Caribbean) that identifies its inhabitants in very particular ways, is to fall into the trap of the actual foreigners who, for so many years, have insisted on marginalizing us by keeping us divided.

Fania's film is full of the small details of life as experienced by Caribbean peoples within the suffocating and alien world of U.S. culture. One scene shows men hiding in the basements of the South Bronx, raising roosters for the cockfights, speaking to them, betting on them, and dealing with them in ways unfamiliar to the Animal Protection Society, which considered this a manifestation of the savagery of inferior peoples. In another scene, on a street of the Lower East Side, Ismael Miranda plays the role of a salesperson in a botanica, a store that sells candles, herbs, and icons used to cast spells on others. Again, from the outsider's view, this is more evidence of the "dark deeds" of these "inferior peoples." The camera also documents the *toques de santos*, religious rituals full of drumming and spectacle where the believers pay homage to the old Afro-Caribbean deities. In other words, the film is full of scenes from life in the streets of this other New York, one that tourists do not visit, a New York full of garbage and abandoned buildings where people do not have access to the smallest benefits of modern development.

Thus, salsa is fully contextualized within the world that defined it. The film includes the scattered elements that inevitably led to a most novel musical expression, even though the son, the foundation and musical core of salsa, had existed for well over fifty years. An especially representative sequence in the film shows a jam session at the Cheetah leading to a bass solo by Bobby Valentín. The dark notes of the bass and the loud clave rhythm being clapped out by the dancing audience serve as background as the camera shifts to a deserted street where a group of boys place a small explosive at the entrance of a building. When it explodes and the boys stampede away, the music changes to the mambo, and the camera gradually returns to the euphoria of the dance. While the reason behind the explosive is not clear, and we could read it as a typical delinquent act, what is most significant here is that this delinquency is part of salsa. Salsa emerged from the same world as this delinquency: Both are a response to the violent oppression of a social environment that treats them as alien.

Obviously, to say that salsa music is the music of delinquency is too simplistic. Rather, the music only articulates that street life, or delinquency, as a particular and defined social fact. Even when it sings the life of the street, salsa goes beyond the street and surpasses it. While delinquents of the Latino sector were the first to adopt salsa music as their own, they are not the only Caribbeans who live in underdevelopment on the margins of progress and who are victims of an otherwise agonizing cultural uprooting. Indeed, the natural audience for salsa music is vast. It is comprised of the most diverse sectors of the popular classes (of which the delinquents are but only a small minority) and of the numerous sectors of the so-called lower middle classes of the region. Yet, the sense of being uprooted is keenly shared among all of them.

At the beginning of this chapter, I argued that the definitive establishment of salsa music as a complete and novel form of music took place in 1971 as a result of the Fania recordings at the Cheetah and of the film *Nuestra cosa*. Never before had salsa been distributed with such commercial force. Never before had this music been adopted so absolutely as the contemporary expression of the urban Caribbean. The old naive and provincial guarachas that expressed life in those large urban centers euphemistically called "great cities" were now a thing of the past. Although this contemporary music shared the same clave as before, it was as bitter and full of irony as the city that produced it. Somehow, all of this became "officialized" by Fania in that summer of 1971. From then on, some of the fundamental characteristics of salsa developed further, and others quietly disappeared, mostly as determined by the double-edged values of the recording industry and its unstable trends. Now we turn to those developments and disappearances.

SIX : THE THING IN MONTUNO

Much has been said about the peculiar fact that New York City was the birthplace of the sound and style that came to define salsa. As many have noted, other Caribbean cities were home to as many or more Latinos than this U.S. city, so it is hard to understand the incredible proliferation of orchestras in New York. It is even more remarkable that those orchestras were able to survive, record albums, and make a name for themselves especially when dependency on New York had desperate overtones for the Latinos who lived there. Yet, that situation explains only the characteristics of a sound, not the many musicians who produced it. Why, then, was New York City able to supplant Havana as the producer of Caribbean orchestras? Why did Caracas not occupy that position, since, with the benefits of its petroleum industry, it had the luxury to cultivate other cultural enterprises? Why not San Juan, capital of Puerto Rico, the land with which the majority of Latinos who produced salsa in New York felt an ancestral identification? Why not Panama City or Santo Domingo? In other words, if all of the traits that generated and nurtured salsa were so wholly Caribbean, why was the city that produced salsa not part of the Caribbean?

In the preceding chapters, I suggested a host of social and cultural reasons why the Latino communities in New York originated salsa. There are, however, seemingly less important reasons that may prove equally significant. Clearly, the new sounds needed musicians who could produce them, and the interesting fact is that the majority of these musicians were in New York at that particular time.

We must keep in mind the conditions that historically have characterized the work of popular musicians in the Caribbean. First, Caribbean orchestras always had one major focus: the dance. The ability to play for dancing audiences—to define oneself in, through, and for them—determined the stability of the orchestras, steady work for the musicians, and the ongoing existence of a variety of dancing venues. When the dances were over, the musicians took their earnings back home: in other words, without dance gigs, there was no food. Thus, until the salsa boom, the record album was always a secondary objective.

These dancing venues were divided into two specific types: public spaces and private parties. In the former, people paid up front and went from club to club depending on the attraction that a particular orchestra offered. In the latter, those two circumstances did not exist. The dancers went to a party for friendship or simple celebration and not for the music per se. The musicians were only a secondary consideration. When musicians have to depend on performing for private parties to make a living, they tend to produce a safer, more neutral sound, a sort of complacent amalgam of all the trends of the moment. There is no innovation. Conversely, a city with a sufficient number of clubs can support a great variety of orchestras, each able to create its own style and sound. When music comes from public spaces, orchestras enter a genuine professional competition, since a venue will only fill up if the orchestra represents a specific attraction for the dancing public. And, obviously, an orchestra that does not pack the house is condemned to failure.

Havana, for instance, had enough clubs and cabarets to offer the public a great number of choices. Music consumers could choose between one orchestra and another, between one style and the next. This diversity obliged musicians to be innovating constantly, creating new styles and combinations of styles, and this could not help but enrich all musical production.

This situation was rarely the case in other Caribbean cities. In Caracas, for example, the local venues were very few compared with the number of private parties where musicians could earn their livings. Only on holidays—particularly during Carnival—did the public venues become primary. Yet, even when this happened, the local orchestras were at a disadvantage because people were more attracted to visiting orchestras, such as Machito playing at the Casablanca or Tito Rodríguez at the Tamanaco. The rest of the year the Venezuelan dancing public went to their familiar and private parties with any old orchestra that could play all the popular styles. Therefore, the Venezuelan orchestras did not spend much time creating their own styles: there were no opportunities for musicians to develop and demonstrate their creativity. In one way or another, other Caribbean cities also limited themselves to private Saturday night parties and repeated this phenomenon. Only Puerto Rico, which maintained a solid connection to its community in New York, was able to avoid this situation.

Previously, under Cuba's musical leadership, New York Caribbeans had developed numerous public spaces where their music could be performed with the necessary flair. This was due to two major factors. First, there was a continuous migration of Cuban bandleaders who came to New York attracted by the creative possibilities that its jazz scene offered. Second, living circumstances in the United States inhibited the possibility of large private or family parties. No Latino had a house big enough to hold an orchestra and dancers, and the costs (and other difficulties) of renting a venue negated the possibility of attempting to host parties. Thus, even with their own deficiencies and limitations, the clubs became a better alternative.

Since the music was to be disseminated and enjoyed from these public venues, to which all aficionados have virtual access, the orchestras had to use creativity and innovation in order to be competitive and develop a public following. Therefore, once Cuba was blocked from participating in its own Caribbean musical scene, only New York was able to supply the orchestras with new sounds. That gave the northern city considerable advantages that allowed it to serve as the site from which those sounds of salsa would be launched.

Nevertheless, when analyzing the emergence of salsa in New York, it is wrong to look at the various causes and reasons in isolation. In previous chapters I tried to show the complex and arbitrary world of Latinos in the "Iron Babel." Latinos were subjected to cultural, social, economic, and political pressures, and the cultural manifestations (including music) that unfolded there served as a confrontation and challenge to those pressures. As already indicated, Latino life in New York corresponded to the living conditions throughout the most populated cities of the Caribbean. In both instances, the same underdevelopment, with all of its attributes and consequences, existed. However, New York was the first city where these conditions were confronted musically—partly because they were felt more acutely and more painfully there, and partly because New York had an ample groundswell of ambitious musicians and orchestras willing to attack those conditions with salsa. This does not mean that the Caribbean did not have musicians or that they were less creative—not at all. It means that their working conditions did not allow for this type of creativity. Once the boom took off, it led to further innovation that would be the hallmark of salsa.

Again, let us recall the critical circumstances that New York offered. The aforementioned boom did not become an authentic, commercial phenomenon until 1974–75, when, throughout the Caribbean, salsa had broken down all of the myths and misgivings that had stood in its way. However, the salsa happening in New York between 1971—that Fania All Star night at the Cheetah—and 1975 offered what, seen at a distance and from a global perspective, may be the most solid and influential of all salsa. In those years, the two most basic and important strands of salsa came together—the barrio inflection and the innovative musical mixing—unrestrained by either formality or "inspiration." This culminated in a stage of rich productivity, abundance, and sabor: that is, the golden age of salsa.

64   All of the life experiences worthy of salsa were let loose: the raucous, the

confrontational, the pleasurable — "The Thing." And it took off from the montuno.

In any overview of that golden age of New York salsa at the end of the 1960s, when the dancing population already had identified a typical and specifically New York sound, the important participation of Willie Colón needs to be emphasized. This was the time when Willie not only was wedding much of the global sound of salsa to his own style and expression but was also gaining in importance. This trombonist from the South Bronx was forever creating new patterns and becoming an inevitable touchstone. This occurred partly because he never abandoned those authentically salsalike characteristics that had enlivened his beginnings: the commitment to play for the people of the barrio and to remain mindful of that as the foremost justification for salsa music. Also, throughout the years Willie consistently aimed at the right place and hit the target. He was always on the go, always ready at the bat, inventing something new and relevant.

Willie's musical life must be divided into three stages. The first began in 1967, with the release of his first album, *El malo*, and continued until 1971, when the Fania group produced his first capital cut. I spoke previously about this period and how, when Willie was still an adolescent, he managed to assert a style that, despite opinions to the contrary, was his own, authentic and effective. The second stage lasted from 1971 to 1973 — from when he recorded the first of his "experimental" albums, *Asaltos navideños*, to the year he dissolved his band. Everything suggested that this was the end of *el niño malo*'s (the bad boy's) musical career. The third stage began in 1975, when Willie reemerged with a string of experimental albums. He first moved into the classic structures of the bomba and the plena, like Mon Rivera, creating ballets such as the *Baquiné de los angelitos negros*. Then he coauthored the most important songs of the Conscious Salsa Movement with another key singer, the Panamanian Rubén Blades. To a certain extent, these three stages represent the entire development of salsa.

Having previously discussed Willie's first stage, let us move to the second, one that is still identified by the sound of two trombones and the singing of Héctor Lavoe. During those three years (1971–73), Willie produced four albums, two of which are considered classics by salsa experts. In these four productions, Willie took two very precise approaches: first, he focused on delving into the traditional sounds of Puerto Rican folk music (bombas, plenas, aguinaldos) and, second, he sought to perfect the notoriously aggressive sound that had characterized his earlier recordings. The first approach informs the two albums of *Asaltos navideños*; the second, the classics *El juicio* and *Lo mato*.

In the case of the *Asalto* albums, Willie's intention was nothing less than to create a new vision of typical Puerto Rican Christmas music within the realm of salsa. To do this, he brought in Yomo Toro as a musical guest. Toro's experience as a guitar player of boleros and of traditional Caribbean music was surpassed only by his work in the folkloric Christmas music of Puerto Rico, of which he was considered an expert and authentic interpreter. Thus, Willie achieved his basic goals through instrumentation: Toro provided the traditional element, while Willie added the New York sound. The first volume of *Asaltos navideños* was a commercial success, and although I cannot confirm the exact sales figures, I do know that it was one of the largest-grossing albums in the history of the company (Fania). The record's primary audience was island Puerto Ricans, but it was especially well received by the older generation, who, despite their years in New York, never felt as comfortable there as their children did. With this album, Willie was able to bridge the generational barrier within the new world of salsa, which was primarily Nuyorican. However, if this first *Asalto* had been only a simple recovery of Puerto Rican Christmas music, the album would have had a limited effect on the global world of salsa. Willie's use of "salsa-salsa" was the very thing that kept that from happening. For example, the first real success that Willie had in Venezuela came as a result of that Christmas recording, which included a salute to Panama through the song that all of the dancers knew as "La murga."

The second *Asalto* album, released for Christmas 1973, did not live up to the success of the first, probably because the song "La banda" had neither the drive nor the following of "La murga." Yet, this *Asalto* went beyond the Christmas and folk nuances of the first, allowing a whole generation of Puerto Ricans who grew up outside the island to preserve an important tradition in the midst of their cultural uprooting. This cultural gain, then, made up for the album's lack of commercial success.

El juicio and *Lo mato*—the other two albums considered classics— were released in 1972 and 1973, respectively. The album covers for both of them present delinquent images, something that always had been a trademark of Willie's. Indeed, by paying homage to the idea of *asalto* (which in Spanish means both "Christmas party" and "mugging"), the two Christmas albums were in that same vein. For example, on the cover of *El juicio*, Willie, Héctor, and Yomo are dressed as Santa Clauses mugging a small Christmas tree. For the larger backdrop of the cover, they used a poorly rendered drawing of the whole band in the guise of a jury bored by Willie's testimony. Wearing gangsterlike sideburns, Willie is on the witness stand facing Jerry Masucci, who is dressed as a judge. (As president of Fania, Masucci never could resist the temptation of free publicity.) The album cover of *Lo mato* was even more aggressive. It depicts a gasoline station where Willie holds a gun to a grayish-haired and apparently defenseless man and threatens, "I'll kill you (*lo mato*) if you don't buy this LP."

These album covers provoked strong reactions. They provided the enemies of salsa with evidence for their argument that salsa was the music of delinquents and, therefore, that it was harmful and led to delinquency. For those who thought salsa could become valuable and prestigious only if it were recognized and accepted by "sophisticated" audiences (whether Latino or foreign), these album covers were equally disturbing and detrimental. For the rest, they were just part of Willie's games, more of those irreverent gestures that characterized him as someone intensely "barrio"—that is, "up to no good." The bottom line is that these album covers gave Willie an exaggerated reputation that hardly represented his real life (although he did like to solve problems by fighting, as once happened in one of his first dance gigs in Caracas). Some began to see him as a dangerous ultra-delinquent, a sort of modern "Jesse James of the Barrio," without understanding that this image was made up, the result of a simple marketing gimmick in which values were intentionally inverted. In 1978, after getting to know him personally, I realized that those album covers were nothing more than graphic representations of the primal feeling—one more infantile than juvenile—that the fifteen-year-old Willie defined through his lyrics: "I'm the bad one here because I'm the one with heart." Somehow, he intuited that the heart (the same tender heart as always), once born in the barrio, had to be nurtured and defended through violence, because violence was the first and ultimate gesture that characterized life in the urban barrios of our time.

Nevertheless, to claim that this sentiment, true as it is, proves that salsa is delinquent music for delinquents is ultimately fallacious. Salsa music itself cannot be considered delinquent, and, furthermore, while salsa did originate in the barrio and delinquency was part of that environment, it was only a small part of it. I mention this not only because salsa's enemies have used this argument to devalue salsa but also because certain defenders of salsa also have tried to argue that delinquent elements of salsa are what makes it good. To suppose a major identification between a music and the environment in which it is produced reveals not only cheap demagoguery but also total ignorance of how things really are and of what barrio life really means.

In any case, Willie Colón devoted himself to singing to the world from which he came, increasingly appreciated and lauded, without being tempted by meaningless praise. From his initial posing as "El malo," Willie went on to deliver, in *Lo mato*, the song that I consider an enduring masterpiece, the all-important "Calle luna, calle sol," with its even more precise definition of the barrio, its life, and its risks. Some of the lyrics run as follows:

> Put your hands in your pockets
> Open your knife
> And be careful. Listen up.
> Lots of guys have been killed in this barrio.

The streets Luna and Sol (Moon and Sun) are two narrow, parallel streets in Old San Juan known for being dangerous: crowded with bars and seedy hotels and full of drunks, prostitutes, pimps, and pickpockets. Clearly the risks represented by these two streets in Puerto Rico are minimal compared with those real dangers lurking in any of the solitary and nameless alleys in that area of New York known as El Barrio. In fact, while most tourists purposefully walk those picturesque San Juan streets, they would never think of going into the South Bronx or neighborhoods like Catia or Petare. Willie, however, preferred to locate his music in the old island streets because that setting allowed him to play with their tradition of violence. By taking them out of their local context and infusing them with a power that went beyond the anecdotes and statistics, he gave his songs more global appeal.

For example, the old Cuban son is full of references to *guapería*. A *guapo* is a good-looking man who hangs out at the corner bar, pinning all of his fame on his smooth-talking boasts about all the women he has had and will have and on his supposed ability to resolve all of life's problems by force. However, once the pleasant neighborhood where he lived was destroyed by social marginalization and economic woes, only nostalgia for those *guapo* days remained. *Guapería*, then, stopped being a mix of smooth talk and tough talk and became physically enacted, posing real threats to others on the corners and in the alleyways.

Violence thus became a daily and inevitable thing, and the *guapo* became an "other," although the streets he roamed were the same as always. Willie Colón capitalized on this shift by portraying, on yesterday's streets, the violence and risks of today. He understood that the same site—the streets—had always been plagued by *guapos*, characters who over time had been changed into hoodlums.

In addition to "Calle luna, calle sol," the album *Lo mato* included another song that immediately took on important meaning: "El día de mi suerte," a bomba also composed and arranged by Willie. Rather than presenting the threatening aspects of the barrio, this song showed its hopes and dreams, which like violence also persistently courses through everyday life. In this bomba, as in "Calle luna," Willie focused on portraying actual experience, repeating the daily phrase that proclaims, with desperate certainty, that one's lucky day will come—that some day before death, despite all of the accumulated frustrations, luck will come. The song is as simple as the hope behind it, and both rely on an insistent stubbornness that makes what is so necessary seem inevitable. It repeats,

> My lucky day will come soon
> I know before the day I die
> My luck is going to change.

Since in 1973 salsa music did not have the radio and journalistic backing that characterized it during the famous boom, neither "Calle luna" nor "El día de mi suerte" were considered "top hits"—that ridiculous phrase that album promoters like to use. Also, even though the album exceeded sales expectations, it was not championed or promoted by experts either, at least not in Venezuela. Salsa fans, however, quickly embraced both songs, whose lyrics and refrains became part of their particular collective discourse. That Willie gave the audience what it needed and demanded and, therefore, had a big hit is evidence of something that few individuals in radio and publicity care to admit: authentic expressions of popular music, even when they can benefit from specific marketing, never totally rely on it. In fact, over time, music audiences and the wider public always recognize what really belongs to them and the music with which they want to identify.

Furthermore, we all know that those famous lists of top hits are nothing more than promotional traps and are full of upstarts and opportunists. Once the boom exploded with its own marketing gimmicks, all salsa music—both good and bad—began to fill those lists. But what concerns us most is that the music that truly matters is never limited or subordinated by the accolades of the market. "Calle luna, calle sol" and "El día de mi suerte" are two good examples of this.

The other six songs from *Lo mato* also achieved the same first-rate level and energy of salsa. They included "La María" by Tite Curet Alonso; a new version of the old montuno "Guajira ven" by the Trío Matamoros; a salsa version of the Brazilian song "Vo so," attributed to Edú Lobo; and the fabulous guaracha "Señora Lola," where the world of the *guapería* reasserted itself in its original spirit: "Mrs. Lola, better tell your husband / To watch his mouth."

The *El juicio* album did not include any lyrics that would allow for speculation about the aforementioned social issues. At that time, the *bachata*[1] alone dominated. That the bachata took over is telling, for its spirit of irreverence and partying is central to and has long determined the music produced in the Caribbean. In addition, those who think that salsa is a simple, elemental, and thus facile music need to be reminded that its ability to absorb the irreverence and partying of daily life and then transmit it with force and clarity was such a complex and difficult task that it has become a standard for distinguishing good musicians from bad ones. Previously I mentioned how Pacheco had a hard time performing music with sufficient sabor. It is equally as difficult to hit the clave of the group and to capture the mood of the partying. To produce something like "Calle luna, calle sol" appears to be much more complex than to produce a song like "El timbalero." Let me emphasize, however, that this is false. The difficulty in both cases is comparable. The standards by which we assign value to salsa áre the same for all of its diverse manifestations. Its famous "social markings" may be more pronounced in some songs or cuts (as in "Calle luna" and "El día de mi suerte," for instance), but they are always there. To downplay that social edge in any piece of salsa would be as griev- ous as to take the heart—the feeling or justification—out of the music.

Many orchestras that failed after the salsa boom, however, had tried to survive by singing bachatas, that is, by falling into the trap of their appar- ent simplicity. These orchestras did not understand that to sing a guara- cha to "the mulatta who eats fire" is just as difficult as, if not harder than, singing one to "the poor worker exploited in the barrio." Thus, a song such as Junior González's "Violencia," full of good intentions but lacking the minimal demands of the form, did not make it, whereas songs such as Johnny Ortiz's "Catalina la O," sung by El Conde Rodríguez, full of sabor, carried the dancers away. Willie Colón's "El juicio" completely exemplifies this. It did not speak of the suffering barrio. Rather, with great eloquence and effectiveness, Willie sang to the "mulattas" and to love. In addition, this was the first album where Willie, as a trombonist and arranger, began experimenting with a style that included a range of harmonic and rhyth-

---

1. Bachata is a Dominican ballad musical style that emerged in the early 1960s and was very popular among the rural and urban poor audiences. Because it was asso- ciated with so-called lower-class people, it was not considered a significant national genre until Juan Luis Guerra recorded "Bachata rosa" in 1991. The bachata is mostly a romantic song performed by guitar-centered ensembles, but nowadays it has been diversified in terms of its instrumentation, mainstreamed, and made internationally popular. Musical anthropologist Deborah Pacini-Hernández has studied the histori- cal, social, and cultural evolution of this genre in her 1995 book, *Bachata: A Social His- tory of a Dominican Popular Music* (Temple University Press).

mic possibilities, a style that later would be identified as one of a kind. The Brazilian influence, for instance, was present in "Ah Ah Oh No" and in "Si la ven," two love songs composed by Willie himself. Likewise, the traditional salsa of the previous decade was felt in "Timbalero" and in the bolero in montuno "Soñando despierto," with slightly more intensity and perfection. Willie also drew on the religious or *santera* world with "Aguanile," while, the old jazzlike tendencies came through in the instrumental "Pan y agua." Finally, "true salsa," the one that would later give its general imprint to the expression, was present in an excellent song, "Piraña," one of the best sones written by Tite Curet Alonso. This mix of elements, tendencies, and approaches gave *El juicio* a special character. Even now, salsa fans consider this one of Willie's best albums. This type of public support has outlasted the brevity of the trend itself.

In order to understand the period between 1971 and the explosion of the boom four years later, we also have to discuss the achievements of Eddie Palmieri. Earlier I noted that Palmieri's avant-garde approach continued to keep him from getting regular work as a salsa musician. He overcame the crisis of the last two years of the 1960s with the production of two incredibly important albums, *Champagne* and *Justicia*, and by confronting the new commercial development of salsa with a frankly rebellious and resolute attitude. Because of that attitude, although Palmieri was a highly influential force in creating a new edge in the 1971 New York salsa world, he did not figure into that world. He already had a reputation for being uncontrollable by those who managed the industry. Undoubtedly, then, without detracting from his (Palmieri's) considerable talents and virtues, once the boom began, Willie Colón became the icon of influence in salsa because he belonged entirely to its boom. He was the one showered with the unconditional support and even favoritism of the desk salseros who managed, controlled, and produced that same boom. Eddie Palmieri, on the contrary, was more and more relegated to its margins.

The first album that shows Palmieri's rebelliousness is *Superimposition*, released at the beginning of the decade. It expresses a sort of salsa inextricably wedded to jazz. Its sales were not that high, but despite negative expectations, the album was not a commercial failure. It did, however, demonstrate a sentiment that was summarized in one review at the time: "Palmieri is too ahead of his times; people do not understand him." And, indeed, people understood him less and less as Fania began to dominate the musical scene. Thanks to the company's commercial "brilliance," Fania increasingly became involved with the traditional Cuban son. Palmieri, on the contrary, was headed the other way: instead of going backward, he was going forward. The majority of the audience, already on board with Fania's music, preferred to leave Palmieri to those insider fans who could understand him. Only at the end of this decade, once the boom wound down and began slowly dying, could Eddie Palmieri return to the open arms of the large and numerous audiences that rightly belonged to him.

Palmieri had gained a solid reputation from his long-ago days with La Perfecta. He had become a complete leader in that he pulled together a cast of musicians who identified with his rebelliousness, and by mid-1971, Eddie was able to put together one of the greatest salsa bands in our time. This band successfully toured the most important U.S. cities, playing a music that knew no limits and that was characterized by its boldness and by the vigorous surge of its rhythms. By this time the phrase "Palmieri's montuno is the montuno of Palmieri, and nobody, nobody can take it and shake it like him" was already famous. Unfortunately, as another consequence of that same rebelliousness, very little of this orchestra's work was recorded. Only one performance, at the University of Puerto Rico, made it onto an album, and it was not released until four years later, in 1975, by the Coco label.

In that decade, Eddie Palmieri established himself as a force to be reckoned with. We could well say that Eddie was to salsa what Miles Davis was to jazz during the 1960s. Just as Davis served as a synthesizing factor for the principal figures who would develop the jazz of the 1970s, so Eddie brought together the most important avant-garde trends that would dominate salsa during the last years of the decade. Just as today's jazz—whether commercial and accommodationist or free and experimental—has very clear connections with the Davis of the 1960s, so today's unconventional salsa music owes much of its strength and attitude to Palmieri, who let loose a rebellion in those years that bookend two decades.

Between the old album of *Justicia* and *Vámonos pa'l monte* (officially Palmieri's last album with the Tico label), Eddie developed the two traits that years later brought him recognition and an enduring place in the salsa that survived the havoc of the industry's boom. The first trait was a grounding in social issues; the second, a continuous, insistent experimentation with new sonorous and rhythmical combinations. The first trait appears clearly in a unique line established from the title cut in *Justicia*, passes through the declarations and statements of *Sing-Sing*, and culminates in "La libertad-lógico." The totality of Palmieri's work from *Superimposition*—which includes live recordings from the University of Puerto Rico and from within the Sing-Sing prison—up to the album *Sentido* in 1973 serves as a remarkably full instance of the second trait.

However, what is most interesting and important is that Palmieri never separated these two aspects. He never sacrificed the message of his lyrics for his musical experiments, or vice versa. He always presented and performed both projects—the cause and effect of his rebelliousness—as a complete whole, unfragmentable and incorruptible. One element contributed to the other, supporting it and increasing it: the rebellious lyrics were sung in a musical manner that also sounded rebellious. Not to have done this would have been a contradiction, and Palmieri would not have lasted in the salsa community. However, those sincere and eloquent demonstrations of a rebellion that was not in the least demagogic or foolish were precisely the life force and influence that Palmieri brought to his music.

I do not want to fall into impertinent and judgmental comparisons, but I do find it necessary to point out some of the differences that characterize the work produced by these two fundamental leaders of their times, Eddie Palmieri and Willie Colón. First, while the former worked at the margins of the industry, the latter never stopped working for it. In addition, while Willie was focused on portraying the reality of his world, producing photographic chronicles that later were transmitted through salsa music, Palmieri sang the direct protest. He dispensed with chronicle and launched right into the argument, exchanging, as it were, the photograph for the film. While both were innovators and experimenters, representing a new trend in salsa, a healthy alternative to the urban music of the times, the musical structures that each used were very distinct. Willie, for instance, always based his innovations on the traditional schemes of salsa; that is, the same ones inherited from the old son (with a part of the theme sung by the soloist and the other developed from the soloist freely riffing with the support of the chorus, i.e., what musicians simply call the son and montuno). Eddie, on the other hand, radically rejected that structure. He was known for his much more daring harmonies and rhythms and for his willingness to let go of the dance as the most important aspect of salsa, an element that Willie Colón never sacrificed.

The sum of these factors determined what came to pass. Willie always had a more direct connection to the general salsa audience, while Eddie was limited to the exclusive world of those salsa fans who understood him. Thus, the overall balance of their influences has to be divided. Even when Palmieri was the first to determine, with adequate forethought and eloquence, what the paths of salsa would be like after the boom, Willie was identified as the one leading the way to new opportunities. Because he launched alternative paths that considered the majority perspective, his role was more influential. However, as I said in the last paragraph, I do not mean to play into the vicious cycle of evaluative comparisons. I intend, rather, to foreground how, in these first moments of the decade, salsa was able to anticipate certain key elements that would be central to defining it in the years to come. Seen from a global perspective, the salsa expression is not reduced to the isolated contributions even of these two important representatives. In reality, there were many who gave of their time and talents and who, in their own ways, created variants of salsa that are equally as important or influential. Yet during the first years of the 1970s, Eddie Palmieri and Willie Colón stood out as the most important figures.

After *Superimposition* came *Vámonos pa'l monte*, with two particularly interesting songs. The title cut was a sort of irreverent statement that represented anyone who preferred a strong and aggressive salsa to the weak and commercial variety. Its lyrics, with direct allusion to the world of drugs, went a bit further than Palmieri's "head for the hills," but it was nothing more than a reaffirmation of his rebellious postures whereby he kept himself far from the pale versions of salsa in which he had little interest. On the other hand, the montuno from *Vámonos pa'l monte*, composed with the support of his brother, Charlie, on the organ, became a classic, an excellent example of an authentic, aggressive montuno. In fact, once he was acclaimed by the nonsalsa media as a jazzlike and authentic innovator of salsa, Palmieri had no other alternative but to reiterate his montunos in the style he had initiated with *Vámonos pa'l monte*. He repeated not only the same intense rhythms but also the very notes and chords of the original. Thus, it would not be an exaggeration to say that much of what was developed and identified as salsa after Palmieri stems from his *Monte*.

The other outstanding song on this album is "La libertad-lógico." More than merely avant-garde, it must be defined as truly political salsa. It shows, for the first time, the Nuyorican confronting the Anglo-American as an oppressive and enslaving entity. There is a famous anecdote about how Eddie came up with the title for this song as "the salsa of freedom." Responding to the question of a surprised interlocutor, Palmieri affirmed, "Yes, freedom, freedom, it's logical!" As I previously noted, the song lacks the traditional structure of son and montuno. Its entire melody derives from only one persistent and aggressive montuno that surges on from beginning to end. Over the insistence of the chorus, Ismael Quintana, the most popular singer at that time, plays quite freely with four phrases, repeating them in time to the increasingly forceful rhythm. I always felt that conceiving the song in this way was exactly right; somehow it gave up a "logical" or coherent line in favor of a supposed lyrical elaboration. Otherwise, the song would have lost the effectiveness of its protest. Indeed, since the song demands freedom from the world that oppresses the Puerto Rican community, and since this demand is desperate and aggressive, the music must be equally so. The song begins with a typical, avant-garde introduction by Eddie, building to a drastic turn that leads to the montuno. Then the chorus joins in with the refrain—"No no no, no me trates así" (no no no, don't treat me that way)—that serves as the motif for the four basic themes. Then Quintana goes on to rework the phrase, "Freedom, sir, don't take it away from me." Breaking with the expected order, a solo by Nicky Marrero comes next. He alternates the traditional timbaleta with the *redoblante*, or the American drum set. Then the second chorus enters, reiterating the universal message of the song—"La libertad, lógico . . . lógico" (Freedom, logical . . . logical). This is then taken up in the trumpet solo by Chocolate Armenteros, who never overused the traditional spirit of the trumpet in the old, Cuban son.

With this arrangement Palmieri brought together two worlds and two sets of life experiences that appear to have little in common: the placidity, ancestry, and freedom that the Caribbean suggests and the harsh reality of the Nuyorican life. The first is represented by Chocolate's trumpet, and the second by the modern arrangement and restless disorder of Quintana's singing. Clearly, Palmieri's music was neither naive nor impromptu, but planned and premeditated, with specific intentions that were both justifiable and understandable.

After *Vámonos pa'l monte*, the Tico label did not come up with an agreement that would allow Eddie to record again. Thus, Tico took the recording of the famous recital at Sing-Sing and issued it in two volumes. The Tico people, who still held the rights over anything that Eddie produced, had no other option but to stand behind this incredibly bold project, although it was recorded on such avant-garde territory. The album included poems by Felipe Luciano (still bearing the oppositional and rebellious image of the Young Lords) and highlighted jazz influences as well as themes of social issues and consciousness-raising. The media thus did not promote either of these albums. Furthermore, the excessively experimental quality of the albums kept mainstream audiences from embracing them. All of this, for one reason or other, marked the end of Palmieri's traditional orchestra. From this point on, Eddie recorded only occasionally, and his public performances were so sporadic and few that the public simply came to the conclusion that Palmieri had left salsa behind. Certainly, he no longer belonged to it.

However, even though Eddie refused to abandon his experiments and avant-garde achievements, he never stopped making music in the context of salsa. In 1973, initiating a new label—Coco—Palmieri released his album *Sentido*, a production that must be understood as a genuine draft of what would be his master work: "Un día bonito," which came out a year later and was included in *El sol de la música latina*. In *Sentido*, Eddie performed only five songs (this aspect alone was radically counter to the conventional commercial album): two boleros, one guaracha, and two distinctly experimental cuts. The boleros, "No pienses así" and "Cosas del alma," represented a continuation of that extraordinarily bolero style that Eddie had worked up already in his famous versions of "Tú, mi delirio" and "Yo no sé." The guaracha, "Puerto Rico," nothing more than a love song to the island, suggested some of what Palmieri was up to. The experimental pieces were "Condiciones que existen" (a sort of salsa-rock whose lyrics, paradoxically, read, "The conditions that exist do not let us sing guarachas, no no") and "Adoración," without a doubt the song that was worth the price of the album. This last song falls into two parts. The first, or introduction, is Eddie's long piano solo, slightly supported by brief interjections of the bass, electric guitar, and timbal. The second part is the salsa part proper, with the scheme of son and montuno. If it is true that the key surprise is the piano introduction, we must also grant that the avant-garde elements are pronounced equally in both parts of the song.

Yet, as I have already mentioned, "Adoración," despite its virtues, is only the anticipation of "Un día bonito," one of the most daring projects in the history of salsa music. In conceiving it, Eddie did not hold back on any elements or areas of influence. In a masterly way, he brought together the best avant-garde jazz of the last two decades with an authentic and classic Cuban *comparsa* that erupts in the middle of the introduction. This forced Eddie's new singer, the rising adolescent Lalo Rodríguez, to sing in the highest registers for the son part, and this established a new style in salsa singing. "Un día bonito" appeared at the height of the salsa fever, yet it became relegated to a secondary tier. It did not fit the commercial norms: the song lasts more than seventeen minutes, more than half of which are taken over by Eddie's long piano introduction. Thus, ordinary salsa followers felt isolated by this new structure. Only the musicians—undoubtedly the only ones fully able to enjoy Palmieri's music—appreciated these experiments and extended them into new variants of salsa that were also rarely assimilated or accepted.

The final balance situates Eddie Palmieri as the black sheep of the family, sent to the kitchen when visitors come and left alone there to create his sounds and his mischief. That is why neither the visitors nor his friends nor even the rest of the salsa family were prepared to understand and accommodate him. However, as usual, that very same kitchen provided a unique space for the exchange of ideas and—in salsa terms—of spices. Palmieri's mischief, after all, offered something special of its own—an essential sound and an indispensable sabor.

Colón and Palmieri, then, serve only as reference points on a spectrum that displays the full range and limits of an uprooting force that swept through salsa at the end of the 1970s. In other words, Palmieri and Colón represent the two extremes of a landscape that was peopled by others also of influence. To that end, since we are still occupied with the beginning years of the decade, I now must mention a musician who, in his own way, also molded some of the shapes of contemporary salsa. I refer here to Ray Barretto, perhaps the best bridge between Colón and Palmieri.

Barretto, already identified as one of the primary innovators in Caribbean music in New York, became a catalyst for the past influences and future hopes that were converging into the salsa sound at this point. Once the structures of the modern charanga ensemble became stabilized as a band of three trumpets and complete rhythm section, Barretto was ready to try any new style that came along. Palmieri modified the nature of his orchestra according to the make-up of its members—an irregular meeting of diverse musicians that made getting regular work or public appearances difficult. Colón would not go beyond the sound his two slide trombones would allow (and recall that neither Willie nor Eric Matos, his other trombone player, were virtuosos). In marked contrast, Barretto had the luxury of maintaining an orchestra of stable and virtuoso musicians, and this enabled him to develop a sound that went as deeply into the most daring jazz influences as it did the most traditional old son-montunos. This made him appear to be a catalyst, putting him in an ideal situation for setting new directions for salsa. Though Barretto's few and occasional compositions hardly qualify him as a composer, he took his place as the logical connecting point between the thematic chronicles of Colón and the forceful arguments of Palmieri. To put it simply, Barretto borrowed from each of them and provided his own synthesis.

Barretto's albums issued between 1970 and 1973 offer a satisfying compendium of everything that happened to the world of salsa, especially in that neutral New York context where salsa existed without Americanizing tendencies and opened itself to a sound that was much more Latin or Caribbean. It did not rid itself of jazz influences—for these were too important and transcended the nationalist considerations—but it rejected the avalanche of pop rock and all of its cultural force. The album covers did imitate many images found on rock albums, but while they displayed hallucinatory drawings and the absurd and laughable metaphysical poses of the time, the music actually included modern versions of such classics as "Guajira guantanamera" or "Bruca maniguá," boleros by Rafael Hernández, and plain old montunos kept hidden under the unpleasant D.R. (reserved rights). Barretto thus attacked everything that could be attacked, impressing a personal seal on all of his musical productions, from the modern sounds—in the famous wave of "Ahora sí" or "Vive y vacila"—up to his classic version of the "Bruca" by Arsenio Rodríguez. This modernizing became the most fundamental characteristic of the majority of salsa that developed after the boom and that later was undermined by the boom itself. The simple modernization of the old Cuban son was sometimes enriched and other times destroyed. Throughout all of this, salsa always referred to the contemporary barrio, the only real sustenance this music had known prior to the days of the commercial explosion.

Ray Barretto, in this sense, again represents a middle-of-the-road position. While both Colón and Palmieri mostly composed their own songs or performed contemporary ones, other figures—such as Harlow and Pacheco—remained dependent on the old Cuban music. Barretto balanced aspects of the old and new without succumbing to what had already been done and without exaggerating the risks of what was to come. This approach allowed him to produce some of the most important albums of this period, such as *Power*, *The Message*, and *Que viva la música*. This last album, released in 1972, exemplifies an important moment in Barretto's musical life. Not only is it the last album that he recorded with his orchestra, which dissolved months later, but it also represents the most polished fusion of all the elements and styles for which he was known. One cut, for example, was a much more ample version of "Cocinando," the song used to promote the film *Nuestra cosa*. Even now, it is considered a good example of what some critics insist on calling "Latin jazz." Meanwhile the guaguancó "Que viva la música"—written by the Cuban Roberto Rodríguez, Barretto's first trumpet at the time—represents a declaration of the most effective principles of true salsa:

> Music is the art
> Of expression with emotion
> The true feelings
> Of the heart.

In addition, this album's cover remains one of the best that the salsa world has ever imagined. Based on a drawing by Walter Vélez, its background is a panoramic view of Manhattan. To one side, Barretto, bare-chested and chained to a conga drum, raises a defiant fist toward a sun with a key enclosed in it. This obvious and elemental symbolism was very compelling to a world that, despite the tropicality of its music, had nothing to do with the palm trees and fabulous beaches celebrated in traditional songs. For New York Puerto Ricans, or Boricuas, reality was exactly as Vélez had painted it. This can also be said for all the inhabitants of urban Caribbean barrios, despite their proximity to the fabulous beaches. Thus, that album cover continued to depict a reality much like their own, easily understood and embraced.

In support of that image, the back cover included a beautiful poem in Spanglish (an important detail) by Felipe Luciano in which he honored the Latin character of the Nuyorican, rooted in the cultural ancestry of a community that desperately struggled not to lose its identity. Granted, this Spanglish provided a framework only for New York's Latino community, since it left out other urban Latinos who did not face as many social and cultural pressures and so did not feel the need to modify their Spanish. However, I must point out two factors here. On one hand, as a direct result of Boricua transculturation in New York, Spanglish functioned as a unique code by which Nuyoricans identified themselves within an immense foreign culture. This was a culture that isolated and imprisoned them, yet one that they could not do without. On the other hand, although our Caribbean cities were not taken over by foreign nationalities, the constant threat of that foreign culture was always present. Therefore, in one way or another, the image of a Latin torso, congas, and chains also resonated directly with all of us. Furthermore, in the same way that salsa represents the unification of Caribbean musics and cultures, it also can offer alternatives for each particular case of cultural uprootedness. This continues to be evident despite the awkward and chauvinistic charges of misconstrued nationalism.

In 1973 most of Barretto's musicians—musicians who had been key to creating and consolidating Barretto's style—left the group in order to start their own. These included Adalberto Santiago, the singer whose voice had become a hallmark of the Barretto orchestra, and the percussionists Johnny "Dandy" Rodríguez Jr. and Orestes Vilató, who had been Barretto's timbal player since the days of the Charanga Moderna. Trumpet player René López and veteran bass player Dave Pérez also left. Almost immediately, all of them formed the core of the emerging Típica 73. Barretto decided to take a break amid the flurry of recordings that foreshadowed the approaching commercial boom. The tumba player, then, produced an unusual recording titled *The Other Road* (*El otro camino*), which was made up of six instrumental pieces with no other intention than to sound like jazz.

This truly excellent album was totally ignored by the salsa community, which did not feel compelled to understand this abrupt change. Fania, which had no interest in breaking into the jazz market and, indeed, no idea how to do so, also contributed to this recording's ending up in a drawer without the fortune or future it deserved. In addition to its other virtues, the album introduced two excellent musicians: the North American flute player Art Webb, who was already known from his first recordings with Chick Corea, and the Colombian pianist Eddie Martínez. The percussionist Billy Cobham also made his debut in the Latin world, masterfully adapting his drums to a rhythmic expression that was unique. A remarkably rich trumpet trio also stood by Barretto: Roberto Rodríguez, the Mexican Manuel Durán, and the Boricua Joseph "Papy" Román. With the obvious exception of the guest musician, Cobham, this band prepared the way for Barretto's inevitable return to salsa after his brief flirtation with jazz.

Before the end of 1973, Barretto brought out an album called *Indestructible*, in which he appeared dressed as Clark Kent with the Superman emblem peeking out from under his shirt. Here Barretto went back to his old strength, to that salsa that was moving toward a balance of both tendencies, in themes as well as in purpose. Tito Allen was, without a doubt, one of the best salsa singers in the New York milieu, and his voice influenced the quality of Barretto's return.

Barretto's definitive hit, his high point in the salsa world and his most mature work, however, came two years later, in 1975, with the release of his collected hits: the famous "Red" album or "the album of the congas," simply titled *Barretto*. In order to record it, the tumba player depended on two singers: Tito Gómez, a young vocalist who recently had migrated from Puerto Rico, and Rubén Blades, who was placing himself on a higher level of salsa music for the first time. The selected repertoire borrowed from the Cuba of yesterday and today. "Ban ban queré" and "Guararé" (originally titled "El guararey de pastorita") were written by Juan Formell, a Cuban bass player and director of Los Van Van. "Guararé" became one of the most spectacular successes of the entire boom, but the majority of the recording was made up of important songs written by two of the most influential and renowned composers of salsa: Tite Curet and Blades himself. Curet's "Testigo fui" is a son dedicated to the courage and honor of the Puerto Rican people, and his "Vale más un guaguancó" is one of the most beautiful songs that this music has ever known. Blades's numbers included the bolero "Esto es amar" and "Canto niche," a song that salutes the eternal Caribbean blackness but that was awkwardly retitled "Canto abacuá" by the New York record producers. This material was presented in the most effective arrangements by a very cohesive band that fully represented the best of the salsa spirit, and all of that makes *Barretto* one of the chief documents of salsa music.

This seemingly inevitable plentitude represented the end of an era. By 1976 Barretto had dissolved his band. Under the leadership of Gilberto López, all of Barretto's former musicians were now isolated and at the margins, trying to survive with their new orchestra, called Orquesta Guararé. Barretto then decided to abandon all the usual structures of salsa and to delve further into the sophisticated world of jazz. He signed an optimistic contract with Atlantic, a powerful international label, and at the beginning of 1977 he released a new recording, significantly titled *Tomorrow*. Here Barretto reproduced part of the spirit that had marked his salsa career. Particularly noteworthy is his imposing version of "Que viva la música," which contains a vigorous exchange of timbales played by the two special guests, Tito Puente and Orestes Vilató, and a fairly satisfactory indication of a new musical direction for him that will be analyzed in the next chapters.

For now all we have left to discuss is the other branch that characterized the first years of this decade. For various reasons that I will address later, this branch, stemming from the traditional son, involved and limited most of the salsa that would be produced during the commercial boom. Performed without modifications or major innovations, the traditional son used only the phrasings of Cuban music from the 1940s and 1950s. In my opinion, two key figures, each with their own variants, served as the creators of this tendency: the Jewish-U.S. musician Larry Harlow and the Dominican Johnny Pacheco.

As previously mentioned, in the 1970s, New York salsa gave preeminence to the son. The Fania All Stars of 1971, who represented an excellent amalgam of all that had and could happen, openly announced (in a rather ostentatious way) their preference for the old styles of the son. Among all of the diverse styles, themes, and influences that were initiated during the final years of the previous decade, only two survived into the 1970s. The first of these was the avant-garde, best represented by Eddie Palmieri and Willie Colón, despite their differences. The second was the classical approach, or to be more precise, the style "encapsulated in the traditional" and inspired by Arsenio Rodríguez. This style hardly ventured beyond the music established by Cuban traditions.

Of course, just as Palmieri and Colón represented two radically different aspects of the avant-garde, so Harlow and Pacheco set the two opposite poles that mark the parameters of the traditional style. Harlow knew how to capitalize on Arsenio's influence to create new sound combinations that were valid and interesting. Pacheco, however, kept his expectations and musical ambitions low and ended up sheltered in what many dancers called—and with good reason—the "modernized Sonora Matancera" or "today's Sonora Matancera."

During the first two years of the 1970s, for instance, Pacheco released *Los compadres*, with his regular singer, Pete "El Conde" Rodríguez, and *Los dinámicos*, with the excellent matancero singer Justo Betancourt. According to Fania, the first album set a sales record and immediately showed the influence of the Matanzas sound on salsa. It included a great part of the repertoire of prior Cuban recordings, and it reaffirmed the strength of that music in the development of montunos. The traditional scheme (of son and montuno) was modified to fit the desired effects of the album: the son part was reduced to its minimum, taking away as much of its importance as possible and giving all of the attention to the montuno.

In this way, much earlier than anticipated, most of Pacheco's cuts were already structured around the montuno and developed with a variation of one or two choruses. (In many cases this second chorus was nothing more than the repetition of the last phrases or words of the first). His cuts also alternated between one or two different mambos and the occasional interjection of a piano or tres solo. The mambos themselves were quite elementary: without major harmonic achievements, they were configured on the repetition of a few notes meant to do little more than to reiterate the beat. Embedded in the phrasings of the montuno, the trumpets and the drums imitated the old Cuban tradition and generally took their solos in the intervals between the choruses. Therefore they were not isolated but, rather, assumed a true leadership role in reaffirming the rhythm. In one way or another, these elements came to characterize what we have called the matancerization of salsa. Though it was one of the first variants to emerge and later dominated the market during the heyday of the boom, this variant of salsa fell out of view and became nearly nonexistent. If we take into account that the recorded songs were basically the same ones published earlier in Cuba, we will understand why this variant, in addition to its musical characteristics, wore itself out by the end of the euphoria and was, in salsa terms, definitely just a trend. Any drive or merits it had were fed only by the publicity and needs of the recording industry.

Harlow released *Abran paso* and *Tributo a Arsenio Rodríguez* around the same time that Pacheco's two albums came out. Both of Harlow's albums are essential for understanding the overall balance of the salsa evolution. In the first album, in contrast to what happened in the matancera style trend, the son was used and molded according to the phrasings and forms of a more modern sound. Consequently, it belonged much more to the salsa community. Composed and interpreted by Ismael Miranda, the song that gave its name to the album became one of the greatest successes of the emerging salsa expression. Equally popular was another song by Ismael, "Abandonada fue," while the extraordinary "Tiburón," by Tite Curet Alonso, helped to complement the contemporary and aggressive phrasings of a son that, without a doubt, tried to accommodate itself to the new styles and the new realities that shaped the life of Caribbean music and its protagonists.

To be sure, this bridge between salsa and the world that created and enjoyed it would never be as direct, premeditated, and effective as that established by Willie Colón, Eddie Palmieri, and all of those who worked with salsa from an avant-garde rather than a traditional perspective. In Harlow's case, the bridge was strictly musical. Any identification with social realities occurred only in the sound patterns, since neither the lyrics nor the themes offered anything relevant to that context. Harlow's songs presented a weak version of *guapería* without the old chivalry of the traditional son or new expressions of the contemporary valiance. The lyrics were only a simple catalog of commonplaces and empty boasts or love spats where the adolescent problems of the singer and the composer were solved in insufficient and inefficient ways with clichéd naïveté.

Nevertheless, Miranda's appearance, his own adolescence and noticeable inexperience in performing the Caribbean song, his intrinsic condition of marginality, and his true stamp as a citizen of the Latino barrio of New York, were strong enough to identify him and the music that he represented as undeniable products of the urban reality that shaped salsa. Thus, Ismael became another member of the family. He went onstage, attended recording sessions, and appeared on the album covers representing an entire community that was like him and felt like him, with all the strengths and weakness of that position.

Harlow's other album memorialized Arsenio Rodríguez and was based on important musical elements, making it much more solid and evocative. As I have already noted, this was the first album that publicly acknowledged Arsenio's influence on salsa, with all of the consequences that this suggested. Of the six cuts, four were original compositions by Arsenio, and two of them were created especially for this occasion. The Cuban's songs ("No me llores," "Suéltala," "El terror y kila," and "Quique y chocolate," later renamed in New York as "Tumba y bongó") were performed in the spirit of the original, but the arrangements that Arsenio's orchestra had initiated were revised using the new salsa phrases and modes. For example, a song such as "No me llores," a fast son-montuno in the original, was slowed down, even to the point of including some bolero elements. This resulted in a very dense and heavy son with a piano solo by Harlow that was certainly surprising and modern and that marked the high point of the shift between historical periods. A similar thing happened with "El terror" and "Tumba y bongó," where the slow tempo of the montunos revealed the first difference with Arsenio's original performance. Even so, 83 the all-important *silences* and mournful choruses that were typical of the Cuban orchestra continued to be honored in the New York versions, in ways in which they had never been used by any orchestra outside Cuba. This was due to the influence of two veterans, the great Marcelino Guerra and Yayo el Indio.

All of this, of course, is of secondary importance when considering the presence of the tres. As mentioned earlier, it is here that the tres becomes officially important as an essential element of the subsequent salsa sound, not only for the traditional (or matancera sound), but also for the avant-garde. If this album dedicated to Arsenio Rodríguez had a star, it would have to be none other than Yomo Toro and his tres, not only because of his solos, but also for the place of honor and foremost significance that was given to him at the time.

Finally, I want to mention the two songs that were composed in New York as a salute to the importance of Arsenio Rodríguez. The first, simply titled "Arsenio," was composed by Larry Harlow and Ismael Miranda and did little more than offer honeyed praises to the Cuban musician. The second, "A todos los barrios," created a beautiful homage to "today's" (contemporary) salsa, which erroneously was already being called "yesterday's salsa." This song was composed by Lázaro Prieto, a bass player with Arsenio who had immigrated to the United States during the days of the revolution and who, like so many other musicians in those circumstances, never fully adjusted to musical life in New York. He ended up driving a taxi throughout the anonymous streets of the city.

In 1972, Harlow's rather insignificant album *Oportunidad* marked the end of Ismael Miranda's association with the orchestra. The next year, Harlow denounced that split and boasted that he would launch a totally new project, something unheard-of in the world of salsa: an opera, a Latin opera, as it was publicized by the industry at the time. Titled *Hommy*, it was a salsa version of *Tommy*, the rock opera by the British group The Who. In the process of composing it, Harlow pulled in each of the characters one by one, forcibly transplanting them from the London neighborhood to the New York ghetto. Tommy, the young blind, deaf-mute man with a surprising talent for playing pinball, became Hommy, likewise blind, deaf, and mute, but with inexplicable virtuosity on the bongo. From here on, the parallels between both operas continued to unfold in absurd ways. Only two good things came of this. One was the song "El mantecadito," which was created with minimal reference to the English text and thus was free and spontaneous, without owing anything to the original. The second, "La gracia divina" ("The Divine Grace"), was a translation of the evil "Acid Queen" from the original score. That "Queen" was transformed in the Latin barrio into a sort of fairy godmother sprinkled with images and poses inherited from Santería and from religious myths rooted in the Caribbean. Except for these two songs, *Hommy* was nothing more than a desperate and ineffective attempt at a comeback using the translation of a story that never made sense for Latinos.

Yet the last word on *Hommy* is not totally negative, despite the fact that this supposed opera was of little interest as a salsa product. On one hand, this was the first attempt to bring a different perspective and another alternative to salsa, one that did not damage but rather enriched it. The failure of the product did not negate its intention. On the other hand, musically it provided a good example of how the son could be dressed up in contemporary styles without the slightest harm to its original expression. This, it seems, satisfied the aspirations of the composers, Larry Harlow and Heny Alvarez, for whom the success of the musical arrangements made up for all of the inappropriate contradictions of the story and the awkward way it was told.

I cannot close this discussion about *Hommy* without mentioning two important figures for the salsa that developed in later years. Marty Sheller, a veteran musician from the United States, had become acquainted with Mongo Santamaría when Sheller was a jazz performer. Sheller later became Santamaría's trumpet player, arranger, and producer. He was also in charge of coordinating all of the musical structures for *Hommy*, and he contributed the majority of its arrangements. He became, then, one of the real heroes of this achievement and, after 1973, one of the most important arrangers in salsa music, responsible for many of its innovations and experiments. Furthermore, his work, even when it was commercially oriented, never diminished in quality. The other figure, already a mythological one throughout the Caribbean and the European continent, was Celia Cruz, the guaracha singer personified. When she sang "The Divine Grace" in *Hommy*, she announced her entrance into the world of salsa as a significant performer.

The reader may ask, But wasn't Celia Cruz always in the world of salsa? Wasn't she one of the first ones? No. Celia had been part of the Caribbean sound and, indeed, one of its founding figures, but until 1973, Celia had never ventured into the salsa arena. Let us leave aside the fabulous music that Cruz recorded with the Sonora Matancera in the years preceding the Cuban revolution. Let us occupy ourselves, for the moment, with her work in the United States beginning with the 1960s and without the Sonora. Celia recorded as a soloist, often accompanied by Tito Puente and his orchestra. She also appeared in a variety of specials and produced some recordings of variable quality. All of this material kept her connected to the dancing audience, but none of these factors made her part of the salsa boom. True, Celia never changed her old Sonora style, so that for her the distance between her way of singing and the new salsa orchestras was always minimal, almost imperceptible. Yet, for the young salsa follower, the fifteen-year-old buying up all the Caribbean music of Willie Colón, Richie Ray, and Eddie Palmieri, Celia Cruz only began to exist once she recorded with Fania, alongside Pacheco, Harlow, and Willie Colón himself. Had these albums not been produced, those young salsa followers (and the larger audience they represented) would never have recognized Celia's voice and presence as one of their own. She would have remained a famous icon of the past, a pioneer whose music did not make it into the modern sound.

Celia obviously joined the branch of traditional salsa not only for musical but also for social and political reasons. At least in the beginning, she did not connect with the alternative music of the salsa avant-garde. Within the traditional salsa, however, it did not take long for her to reach the furthest end of its (accommodationist) extreme. If previously I defined this salsa caught up in the furor over the traditional as matancerization, it would follow that Celia would be at the forefront of this style. The emergence of this style really began in 1974 when Celia recorded an album with Pacheco's orchestra, an album that significantly propelled the traditional style into the forefront of the recording boom.

Pacheco's orchestra was not the Sonora Matancera, but it came close. The wind section was based on two trumpeters playing in the high registers without any clear distinction between first and second trumpet. Each alternated so that their mambos, simple in appearance and in harmonic propositions, were tremendously powerful and effective. Beyond the two trumpets, the rest of Pacheco's orchestra was one rhythm section. As in the case of the Sonora and of all the other groups that performed the son following Arsenio's innovations, the percussion consisted only of a tumba player and a bongo player who dealt with the montunos with a handbell. Pacheco, the main singer, handled the rest of the percussion: the maracas and the guiro. The rest of the rhythm section included the piano, bass, and tres. The piano had to be acoustic, since an electronic instrument would distort the traditional nature of the music. The bass was also preferably acoustic or, lacking that, a bay-bass (an electric bass shaped like a counter-bass, but never a bass guitar or conventional electric bass, for the same reasons stated above). The tres, as already mentioned, provided the most definitive nuance of the traditional salsa sound. This may be the only real difference with the original Sonora Matancera, where the tres was never included and where the director, Rogelio Martínez, was never heard playing his own instrument, the guitar, either on recordings or in public performances.

Pacheco's orchestra, then, extended the life of the old Sonora through this modern variant. With the slightest nuances of difference, this kind of orchestra served as the platform for Celia Cruz's stardom.

Their album, titled *Celia and Johnny*, was full of old sones. Cruz also sang the old and beautiful bolero "Vieja luna," a song from the black folkloric tradition of Peru; "Toro mata"; and only one autochthonous song from the Nuyorican salsa—perhaps the best cut of the entire album— "Quimbará," penned by the late Junior Cepeda. This song is still unbeatable. Celia's intelligence and sabor in playing with the montuno, as well as the extraordinary arrangement, made this one of the most anthologized cuts of salsa music. The lyrics, drawing on the old tradition of celebrating music itself by giving it primary emphasis and by rooting it in everyday life, represented a microcosm of everything that had happened in the Caribbean rumba:

> Quimbará Cumbará
> Cumbaquim Bam Bam
>
> . . . .
>
> The rumba is calling me
> The bongo says I have to go
> I'm waiting for the moment
> To sing a guaguancó
>
> . . . .
>
> My life is so much
> The good rumba and the guaguancó.

In the 1970s, Celia recorded four albums with Pacheco, and the first two are the best of the series: the one mentioned above and *Tremendo caché*, released in 1975. The rest, which came out of the fever of the recording boom, lacked importance because they were mere copies of the past, without any unique features. I will discuss these in the next chapter, for we need to see them within the context of the boom. For now it is more relevant to note that, in 1974, the other variant of the traditional salsa was also being produced, one that would try to add innovations to the traditional cadences. This was the same year that Larry Harlow recorded what would be his most important and successful album: *Salsa*.

This recording brought together three very valuable and special elements. First, most of the recording industry officially accepted and used the term "salsa" for the first time. Before then, the term had been bandied about in a sporadic and haphazard way. Albums that used the word on their covers never gave it much meaning, and direct references to the term "salsa" were never deliberate or clearly intentional. By naming his album *Salsa*, Harlow reflected a generalized feeling within the community of salsa followers that had not yet been wholly or, let us say, officially affirmed. After Harlow's record, Fania proclaimed itself a salsa company, and when it produced a second film in 1975, it was simply titled *Salsa*. In this way, the term was exported not only to the Caribbean community but also to U.S., European, and Japanese audiences who were beginning to respond to this proliferation of record albums. While the albums produced in 1974—and, indeed, many produced earlier—could have been called salsa, Harlow's achievement lies in his seizing the opportunity. He was the first to infuse the term with an intrinsic value, and he did so without offering any secondary explanations or excuses.

The second contribution of this album was that it represented the culmination of Arsenio Rodríguez's influence on a truly contemporary sound. In the famous *Tributo* album, Harlow's music still had sounded halfway between Arsenio's style and the oncoming new salsa. Luckily, he closed the gap three years later in 1974, with *Salsa*. North American trombonists Mike Gibson, Sam Burtis, and Mark Wenstein were responsible for the majority of the arrangements. They realized that the New York salsa was a valid development of the jazz they had been playing and that, with their modern arrangements, they could contribute to this new vision and treatment of the old Cuban son. They kept the traditional structure of the son and the montuno, but the mambos that were interlaced with it reflected a way of conceptualizing that structure that was very different from what Lily Martínez, the old arranger for Arsenio, had established. Likewise, the piano, trumpet, trombone, and bass solos were imbued with a totally contemporary spirit, quite far from the patterns of tonic and dominant chords that had characterized the musical elaboration of the traditional son. It is worth noting that this type of innovation was also very different from that of Palmieri, Colón, and the other avant-garde musicians. It did not pretend to escape the world of the son or to modify it with any variants that would risk taking away its virtues.

The third element that gives the *Salsa* album a very special character is what has been called "the rebirth of the charanga." From the first years of the 1960s, the charanga ensemble had virtually disappeared from the Caribbean world (except, of course, in the Cuban context). It was, in effect, only during the developing boom that the charanga came back into favor with music lovers. Although Harlow's orchestra was not technically speaking a charanga, his album *Salsa* created this opening. Two of the songs from the album were especially influential: Arsenio's "La cartera," which eventually became Harlow's most successful cut, and "El paso de encarnación," penned by Richard Egües, the exceptional flute player from Orquesta Aragón. In order to work with those two songs, Harlow adjusted the traditional structure of his orchestra (a pair of trombones, a pair of trumpets, and a complete rhythm section) by adding violins, one of the basic features of the charanga ensemble. Thus, Harlow was able to combine both formats: the salsa and the charanga bands. This was also possible thanks to the involvement of the U.S.-Jewish musician Lewis Khan, Harlow's regular trombonist, who was able to play the violin equally with utmost facility. A further note on Khan's virtuosity is that he was able to deliver a pair of very satisfactory solos, although he had no previous charanga experience. Taking advantage of the electronic system, the amplified sound of one violin gave the sensation that there were many, or at least the two violins essential to any respectable charanga. With "La cartera" and "El paso de encarnación," the salsa audience began to recognize the possibility of violins, and, as with the complete re-incorporation of the charanga, they became accepted as part of the salsa world a few years later.

As 1974 came to a close, it marked the end of the initial stage of the recording boom. During the first years of the 1970s, salsa began to define itself through its two fundamental variants—the avant-garde and the traditional sounds—and many musicians and orchestras tried, in one way or another, to capitalize on one of those tendencies. Some, hastily and without any vision, were not able to ground themselves. Others, however, despite a lack of publicity or distribution, did manage to slip into a particular modality that allowed them to take important musical steps. This was the case of a modest orchestra that stuck with the traditional sound but brought in avant-garde lyrics, thereby making its own contribution to the period just before the boom: Ernie Agosto and La Conspiración.

A brief mention of Agosto is essential to this book. The first album that his group released was called, simply, *La conspiración* and appeared around 1970 under the direction of Willie Colón. Its musical quality was poor, since the members of the band had not worked through the influence of the boogaloo; nor could they handle the basics of musical performance. However, even though this recording hit the streets without making use of some of the most important nuances of the previous decade, it did address the most important social and political issues of the immediate past. This in itself was valuable, since what had happened in the 1960s had never been sung about in such a direct way. A bit behind the times, but at least, finally, here was an album that summarized the world and experiences of the Young Lords in the chronicles of salsa. Songs such as "La voz" talked about "the voice of youth, the youth that does not want an establishment, the youth that has a voice and will be heard," and the montuno of "Tengo poder" revolved around the challenge of "I have power, power to conquer." In addition to striking such a tone, the name of the orchestra already suggested a rebellious, irreverent, and even subversive attitude. A personal anecdote may be useful here: In 1975 when I produced *Quiebre de Quintos* for National Venezuelan Radio, the officials of the radio station censored my program because it contained "music that incites political rebellion." That censored music was nothing other than the incipient, intelligent, and upbeat salsa of Ernie Agosto.

In 1972 the orchestra split apart, following that unfortunate tradition of so many small salsa bands. Martín Galagarza, bongo player and codirector, left to form a new group, La Conquistadora. Agosto, however, continued on and recorded a second album, *Ernie's Conspiracy*, which was less political than the first but much more infused with good salsa music. The group did not lose much with the split, mostly because the singer, Miguel Quintana, stayed on. Quintana was one of those unknown and congenial figures who time and again forced us to listen to the old albums. He was also an old Cuban veteran with a timbre in his voice similar to Cuní's but with a unique and powerful style. It is still difficult to explain how Quintana was able to jell with the spirit of La Conspiración, a young orchestra of mostly inexperienced musicians performing music that was a long way from the placid son that Quintana was accustomed to. However, Miguelito (the musicians used the diminutive form in evident irony about his age) not only adapted perfectly well but ended up being the only possible singer who could maintain the irreverent spirit of La Conspiración. Seen from this perspective, the musical life of Quintana continues to be a mystery. Inexplicably, he never had much success in the Cuba of the 1950s; indeed, when he began to record with La Conspiración, many in the music world were skeptical. The attitude in New York was that any Cuban singer who did not come with fame came with nothing. And Quintana, despite his New York recordings, remained unknown, mostly because orchestras like La Conspiración never attained the benefits of popularity.

Quintana recorded a total of four albums with Agosto: the two I mentioned above, then *Cada loco con su tema* in 1974 and *Afecto y cariño* in 1976. These last two albums were of lesser quality and less musically grounded than the first two. After Quintana left the group, La Conspiración became lost in the waves of repetition and a lack of creativity, and their demise coincided with the fading of the boom. Ernie Agosto no longer wanted anything to do with the political issues of his first albums, and the limited ability of this band, once known for its straightforward barrio flavor, meant that it ended up isolated, producing records that do not deserve to be remembered.

To the south of New York, Puerto Rico continued to produce a salsa that despite its own particular nuances still lagged behind the sounds of the north. Similar things were happening in Venezuela, Santo Domingo, and Panama. New York, as I indicated at the beginning of this chapter, was the only city with the conditions to support any experimentation with the new Caribbean sounds. Thus, while the city exploited the commercial boom, it remained the necessary capital of salsa, the city where the avant-garde and the traditional sounds converged. This privilege, however, did not last long, and from 1975 on, the Caribbean refused to stay in second place. Puerto Rico abandoned its dependency on the New York sound and created a very particular salsa of its own, a salsa that proved to be both interesting in spectacle and in the music. In the same way, Santo Domingo and Venezuela began to serve as primordial places both for the production and development of original salsa and for their own audience support. All of this happened during the boom, in the wake of the salsa force that soon took over everything in the region.

SEVEN :
THE BOOM

In the fall of 1973, the Fania All Stars gave the largest salsa concert ever in New York, so large it was held at Yankee Stadium. The audience still had memories of the Cheetah event, and the four albums that came from it had become part of their personal celebrations and street-corner gatherings. Those songs were played over many radio stations throughout the city, and the film *Nuestra cosa latina* was being shown throughout the Caribbean to great applause by fans everywhere. Now it seemed that Fania was back to create another landmark with even higher aspirations to carry salsa even further beyond the confines of the barrio. As a complement to the main concert, Fania advertised performances by Típica 73; El Gran Combo de Puerto Rico, appearing by special invitation; and Mongo Santamaría, whose prestige in the jazz world was sure to attract non-Latino audiences.

Yankee Stadium, the most famous of all baseball parks, was on the verge of being remodeled, so the proprietors easily agreed to rent it out for this night of salsa. There was, however, one very important stipulation: the audience could not go onto the field. The promoters set up a very tight security system and put the stage right in the middle of the field. It was an immense and very elevated stage that stretched from first to third base. And the concert took place.

At first everything went smoothly. La Típica, a new and practically unknown group, opened the concert, but they did not inspire much enthusiasm. Then Symphony Sid—the same gray-haired and raspy-voiced spokesperson who had served as emcee at the Cheetah—announced Mongo's entrance. The Cuban conga player and his band performed six pieces rich in sabor and full of a quality that later was captured in an excellent album on the Vaya label titled *Mongo Santamaría Live at Yankee Stadium*. El Gran Combo concluded the opening act with their captivating choreography, old hits, and the powerful voice of Andy Montañez. The audience, estimated to be nearly 40,000 strong, began to get restless, and people threw themselves against the security fences. The long-awaited Fania All Stars were supposed to come on next, but several minutes passed and still the stage remained empty. After a while, just as the audience was about to erupt, the emcees began to introduce the musicians, one by one: on trumpet, Víctor Paz, Ray Maldonado, Luis "Perico" Ortiz, and Roberto Rodríguez; on trombone, Lewis Khan, Barry Rogers, Reinaldo Jorge, and Willie Colón; on conga, Ray Barretto; on timbales, Nicky Marrero; on bongo, Roberto Roena; on bass, Bobby Valentín; on piano, Larry Harlow; on cuatro, Yomo

Toro; special guests, Jorge Santana on electric guitar and Billy Cobham on drums; the singers, Ismael Quintana, Justo Betancourt, Santitos Colón, Ismael Miranda, Pete "El Conde" Rodríguez, Héctor Lavoe, and Cheo Feliciano; and finally the director of the orchestra, Johnny Pacheco, who came onstage with his small flute.

The All Stars began with a thunderous fanfare that completely silenced the entire stadium. Then Pacheco began to sing in a joking tone, inviting the musicians to begin to jam and stomp around.

After a pause came the shout, "Harlow . . . !" and the piano and rhythm section took off. This launched the debut of "Congo bongo," a cut based on jamming that had at its core a battle of the congas between Ray Barretto and Mongo Santamaría.

But the music did not last long. The scream that initiated it also inspired the crowd to throw itself more violently against the security fences and to stampede across the field. The musicians barely were able to complete their first song. The police had to resort to clubs, and in a few minutes the stage was empty again. "The concert is over," scolded one of the emcees, and so the much desired party ended just as it was really about to begin.

As before, Jerry Masucci had called on León Gast to film this event. Masucci wanted to make another film, a new production that would supersede the commercial ambitions of the first. They used only the musical presentations from the Yankee Stadium concert, and the mayhem and the rest of the music was eliminated. They believed that they could select the right elements to attract new audiences, open new markets, and make salsa—more than a modern musical expression from the barrio—the latest fad in the international pop music scene. They called their new film *Salsa*, and they intended for it to show the history of this musical expression.

They chose Geraldo Rivera as the narrator. Rivera was a Latino journalist who had gained success in U.S. television for his gritty exposés on the social ills of the United States. He guaranteed the producers an audience that would not necessarily be limited to Hispanics. Yet the initial problem was that Rivera, despite his success, was another U.S.-American, another gringo who did not understand fully the depth of what the barrio and its music meant. Thus, while in *Nuestra cosa* the intent was to get closer to the barrio, the idea in this second film was just the opposite: the less the barrio appeared, the better. The history of Latin music became something else, something far removed from that life of misery and marginalization.

This history invented by the producers and narrated by Rivera went as follows: First, salsa came from Africa, where the drum was born. (On the screen we see some black people, apparently from the Congo, dressed in colored robes and speaking a foreign tongue while they perform some supposed ancestral rite to bless the skins and the drums). From there the drum came to America in slave ships. (Here let us remember that for the United States, "America" comprises only that territory between Canada and Mexico, and everything else is something different, like a subcontinent, "South America" or "Latin America"). In this America, the drum was liberated from slavery, and thus African music was born in America (the United States!). The same thing happened in other parts of the region, and therefore in the Caribbean, the same African music emerged. (Also remember that in the eyes of the United States, the Caribbean consists more or less of those islands south of Florida that are considered the property and extension of U.S. territory). As the years passed, Caribbean blacks migrated north to America and became Americans. Most of them arrived in New York City and made their music there. This is how, according to Masucci and Rivera, salsa came to be born in the heart of America and is, therefore, American and nothing but American.

Having swindled the history in this way, the film then launched into its true commercial hook: how this "American" music, originating in Africa, became so popular with U.S. audiences. Next the film reached into the Hollywood archives: We see Mexican *charros* (who were neither very Mexican nor very *charro*) on horseback attacking a bar in the West. We also see Groucho Marx flirtatiously dancing and joking with a "señorita." Then Al Jolson sings his "Latin from Manhattan" ("She's a Latin from Manhattan, she's the sweetest dancer, she's a nice young woman wooo"). Dolores del Río, who appears next, was indeed a very beautiful and important entertainer, but what did she have to do with the music and, particularly, with Caribbean music? The same goes for Carmen Miranda, with her plastic pineapples and her coy and uncomfortable strutting. The last straw of this absurd history of Latin music was Desi Arnaz singing his very mediocre version of "Babalú" while dragging his gringo conga around a luxurious Hollywood ballroom.

Since the United States sees itself as it is represented in its movies, the Latin music and the image of the Latino/Latina depicted in those old films are also a central part of American life. Thus, Rivera spouted the lies and claimed that the dances that had excited and seduced so many generations of Americans were also Latin. Mambo fever, the cha-cha (which is not the cha cha chá), the rumba, and the conga all were included in the screen images of the 1940s and 1950s. Rivera then narrated how that same history and evolution was culminating in the new fever, the euphoria over salsa. While the film did note that salsa music had been cultivated in the Latino barrios, it never gave any reference to the social meaning of the lyrics or to the people who considered the music their own. Thus, salsa music was divorced from the barrio, from the Caribbean, and from the people who lived and had lived there. Salsa was now an American music, as American as Hollywood. One day it arrived from Africa, and the next day it went to the movies and became "glamorous."

The producer's intention was clear: for the salsa industry to reach the million-dollar mark in profits, it had to get beyond an exclusively Latino market and penetrate the larger, U.S. one. From there, it could become a genuine mass trend that would reach even European audiences. In order to achieve this, the Fania entrepreneurs felt the need to change radically the image of salsa music. The first film, *Nuestra cosa*, was too much of a hindrance. It spoke of the barrio, of how salsa emerged and developed on the margins of society, in impoverished and disadvantaged neighborhoods rather than in the glitzy environments of the powerful U.S. popular culture. It was essential, then, to produce a film that would say exactly the opposite: that salsa was a fundamental part of that pop culture, that it was likely to be embraced by majority audiences, and that it had nothing to do with the minorities and their repugnant misery. This, and this alone, became the fundamental characterization that fueled the so-called salsa boom, a boom that did increase its market share effectively but that also stripped away the true social values and raison d'être of salsa music.

Thus, if *Nuestra cosa* announced the definitive emergence of the new music of the barrio, the second production, *Salsa*, proclaimed the birth of its commercial explosion. These two lines began from the same point, but their concepts of salsa diverged until they were nearly 180 degrees apart. In a few cases, the true salsa took advantage of the new life that the boom's advertising campaign offered, but most salsa remained hidden or ignored in ineffective, sterile, and outdated molds. However, an overall assessment of the boom is not that simple. Despite its negative impact on the music itself, the boom did offer some important benefits. Because of it, salsa (in one style or another) was able to reach untapped audiences, even Latin American ones, who previously had remained indifferent to it, tired of the pervasiveness of U.S. culture. Owing its existence to mere publicity and hype, the boom did not last long, but it did make room for that other music, the authentic salsa. This emerged in the years that followed, but first we have to examine that process, assess its parts, and listen to its successes and failures.

The Stars of Fania

The salsa boom can be analyzed best from the standpoint of the stars of Fania, particularly those All Stars of the record company who by 1973 made up what was considered the best band in the world and the most important contemporary influence on Latin music.

Fania had not released any new productions since 1972, the year of the Cheetah recordings. The 1973 concert offered a new opportunity, but for the most part none of its music was worth publishing. Jerry Masucci, then, called all of the musicians into the studio, and there they recorded the album *Latin, Soul, Rock*, which they released in early 1974. This album revealed the new musical trend that the company was going to follow. As suggested by its title, it tried to represent the convergence of styles that dominated the international pop music market at the time. The new product, "Latin Music," was a sort of rock with congas that accommodated rock and soul with its common and accessible melodies while adding one rhythmic flourish or another. Clearly, the idea was to try to capitalize on the popularity that guitarist Carlos Santana had created with his successful Latin rock. Thus the Fania group, which, from 1971 on, had become the premier salsa orchestra, abandoned salsa overnight in favor of a musical expression that was never more than secondary.

To record this "crossover" album, Fania invited various stand-out musicians from the rock and New Jazz scene (which by this time was closer to rock than to jazz, properly speaking). These included Jorge Santana, Carlos's brother, who was also a guitar player but with less talent than his famous brother; the U.S. percussionist Billy Cobham; and the European pianist Jan Hammer. The latter two were from the Mahavishnu Orchestra of John McLaughin, a group well known for performing intelligent fusions of rock and jazz. The fourth musical guest was Manu Dibango, an African saxophonist who had very little renown and importance, even though he had already established a beat of his own, the Soul Makossa. The fifth guest was Mongo Santamaría, who, despite his virtues as an Antillean conga player, belonged more to jazz than to Cuba—at least this was the perception in the U.S. music world that made these kinds of distinctions.

This group of musicians recorded side A of the album, a side that had little long-term effect either on Latin audiences or on the U.S. listeners that it was so anxiously trying to seduce. Side B, however, was more successful. Even though it included the unbearable Makossa rhythm by Dibango, it also presented "Congo bongo" from the Yankee Stadium performance, and that was its main attraction. The real draw, however, was the "El ratón" cut, an old montuno composed and recorded by Cheo Feliciano in the days of Joe Cuba's sextet and performed by Fania at the Roberto Clemente

Stadium in Puerto Rico. "El ratón" was the first great success of the salsa boom. It not only saved this lopsided album from obscurity, but it also allowed Fania to increase its sales. Although "El ratón" did not break the barrier and gain access to mainstream U.S. listeners, it did open up some Latin American audiences that had been less attracted to or identified with Caribbean music. In Venezuela, for instance, the case of "El ratón" was extremely important. For the first time, the so-called sophisticated radio stations (mislabeled as "juvenile") that catered to upper-middle-class listeners allowed this salsa music into their exclusive and arbitrary musical programming. The middle class, then, began leaning toward salsa and letting themselves be moved by it, without the past prejudice they had against listening to "La murga" by Willie Colón. This Venezuelan example is not an isolated one. The same thing happened throughout the elitist Caribbean middle class that had been so intent on denying its true cultural legacy.

Among the elements of "El ratón" that allowed for this unique achievement was its complex musical arrangement, one much closer to Santana and to rock than to true salsa. This arrangement served as a passport to those audiences who thought of rock and U.S. music as synonymous with quality music. But the arrangement was only the beginning. There was also Feliciano's own interpretation, his pleasant and penetrating voice, and the free style with which he was able to glide above and beyond the melody and the montuno. In addition, Santana's electric guitar solo—actually a quite simple and mediocre one—was rock and roll to the end, enough so to be accepted by the disc jockeys who loved Stevie Winwood and Eric Clapton. The final element was the roguish chorus that sang over the long montuno: "Echale semilla a la maraca pa' que suene" (Throw the seeds in the maraca so that it can play). This chorus became a legacy of the youth culture. The simplest mention of it signaled the acceptance of salsa, of that Latin trend, as a part of the modern and as a style apparently so close to rock that the musical distances effectively disappeared. The chorus, in fact, became a refrain that suggested a host of double meanings, most of them related to drug use and delinquency. (For example, to "throw the seeds" meant to put marijuana in something). Latin American rock-and-roll lovers spent long nights coming up with alternative interpretations for all of the lyrics to "El ratón," and indeed the lyrics did have double meanings that were hardly understood by the disc jockeys and their usual audiences: "My cat is complaining / That it can no longer play."

The rat and the cat in the lyrics especially took on all sorts of possible meanings. Once when Cheo Feliciano came to Venezuela in the midst of the hype over his song, a disc jockey from a youth station asked him about the rat's "philosophy." The singer replied with a pause and a stutter, which suggested such a term was both a compliment and a foolish comment. Feliciano ended up saying, "Well, it's not that there is a philosophy. There's a male cat, a female cat, and a rat. . . . I don't know, I think people understand me, and they understand that—that's all that happens, nothing else." But Feliciano was being unfair to the public. He had not realized that his song had reached audiences who had to present themselves as sophisticated but who had already lost the ability to interpret intelligent lyrics with obvious double meanings that are so common in Caribbean popular music.

The confusion increased as "El ratón"—which by then represented the whole salsa boom—appealed not only to rock-and-roll fans but also to academic and intellectual sectors. They speculated beyond the drug metaphor and interpreted the song as a direct political analogy. In this reading, the cat represented the Puerto Rican people who want liberation. But the rat, representing the police—the oppression of imperialism that was always identified with rodents—comes in, "jumping from any net," to break up the attempt at liberation. Thus, Feliciano's "El ratón" offered something to everyone. The fabulous and fertile world of interpretations that emerged from this song was evidence of the immense speculative richness that Caribbean music can offer. Now it was also being surprisingly discovered by the "colonized" middle class of the region.

The cat, however, was much more ordinary. His dilemma was not about drugs or politics, but simply about everyday life and love. The story told in the montuno—as Feliciano would clarify later—is the story of an individual (the male cat) who has an affair with another woman (the female cat). The lesson in the story is in the gossip that spreads throughout the neighborhood, unveiling the clandestine actions of the adulterous cat. The one who discovers these actions is the rat, the old gossipy woman who, as the lyrics say, "jumps from any net." And that is all; the rest was the result of long nights and wild imaginations.

Beginning in 1975, the Fania All Stars released two volumes titled *Live at Yankee Stadium*. They appealed to their faithful fans by using a photo of the interrupted New York concert for the cover. The music, however, had been recorded during various concerts at the Clemente Coliseum in San Juan, Puerto Rico, without the hype and spectacle of that original gathering in New York. These albums marked a return to true salsa, although the overall quality of the music was inferior to that of the Cheetah albums.

Each volume had five songs. The best cuts on the first are Curet Alonso's "Pueblo latino," sung by Pete "El Conde" Rodríguez, and "Mi gente," a festive composition by Johnny Pacheco that introduced Héctor Lavoe in his new role as soloist. Over time, this song would become one of the funda-mental hits in all of salsa.

The most important songs from the second album were the ones by Ismael Quintana and Justo Betancourt, who were now officially part of the All Stars. However, what really made these records unique, popular, and profitable was nothing other than the presence of Celia Cruz. On the first record, she interpreted a song that Johnny Pacheco had composed expressly for her. Its montuno—"Vamos a gozar con la Gracia Divina" (Let us have fun with the Divine Grace)—was a direct allusion to Celia herself and the proliferation of nicknames that the salsa world would give her.

The second volume featured a new version of José Claro Fumero's theme "Bemba colorá," which Celia herself had recorded previously with Tito Puente's orchestra. This second version, though inferior to the original, spurred the mythical aura that came to surround the figure of Celia. Bobby Valentín's arrangement was conceived in such a way that Celia could show off the unequalled power of her voice. The Fania All Stars catered to her un-conditionally, and so did the whole Fania recording company, eventually creating an adoration of Cruz that was unusual in this musical world.

After 1975, Celia Cruz became the most important figure in that record company, allowing it to gross outrageous sales. She was a guaranteed moneymaker for any project, especially when the boom began to fade. In the previous chapter I noted that Johnny Pacheco and his orchestra was the first to record Celia during the beginning of the traditional (or matan-cera) trend. Now we will see how Pacheco himself, together with other stars from the Fania empire, came back to Celia in order to guarantee their survival during the hard times. For a good music lover, the Celia from the Cuban days of the Sonora Matancera will always be much more attractive and interesting. In some ways, these new recordings limited her, so that she lost some of her old force and creativity. However, for the new fan—for the young person who discovered Celia after listening to Aretha Franklin and Diana Ross, for example—Cruz represented the high point of a par-ticular music and a particular style.

Now let us return to the Fania All Stars. In 1976, after a series of tours throughout the United States, Puerto Rico, Panama, and Venezuela, the orchestra recorded its last salsa album: *Tributo a Tito Rodríguez*. Com-mercially, this album was intended to connect the old style of the Puerto Rican singer with the new trend that Fania had created. Previously, Tito's style had been the most important and successful expression of authen-tic Caribbean music, and his sales and prestige were untouchable. This new project, however, oversimplified the music and thus was doomed to certain failure. Fania took Tito's old songs and had new singers interpret them without adding any creative updates. Thus, Héctor Lavoe and Justo Betancourt, for instance, tried obligingly to re-enliven songs such as "Cuando, cuando, cuando" and "Cara de payaso," respectively, at a time when Rodríguez's own powerful and authentic interpretations were still unsurpassable.

The only cut that transcended Rodríguez's original recording was "Vuela la paloma," an old classic penned by Félix Reyna. Fania transformed this song by presenting it as a jam session where each singer, alternating with the chorus of the montuno, saluted the memory of the late icon. Along with this version of "Vuela la paloma," the dedicatory album made one other important contribution: the presence of the Panamanian Rubén Blades, who, in two short years, would redefine the style and the music of salsa. From this album, I would like to highlight his rendition of "Los muchachos de Belén." Here Blades gained the advantage over his orchestral companions by finding a way to salute Tito without being absorbed by his shadow. Thus he was able to create salsa music that broke free from the immediate past.

After this album, in 1976 Fania immersed itself in its new style, the one that led to the sad and irrevocable demise of its famous stars. Already the company had signed a contract with the powerful media giant CBS to have its Columbia Records produce and internationally distribute the "Latin" albums of the Fania All Stars. For Jerry Masucci and other managers, this was the master stroke that would allow them to invade the United States and, from there, the European markets as well. To do so, they decided to alter drastically the character of the music and return to the standards implicit in *Latin, Soul, Rock*. Ironically, that music already had been made considerably less "Latin" so that it would seem more "American," despite the loss of intrinsic values such a change implied.

The first album with the CBS label had a very feminine title: *Delicate and Jumpy*. The Stars were limited to the rhythm section: Papo Lucca on piano, Ray Barretto on the congas, Roberto Roena on bongo, Nicky Marrero on timbales, Bobby Valentín on bass, and Johnny Pacheco directing. In addition, CBS brought in Stevie Winwood, a prestigious guitar player from the old rock era. This invitation was an attempt to gain other audiences, but his presence was scarcely felt in the music, which was of very poor quality. In fact, it sparked minimal interest for either of the two audiences—U.S. or Latin—and thus it doubly failed. Once, while I was responsible for the program *Bachata* on Radio Aeropuerto, I was able to interview Roberto Roena. I asked him to comment on that album and the reasons behind such a terrible production. Roena agreed with my assessment and tried to excuse himself by saying that he was only a musician hired to play the music that was placed in front of him. He went on to say,

> They brought us (the six musicians from the rhythm section) together in New York to record this. . . . Then they took the tape and added everything else—the U.S. drums, the electric guitar, and the brass. . . . None of us liked what they were taping, but what could we do, you know? They're the ones in power. . . . Still, in those jam sessions, while we were recording that garbage, we did some jamming and that was really, really good, heavy. . . . I don't know. Jerry said maybe they would include that jamming in a record. . . . But what came out was really bad. It reminds me of supermarket music, that music they play while housewives do their grocery shopping and it is totally useless because those ladies don't even pay attention to it. . . . It was really, really bad music.

I waited in vain for that jamming record that Roena had mentioned, but instead the Fania entrepreneurs continued to produce albums of supermarket music. Each release further eroded the true essence of the Caribbean music that, now badly disguised, they wanted to sell to the gringos. In 1977 they released a second album with CBS, *Rhythm Machine*, with equally poor music, even though the entrepreneurs, who recognized the failure of the initial album, were beginning to see the need for a change, for a new and important musical change. Indeed, the producers had to acknowledge that Latin music, despite its being dressed up in "American" sounds, was attractive only if it was effectively Latin. This was why they decided to include a salsa number, a real one, one that in the midst of their failure would guarantee them better audience response and better sales.

They turned, then, to Rubén Blades, who offered one of his own songs, "Juan Pachanga," which became an essential and vitally important touchstone. In order to measure its virtues, we must analyze both its arrangement and its lyrics. As to the first, the music was performed by an extra-large orchestra, which included a new section of violins with the traditional structure of trombones and trumpets. In contrast to the old Cuban tradition of charanga music, these violins served a melodic rather than rhythmic role. This alone created a completely distinctive and attractive new sonority. Another featured instrument was the acoustic guitar, which added new effects to conventional salsa recordings. Played by Blades himself, the acoustic guitar also contributed to a significant difference in sound. However, the real long-term importance of these contributions lies in the ways these instruments were integrated into the conceptualization of the song. The initial arrangement was the product of Jay Chataway's work. Famous for his arrangements for Maynard Ferguson and other important figures in big-band jazz, Chataway molded this theme to a structure different from that of the usual salsa. Instead of working the "initial theme, son, mambo, montuno, moña, final theme" approach, Chataway developed the following variant: His initial theme was really a piano improvisation; then came the son, directly followed by the montuno without the mambo transition, and then the final theme, once again developed through the free jamming of the piano. This arrangement sparked immediate enthusiasm, since there was an undoubted richness and quality in its harmonic propositions, and since it truly represented a valid and effective opening for the fusion of salsa with rock music (or with jazz). There was only one problem in this arrangement, and it was a truly serious one. It was not "in clave." In other words, it was a perfectly harmonic piece and well structured, but it had no grounding. It floated, as it were, without any rhythmic foundation and thus without any rootedness or meaning.

I have mentioned several times the incredible importance of the clave—how it defines and justifies nearly the entire body of music from the Caribbean. To say that something is "out of clave" is to declare that it is wrong, pointless, broken—it is nothing. Chataway's arrangement, then, had to be put right, reconnected with that authentic world that characterizes and identifies salsa music as salsa music. And for this to happen, it had to be put "in clave." Louie Ramírez responded to this challenge and modified the arrangement in such a way that it could be said, in fact, that he created a new one. Ramírez successfully found a way to respect all of the harmonic virtues of the original arrangement while adding the essential clave rhythm that lent a particular musical meaning to "Juan Pachanga." The structure proposed by Chataway was maintained, but now it included all of the mambos needed to bridge the son and the montuno and the other diverse parts. Likewise, Ramírez also included bass and vibraphone solos—those important salsa solos that were absent in the original version. He thus created one of the songs that came to represent an avant-garde achievement, one that quickly triggered numerous and fruitful imitations.

The other element that gave "Juan Pachanga" a special meaning was its lyrics. Following one of the most persistent features of Caribbean music, the lyrics were presented as a chronicle, a portrait of daily reality, insistently repeating its ongoing customs. This reality was represented by the protagonist, Juan Pachanga, a continuation of the typical hero of the barrio. This happy-go-lucky rogue transcends time and place and changing fads, ever seducing women and joining any street fight that arises, always coming out a winner. Any review of Caribbean music leads us to a world full of opportunists who, with an obstinate joy, are capable of overcoming their daily circumstances. However, the chronicle of today's rogue had to be different. In order to acquire any real contemporary and true, lasting value, it had to have a different spirit, one that would offer new, critical nuances without modifying the essential pattern of the traditional chronicle. Thus, this opportunist was now portrayed at the lowest point in his life. For the first time, the happy pleasure seeker feels pain inside; for the first time he is discarded as a role model. Here was a turn and tightening of the screw without a betrayal of the tradition: he was presented with a true mixture of his intrinsically tragic situation and his famous happiness. This is the Juan Pachanga that Rubén Blades sang about:

> Everybody swears that Juan Pachanga's really happy
> But he carries the pain of betrayal in his soul
> And only drink and smokes and drums can cure him.

In 1978 Fania was still producing albums under the CBS label. The third in this series demonstrated the same musical mediocrity that once more had become predominant. The album was titled *Spanish Fever*, in reference to the popular disco music that had emerged from the film *Saturday Night Fever* with John Travolta, the new idol of international pop. Despite having recruited musicians such as Maynard Ferguson, Hubert Laws, and Eric Gale, and despite having included more salsa numbers, Fania preferred to market the album as part of the new disco trend. The musical achievements of that trend, however, were marred by the ridiculous and by the loss of Latin tradition. The salsa songs featured Ismael Miranda and Rubén Blades, with his new cuts, "Sin tu cariño" and "Coromiyaré," a rather sophisticated jam session effectively composed by Johnny Pacheco. So, again, Blades survived, although without the sales hit or influence of his "Juan Pachanga," but the rest of the music was once more ignored by music lovers on both sides (the Latino and the Anglo). Now the demise was obvious. The Fania All Stars, who had created the euphoria in 1971, were now helping to snuff out the trend by overshadowing it with clumsy musical efforts. Those responsible, however, were the same as ever: the entrepreneurs.

The agenda of opening new markets for the new sounds failed. Yes, the Caribbean middle class was finally attracted to this boom, but numerically speaking, they were never an important or significant percentage in terms of the goals of the record companies. Fania, with its prepackaged music, its soft, rosy colors, and its feminine-like complacency, was not able to captivate the North American public, let alone the old idea of the European market. The flashy tours organized by Masucci and Ralfi Mercado (the promoter and agent for almost all of the orchestras and bands within the company) that took Fania to remote and incredible places, such as Africa and Japan, came to nothing. Like throngs of sheep, the international audiences consumed the tastes that the major record companies fed them. But despite contracts with Columbia Records, Fania never benefited from that exclusive arrangement, though that definitely influenced the music that it produced, recorded, and released. The music was nullified from its very conception, unable to spark any interest in the large, international audiences who, by the way, preferred the originals that Fania so awkwardly tried to imitate. Nor did it create any interest among the Latino audiences who saw this new Fania music as a betrayal, an inexcusable treason that was appropriately punished with low sales and with an indifference equal in enormity to the size of their blunder.

We can trace the cycle of the famous salsa boom from the film *Salsa* up to these final productions of the Fania All Stars. From this cycle, we can measure the boom's successes and failures. All of this concerns the surface, however, and now we will look into the depths, where, despite the lingering influence of the Stars, there emerged particularities and variants that need to be analyzed on their own terms. These, really, are much more interesting than the material we have covered so far. In fact, now we will see where the real salsa developed—good or bad, as it may have been, it was salsa to the end.

During 1972, when the Fania monopoly was enjoying the success of the All Stars, when the film *Nuestra Cosa* was being touted as the most significant event in the world of Latin music, and when album sales were exceeding expectations, the company decided to change its politics of promotion and management of artists. Fania also had a number of orchestras that had established solid reputations. But this was not enough; the company wanted to do more. It was clear to everyone that the ones who had benefited the most from that first gathering of the All Stars were the singers, the young singers who had their own public identities and who had requests to perform without the orchestras. The solution was obvious: Fania had to make the singers independent agents and let them find their own orchestras so that they could chart their own courses. Then the company could expand both its number of artists and the size of its record catalog. And that was exactly what happened.

The first singer to become independent was Ismael Miranda. In the previous chapter, I mentioned the last album that he recorded with Larry Harlow's orchestra, the album *Oportunidad*, which was conceived by the producers as a sure springboard for the young singer. Ismael's face filled the album cover, while its grooves contained the eponymous cut expressly composed for this album by Curet Alonso. The album, as a whole, was not of much interest. What undoubtedly stood out was the cut "Señor Sereno," a guaracha penned by Ismael himself, through whose lyrics he announced, "I'm no longer twenty-one, you can't order me around."

Perhaps because he was the first singer to become a soloist, Miranda enjoyed better treatment, and Fania planned his work and repertoire with more care. Their first move was to form a new orchestra, one that curiously had the luxury of bringing together a good number of young musicians who, in a few years, would make up the major part of the New York avant-garde. The orchestra was named La Revelación and included, among others, Nicky Marrero on the timbales, Frankie Rodríguez on the tumbas, José Raúl (Joe) Santiago on bass, Oscar Hernández on piano, and on the tres, the virtuoso Nelson González. They quickly jelled, and by 1973 they presented their first and only album, *Así se compone un son*. This was, it seems to me, the best album that Ismael Miranda ever recorded as a soloist.

The first difference that listeners noticed was Ismael's voice. After the sharp timbre of an irreverent young man, so characteristic of his work with Harlow's orchestra, Miranda now offered a much deeper voice, illustrating a determined maturity and a keen desire for a change in his image. The audience, however, was not upset with this change but continued to support him. This occurred because, far from being dishonest, the album encouraged listeners to raise their expectations. It was conceived of in an experimental way, although the band's predominant spirit was imbued with the traditional sound (under the direct influence of Arsenio Rodríguez). Ismael contributed three of his own songs. The first, "Ahora sí," a challenging duel-like son, announced the young man's new beginning with the lyrics, "I hold the machete in my hand, let's see who's got more. . . . Now, yes, let's see who's got more." His second song, a salute to Colombia, offered no fresh elements, but the third was the cut that gave the album its name, "Así se compone un son." This song proposed a sort of musical recipe for preparing the music, or, better said, the salsa:

> To compose a son, you need a motive, a constructive theme, and
>   inspiration.
> Then you add the sabor and you apply it to the theme
> And with this approach you will never fail, brother
> Oh, but give it inspiration and Cuban sentiment
> Listen to it well. . . . That's how you compose a son.

In addition to these compositions, Ismael resorted to other possibilities, and Curet offered a "Sonerito." Ismael also included the merengue

"Ahora que estoy sabroso," an old song from Arsenio, and, most importantly, two boleros. The merengue was unusual because at that time salsa rarely dared to perform the *Quisqueya*[1] beat (as the Dominican Republic is vernacularly known), but to have Ismael, who was just starting out, performing a bolero was especially significant. During the Harlow days, he hardly ever sang or recorded boleros. The few that ended up being published were always weak, poorly selected, in worse arrangements, and generally ill conceived. Yet, this did not affect Ismael's reputation as a sonero too negatively, since he was an established guaracha singer. As I mentioned previously, the guaracha and the son were the leading genres for salsa, whereas the bolero was always a secondhand form. Despite this, the bolero held a special attraction for Miranda, and in this, his first personal production, he wanted to show that. He also sang "Sálvame," an old bolero arranged by Luis "Perico" Ortiz. This is an important detail because, as far as I know, this was the first salsa arrangement officially attributed to Perico, who went on to become one of the most extraordinary and influential arrangers of salsa music.

Yet the most dazzling bolero was "Las cuarenta"—not an original, but a very old and extraordinary tango composed by Gorrindo Grela. The first striking element of that recording was Ismael's vocal harmonics. He used a mature way of saying the lyrics, and in the old world of boleros, it was understood that some songs were better spoken than sung, though to do so was much more difficult. Ismael displayed that talent, but unfortunately he did not do so again during the rest of his career.

The second key feature that made the "Las cuarenta" bolero so special was Marty Sheller's arrangement, and I still consider it one of the most extraordinary arrangements ever produced in the world of boleros. Sheller's arrangement capitalized on the clave rhythms that Rolando La Serie had set for it when he initially recorded it at the end of the 1950s in Cuba. Sheller, however, impressed on it all of the bitterness, maliciousness, vitality, and power that were imperative in salsa. Thus, Sheller's arrangement presented the ideal framework, Miranda's voice served as the perfect conduit, and this combination resulted in the truest flavoring of the song: the lyrics. Through the effects of salsa and the urban popular music of the continent, these lyrics acquired a most special resonance.

The first thing that stood out in the lyrics was Grela's painful portrait of the barrio. The barrio, of course, was the foundational factor that identified and connected all Latin American music in the twentieth century.

1. *Quisqueya* is the indigenous name for the Dominican Republic, similar to *Borinquen* for Puerto Rico.

It is extremely important to note how that old barrio in Buenos Aires— the old neighborhood—found a direct and automatic counterpart in the modern barrio of salsa. In the case of "Las cuarenta," it was the New York barrio, the same one that produced identical living conditions, despite the passage of time. While certain *lunfardo* voices (those associated with the Buenos Aires underground) were a bit displaced in the new context, most of the lyrics—their meanings and intentions—remained clearly in force, even in contemporary times. Thereafter, the song presented the personal failures of a resident of the barrio, balancing a long list of accumulated deceptions that arise from the pain of living in that part of the city. ("Hope was my lover; disappointment, my friend").

This all-important balance was transported exactly, without any problem, from one extreme of the continent and of Latin American life to the other. And that, to be sure, was the meaning and motivation behind salsa as popular music—as an authentic and sincere popular music. It did nothing more than reflect the world from which it emerged and which it addressed. Regional specificity and diverse tendencies and influences that color each historical period and its expressions are never sufficient to erase that primary and fundamental condition of popular music. Of course, the path was full of pitfalls, of false expressions that were disguised as the popular in order to fulfill the temporary needs of the recording and marketing industries. But, fortunately, those same imposters never last; they fade into a deserved oblivion with the passing generations. When the industry became more important than the barrio that produced the music, that same salsa music also fell victim to many pitfalls and disguises. Nevertheless, the authentic expressions successfully overcame those obstacles, since the music identified itself as the unique and definitive expression of a unique and definitive people. That is why salsa could absorb the tango. In fact, any barrio was able to nurture both salsa and the tango. Thus, even with more than fifty years of time and distance—from Buenos Aires to the Bronx, where numerous Latinos were living in misery—the continuous popularity of "Las cuarenta" by Gorrindo Grela was apparent: "Old street of my barrio / There, where I took my first steps."

In the following years, Ismael Miranda continued to release album after album, although the quality of the music progressively declined. This was influenced by the notorious demise of Orquesta Revelación. By 1974 the band no longer existed—the singer and the musicians never agreed, and some charged more than others, which always causes problems. Therefore, from that point on, Ismael was forced to sing with random orchestras or with fly-by-night bands that did not practice enough and were hardly in a position to follow up on the success of his first initiative. Under these conditions, the album *Ismael Miranda en fa menor* appeared. It was produced without any of the aspirations of the singer's former work, although listeners continued to buy it. With that album, however, Ismael popularized his song "Borinquen tiene montuno,"; Curet's bolero "Nervios de acero," and Rubén Blades's charanga "Las esquinas son." In this last song, and despite the weaknesses of the album as a whole, the barrio was once again a central subject.

Around this time Ismael Miranda was considered the most important of all the Fania singers. As a soloist, he brought in the most sales, and the owners and producers had very high hopes for him. His image, however, started changing radically. That and the decreasing musical quality of his albums translated into a loss of devotion from fans and dancers. His album *Este es Ismael Miranda*, released in 1975, illustrated this. Capitalizing on his old and ridiculous image as Fania's pretty boy, the singer appeared on the cover dressed in a fancy white outfit in the style of the ballad singers. On the back cover, the ever-kitschy brandy cups and window blinds completed the banal picture. The music, however, had some redeeming qualities. It included two of Miranda's own songs, "María Luisa" and "La cosa no es como antes," and another important composition by Rubén Blades, "Cipriano Armenteros," which became the album's top hit.

Yet the interest in Ismael Miranda ended there, since what followed was progressively mediocre. This resulted from a lack of clarity among the producers and from Miranda's own decision to stick with his pretty boy image. Because he did not anchor himself in the old roots or return to the values of the barrio and the popular reality that informs a truly forceful music, he was dismissed in a world where divas and false idols simply have no place. Despite the fact that Blades and Curet Alonso continued to compose for Miranda, he did not develop the forms and styles that would attract an audience that already had abandoned him. Ismael then opted to sing the very mediocre songs of the very mediocre Brazilian Nelson Ned. He tried to find flair in Jorge Millet's arrangements, which, despite their quality and ostentatious forms and harmonies, did not offer much in terms of either salsa or sabor. Thus, Ismael—sometimes consciously and at other times as the result of an inevitable inertia—ended up bringing together all the elements that actually undercut salsa and authentic popular music. His unfortunate failure, therefore, automatically followed. Faced with the mediocrity of his last albums, listeners preferred to return to his old recordings, such as "Abran paso," "Señor Sereno," and that fabulous son whose montuno lyrics said, "You played with me but not with my heart." The rest of his music was easily forgotten.

108　　Previously, before the end of 1973, in the midst of its commercial expansion, the Fania Company had suffered one of its hardest blows. Willie Colón, the best representative of the new sound, the most established of all Fania artists, and the one with the most solid sales record, decided to disband his orchestra. After numerous successes, such as *El juicio* and *Lo mato*, he opted for a temporary retreat. It seemed that he was undergoing a difficult personal crisis. This left the producers with no other option than to continue exploiting his old image, and so the second of the star singers, Héctor Lavoe, was given the opportunity to become a soloist.

Lavoe's first album, *La voz*, was released in 1974. It had the direct support of the rhythm section from Willie Colón's old orchestra, which was now, of course, simply Héctor Lavoe's orchestra. However, they needed a new sound, so the old structure of the two trombones was enlarged to a brass quartet with the addition of two new trumpets. This musical team consisted of Colón's former musicians—Professor José Torres on piano, José Mangual Jr. on bongo, and Milton Cardona on congas. They also added new figures, such as José Febles, a young arranger and trumpet player; José Rodríguez, the old Brazilian trombone player; Harry D'Aguiar, also a trombonist; and Ray Maldonado, another virtuoso trumpet player. In contrast to Ismael Miranda's situation, all of them were a constant source of support for Lavoe, and this, of course, translated into the stronger and richer music that he was able to produce as a soloist.

The group's first hit was a composition by Héctor and Willie titled "El todopoderoso." It illustrated Willie Colón's new interest in salsa songs arranged from a freer and wider-ranging perspective. Despite all of the avant-garde traits of his earlier work, his new material was much more open and unburdened by previous expectations. Without the pressures of directing a band, Willie was able to dive into a new direction and totally dedicate himself to the production side of things. This first album that he produced for Héctor was only the beginning.

Three elements combined to make "El todopoderoso" a success. First was Lavoe's voice and his aggressive and irreverent style in singing the guaracha. Forcing the modulations, he made his singing a continuation of the clandestine speech of the barrios. The second element was Willie's arrangement, which brought new forms and harmonies to salsa. A Venezuelan critic once characterized this "Todopoderoso" as the first example of the new Gregorian salsa, an obvious reference to the most peculiar mambo that Willie Colón had written. The third element was the theme, one of an impressively popular nature that had never before been taken on in such a holistic and convincing manner. Of course, the reader will note that a religious element always had been present in salsa, as it has been in all Caribbean and Latin American musical expressions. However, in terms of salsa, the religious element was more clearly a reference to Santería, to the black religions from Cuba. Even when variants of salsa alluded to Christianity, it was always done uniquely in the context of that same Santería. This element was especially emphasized in "El todopoderoso" where religion is referred to but without mentioning Santería explicitly, and this, in its own ways, was important. The song begins,

> How he was spit on
> How he was pushed around
> How he carried the cross.

After the montuno, the singer asserts, "The Lord is all powerful."

In the song, Willie and Héctor presented a Christ figure that was much more embedded in popular superstition than in the official doctrines of the church. This has been a constant throughout Caribbean popular music. A few months later this approach was confirmed and even considerably exaggerated when Ismael Rivera released his guaracha "El nazareno." In this song another popular Christ, in this case a black one, moves with uncanny familiarity through the everyday spaces of the barrio.

Curiously, the second great success of La voz, "Rompe saragüey," also centered on a religious theme. This was an old Cuban son, surely nuanced by the facts and characteristics of black Santería: "You can't play around with the saints / You can't play around."

Arranged as a slow and heavy son montuno, this cut featured two performers: Markolino Dimond, the pianist, who played an elegant and ingenious solo, and Héctor Lavoe, who achieved in "Rompe saragüey" one of his best moments as a singer. With this tune, Dimond established himself as a classic figure among the fans. They quickly and surprisingly memorized his solo, even though, as we all know, the great majority of solos usually remain at the margins of mainstream audiences who barely acknowledge them and even more rarely memorize them. As for Lavoe, he had enough talent to capitalize on the phrasings of the chorus and the montuno in ways that fully satisfied everyone's expectations.

The rest of the album included another montuno, some boleros, a number of guarachas, and a rewriting of the theme, "Mi gente." Willie Colón's arrangement of the guarachas gave further evidence of his love for Brazilian music. Despite the virtues of the recording as a whole, the "Mi gente" rewrite unfortunately ended up without any of the vitality or joy that came through in the live version of the Fania All Stars. Before concluding my comments regarding this first album by Héctor Lavoe as a soloist, I have to mention the boleros, "Emborráchame de amor" and "Tus ojos." In the past both Héctor and Willie had dedicated very little energy to the misnamed *romantic* music, but here they chose one of its most rudimentary—and therefore more popular—variants: the song of the corner bar in which the frustrated lover finds a last refuge in a waitress-turned-confidante. In the specific case of "Emborráchame de amor," a very old bolero by Mario Cavagnaro, the singer and arranger collaborated to present a modern and polished image of that corner bar of old. Tradition already suggested that this formula would be commercially successful, since in Caribbean music the use of the corner bar as a refuge from a lost lover or a love affair gone bad is one of the most powerful and pervasive constants. "Emborráchame de amor" drew on this tradition explicitly, aggressively, and painfully, without any concessions:

> But no, don't ask me anything
> Just do it, please, if you will
> Let's drink from the cup of dawn
> And in this night of sin
> Get me drunk with your love.

With *La voz*, Héctor Lavoe established himself as one of the premiere singers of salsa. His old popularity increased and his reputation solidified. Ismael Miranda and he were the best-selling duo in Fania, a duo born in salsa, who, therefore, could sing it with much more authenticity and popularity than any other soneros. After 1974, however, Héctor began to have a certain advantage over Miranda. In Lavoe, the presence of the barrio was much more pronounced, and the changes in Ismael's style, as I already noted, led him further and further into an assumed sophistication and finesse. Lavoe, on the other hand, never changed his style significantly; he added only slight variations that emphasized his sensibilities as someone marginalized. He was clearly a barrio singer from the streets who could never assume a sophisticated expression. In just a few years, this difference between them began to exact a price: Miranda lost visibility, while Lavoe's presence became ubiquitous and extended further than that of all his New York colleagues and onto the same level as the big names in Caribbean music.

An additional difference between Miranda and Lavoe was also evident in the internal workings of production and management. While Miranda showed professional behavior throughout, submitting himself to a rigorous and systematic work schedule, Lavoe turned irresponsibility and disorder into defining characteristics. This meant continuous and uninterrupted production for Miranda, whereas Lavoe, despite his fantastic sales figures, recorded albums at the most every other year. Thus, while Ismael released six albums between 1974 and 1978, Lavoe recorded only three. 111

Despite this disadvantage, Lavoe ended up winning the game, because he sold more records than Miranda, whose records disappeared soon after the publicity for them ended. Furthermore, all of Lavoe's albums made themselves unquestionably and continuously relevant and, it seems, indomitable.

In 1976, Héctor Lavoe's long-awaited second album, *De ti Depende*, was released, and it was much more successful than the first. Once more, Willie Colón was both the producer and the arranger, repeating his experiments and innovations. Without a doubt, the best cut was "Periódico de ayer," one of the most successful compositions by Tite Curet Alonso. For his arrangement, Willie followed the patterns that Louie Ramírez had developed a year before, in which the strings played a dominant role. Most often in Caribbean music—and exclusively in the traditional or charanga orchestra—a couple of violins were used to fill in the rhythm, more to support the percussionists than the flutist or the singers. In other, though less common cases, the strings functioned as a supplement to the arrangement and orchestration of boleros.

Now, however, the festive music of the guaracha began to use the violins in a melodic rather than rhythmic role. This innovation came out of salsa. The first concrete example was Rafael Hernández's son "Canta canta," recorded by Cheo Feliciano using an arrangement by Louie Ramírez from his 1975 album, *El Cantante*. (Fania published this "Canta canta" without repeating the verb.) The second example was this "Periódico de ayer," and many other examples followed in future arrangements performed by the avant-garde orchestras of New York and the Caribbean.

The reader may object that in Cuba, as long as twenty years ago, figures such as Armando Oréfiche and Ernesto Lecuona had used the violins and other string instruments in ways very similar to those that developed in salsa. I would point out, however, that those Cuban examples, far from representing global tendencies, were always isolated experiments that had no support from dancers and music fans. Furthermore, even when the violins were used for identical purposes, significant differences of meaning and criteria were always evident. What was initially "precious" or mere sophistication was now a direct attempt at modernization.

At the time, "Periódico de ayer" represented Willie Colón's best arrangement, as well as the most unusual lyrics by Curet. Its play with the newspaper story, its identification with everyday love and its outcomes, and the manipulation of a double meaning, inevitably colored by the guaracha, went well beyond the standard love story and the same old journalistic news. For his part, however, Héctor Lavoe did not augment the quality of his singing. Although, admittedly, his skills displayed a high level of effectiveness and originality, Lavoe did not capitalize fully on the potential that Curet's lyrics offered, and, in the end, his singing sounded the same as always. Rather than show off through the montuno in new or creative ways, Héctor chose an easier option of resorting to *radio bemba* (oral) improvisation, which he used to little advantage in the final recording. Thus, Curet's lyrics remained limited to a simple journalistic allegory, without the much-needed elaboration that they demanded. Despite the singer's shortcomings, however, Willie's arrangement made "Periódico de ayer" an almost guaranteed success. The music lover *felt* the novelty and supported it fully. Salsa, swinging into the full sail of the boom, began to delve into new and alternative sounds. This was extremely healthy, opportune, and necessary, since the mass production of Latin music was becoming saturated with repetitive imitations and growing stale by clinging to old criteria. "Your love is like yesterday's newspaper / That nobody reads any more."

In addition to "Periódico de ayer," the 1976 album also included the song "Vamos a reír un poco," composed by the Venezuelan Rico Quintero. Quintero had made it to New York thanks to Perucho Torcat, who included him on the album he produced with Barretto and Eddie Palmieri. The rest of the songs on this album were arranged with great quality and style, but only "Mentira" offered anything important. It was a new salsa rendition of an old son by Ignacio Piñeiro that had been published under the fuller title of "Mentira, Salomé."

In regard to "Mentira," let me share an anecdote that took place in Venezuela in the midst of the hype over this song. The arrangement required a long and well-performed conga solo at the end. The solo (performed by Milton Cardona) developed during the montuno with the continual support of the chorus, who, measure by measure, repeated only the word *mentira*. It so happened that a journalist in charge of the entertainment section of a very important newspaper in Caracas harshly criticized the song. People knew his aversion toward salsa, which he openly indicted as superficial and vulgar, without any quality or style. According to this journalist, "Mentira" was the ideal example to confirm his view. With a dogged patience that could have been put to better uses, he dedicated himself to counting how many times the word *mentira* appeared in the montuno. He concluded that it appeared more than fifty times, and that, therefore, the song was pointless and annoying, since all it said was *mentira, mentira*, without any other substantive content.

This is an interesting anecdote not just because it illustrates an aggressive journalistic bias that opposed (and still opposes) salsa and favored North American and European music as what we should value and identify with instead. Of course, such criticisms were inevitable, given the inferiority complex that arises from a sense of cultural underdevelopment. I am interested, however, in another detail: the clumsy and arbitrary criteria used by some supposed critics and experts to cast doubt on and even eradicate salsa with their weak and flimsy arguments. The journalist above, rather than focusing on what the song really suggested, preferred to focus instead on the minor aspects of the song. Perhaps this was due to ignorance. I do not know what this journalist considered a good song to be, what categories he used, or what criteria guided him. Certainly, for the purposes of salsa, he did not apply any appropriate criteria. And that is precisely the problem: as a particular popular musical expression, salsa has its own traits, meaning, and purposes, different from those associated with U.S. pop. Thus, it is wrong to use the criteria of one to judge the other—for example, it would be wrong to look at Héctor Lavoe through the same lens we would use for Elton John. The distortion is complete because these are two radically different expressions that under no circumstance allow for comparison. Yet, that was the approach taken by this journalist. He confused his lenses and ended up with a shortsighted view.

Of course, in the end, this anecdote offers only a curious footnote. The journalist did not win his battle; on the contrary, the public mercilessly rejected him. What remains important, however, is that this journalist—like many others in the media and in charge of social commentary—engaged in an absurd questioning of popular expressions that he never understood wholly or properly. Cultural underdevelopment paid its price. The great majority of music lovers and dancers—who, despite media pressures, are able to maintain a certain level of authenticity and individual identity—did nothing more than smile at the uneasiness of those "experts" who teetered between their own inferiority complexes and the larger social reality. The journalist wasted his time counting the *mentiras* in Lavoe's song without ever recognizing the real substance of the music: the supreme tumba solo of Milton Cardona and the exuberant vitality of the montuno. His actions were comparable to going to a museum only to look at the frames without ever seeing the paintings inside them. What a pathetic waste of time.

As for Héctor Lavoe, by 1977 he was *the* singer of salsa. Various factors distinguished him from, for example, Ismael Rivera and Cheo Feliciano. They had been performing their own styles long before the salsa explosion—styles that were, each in their own way, too unique or unusual to fit into any general category. On the other hand, Oscar D'León and Rubén Blades—the two soneros who later took over the salsa world—were not yet even in the background of the Ponce-born Lavoe. D'León was still too limited to the Venezuelan scene, and Blades had not taken off as he would after his recordings with Willie Colón. Lavoe, then, had the field to himself. His only competition came from Ismael Miranda, the only other singer also considered to be born in, for, and through salsa, but, again, Miranda's growing sophistication was already pulling him away from his barrio roots. Thus, Héctor's calendar filled up with requests to perform for New York dances, to give concerts, to make television appearances, and to travel all over the Caribbean, especially to Venezuela, where he was adored.

In the midst of his fame and success, however, Lavoe's personal chaos increased. He arrived late to the dances; he was careless about his vocal health; he did not worry about developing his abilities; and he displayed such irresponsibility that he annoyed all the entrepreneurs of the region. Lavoe's main problem was his supposed drug abuse, a vice that forced him to postpone, for months at a time, recording an album that remained perpetually unfinished. The final crisis was not long in coming. By mid-1977, Lavoe had to retire from public view because, it was said, he had become irrational. The recording was left undone; concerts, dances, and other scheduled appearances were canceled; and the rumors circulated widely, all with the usual exaggerations and no small dose of ill will. No one ever knew for sure what had happened. Some said that Lavoe had lost his voice; others claimed that, out of envy, his enemies had "done a number" on him, and Héctor had fallen prey to black magic.

At the time, I was producing the program *Bachata* for Radio Aeropuerto. In an unaired interview, a close friend of Lavoe's professed that Lavoe's health would improve, and, once "healed," Lavoe would return to Caracas. In using the term "healing," he was referring to the work of a well-known Cuban *santero* through whose prowess all of Lavoe's ills from the "curse" would be lifted. During this time Lavoe's whereabouts were unknown. The public insistently called for him to perform, but the producers and entrepreneurs made all sorts of contradictory excuses.

Just before the year was out, Lavoe resumed his career, but in Venezuela people said he was weaker, without the vitality or control he had sung with before. Those closest to the singer confirmed that during his absence he had been forced to undergo intense treatment in a psychiatric clinic in Madrid, which released him after a couple of months. Of course, thereafter Lavoe was the victim of a cruel press that refused to refrain from spreading gossip and rumors. Héctor emphatically denied his supposed drug vice, mentioned some illness and the exhaustion from excessive work, and, in that way, got away with it. But in the eyes of the public, a shadow of doubt remained, along with the contention that, for whatever reason, Lavoe was clearly not the same as before.

Finally, in 1978, the long-awaited album by Héctor Lavoe, *Comedia*, was released. It was smartly illustrated with a photo of Lavoe in roller skates dressed up as the Charlie Chaplin figure "Charlot," or "Carlito." The album was an overnight success, and it contained the very important hit "El cantante," composed by Rubén Blades. Here Willie Colón repeated his experiments with the violins and produced an extraordinary arrangement, much more mature and polished than his earlier "Periódico de ayer." Lavoe (despite all of his problems) was, of course, an established and veteran singer. On this album, he enhanced his singing style by making it sound more pained, irreverent, and streetlike, and, therefore, it was more effectively riveting. However, the element that most turned "El cantante" into a salsa classic was its lyrics, in which Blades unflinchingly described the circumstances of the salsa singer, the popular idol who sways unsteadily between the popular myths about him and his own painful, private suffering. Of course, after Lavoe's crisis, such lyrics sounded like a public confession. Beyond that specific example, however, the lyrics of "El cantante" could apply to a number of cases, even if they were less dramatic and less known. In any event, the myth was uncovered and the pedestal destroyed, which, in the popular arts, is always meaningful.

I'm the singer who you have come to hear
I'll bring you the best of the repertoire
And sing to our life of laughter and pain.

Despite the difficulties surrounding its production, the album *Comedia* became Lavoe's best recording to that point, particularly thanks to Willie Colón's influences. He gave full and equal attention to each number and imbued all of his arrangements with an experimental or avant-garde sensibility. Colón's "El cantante" was especially significant, but his son "La verdad" and Perico Ortiz's arrangement of the bolero "Comedia" also contributed to the album's success. Equally important were the version of Eliseo Grenet's "Sóngoro cosongo" by the young pianist Edwin Rodríguez and the sones "Tiempos pasados" and "Bandolera" by trumpet player José Febles (the musical director of Lavoe's orchestra). This last song was especially notable for an arrangement that had no major percussive elements—except for Mangual's bongo and Eddie Montalvo's tumbas—and for having at its center an exceptional piano solo by the virtuoso Professor Torres.

By 1979, Héctor Lavoe felt that he had overcome his crisis, but by then the competition with Blades and D'León had taken away the exclusive leadership that he had held for the last two years. Still—and this was particularly true for the New York audiences that supported him unconditionally—Lavoe remained one of the fundamental figures of salsa in the 1970s.

He personally embodied the highs and lows, the virtues and vices of the music. The wide array of situations and life experiences that salsa speaks to cannot be represented fully by any one singer. However, Héctor Lavoe—who became a professional musician in the middle of his adolescence and who rose from humble obscurity to the vertigo of sudden fame—is a prime example of what happened during the 1970s when, with the power and authenticity of its montunos, the Caribbean barrio invaded New York.

In the preceding chapter, when I defined the central styles and tendencies that nurtured the development of salsa during this decade, I identified two fundamental trends: the avant-garde and the traditional style. I have made it clear that the latter represented the majority of salsa produced at the height of the commercial boom. While this was the direct result of the criteria imposed by the Fania monopoly, one figure within the company represented, all by himself, everything that this tendency meant. That was Johnny Pacheco, the explicit promoter of the matancera style of salsa.

I also commented earlier on the albums that Pacheco produced in 1974—a key year for marking the take-off of the boom. Those albums were *Celia and Johnny* and *El Conde*, which introduced Pete "El Conde" Rodríguez as a soloist. Both albums were performed by the Dominican's orchestra, although this acknowledgment was deliberately ignored on the second album. The company, as mentioned before, had developed a plan for expansion, which meant that the artists and orchestras had to multiply themselves, or seem to—a trick that led to a number of other deceptions. Thus, the first album with El Conde Rodríguez as the leader was, in fact, just a recycling of one of the many that he recorded as a singer with Johnny Pacheco's orchestra.

After this production, however, El Conde went his own way. From here and there he gathered together a number of talented musicians to form his own orchestra, one that repeated, element for element, the traditional structure of Pacheco's band: two trumpets, conga and bongo, piano, bass and tres. To listen to El Conde, then, was pretty much to listen to Pacheco. Even many of the arrangements in the singer's repertoire were the same. In this way Fania achieved its goal of getting two orchestras out of one—two identical bands that were presented to the public as though they were two different ones.

As the boom continued, El Conde Rodríguez remained one of the representatives of the matancera style salsa, but some caveats must be noted. Amid his musical limitations and the pressures of his commercial situation, he did try to innovate, to find alternatives, even if he did not always succeed. On his first album, for instance, while Johnny Pacheco offered his old song "Los compadres" (referring to the brothers Lorenzo and Reinaldo

117

Hierrezuelo, his old compadres of the Cuban son), El Conde performed new songs by Curet Alonso—"Babaila" and "Un toque pa' yumbaó"—with distinctive new phrasings and purposes. Granted, those cuts showed no drastic or radical change; the differences were only those of nuance. But those same nuances, once the boom forced musicians to imitate a good part of the old Cuban repertoire of the 1940s and 1950s without any modifications, acquired a special, if negligible value.

El Conde Rodríguez, who shaped his vocal style according to the Cuban demands of Pacheco's orchestra, ended up in a very tenuous position. He did not belong wholly to the traditional or matancera style salsa, nor could he be considered part of the old, fundamental school of authentic Cuban soneros. This situation, however, was not unique to Rodríguez. The hype of the boom thrust many salsa singers onto album covers and into supposed starring roles overnight. In the middle of that swell of "stars," El Conde, however, started to shine. Indeed, he was one of the first figures to swim in both seas: Cuba and salsa.

In 1976, when salsa reigned supreme throughout the most isolated corners of the Caribbean and was replicating itself incessantly in all the Latino neighborhoods of New York, riding high on the euphoria of the boom, El Conde released his second album, *Este negro sí es sabroso*. It included one of the most listened-to hits of salsa: "Catalina la O," composed by the young Puerto Rican Johnny Ortiz. Here, the old image of the ideal mulatta, the woman desired by every man, was once again sung about in clave rhythms that delighted the dancers even as it perpetuated the myth:

Catalina La O
Catalina La O
With a cadence of silver
With a necklace of warmth.

From another view, upheld as one of the most authentic Fania All Stars in the salsa world, El Conde Rodríguez embodied a direct representation of the traditional or Cubanizing trend. He watched the ongoing recording boom from a very comfortable and stable position. Though, with the exception of "Catalina la O," he never broke any sales records, unlike other salsa stars, he also never slipped to the lowest levels of popularity and support. His third album, *Un toque de clase*, released in 1978, was again buoyed by Tite Curet Alonso's compositions and the same matancera style. Though produced with indisputable quality and good taste, the album was not championed by the public. It appeared during the crucial year of the boom, when most of the productions were repetitive, lifeless, and dull.

This naturally forced music lovers to reject any music that seemed identical to the usual fare, even if the publicity and marketing claimed the contrary. El Conde's album, thus, fell onto fallow ground and had no significant effects. Well into 1979, El Conde became one of many salsa figures who wandered New York, playing sporadically at dances and making occasional personal appearances that were never very noteworthy. Many of those musicians tried to live on their past fame, but without a fresh breath, that fame could not sustain itself indefinitely. This final stage, so close to anonymity, was common for many of the stars who, years earlier, had invented the boom.

What happened to El Conde Rodríguez was more or less repeated by Ismael Quintana, the singer of the preceding decade who had given a voice to Eddie Palmieri's explosive premier. Quintana was one of the singers who joined Fania during its expansion. Until 1973 he had remained stable even amid the many experiments and difficulties that had plagued Palmieri's orchestra. In 1974, however, Quintana separated from his former leader to look for greater security. He then signed on with Fania and was included in their catalog of artists under the new Vaya label. With Vaya, he released his first solo album, *Ismael Quintana*. That album allowed him to distinguish himself from others in the company and to begin exploring new sonorities and other innovations.

His experience, however, was not very positive. Not only was Fania unable to promote him sufficiently, but the majority of the public still believed that Quintana's voice only had meaning if it were improvising on Palmieri's montunos. All of Quintana's earlier work represented an immense weight that he could not get out from under. He inevitably fell into producing one commercial album after another, albums that were easily forgotten as the boom wore on. Because he was a regular member of Fania soneros, one of his new songs, "Mi debilidad," was included in the film *Salsa*, but this did not help much. Ismael still felt out of place. He also felt left out in the cold as younger audiences began to champion new idols with their fresher styles.

It would be unfair, however, to include Quintana among those singers who, in the midst of the boom, became overnight stars. His case was different. He deserves his rightful place as a pioneer who tried to forge a new style for the Caribbean song. During the 1960s, when Palmieri struggled to take the guaracha and the son down a new path, he needed a singer who could adopt that path as his own, and that singer was Quintana. His hoarse voice and his way of playing with words in the montunos made him a completely unique figure. Of course, the caliber of Palmieri and his band,

La Perfecta, and the demands of their musical projects created a kind of dependency among the musicians involved. In the end, this hurt Quintana who, once he became a soloist, felt cut off and unsupported.

Despite these problems, Ismael produced one of the best albums of the boom, although he never credited himself for any of the All Stars' successful albums. That album, released in 1976, was titled *Lo que estoy viviendo*, after one of Quintana's own compositions. For it, Quintana used what was considered the most excellent of salsa band configurations: a pair of trumpets, two trombones, and a complete rhythm section. Since he did not have an orchestra of his own, he relied on the musicians who recorded most of Fania's productions. These musicians included Papo Lucca, Johnny Rodríguez Jr., Nicky Marrero, Roberto Roena, Eddie "Guagua" Rivera, Ray Maldonado, José Febles, Luis "Perico" Ortiz, Héctor Zarzuela, Tom Malone, Reinaldo Jorge, José Rodríguez, Leopoldo Pineda, Harry Vigiano, Lewis Khan, and many others whose names can be read on the back covers of the albums published in those years (when the producers were decent enough to credit them).

Some of these musicians took part in *Lo que estoy viviendo* with all of the flash and fanfare that is possible when good musicians work with good music. I say this because many of these same figures wasted their talents on mediocre albums that were planned around lackluster repertoires using awful arrangements. Quintana managed to bring together all the necessary elements to make his album a significant one. Even so, he was the victim of a system of promotion and distribution that already exclusively lived off of kickbacks from radio stations and catered to the arbitrary tastes of their staffs and to the supposed criteria of not a few newly minted "experts."

In the years that followed, Ismael continued to perform for Fania, producing, as if under an inertia, new albums that never matched the level of his work in 1976. Thus his career faded into indifference and he ended up in virtual anonymity, despite the memories of his glory days with Palmieri.

I continue this summary of the Stars with Justo Betancourt, another singer with enough unique traits to escape rigid categorization. In previous pages I mentioned his initial work in the New York Latino scene that followed his solid experience in the old, Cuban guaracha. He then managed to incorporate himself into Fania as a leader and a soloist in the matancera style well before the company adopted it as the required mode for all of its singers. He produced albums that continue to shine, albums that are whole and unblemished. Betancourt also tried to maintain himself in that same way during the initial years of the decade when he released three quite satisfactory albums. The first was *El que sabe sabe* (1971), whose title directly referenced all the young salsa singers who, though just starting out, demonstrated a generally pretentious independence and unjustifiably arrogant poses in their stage appearances. The second, *Los dinámicos*, released at the end of that same year, was produced with Pacheco's orchestra. The most important of all, *Pa bravo yo*, was released in 1972. Let us turn to this latter one as a basis for understanding Justo's significance in salsa music.

When I last referred to El Conde Rodríguez, I mentioned his tenuous position between the phrasings and styles of the old Cuban guaracha and the requirements and essential traits of the new salsa. It is interesting to note, then, how Betancourt more easily overcame that same challenge. Not only did he fully address his Cuban roots, but also, with his clear virtuosity, he completely took on the salsa approach. Justo, in responding to those elements of salsa that had entered the old Cuban arena, became a singer par excellence, an authentic sonero who was able to move from one side to the other while exhibiting clearly the character of each. For a singer who was "made in New York," this was a difficult thing to do. Generally, either one extreme dominated—as happened with most soneros—or the uncomfortable straddling between the variants overcame the singers. As aforementioned, this matancero singer avoided both pitfalls.

For instance, the son "Pa bravo yo," composed by Ismael Miranda, had a theme that respected the style and structure of the traditional Cuban son but that was created from the perspective of salsa, as was the tendency at the time. Its lyrics were confrontational and disturbing, with aggressive phrasings and an extensive montuno that fought the chorus so that a kind of attack was reflected in the lyrics and the rhythm. A conventional singer would have worked through this theme by first presenting the initial part of the son in a flat interpretation, without any major variations or flourishes, and then offering a disorderly, even incoherent, repetition of two or three phrases of the montuno. Any reader familiar with the typical sounds of salsa produced during the boom would recognize this as the most obvious trait among the majority of nondescript singers. Betancourt, however, found a different solution. He approached the son with the old, Cuban style, taking full advantage of the range of liberties allowed a singer who knew how to play with all the melodic possibilities. He brought to bear a totally salsa style for the montuno, alternating phrases without repeating himself, playing smartly with any opportune phrase, even changing the rhythms, if need be, to show off between the measures of the chorus. Inspired by Justo's ability, many singers tried to imitate him, but they never achieved his results. While Justo went on playing with the montunos by including old bolero melodies and adapting lyrics from classic songs, many second-rate singers who tried to imitate his style produced only pitiful and misguided improvisations that had nothing to do with the song's theme. For any vocalist committed to this type of music, there is no skill more important than the ability to sense and seize the right moment—that is, knowing when to lead the chorus and when to stop it, when to throw in a joke that will animate the band or the phrase of an old bolero, some virtuoso taunt—in brief, knowing what to do and, most importantly, when to do it. As it happened, few singers at the height of the boom had the slightest idea of how to pull this off. As a result, there are plenty of albums full of shouts and screams that brag about a "sabor" that they simply never had.

Almost every one of Justo Betancourt's salsa recordings is an eloquent example of the contrary. This expedient sonero was full of the real salsa, the real Caribbean. Before concluding my remarks on this Cuban singer, let me comment on the lyrics of a song composed by Miranda—lyrics that, with Betancourt's interpretation, acquired very special nuances. These lyrics repeated a constant in Caribbean music: the self-identification between the one who sings and the music, in all of its contexts, its legacy and future. Salsa music is full of lyrics in which the sonero invests himself with the old spirit of the Caribbean *guapería*. Of course this pose is a very precarious one, since, in many cases, it ends up as banal chest-beating or as a simplistic and alienating defiance that turns out to be both ridiculous and pointless. To address this tendency, salsa initially turned to previous Cuban and Puerto Rican compositions, rather than developing its own treatment of this theme. This background should make clear the importance of "Pa bravo yo" as one of just such exclusively salsa-based treatments:

> I am brave . . .
> I who am a dark-skinned mulatto
> I have my head on straight
>
> .   .   .   .
>
> I have African blood
> And I sing with skill
> I am brave.

In 1976, after releasing his *Justo Betancourt* (1974) and *Lo sabemos* (1975), Justo joined Mongo Santamaría to record one of the most unusual recordings of the salsa boom: *Ubané*. According to the producers (Marty Sheller and Mongo himself), the idea was to return to the fundamental style of the Cuban guaracha of the 1950s. Their logic was clear: since salsa was now mostly known for its "Cubanization," the most prudent thing to do was to take the road back to its beginnings and show that the path from Cuba to salsa had been a smooth one. After devoting more than fifteen years to jazz, Mongo returned fully to "the kind of music you could dance to." For the recording, they called on some of the most important musicians around, most of whom had been released from the Fania monopoly. Among the participants were Víctor Paz, Manny Oquendo, Orestes Vilató, Patato Valdez, Julito Collazo, Bobby Rodríguez, Andy González, Justo Almario, José Madrid, and Virgilio Martí. For the first time in New York, the orchestra broke with the traditional salsa configuration and added a section of saxophones to the combination of trumpets and trombones. The rhythm section was much fuller with the doubling of a *quinto* player and two tumba players—a basic requirement of the real Cuban rumba. To achieve this objective required the presence of Justo Betancourt, the only singer proficient in the New York salsa style and, therefore, capable of fulfilling the aspirations of the project.

Despite these elements, the recording was a failure. The majority of the burgeoning audience that followed the dictates of the boom rejected those adaptations. However, despite its commercial problem, the album continues to have important, indispensable value. Observe the following: The salsa music that developed in the second half of the 1970s was conceived exclusively from an urban perspective. It was the music of the barrio and for the barrio. It was from there and from that point on that all of the elements that define salsa in the 1970s came together. And since salsa was seen as a supreme and culminating expression, it had the luxury of involving music that was not urban, as well. Thus, the old Cuban son that emerged outside the urban realm was wholly absorbed by salsa. The path went, then, from the city to the Caribbean countryside, or more precisely, from the city (the Latino barrio) to the urban expressions that emerged from other cultural circumstances (jazz, for example). Of course, the finished product was always salsa, since salsa was already an open expression that infiltrated and forced a connection with everything that it touched. But as we have seen in this chapter, the boom momentarily limited this same salsa, this open expression, by reducing it to the same, repeated mold. Once salsa entered the period of prolific, moneymaking recordings, it found itself divided between the avant-garde styles, with their very specific and particular traits, and the traditional styles, which we will discuss later. For now, let me reiterate that these are not the same styles that succumbed to matancerization. On the contrary, these styles developed from the charanga and the old mambo, from the glamorous big bands of the 1950s, and from the traditional Cuban bands. In all, the music was created from an urban perspective. Granted, there were some failures, as when an urban singer in the vortex of the city was forced to sing as if a country bumpkin crooning about the pleasant, bucolic life in the hills. However—and this is worth noting—in the midst of the boom, the urban musicians, particularly the old Cuban veterans, opted for an alternative path, one from the countryside to the city, while still making salsa. In the next chapter I will discuss the group that was an excellent representative of this tendency: Grupo Folklórico y Experimental Nuevayorkino (the Nuyorican Folkloric and Experimental Group). At this point, to continue with the boom and with the salsa that Fania produced, let us return to *Ubané* by Mongo and Betancourt, an album that also turned salsa on its head.

Ubané was a way of bringing Cuba into New York, rather than the other way around. The album tried to avoid the traditional son that for so long had fed into and dominated salsa. Instead, it chose the old guaracha, arranged in the festive and almost naive style that had characterized the final years of the 1950s. Songs such as "Cantándole al amor," "Serpentina," and "Vengan pollos" fit the mold nicely, and "Vengan pollos" also leaned toward the phrasings of the pachanga. Perhaps that approach led to the album's failure, since the salsa public did not relate to those styles. Even so, these guarachas could be viewed as a preface to the album, whose really important cuts came a few grooves later with three particular songs: "Ubané," the eponymous guaguancó; "Manana," a highly crafted son; and "Cumbia típica," an effective and faithful transplantation from country to city of one of the richest and most important genres in the Caribbean musical spectrum, the Colombian cumbia.

The son was another salute or homage to Manana, the legendary Cuban *rumbero*. It was arranged brilliantly in pure salsa style by Javier Vásquez, the Cuban pianist and arranger who provided accompaniment for Ismael Rivera and his Cachimbos. Vásquez infused the son with characteristics from the avant-garde Cuban music of the 1950s (in the style of Bebo Valdez, for instance). To achieve an obvious salsa feel, Vásquez retained the montuno (something rarely done in the Cuban recordings) and developed all of its possibilities. He accomplished something radically new: an idea of what an authentically Cuban salsa could sound like, rather than a Cuban music imprinted with New York salsa, as usually happened.

In the case of "Ubané," the title cut, the achievement was less noteworthy. This guaguancó, which had become a standard salsa orchestra recording, was presented without any significant updates. Mongo's proposal to approach the guaguancó in a straightforward way, without apology, was dismissed in favor of a hybrid: a pure guaguancó rhythm (imagine what this rhythm, performed by three tumba players such as Mongo, Patato, and Julito Collazo, sounded like), but with radically modern harmonies. Once again we have a middle-of-the-road project that was neither salsa nor guaguancó, which is probably why the public rejected it. Still, something good did come of this: The guaguancó, in addition to its latest sophistications, retained its Cuban origins. From a salsa perspective outside Cuba, this was very important.

"Cumbia típica," the third song from *Ubané*, exemplified salsa turned upside down, but in the salsa world, it did not elicit any major reaction. Even the musicians, who considered it part of a failed project, preferred to ignore it rather than to follow its risks. I always thought, however, that in the long run this cumbia represented the best of this album. It is a piece that, seen fairly, anticipated the more distinct paths of salsa. Mongo's pianist, José Madrid, composed and arranged it. As its title indicates, the song is the most *typical* possible, for its harmonies and concepts come out of the best Colombian tradition. Nor did the producers cut any corners when it came to the percussion performance. They invited five coastal drummers, true cumbia experts, and they also used traditional instrumentation. From the opening measures, the listener feels shaken by the freshness and vibrancy of a well-known beat, but one rarely heard in all of its authentic sonorities. Grupo Folklórico later seized on this valuable contribution, and audiences that had been taken with the modern phrasings of salsa responded to its truly original forms. They also recognized in them the real musical reasons behind their taste for salsa. This cumbia, despite its traditional title and intentions, was developed for a modern, urban, and salsa context. Thus, this mix: Betancourt's radical salsa style of singing and Justo Almario's flute added to the Colombian drums. Almario, a virtuoso instrumentalist from the Colombian coast, performed a solo that wound its way through the jazzy paths of the contemporary avante-garde without departing from the music's traditional spirit. With a balance of traditional validity and the freedoms of salsa, this song created a perfect and happy whole.

In the next chapter we will see how the alternative that this salsa initiated became one of the best solutions for continuing as a unique musical expression once the boom faded. *Ubané*, having been there near the beginning of the boom, serves as a good example of this. Obviously, the project was not the last word. The ambition to make salsa both accessible and profitable limited the actual possibilities of the album, and, amid the hype, there were very few fans who accepted the album on its own terms. Thus, as I noted, the "Cumbia típica" was sadly overlooked, even though it established a precedent.

By the end of 1976, Justo Betancourt had proven himself with productions of this type and felt limited by the New York scene created by the boom. As a way out, he separated himself from Fania and moved to Puerto Rico, where a freer and more modern sound was emerging. There he created his own orchestra, Borincuba, with young musicians who were not yet contaminated by the headiness of New York fame. Betancourt began 1977 with the album *Distinto y diferente*, in which he drew on the best spirit of the old salsa (by this time the original and vigorous salsa of the early years of the 1970s was already referred to as "old"). This album included one of the most successful hits of the entire boom, the song "No estás en nada." According to Justo, no matter what happens, people will continue to dance and to listen to good music, the good salsa:

> You're not cool
> You're just not cool
> Despite all your efforts
> You're not cool.

These apparently disorderly lyrics were intended to affect someone other than the "haughty woman" to whom the song refers. Sometimes a double meaning is the best tool that musicians have when they need to say things that the industry might censor or when they want to criticize the industry. "No estás en nada" could well be an example of this.

Living in Puerto Rico, free from all the hoopla and rumors that surrounded the other stars of the boom, Justo Betancourt remained one of the most authentic interpreters of the *true salsa*. He made his own decisions about the music and produced what he wanted to produce. Justo's salsa maintained and advocated all of the same characteristics that had been present in the boom's fabulous beginnings. By the end, as I shall demonstrate, only the best salsa survived, and "Presencia," from Betancourt's 1978 album, confirmed this. The song itself, composed by Curet Alonso, included a son written by Rafael Hernández in those old glory days of entertainment that were mythologized throughout the hemisphere.

> Don't nobody question my presence
> Don't nobody take me down
>
> . . . .
>
> I'm the soul and consciousness of an Antillean
> I've got a privileged heart.

Also during those days, many boleros were produced en masse, and many of them ended up dramatized in Mexican cinema. There was no distance between the cultures: Anyone could sing along with the Caribbean rhythm or with the melodious Mexican boleros, with the arrogance of rancheras or with the spiteful pain of the southern tango. At this point, North

American and European cultures had yet to provoke a damaging inferiority complex among Latin Americans, as discussed earlier. After that, we were able to look back on the legacy of that fabulous golden age and its impressive repertoire of popular music, and those earlier generations know that history by heart.

In some way, salsa music had to absorb part of this old spirit, to inherit something of that flair. Contemporary circumstances were considerably different from those that gave way to a swaying and sweet love, and in salsa, aggression always takes precedence over sweetness; fierceness is more important than melodiousness. However, these radically opposed differences were not enough to weaken the link, the possibility of bringing together the past and the present. In this case, it is not just about the old Cuban guaracha, but about the old spirit: Was it romantic and dreamy or cinematic and idealized? Or was it something elegant and reticent that characterized the musical production that the film and recording industries spread across Latin America in the 1940s and 1950s? Despite the barrio—and its rawness and misery—salsa music could not ignore those seductive images. Of course, the fusion was difficult and risky, since, despite everything, salsa had to continue being produced in the language and for the audiences of salsa. In other words, it could not disappoint any of the expectations for contemporary sound and vitality. This meant that salsa had to become more sophisticated in its forms and relate to the old spirit, but without, in any way, betraying the new one.

From the perspective of the Caribbean in New York, only one figure was able to meet both demands, and that was Tito Rodríguez. On one hand, his *hot music* was the best music produced up to that point. On the other, the public identified completely with his romantic music—his so-called romantic boleros—that surpassed even the brilliant expressions that had seduced so many Latin American generations. But Tito, as was well known, never repeated himself, and the salsa world may have been looking for a copy, a second edition.

Yet the need to reflect the old spirit was still there, so the industry had to find performers who were willing to fill that niche. One such performer was Vitín Avilés, an experienced Puerto Rican singer with plenty of talent for smoothing the way between the guaracha and the bolero. Vitín's vocal timbre, in fact, was very similar to Tito's, and, in certain ways, this masked the very real differences between them. The same could be said of Santitos Colón, the best *bolerista* in Tito Puente's orchestra and the singer Fania tried to use to forge a connection with the past. But both Vitín and Colón lacked the roots and the incisiveness to create a lasting bond with the audience, and both of these singers soon fell out of favor. They did not belong meaningfully to salsa or even to the New York rumba that was its direct antecedent. The same also happened with Vicentico Valdez—one of the best bolero singers from Cuba—who was part of the Latin scene in New York. Clearly salsa would not have gone far with these singers. To forge a true connection or bond required something that was definitely salsalike.

But that type of bond cannot be made to obey a musical producer's plans. We are playing with something here that is spontaneous, fluid, and free, in line with the tastes of an expansive community that takes pleasure in its own authentic musical expressions. Tito Rodríguez, for instance, did not respond to any entrepreneur's "innovation." The impressive reach of his music and its ability to touch his audiences followed genuinely from those natural connections that cannot be affected or fostered by images created in and for the industry. Therefore, if salsa wanted to cross over, it could do so only through a figure whose own personal traits were sufficient enough to meet the requirements of both music and audiences. Such a figure, who, from the pain of the New York expression, was prepared for the Caribbean and embraced by salsa as one of its first and authentic idols, was none other than Cheo Feliciano. Only Feliciano was capable of carrying on the old style of Tito.

Understand, however, that Feliciano did not come to prominence in salsa until 1971, just as the decade began, when the Fania Company signed him on as their most important singer. We exclude Feliciano's previous work with Joe Cuba and his sextet—significant work that defined the later style of salsa—first, because salsa had not been defined as such and, second, because, though clearly talented, Cheo was yet to enjoy the popular following that later flocked to him. The Cheo that had a real impact on salsa audiences was not the Cheo of Joe Cuba's sextet but the salsalike Cheo of "Anacaona," "Naborí," and "Canta," the Cheo of boleros and sophisticated rumbas, with their fine and delicate phrasings that gave up none of salsa's vitality or power. It was this Cheo who bridged the old spirit of the popular music of previous decades and the kind of salsa that was now inundating the region.

By 1980, Cheo had released eight albums as a soloist. Two of them contain boleros only (*La voz sensual de Cheo* [1972] and *Buscando amor* [1974]); one offers Christmas songs (*Felicidades* [1973]); another collects his top hits (*El arco iris de Cheo* [1977]); and four albums present true salsa, with guaracha and bolero mixes and other rhythmic experiments (*José "Cheo" Feliciano* [1971], *Con la pequeña ayuda de mi amigo* [1973], *El cantante* [1976], and *Mi tierra y yo* [1978]). In all of them, Feliciano revealed the highly unique style that distinguished him from other New York singers. As mentioned before, in his first two productions, Cheo worked with a small ensemble and with the same basic sound as in his days with Joe Cuba (i.e., vibraphone, piano, complete rhythm section, and the additional salsa-style guitar player who alternated his electric instrument with the traditional tres). Good taste is the chief characteristic of both albums. Cheo accords enough propriety to his boleros—situating them as a direct elaboration of what Tito had already done—while also connecting himself fully with the son and the guaracha through his melodious style. He did it all. Curet Alonso had defined these characteristics already in a challenging salsa form, in this son expressly composed for Feliciano:

> So that you can play
> I brought you a son
> So that you can play.

In 1976, with a big orchestra behind him, Feliciano released his album *El cantante*. The album cover displayed what was by then his symbol, a red rose, since he had taken on the role of the "romantic balladeer," a role that related him directly to the old entertainment figures of the continent. The opening number was the old son "Canta, canta" by Hernández. Cheo, of course, was not in the same circle as Lavoe and Miranda, nor could he be categorized with El Conde and Betancourt. He had nothing to do with Bobby Cruz or Ismael Quintana, and, likewise, even though he and Ismael Rivera shared the same rootedness and quality, it is clear that the distances between them were quite vast. Feliciano, therefore, had the privilege of operating on his own terms and presenting his own singular style. In the bolero, there was no one in the wings, and nobody dared to imitate his re-creations of sophisticated and refined guarachas. This is why Cheo felt able to experiment freely, doing things that many of his colleagues would not allow themselves to try. For example, also on *El cantante*, Feliciano recorded the cut "Poco a poco" by Aldemaro Romero, based on an exceptional arrangement by Jorge Millet but translated from its original "new wave" style into an intricate, mambo rhythm or clave.

One might think that all of these characteristics would have made Feliciano the most important salsa singer of all time, but this was not the case. Cheo never lived up to his recordings, which, after 1976, were poorly and almost reluctantly produced, perhaps because of his difficulties inside the company. He also suffered from not having a stable orchestra of his own—one accustomed to his sonero style and able to capitalize on the arrangements of his repertoire. Instead, Cheo had to work with whatever band was put together for the occasion, bands that were often comprised of second-rate musicians or bands on prerecorded tracks. Neither case permitted the singer to show off his talents. In Caracas, for instance, Cheo's concerts were consistently bad. In his first major perfomance, during the heyday of "El ratón," Cheo performed on television with an orchestra that had not rehearsed the songs completely. This glaring blunder caused great disappointment among the audience. His later performances were no better. The lack of communication between Feliciano and his musicians was obvious as soon as one heard the opening measures. As a final straw, it was obvious that Cheo did not always take care of his voice, since he sounded hoarse on many television shows and during his concerts at the Poliedro. Everything that was so wonderful on his albums was drastically diminished or undone in his live performances.

The poor production and mismanagement that led to the demise of many of the best salsa singers of that time was the direct result of bad planning by an industry avid for fast and easy money. Because Feliciano was one of the most promising performers, his case is perhaps the most tragic. To disentangle what truly happened is a difficult task. The politics of Fania—and, really, those of most salsa record companies—took place under such a thick veil of secrecy that no one will ever know exactly what the salaries of the artists were or, more importantly, the details of their sales records. This lack of certitude, of course, led to the wildest speculations, and those rumors were exacerbated by the artists. Ismael Rivera, Cheo Feliciano, Rubén Blades, and Eddie Palmieri, among others, constantly protested. In the words of Rivera, "We are treated as in the times of slavery and the whip." Palmieri expressed a similar complaint when he objected to the absolute lack of respect on the part of the management toward artists and their work.

We will return to this issue later in the book, but for now it might prove interesting to review some of the significant irregularities and chaos that characterized the work of the record companies. That work, rather than benefiting the artists, damaged them and progressively destroyed their potential. Cheo's particular problems began in 1975, the year he completed his last important record (*El Cantante*), without the collaboration of Curet Alonso. Cheo's differences with the record company, of course, had to do directly with salaries. Cheo therefore (as did Betancourt later) decided to abandon the Fania Stars, move to Puerto Rico, and keep himself on the sidelines, singing occasionally in little recitals where he distributed his signature red roses to his fans. This is the unfortunate image we still have of him. Thus, what could have led to a phenomenon of popular music across the continent was relegated to a few albums preserved and appreciated by music lovers alone. Subjected to the same punishment as Barretto, Rivera, and Palmieri, Feliciano had to pay an unfair price for his rebellion against the corporate record world. These musicians were never offered the freedom to create new musical works, were never provided with the minimal conditions necessary to improve that music's quality, and were never given the basic guarantees for the economically and socially stable life that every worker deserves. Clearly Cheo did not submit himself to the "whip," and therefore he ended up marginalized. Years later those familiar with Cheo's case and with the internal politics of Fania said that, like many others, he had given his life to the company and, ultimately, would never be free of it. For too long he remained stuck in an abusive relationship, and that cut short the opportunities for fans to enjoy his full talents. The history of salsa—the history of the boom—is full of these troublesome scenarios. This book is only recounting the things that actually happened.

His last album—*Mi tierra y yo*—produced without the ease of his previous work, still evinced that latent quality that, despite his personal grief, continued to be a hallmark of this singer. The guarachas speak for themselves, while "Obra maestra," by Curet Alonso, and "Quién sabe" show us, one more time, the best bolero singer ever to have emerged from the salsa boom. To conclude this discussion of Feliciano, let me reference the lyrics of a waltz (apparently the only one in salsa recordings), "Ansia loca," based on a well-crafted arrangement by the young Wisón Torres Jr., who mixed the cadences of an old Puerto Rican *danza* with the traditional bomba. Cheo recorded this as another homage to the Puerto Rican woman, the Caribbean woman who, with all of her scheming and wiles, continues to inspire so much fabulous Caribbean music. This theme also continues to suggest the bridge between the past and the present that I mentioned at the beginning of this section. Despite the clumsiness of commercialism, that bridge connected the bucolic and the melodious:

> I want the love of a dark-skinned woman
> One of those women from my homeland
> Who hides in her soul
> A bounty of warmth and kisses . . .
> A bounty of warmth and kisses . . . .

In the summer of 1977, during a session of my radio program, *Bachata*, Larry Harlow shared the following anecdote:

> When I recorded *Hommy*, nobody understood anything. . . . It was 1972, and Ismael (Miranda) was no longer in the orchestra, and I was preparing something big, something "heavy." . . . I used to work on the music, and, with Marty Sheller, we recorded it in parts. . . . You know, nothing like that had been done in salsa before, and people said that I was crazy. . . . We had everything—violins, a big band, Cheo singing one

131

song, Justo another, El Conde, Adalberto. . . . Forget it, nobody understood what was happening. . . . And I wanted to include Celia. I wanted
her to record the song by the woman, "the Divine Grace." . . . To me,
she was the only one who could sing it. But she was in Mexico and had
nothing to do with salsa, so I sent her a cassette with the music for the
song so that she would learn it, you know, so that she would get used
to it, more or less, and that way we'd save some time when she came to
New York for the rehearsal. Now what really impressed me—me and
all the other musicians—was that Celia did not rehearse anything. . . .
That lady was a genius, the best singer ever. . . . When I asked her if she
wanted to rehearse, she said no, that we should go straight to recording
it. . . . And then, well, we started to record. . . . And that version on the
album was the first and only one that we recorded. . . . Celia did not
rehearse at all. She sang that song from beginning to end, without any
mistakes, without having to go over anything. . . . I was so surprised that
she was ready to record right away, without any adjustments. . . . I had
never seen anyone like that—she's the only one who's done this—sing a
whole song without rehearsing it, as if she knew my orchestra by heart,
as if she was inspired and everything. . . . Forget it, Celia is one of a kind,
the grandest.

This anecdote reveals why Celia took off when the boom emerged. In previous chapters, I discussed the importance that *Hommy*, the album that
Celia recorded with Pacheco in 1974, had for the beginnings of this new
expression called salsa. Also important was the *Bemba colorá* album that
she recorded with Fania. Now we have to examine the rest of her work—
two more albums with Pacheco and one with Willie—and the growing fan
base she accrued throughout the years.

The salsa that developed during the boom had little in common with
the music that initially had shaped it. The industry forced musicians to
follow safe and easy formulas, and so the old Cuban guaracha increasingly dominated the repertoire. Not only because of her exquisite virtuosity but also because of her imposing musical personality, Celia Cruz
possessed all the attributes necessary to represent the old Cuba fully. Of
course, she also had plenty of other qualities that prepared her to take part
in diverse experiments and innovations, as her work on *Hommy* and the
album with Willie Colón made clear. Fania, however, and, under its label,
Johnny Pacheco himself preferred to avoid such risks. The matancerization approach was generating numerous successes, so they saw no reason to change direction. In 1977, Fania produced *Recordando el ayer* with
Pacheco's orchestra and the participation of Celia, Justo Betancourt, and

the extraordinary Puerto Rican pianist Papo Lucca. That album was full of sabor, but to the extent that it catered to the matancera style, it was also a disappointment. It was, however, an immediate hit, and the music in it is undoubtedly good. But again there is a very important "but" to this album that we cannot ignore.

As its name, *Remembering Yesterday*, indicates, the album pretended to evoke the past, which is quite legitimate for salsa or any other musical development to do. The problem emerged, however, when that evocation was presented as "the best of salsa," which, of course, was a contradiction. Note: clearly the entire range of Caribbean music of the twentieth century—and especially the son—provided antecedents for salsa. To acknowledge those antecedents was healthy, if it meant interpreting them in ways that *enriched* the original expression. This was what good salsa orchestras did—they capitalized on their musical legacy in order to *justify* and solidify their own expression even more. So far, so good. But what emerged next was questionable: The old expression was reproduced and imitated to the letter without any type of innovation, without any new element that revealed the music's contemporary circumstances. One could argue, in favor of this variant, that *replicating the past* is completely valid in any artistic expression as long as one respects the totality of its elements and details. And this is true. It is unacceptable—even false and disingenuous—however, to mask this reproduction of the past as the legitimate and authentic expression of the present. Yet, that was precisely what happened with *Recordando el ayer*.

The Venezuelan group Sonero Clásico del Caribe, for instance, had been recording the son in its purest forms consistently for years. Guided by an ironlike orthodoxy, they sought to reproduce its smallest details, and the music they produced was scrupulously valid, mostly because they never tried to sell it as salsa or as contemporary music. Any audience that listens to Sonero Clásico knows that they are listening to a fabulous evocation of the past, one with no pretense of being a form of contemporary salsa. Again, let me be clear. What I object to is not the recording of old music, but when that old music is recorded without any modifications and when, through this, the musicians dupe an audience that lets itself be swayed by the suggestion that they are experiencing a new musical trend.

Recordando el ayer was an excellent example of these commercial intentions. Because the album was a good collection of the old Cuban guaracha (especially of the Sonora Matancera), the deception was even subtler, since it was recorded and presented in an impeccable form and, moreover, performed by musicians of the first order. That combination of elements also easily explains the success of the album. Once again, Pacheco was able to meet his highest sales goals. Celia continued to demonstrate her virtuosity, and the achievements of Betancourt and Papo Lucca helped to complete a perfectly rendered idyll. Add to these the participation of musicians such as Perico Ortiz (first trumpet), Johnny Rodríguez (congas), and Charlie Rodríguez (tres), and you have an album that had it all. But here again it is worth being more precise: the album was *good*, and if it had been presented simply as an evocation of the old, matancera music, I would consider it as excellent and worthy of being anthologized. However, the intent to misrepresent its contents forces me to dismiss it. Indeed, this was how salsa started to become discredited, and this easy way out eroded much of salsa's sensibility and significance. This example reinforces the need to keep clear the true aims of the music. Salsa, as I have said repeatedly, is a specific musical expression, and as such, it has its own characteristics and contexts, which under no circumstances should be conflated with those of the old Cuban son. Yes, we are dealing with very similar musics, with expressions that share the same Caribbean lineage, and this evolution has to be respected. However, Ignacio Piñeiro composed his "Suavecito" during the 1920s, not in 1978, and that fifty-year difference is too important to ignore just to satisfy the recording industry's desire for profits.

Of course, we are talking about a trend that took place within salsa while the boom was exploding. Trends in and of themselves are never bad; the cultural industry simply uses them to sustain itself. The problem arises when those same trends are exaggerated. (In Venezuela, there is a common expression that "when the radio seizes on a song, it ends up making it an annoyance.") Other expressions that may be authentic but not trendy are overshadowed by these exaggerations and then discredited and dismissed. In the case of salsa, this distinction is extremely important. The matancerization of salsa was a trend, and that was fine. However, that same trend started going overboard and, through the industry's marketing manipulations, ended up being identified as salsa itself. Having said this, I understand that those responsible for a trend are not necessarily the same ones responsible for its overreaching its bounds. This was the case with Johnny Pacheco, one of the best promoters of the trends connected with Caribbean beats.

To say, for instance, that Pacheco invented the charanga ensemble is absurd. However, its popularity did increase when his orchestra was leading the music world. This occurred also because, in the minds of the New York audience that continued dancing to the charanga style after the United States cut off relations with revolutionary Cuba, the charanga only achieved popularity when it was dressed up in the trendy nuances of the time. A similar thing happened during the salsa boom, when a growing audience began to think that Pacheco invented the Cuban son and other popular folk music. Of course, the Dominican never claimed to be the author of those forms; in fact, and to his credit, his best achievement was to have invented a trend based on what was already there, and that was the only authorship that Pacheco claimed.

Along those lines, Pacheco brought out some albums that were very important for the salsa boom. He added to his first two productions with Celia by releasing *El maestro* in 1976 and *El artista* in 1977. Both of these were enhanced by the power and vocal strength of his new sonero, the Cuban Héctor Casanova. These two records clearly attempted to continue the old tack that Pacheco had inaugurated with El Conde Rodríguez, though in some ways this project was seen as even more superior than the first. Not only did Casanova offer a much more Cuban style of improvisation with the *soneo*—one more defined and aggressive—but Pacheco himself, aided by the arrangements and orchestral direction of Perico Ortiz, finally threw himself into refashioning the old Cuban music that continued to nurture his repertoire.

Until 1973 Pacheco's albums were characterized by a battle cry, launched, as it were, in some of the montunos, such as "Pacheco . . . and his *new* tumbao." In 1977, however, that cry radically changed to "Pacheco and his tumbao *of old*." Curiously, both cries were shouted out over a music that remained basically the same, with the same son on every album. This detail exemplifies what was happening to Pacheco's orchestra and, beyond it, to the matancera style more generally. In the albums he released during the first years of the decade, Pacheco worked with a style that was new or unknown to most Caribbean audiences. (Non-Cuban musicians younger than twenty would have had no idea who Chapotín was or what Arsenio had done or about the island tradition known as conjuntos. For them, "Matancera" referred only to an old orchestra, while the only new and important thing in music was what the rebellious young musicians were doing in New York). In light of this and to connect with music from the New York recording empire, Pacheco said that he was playing something "new," the "new tumbao," the next thing to follow the fever for the charanga. Even so, once the matancera style became a trend of recognizable caliber, Pacheco felt the need to make modifications. In a smart move, he aligned his style even more with popular folk music mixed with a certain modernity of arrangements, especially in the fabulous solos of his guest musicians (especially Lucca and Perico himself) and in the flavorful soneos by Casanova. Thus, even though the music remained the same, Pacheco now proclaimed it the "new" tumbao "of old."

Taking on this spirit in *El maestro*, Pacheco recorded two slow and heavy montunos that illustrated all of the traits mentioned above. Perico's trumpet in "Simaní" is excellent, as are the soneos created by Casanova in "El faisán," composed by Pacheco himself. The same strain was preserved in *El artista*. Its old montuno, "Esa prieta," popularized by Benny Moré, contributed to the album's success. In 1978, trying to reach a new audience—especially the Mexican one, one of the region's most important markets—Pacheco brought in Luis Silva, the veteran Mexican guaracha singer who, in previous decades, had formed part of that famous duo Lobo and Melón. He even titled the album *Llegó Melón* (*Here Comes Melón*). A fine rendition of the flamenco rumba "Don Toribio," by Peret, also helped to draw a sufficient audience, while Melón's melodious style, full of those guaracha-like scats in the matter of "da-bidi-di-dum," added a *new* technique to salsa singing. Basically, Melón had nothing to do with salsa. His way of singing the guaracha and the son was dripping with the rumba style disseminated by a Mexican cinema full of borrowed "Americanisms." That style, therefore, could hardly be continued in the new salsa. Despite being full of repetitions and using less-talented singers, Pacheco's album with Melón did give music lovers a sort of necessary respite between trends.

That blend of elements also gave Pacheco value in the salsa world. He was, in the end, the leader of the matancera style—a fact that alone already afforded him a very important place in the larger world of salsa. Of course, those values diminished when that same matancerization—a passing fad, after all—was exaggerated as on the previously discussed album *Recordando el ayer* or in some of the cuts that Pacheco included on *El artista*. This was the case with "Corso y montuno," the album's biggest hit. Signed as an original composition by Pacheco, it was nothing more than a random assortment of old Cuban choruses, all sung over the same endless montuno. The title comes from El Corso, the most famous salsa club in New York, where Pacheco's orchestra routinely played. The theme follows suit: the same montuno endlessly repeated night after night at the same club. Still, it was a hit, one sure to motivate the audience to dance, and that was fine. It was not fine, however, to claim as original a composition that was not so. ("Corso y montuno" was a potpourri, nothing more.) Nor was it fine to set up the same old trap of presenting the old as if it were new and to snare an audience that aimlessly followed the boom and its music, a music that was more and more incapable of conveying and carrying on the authentic meaning of salsa as a unique expression.

The case of "Corso y montuno" was repeated, with the same intention and the same results, in "El bajío," another potpourri of montunos recorded by Pacheco with Celia Cruz on the album *Eternos*, released at the end of 1978. Thus, what seemed virtue on one hand became a defect on the other, again resulting in contradictions. *Eternos* represented the virtual exhaustion of the whole matancera trend. As of 1980, it was also the last album to feature the combo of Celia and Johnny, but the album's quality was quite inferior to their previous ones. This was not because of a lack of talent in the singer or any measurable decline in the quality of the arrangements; rather, the same old Cuban vein had run dry. Audiences were seeking something different, something really new, something representative of the urban and contemporary world of salsa.

Apart from the matancera style, the end of 1977 saw an album that presented a very different Celia Cruz singing Brazilian music and Mexican rancheras in salsa arrangements with an orchestra of a distinct sonority. This album took advantage of the great myth of the matancerization trend, which was supposedly expressly trying to escape that category. Titled *Sólo ellos pudieron producir este album (Only They Could Produce This Album)*, it was recorded by Celia Cruz with Willie Colón's trombone orchestra. Of course, some of the repertoire came from the old Cuban expressions, including a new version of the classic Celia and Sonora cut, the "Burundanga." This time, though, the music was focused through the lens of salsa, without any intention to reproduce or imitate what the Cubans had done already. That was the album's real success—it *was* something new. From the salsa arrangement of the very famous Brazilian cut "Usted abusó" to "Tú y las nubes," one of the most extraordinary compositions by José Alfredo Jiménez, everything was presented in an effective and daring arrangement by Perico Ortiz with a dazzling Celia. Here the bossa and the ranchera met the bomba "A papá" and Johnny Pacheco's merengue "Pun pun catalú." This demonstrated, once and for all, that salsa had to draw not just on the old Cuban music but on the whole Caribbean musical tradition. This included the richness of Mexican music, which, as an authentic, popular Latin American music, offered numerous features or elements for the modern salsa expression to adopt.

As Celia moved through the world of salsa, performing in a variety of styles and genres, the dynamism, power, and quality of her voice were barely affected by the passing of time. She was already the greatest celebrity and the most important and influential pop figure in every mode of salsa. At each of their events, the Fania All Stars announced her as the main attraction, and at the emotional high point of any concert, the emcee shouted, "the goddess of Latin music," one of her many titles. In September 1978, the Ralfi Mercado and Ray Avilés Company boldly offered two back-to-back concerts at Madison Square Garden, one of the largest venues in New York City. They solicited a number of Fania Stars to perform with their respective orchestras on both nights, but the only star to do so was Celia, the only one also capable of attracting a significantly large audience. On the first night she performed with Willie Colón, and therefore she sang the salsa repertoire. On the second night she was backed by Johnny Pacheco's orchestra and offered songs in the popular folk style. The combination was perfect, representing fully the salsa boom. On both nights, as always, Celia was impeccable, enchanting a new audience who could not help but surrender to her newest forms and her improvised soneos.

Celia traveled beyond New York, throughout the Caribbean, singing with various orchestras. In Venezuela, she even reunited with the old Sonora Matancera in a performance that was truly historical even though the public did not know enough to appreciate that moment for what it was worth. Celia also went to Mexico, and there, alone, she revived a good part of her old fame. Mexico accorded her a distinction and a level of support that none of her cohorts from New York salsa ever received in that country. In February 1979, in a recital at Radio City Music Hall, I saw her singing a homage to Benny Moré. That night, with Tito Puente's super-orchestra, Celia sang the old bolero "Encantado de la vida" in a duet with Cheo Feliciano. Later she changed outfits and appeared onstage in her Cuban rumba dress, the one with the long train that was reproduced on so many of the Sonora album covers. Celia sang "Yiri yiri bon" and then asked for silence in order to sing another bolero, "Me acuerdo de ti," a sort of lament for the old glories of the Tropicana cabaret. That night, music lovers were able to contemplate the total image of what Celia Cruz meant to the world of Caribbean music.

When she was announced, the thousands of people who filled the immense hall gave her such an ovation that their adoration for her was strikingly clear. There she was, teaching us how to sing, how to speak *truthfully*, and how to breathe and articulate the Caribbean rumba. Celia improvised the past with "Yiri," and she whispered the present, also intimated by Cheo, with the bolero. She insinuated that this step, of course, followed the nuances of another bolero, one reminiscent of the traumas, frustrations, complexes, bitterness, and anger of a political event that divided Cubans and Latin Americans into two groups, an event that divided the contemporary history of the continent into a before and an after. Celia's musical leadership led her to take on an inevitable political leadership. She had left Cuba and she sang to the exiles, but she also sang to those who had stayed behind. Her political role, however, harmed her in some ways. In general, the Latino youth who lived outside the Cuban revolution ignored the problem, and those who did engage it, were sympathetic to the cause. The rest, the exiles, who in the early years of the 1960s called for an immediate return to the island, gradually started to distance themselves from that dream. Miami—the "Cuba" that developed outside the island—was never fertile soil for salsa (whether it cheered or jeered the revolution). The generation of young Cubans born or raised in the United States felt considerably far from everything that their parents' world had included. The sad truth was that they were already "Americans," completely U.S.-Americans. Their middle-class status also separated them from the Boricua youth whose impoverished and marginalized life in New York inspired the creation of cultural expressions increasingly Caribbean ("We have to return to our roots" was their general motto). All in all, then, Celia's critiques fell into a vacuum. Her disavowal of socialist Cuba connected with only a minority of her audience and had very little to do with the rest of salsa. That night at Radio City, the example was clear: The same audience who had given her an initial standing ovation responded to her nostalgic bolero with hesitant, awkward applause. Moreover, Celia was singing about the Tropicana (the old image of the island cabaret), in a homage to Benny Moré, a pop icon who, very differently from her, had chosen to stay in Cuba, with the revolution and with all of its hardships and hopes.

Shouldering her sadness, Celia Cruz still continued to sing the rumba, to entertain at dances and carnivals, and to let shine the majesty of her voice. She was a gift to salsa, a figure who came from the old guaracha and who knew how to prolong its spirit through the turbulence of the present times. It would be a lie, though, to say that she was the best of salsa. Celia was, more accurately and undoubtedly, the best *guarachera* ever known, both before and possibly after salsa. But Celia was not salsa; she was, simply, a unique phenomenon.

The Other Stars

In 1975, motivated by the success of the Fania All Stars, the executives at Tico and Alegre decided to hold a mammoth concert reuniting the other stars—their stars—who very much reflected the spirit of New York music before the Fania-induced explosion. From that concert they produced the album *Tico-Alegre Stars Live at Carnegie Hall*. The cover listed all the big names: Tito Puente, Charlie Palmieri, La Lupe, Ismael Rivera, Joe Cuba, Vicentico Valdez, Vitín Avilés, Yayo el Indio, Javier Vásquez, Alfredo "Chocolate" Armenteros, Héctor Rivera, and Israel "Cachao" López (whose miniaturized photo appeared on the cover, although his music was not included on any of its grooves). All in all, these were the veterans, those masters who had the opportunity to make the New York scene an authentic bridge between the music of the past and the music of the present. This album returns us to those earlier chapters about the 1960s, when salsa was not yet called salsa, and the musicians were trying in various ways to develop new styles and new sounds.

But Tico's attempt fell on deaf ears. The album's return to the past mistakenly ignored the achievements of the first half of the decade and—thanks to Fania's interventions—such oversights were not well received either by the audience or by the music. Just what did the album contain? Two cuts with Puente's orchestra (one an instrumental and one a bolero sung by Vicentico Valdez), a song recently produced by Joe Cuba, a Brazilian theme badly rendered as salsa and sung by La Lupe, a guaracha by Charlie Palmieri sung by Vitín Avilés, a romantic son by Yayo el Indio, a song by Bobby Capó with Ismael Rivera and his Cachimbos, and a jazzlike jam session directed by Javier Vásquez. We can use this album to examine what happened to this other group of talented New York musicians, who at a certain moment in their careers exerted (and have gone on to exert) a natural leadership over certain aspects of the salsa expression.

Let us begin with Palmieri. We have already seen how, by the end of the 1950s, Charlie Palmieri had achieved a stable orchestra, a charanga that was ready for the next burst of that style. Palmieri's Duboney Orchestra had Pacheco as its flutist, and he soon became the dominant leader of the charanga style. Latin American history often offers similar examples of political leaders whose potential ends up lost in a corner of memory because they failed to seize the moment or were unable to ride the wave of opportunity. I believe this happened to Charlie, who was, without a doubt, one of the best pianists in the Caribbean expression, both in and outside Cuba. Why didn't *he* develop the new trends, since he had all of the necessary conditions to do so? The answer is difficult and has as much to do with the business of the music industry as with the music itself. The Duboney Orchestra, for instance, was always at the leading edge of the charanga style, and most of its albums from that time are counted among the best. Later, when the charanga trend had run its course and the city began to demand a new sound, Palmieri adapted to a more North American structured orchestra, taking advantage of new brass combos. These were the days when his brother, Eddie, was surprising and amazing audiences with his own experiments and innovations, with his dissonant and raucous trombones. Charlie's virtuosity was undeniable, and so was his ascendance over many of his musical colleagues. But he remained on the second tier with productions that never really stirred the listeners. His image was considered cold, not one that could spark the emotions and euphorias needed to maintain a following for his type of music. In his favor, however, we must acknowledge the fabulous jam sessions that he directed with the best musicians at the time, especially as documented by the initial albums of the Alegre All Stars. But none of that was enough to attract a sufficient number of dancers or record buyers. Already at a frank disadvantage, Charlie Palmieri entered the new decade when the younger musicians—who were, for the most part, considerably less talented or less capable of producing quality music—boldly began to determine the contemporary paths of Caribbean music. And Charlie once again only minimally changed his style.

A review of some of the albums that he produced during the 1970s—*El gigante del teclado*, *Vuelve el gigante*, and *Adelante gigante*, for instance—reveals the sad evidence of wasted talent. One must listen to all of these productions with intense attention in order to select the best of the isolated grooves, since most of them were undermined by Charlie's insistence on performing the montunos on the organ. Quite simply, some instruments have very select musical functions. That same organ, for instance, did not disrupt Eddie's *Vámonos pa'l monte*, but it was frankly intolerable in a series of sones and guarachas where its long and heavy notes took away the vigor and vitality of the beat. This criticism—which any music lover would agree with—was shared with Palmieri by many of his colleagues, but the master persisted. Of course, to blame the organ alone is as arbitrary as to dismiss Arsenio's old recordings because certain deficiencies in the sound lent a blandness to the albums. The instrument is only one element of a strength or weakness that lies in something deeper.

There, precisely, was Charlie's problem: His conception of the music was simply not in the same vein as that of salsa. Palmieri, sensing the growing Matanzas-like trend, recorded a great deal of old, Cuban music. He reproduced sones, guarachas, and classical boleros; but nothing ever came of it, and audiences had plenty of reasons for remaining indifferent. Johnny Pacheco had beaten Palmieri to the punch. Hence, the apropos analogy and expression I used before: The one who succeeds is the one who senses and seizes the moment, the one ready to ride the wave of opportunity. While Pacheco anticipated and clearly foresaw the new trends, positioning himself as a leader of the avant-garde, Palmieri remained enveloped in an unfortunate inertia and again came in second, losing the ground that once had belonged to him in so many ways.

The album recorded live at Carnegie Hall presented Charlie's orchestra through the son "Son tus celos." The cut is truly full of sabor. Avilés moved gracefully through the montuno, the band respected the clave, and there was a level of quality sustained from the beginning to the end. But this cut, staged for such a special occasion and with the grand claim of making history, was performed without any sense of risk or glory, as if it were being played for any old dance after three in the morning. This was because, despite all of the factors just mentioned, the orchestra lacked cohesion, one of those intangible forces that make the music lover pay attention, listen keenly, and return to the cut over and over again. Sabor alone was no longer enough now that the new salsa trend had taken over.

Years later, around 1978, when the salsa audience justifiably was losing its admiration for some earlier figures, Palmieri produced an album that capitalized on the voice of the Panamanian sonero Meñique. The result was pretty much another disappointment. Of course, the album cannot be dismissed as easily as we have done so with other productions of the same time—as truly terrible. On the album, *Gigante*, there are a couple of piano solos that are worth listening to again and again. As I noted earlier, any short list of the Caribbean's best pianists would have to include the name of that heavy, gray-bearded musician Charlie Palmieri, a leader who unfortunately did not keep up with the times.

Already by 1977, the salsa boom had made a strong impact on the Venezuelan public. In February of that year, Radio Capital, a pop (or youth-oriented) radio station that was considerably opposed to any "Latin American" music (obviously including Venezuelan music), tried to jump onto the bandwagon of the new salsa fever. With great fanfare it announced a concert by Joe Cuba and his sextet at the Poliedro. It happened that the sextet, with its worn-out view of salsa, was quite accessible to listeners of pop. Ten years prior Joe Cuba had set in motion the fusion of the son with the boogaloo and the commingling of English and Spanish—that is, the salsa that had made it into the mainstream record industry of the United States. He had recorded the original version of "El ratón," a salsa number that was completely embraced by all the radio stations. In other words, to a certain extent, Joe Cuba represented salsa that was less regional, a little more "in" and gringolike. The concert took place, and the audience's disappointment was obvious. The group Dimensión Latina, invited to perform as a nod to national pride, saved the event, but the famous sextet, that evening's attraction, turned out to be a fiasco. This was hardly unexpected by those who knew the album behind it all—*Tico-Alegre Stars Live at Carnegie Hall*—which already showed that Joe Cuba was not even a shadow of his formerly fabulous self.

Let us review what this group produced in the 1970s (up to the first months of 1979, when I was writing these paragraphs). Of their four albums, three were released between 1970 and 1973: *Recuerdos de mi querido barrio*, *Bustin' Out*, and *Hecho y derecho*. The last album, which was inexcusably not recorded until three years later, in 1976, was *Cocinando la salsa*. This album appeared after the Tico label had been taken over by the Fania monopoly, meaning that the album was forced to comply with the new musical criteria of the company, and that was a real pity. Joe Cuba relied on the voice of Mike Guagenti, a sonero without any unique talent or recognition, but one established enough to fulfill the basic functions he was assigned. Cuba also drew on the always effective repertoire of Jimmy Sabater, and he accepted the new musicians who were called in to complete this lackluster album. The repertoire reprised some of the old successes of the conga player and incorporated some new compositions by Guagenti himself that remain forgotten. What went wrong? Why, ten years after those fabulous albums of *Bailadores*, *Estamos haciendo algo bien*, and *Bang, Bang, Bang*, did they lower their standards and produce such a poor product that it triggered only nostalgia? Where was the old spirit of *Alafia*, that declaration to uphold the "en clave" principles of the son? What stroke of fate was capable of eradicating all of the virtues and leaving behind all of the sins? The most unfortunate thing about this is that no answer was offered, not even by the musicians themselves. Suddenly, all the blame shifted to the environment, the same one that ten years earlier had hailed the group as an irreverent and easygoing ensemble, a worthy representative of all that the new music of the urban Caribbean embodied.

By way of analogy, let me remind readers of the histories of many boxers who one fine day achieve everything they want, with the easiness of one lucky blow, but once things change, end up mercilessly falling back down to the ground or the level from which they came. The world of popular musicians may not lead to the fame and luxury that, with a single blow, a fortunate boxer can enjoy, so for the musicians the ground they fall back to may be less hard. But the loss is the same. There is a change of fortune that is not controlled by the protagonists and that victimizes them either way. It is possible that Joe Cuba, like so many other good musicians—indeed too many, to tell the truth—ended up overwhelmed by a capricious indifference. This is the only way we can understand the gulf between his musical production that began and ended these ten years.

> If you bring to me
> Your son and your lucumí
> If you do the bembé
> And dance the abacua . . .
> Ban ban bancó mama . . . .

The son simply titled "Lucumí," released by the sextet in 1973, showcased the virtuoso singing of Willie García. An epileptic and strident rock-and-roll version was included in the album from Carnegie Hall, showing again that a brief two-year period was enough to mark the group's decline. Right up to that album of 1973—*Hecho y derecho* (*Doing It Right*)—however, the sextet had something to contribute to salsa, but from that point on they returned to the policy of reprising old hits (most often, the classic "La calle está durísima"). Still, they did include one new number that continued the initial wave of *Alafia* and that was the son that gave the album its name, "Hecho y derecho." Here a challenge was offered and, with it, a defiant new definition for the world of the barrio and for the gamut of characters who embodied, created, and enjoyed salsa.

In effect, the lyrics of "Hecho y derecho" convey a certain disorder. They lack that so-called logical coherence expected by those who see things from the other side. It was, however, that same arbitrary nature of elements that translated, occasionally, into the fierce grounding required of this type of music with all of its social implications. Here a particular code was used to suggest a closed world where many things are understood completely in an instantaneous flash of insinuation or snideness. Ever since the rousing days of his best music, Joe Cuba had been a master at playing with the obscure retorts of a special language that says it all even while the outside world remains unsure of the meaning, and that talent, so important within the cultural expression of salsa, gave the name of Joe Cuba and his sextet a predominant place in the final assessment of that musical world. The old albums still hold that place, and they allow us to forget the unfortunate character of his last stage.

Let us return now to the Carnegie Hall album. In addition to the son by Charlie Palmieri, side B presented another one with the same orchestra backing Yayo el Indio, whose powerful voice gave him a regular sonero role with the Sonora Matancera in its later years. Despite his vocal talent, however, Yayo never established a steady following among audiences, and, whether in the Sonora or in the many diverse New York groups with which he recorded, none of his music can be linked with the spirit of the salsa trend. His lyrical style of sones was born in the Havana orchestras of the 1950s that had little impact on the violent and turbulent world of salsa. That is why Yayo was seen less as a lead sonero in salsa and more as a good singer of choruses. His full voice, with its uncommonly low register, rare among the new vocalists, made him an ideal singer when the old choruses of the dense and ponderous Cuban son needed to be reproduced. Therefore, Yayo el Indio was thrown in as a big star in the Tico-Alegre productions, but nothing ever came of it.

What completed the album was a totally extemporaneous jam session, more in the style of the Fania of 1971 than in the style that had been perfected in the 1960s. There are some good solos, to be sure, but these offer very little of the salsa tonalities that were sweeping through the streets in 1975. The cut that really did spark a sense of power and rootedness was

"Dormir contigo," an effective and plaintive son, one of the best of the extensive and sharp repertoire of Bobby Capó. It was sung with all the quality and vigor required by Ismael Rivera and his Cachimbos orchestra. However, let us leave the cut "Ciudadano de la calle calma" for later, since some of the elements it presents are better analyzed outside the salsa trends and personalities I am now discussing.

With the exception of the cut by Joe Cuba, side A of the album was performed by Tito Puente's orchestra, beginning with a showy version of "Así hablaba Zaratrusta," retitled as "La odisea de Tito" after the 2001 space-odyssey films. Tito, of course, is one of those personalities who surpasses any categorization. Many of the major productions of Latin music in New York were indebted to his initiative and creativity. At that time he was also undoubtedly the Caribbean musician with the most records to his name. (He recorded more than thirty albums for the Tico label alone, not to mention all that he did for U.S. record companies and for the first Latin recording companies established in New York, for whom he served as a principal artist. At one time Puente himself confessed to us that he was approaching his 100th album. Since that conversation, he has released three more albums and may, then, have already reached that number.) In addition, Puente was one of the fundamental figures in the Afro-Cuban music produced outside Cuba. This privileged position obviously frees him from any second-guessing and renders other random critiques meaningless. Tito is beyond all that. What is most relevant to us, then, is to mention the extent to which Puente's music, despite the artist himself, was, at any given moment, absorbed by the salsa hype.

In an uncaring and difficult market that made it impossible to support an orchestra with more than ten musicians, Puente was able to maintain his big band, captivating both dancers and concert-goers. The public, however, had become accustomed to the sound of small bands—trombone and trumpet combos—that were gaining more visibility than the old super-orchestras. Still, Puente persisted. In some statements given to *El Universal* newspaper in Caracas in 1977, the master declared that he did not care about salsa because he did not do salsa; he did "Antillean music," not salsa. His many years of making music gave his words a great deal of authority. And although personally I define salsa as the contemporary culmination of all Caribbean expressions, Puente's opinion—especially at the time it was articulated—had a good deal of truth to it. For the Matancera-style boom, salsa was exclusively the old, Cuban son that, due to the whims of entrepreneurs and their publicity, erased with one stroke the rest of the musical richness of the Caribbean. Faced with such arbitrariness, it was prudent to set some clearer boundaries. And that was what Puente did. Confronted by a mediocre and commercialized salsa, a salsa that was awkward, repetitive, and imitative, the master had to take an opposing stand. Therefore, Tito said he was not doing salsa and tried to maintain this stance. He was always, however, among the most innovative and creative musicians.

As long as Tico remained an independent company, Puente was able to continue developing his signature sound, recording showy experiments with his big Orquesta de Concierto. (An example of this was "La odisea de Tito" and other danceable numbers accompanied by prestigious singers, as in the case of "Changó" with La Lupe at Carnegie Hall.) He also refigured the traditional world of the bolero with intricate arrangements (as recorded in that same concert, this time with Vicentico Valdez). All of these productions exhibited quality, although they progressively lost favor among the fans once the new salsa stars began to dominate. Puente, however, from his acclaimed position as a leader and avant-garde musician, ignored those signs.

Once the Tico house was taken over by the Fania monopoly, a change was inevitable. Puente fell easily into the fabric of salsa as seen in the five albums that he produced based on this new criteria: *No hay mejor*, *Los originales*, *La leyenda*, *Tributo a Beny Moré*, and *La pareja*. The first three featured his former vocalist, Santos Colón; the fourth used a gathering of star-singers; and the last one had La Lupe singing sad approximations of her former glory. All of these albums revealed a significant sacrifice, since in none of them did Puente continue his spectacular experimental style. Instead, the albums were pitifully reduced to what a Fania entrepreneur defined as "music for dancing . . . just for dancing." With the exception of the album honoring Benny Moré, the others were of considerably lesser quality than any of Puente's previous albums.

I make special mention of the album *Homenaje a Beny Moré* partly because it escaped the dreadfulness of those last years and partly because it earned Tito Puente a Grammy award. With great arrangements by Eddie Martínez, Louis Cruz, Jorge Millet, Marty Sheller, and Puente himself, the album included some previous successes of the sonero from Lajas (Benny Moré). For the vocals, they called on all of the company's good soneros— who, with the exception, of course, of Celia Cruz, were very scattered and doing unsatisfying work. Thus Junior González (who for some time had enlivened Tito's dances) sang "Se te cayó el tabaco," Adalberto Santiago sang "Camarera del amor," and Ismael Quintana, "Francisco guayabal." "Bonito y sabroso" was sung by Néstor Sánchez, while Santos Colón delivered "Dolor y perdón." Recently acknowledged by Fania, which gave them the major roles they deserved, Luigi Texidor and Héctor Casanova did the vocals for "Santa Isabel de las Lajas" and "Baila mi son," respectively. The ultimate hook was, once again, Celia Cruz, who recorded "Yiri yiri bon" and the bolero "Encantado de la vida" in an extraordinary duet with Cheo Feliciano. This was the same repertoire presented at the Radio City concert, and the album brought together various important elements. These included, first, the use of diverse singers (a privilege that Fania had reserved only for its already discredited orchestra, the Estrellas de Fania). Second, the effective production of Louie Ramírez led to a great repertoire and arrangements, and third, all of the material was presented with quality and with a definite sabor. With this album, Tito Puente came out of the shadows to which the salsa boom wrongly had relegated him.

Certainly, the Grammy award was the ultimate boon for Puente, but, to be honest, this album is far from representing the best of his musical abilities. Still, everyone knew that the award was not so much for that one album as it was for his entire musical achievement. For the world of popular music in our time, the Grammy is something like the greatest honor, the best recognition of one's work. For many years Latin music (and, within it, Caribbean music) had been openly ignored by the academy that gives out the awards. It was only in 1975 that they opened up the new category of "Latin music," which was understood to refer to salsa music exclusively. From one perspective, this new category can be considered an example of a kind of fascist labeling that marks "ethnic music" as secondary or lesser. Personally, given the kind of music that we like, it seems that the importance of this award has been overrated. Eddie Palmieri received two consecutive Grammies because his albums are closer to jazz, not for what they represented for salsa. For the same reasons, Mongo Santamaría was the second Latin Grammy recipient. Therefore, by 1978 it was clear that Tito Puente ought to be acknowledged. But, as I have said already and say again without any exaggeration, even that award was too small for the "King of the Timbal."

In 1979, when the salsa boom was riding its last wave and trying to overcome a critical lack of authentic stars (since only four or five were able to meet the demands of the mass audience), Tito Puente reemerged as the "father of 'Latin music,'" as the "master" capable of offering some of the long-lost quality. At this point, the producers and entrepreneurs began to acknowledge his talent and musical value. Thus, on the evening of February 10 of that year, on one of those bitterly cold New York winter nights, the famous concert at Radio City took place, the same concert that I mentioned when we were discussing Celia Cruz. The event was aptly named "La Perfecta Combinación de la Salsa" (the perfect salsa blend). On one hand, it included the key representative of the present through Willie Colón in both of his phases, the old roots with Héctor Lavoe, and the emerging ones, importantly and clearly defined by Rubén Blades. On the other hand, it also included the traditional expressions of the Caribbean music produced in New York with Tito Puente and his orchestra taking over the whole stage, performing his album of homage to Benny *live*. That night was a good reminder of all that salsa and Caribbean music was and had been. Blades defined the new path with his "Pedro Navaja," "Plantación adentro," and "Siembra." Willie dressed it up in the best of the golden age of early salsa with a royal potpourri of "Che che colé," "Calle luna," "La murga," and "Barrunto," all sung by Lavoe. Finally, Puente built a towering performance out of the glories of yesterday and forever. I can still see the set of three timbales (six drum heads in total) on which he displayed a virtuosity so masterful that all of the applause and adulation seemed pale in comparison. No wonder he is considered the King, El Rey. Although in this world and in Caribbean music there is no nobility, no royal lineage, his particular title was absolutely fitting.

Let us return one last time to the album *Tico-Alegre Stars Live at Carnegie Hall* as our basis for examining the musical production of the other stars in the Latino music world in New York. The only such star left to discuss is the irreverent La Lupe, a sort of misunderstood genius of the bolero and the guaracha. "La Yiyiyi," as her fans used to call her, had her moment, but beyond that moment, she did little else. She did not even repeat her success; instead, she took shelter in her previous fame. This may be partly due to her own life, "a real earthquake," as some of her close friends described it. However, for the purposes of this book, that does not matter much. I prefer to analyze her music itself and *its* circumstances, which may offer some reasons for her demise.

After an increasing number of albums led La Lupe to the height of popularity, the singer began to set herself apart. She stopped recording with Puente, and that was her first mistake. Thereafter, she relied on comfortable, unambitious productions, leaving her diehard fans to make the sad realization that her subsequent albums varied only by one or two boleros and did little else to satisfy their expectations. Like many of her fellow musicians, the so-called Queen of Latin Soul paid the price of salsa's too-rapid explosion. There were only two alternatives: to strengthen the old foundation or to throw oneself fully into the new trend. La Lupe plainly stayed stuck in the middle.

In 1974, trying to revive her initial success, La Lupe recorded an album titled *Un Encuentro con La Lupe*, with compositions by Curet Alonso. Though it included some good sones and guarachas, this album indicated what was happening. It was clear to everyone that salsa was taking over, so they tried to reassert a biting force in the boleros; but that gesture went only halfway and was, frankly, pointless. After the extraordinary "Puro teatro," La Lupe recorded "Más teatro? . . . Oh no!" a bolero that had very little to do with its antecedent. Similarly, even though guarachas such as "Sin maíz" and "La mala de la película" made money, they were insufficient next to productions that were true moneymakers. This is just one more reason why it is preferable to return to her old albums.

Three years later, La Lupe had become one of the many stars of Fania and attempted again to regain her glory. "Qué te pedí" was a classic that did not exist for the new fans of salsa, so La Lupe had to conquer new territory that did not belong to her. Embedded in that gigantic web of the recording monopoly, however, and having to follow its criteria—criteria that were already depleting the salsa fever—there was little that La Lupe could do. Her last album (that I am aware of), *La pareja*, recorded at the end of 1978 with Tito Puente's orchestra, shows again the steady decline of those years. To the fan who considered her album *La excitante Lupe con el maestro Tito Puente* a gem, the *Pareja* production by the same pair ten years later was almost an embarrassment. Given the importance of these two figures, it is worth repeating what I asserted earlier: The musicians are only minimally to blame for this falling off. I point, rather, to those on the commercial side.

La Lupe, however, undoubtedly considered one of the best interpreters of the Caribbean bolero, did imbue her shaky last production with some of her own talent. When she encountered a good bolero, she knew how to articulate it with the power and flair that it deserved. In the end, the mediocre arrangements were not so important, and she always managed to do what was necessary to take the drama of the music to the heights where it belonged. Examples of this are the two boleros "El verdugo," by Curet, and "Cualquiera," by Lolita de la Colina. The first exemplifies the feeling of cruel and agonizing abandonment with which La Lupe so greatly identified. Curet wrote this expressly for La Lupe's singular mastery:

> You are my hangman despite your moral force
> Because alone, alone, I'm doing well
> And knowing this is fatal for you.

The second bolero, a fierce composition by the unusual de la Colina, who was best known for this piercing love song designed to get under one's skin, completely reflected La Lupe as a bolero singer:

> Anyone can give you the things you wish for
> Anyone who abandons her hold on your chest

And later forgives you for returning to my bed
. . . anyone . . . .

La Lupe's rendition, included on her album *Unica en su clase*, was a true classic; indeed, only she knew best how to interpret these types of boleros.

To return to the larger context, for the Venezuelan, Panamanian, Dominican, Colombian, and Puerto Rican music lover, the city of New York was a big puzzle. Too many of its images were conflated. After the forced closure of Cuba, the city became the contemporary mecca for all of the music that is now wholly subsumed by the category of salsa. Music lovers had heard about the Palladium and the days of the pachanga and the big orchestras. They knew very well that many of the great figures of that musical expression, for one reason or another, had ended up in New York. And they assumed that they were all happy there, living in the luxury that came from their music. From a distance, the myth of all of these "musical legends" grew considerably. Living in New York was almost like living in heaven, the publicity suggested, and many of the movies we religiously watched from our childhood onward confirmed that. Distance created the fantasy of that cultural capital as a happy city where all musical forms held hands and smiled at one another. To create cultural expressions in New York, then, seemed as easy as throwing oneself downhill on a toboggan. One enjoys the thrill of being at the top with the illusion that the rest of the world is waiting at the bottom.

In Caracas I met many young musicians who had one great ambition emblazoned on their foreheads: New York. They made music in the barrios, using even the tiniest apartment as a rehearsal studio. Sometimes they were lucky, and their little orchestra would get hired for a small dance, or they recorded a bad album that never was aired. They—the most loyal music lovers one can imagine—were also the ones who religiously bought and discussed those albums; they studied them and learned their music by heart. For them, New York was like a phantom. After watching *Kojak* and after listening to all the lies that our undignified cultural industry construed, they continued to see New York as the end-all and be-all of their every aspiration.

But, as always, the myth veiled the harsher realities. In the underdeveloped Caribbean, the focus was only on a few famous Latin musicians and their supposed victories in that "modern capital." However, not much was said about the others, the immense majority who wandered the streets anonymously and never belonged to the city. This was where the clash began; this was the precise moment for dismantling those fantasies. Certainly, a great number of Latinos lived in New York then; in fact, one of every eight New Yorkers was a Puerto Rican. But what was not said was that these same Latinos lived in the utmost misery, a misery worse than that of musicians in the Caracan barrios who dreamed about making a fortune. Moreover, the latter at least lived in their own country, in their own cultural world. Those in New York, whether they had U.S. citizenship or not, continued to be tossed aside and unappreciated by the "legitimate" native-born, white Americans who still viewed them as bothersome intruders. Misery, then, was perhaps more painful in New York.

From time to time during this period, the devout fan of salsa may have asked him- or herself about the fortune of Pete Rodríguez (who sang about Micaela who one day disappeared), of Johnny Colón, or of Joey Pastrana. Whatever happened to Kako? What is Héctor Rivera doing now? What became of Rolando Valdez, who once so proudly proclaimed in the old Cuba, "There is only one feeling"? What are those stars, the old and unsurpassable masters, up to? Is Fajardo well-off? Is Patato doing okay? Do they feel up there in the United States our same devotion for the exquisite trumpet of Chocolate Armenteros? Do people there really know how to appreciate the talents of our musicians? Do those people properly respect the immense value of the figures who live there now? Such questions must have begun to pile up, only to be reduced to one sad answer: In the U.S. scene, our musicians were not really idolized, and their lives were not only bad but in some cases far worse.

One night, while I was riding one of those old trains between Brooklyn and Manhattan, I ran into a familiar figure: a short, stocky black man sitting at the other end of the car. He was carrying a unique suitcase, the kind used for bongos or small timbales. It was after 11:00 P.M., and the musician still had a toothpick in his mouth. I had no choice but to approach him, and as I did, I had no doubt who he was. "Papaíto, how are you?" He responded, surprised, with a bow: "Very well, sir, and you?" Amid the rumblings of the train, we tried to talk. This man traveling amid the indifference of the other passengers was none other than Mario "Papaíto" Muñoz, timbalist for the Sonora Matancera, an exceptional percussionist who elicited extensive praise from true music lovers of the Caribbean. In Caracas or Panama or Santo Domingo, they probably assumed that such a man would be living peacefully and happily. But in New York, he shared only in the anonymity of the subway, his renown recognized only by a few while the rest of the world patently ignored him. Papaíto told me that he was on his way to Brooklyn to play at a dance in one of those third-rate clubs where knives jump as fast as the rum, and where the marijuana and the cocaine freely flow. I decided to go with him in order to confirm what I already feared: the indifference of a dazed audience that neither he nor his music deserved. That night Papaíto played as he always did—marvelously, exceptionally—but no one recognized his brilliance. The audience barely applauded at the end of each cut; the musicians meant nothing. Despite the respect that Papaíto garnered abroad, here he was just another rumba player, one of those nameless and forgotten black drummers who serve only to spice up the evening. I imagine he is still out there, playing a fabulous rumba that fades to nothing, which is the worst kind of rejection of all.

I share this anecdote because I witnessed it personally. New York, however, offers many others like this, or worse, that take place repeatedly as if an ordinary part of life. Other musicians, so as not to sacrifice the dignity and respect that they rightly deserved, decided to leave New York or, in more disheartening cases, altered their playing to fit other musical expressions that had nothing to do with the Caribbean. This was the case with Marcelino Guerra, who left for Madrid, and Cachao López (who was, without any exaggeration, one of the best bass players ever), who moved to Las Vegas. Víctor Paz, the exceptional Panamanian trumpet player, abandoned salsa to play conventional U.S. music, while Alfredito Rodríguez—one of those Cuban pianists capable of doing the impossible—ended up having to deal with all kinds of foolishness and rejection. Alejandro "El Negro" Vivar died in Miami in a car accident, and nobody said anything. Lino Frías—the former pianist with Arsenio and author of "Mata siguaraya," a candidate for the best example of the Caribbean piano—continued having his daily coffee all by himself somewhere around Broadway and Fifty-fourth Street.

By the end of 1976, when the salsa boom was offering albums that pretended to represent authentic Cuban roots, the entrepreneur Martin Cohen decided to bring together some of the genuine masters. Cohen was part of a company called Latin Percussion, the maker of all the Afro-Cuban and Caribbean percussion instruments. He wanted to show the other side of the story: a music that was not salsa (and did not pretend to be) but one that represented a real Cubanness. They released the album *Ready for Fredie's*, with Carlos "Patato" Valdez as its star. He was backed by Alfredo Rodríguez, Orestes Vilató, Julito Collazo, Bobby Rodríguez (the old bass master), Mario "Papaíto" Muñoz, Nelson González, and Joseph Manozzi, a young trumpet player of Italian descent who had cultivated the purest forms of the Cuban son in the New York scene. What they produced quickly became a classic, especially the son-montuno "La ambulancia," composed and sung by Papaíto.

The son "La ambulancia"—roguish, witty, and beautiful, a sort of surrealist lament of love—exemplified the virtuosity of Patato on the quinto, Nelson on the tres, and, above all, Rodríguez on piano. It was followed by a princely guaguancó by Augusto Lores, sung by Patato himself, and then the chorus repeated, "The ambulance is taking me / the ambulance . . . ."

Some time later, a second album appeared, with a title that reflected its pretensions—*Autoridad* (*Authority*)—and with Patato, his tiny hands and signature hat once again on the cover. This album was much more focused on the rumba. There was no piano, no bass, no trumpets—only drums, the quintos and congas, which emphasized the guaguancó itself. This album incorporated another very special musician, Virgilio Martí, a veteran Cuban rumba player and composer of painful love songs who for a good while was in charge of accompanying the legendary Tongolele in her rumbas. *Autoridad* included one of Martí's guaguancós, "Alma mía," an actual poem whose verses served to inspire each of the percussionists.

Now my poor soul
Tired of living
Takes to the whining world
The love of its feeling. Silence.

In July 1976, René López, a savvy and devoted Puerto Rican musicologist and producer, brought together a group of the best musicians around and placed them under the direction of the master Israel López, the great Cachao. The idea was to revive the spirit of the old Cuban jam sessions that Cachao had recorded during the 1950s. With amazing genius, they determined the whole repertoire in a couple of sessions. Cachao put together a traditional charanga orchestra with the violins of Félix "Pupi" Legarreta, Alfredo de la Fe, Eddie Drennon, Yoko Matsuo, and Carl Ector. Patricia Dixon was the cellist, and the rhythm section included Julián Cabrera on the congas, Rolando Valdez on guiro, Osvaldo Chiguagua Martínez on timbales, and the masterful Charlie Palmieri on piano. Gonzalo Fernández contributed his exquisite folkloric flute playing, and Cachao himself, of course, was responsible for the acoustic bass.

This group recorded three danzones that Cachao had composed in the long ago days of the orchestra of Antonio Arcaño: "Adelante," "Se va el matancero," and "Jóvenes del ritmo," enhanced by the best new recording techniques and developed fully, that is, without limiting any parts for commercial reasons. The result was an authentic and important milestone. Alongside these danzones, Cachao presented the jam session itself in "Descarga cubana," "La trompeta y la flauta," and "Trombón melancólico." Those cuts featured such prestigious musicians as Lino Frías, Chocolate Armenteros, El Negro Vivar, Manny Oquendo, Andy González,

José Rodríguez, Barry Rogers, Nelson González, and that incomparable team of percussionists—Patato, Papaíto, Collazo, and Martí—along with vocals by Totico, Rafael Felo Barrio, and Roberto Torres. The rest of the repertoire was complemented by "Centro San Agustín," a danzón-cha, a very unusual version of "La bayamesa" by Garay, and "KoWo-KoWo, güiro" by Julito Collazo. These sessions were meant to be only the beginning of an extraordinary series of releases, but in the end, having to depend solely on the energy of the musicians and given the penny-pinching of an industry that undervalued their project, they never met again.

René López struggled just to produce the material for two albums (*Cachao uno* and *Cachao dos*), and they never made it to the radio or onto the list of favorite hits, although they should have a privileged place in any respectable record collection. The mediocre nature behind the commercial boom was apparently insurmountable and did not allow for these types of successes. Félix Cortés, who wrote the notes for those two albums, commented on the surprising fact that it would take Cachao, who had been a fundamental figure in Caribbean music, more than thirteen years to get all of his music recorded in New York. Cortés bemoaned what had happened, especially since the industry had recorded, instead, a great deal of music that was considerably inferior to what Cachao and all of those old Cuban characters had produced. This continued to happen without anyone batting an eye.

In the end, we are left to draw this conclusion: Certainly, the explosion of salsa brought to the community some important figures, artists who legitimately represented the feelings of the Caribbean. However, along with those genuine stars, the industry promoted others who made hardly any relevant contributions to this musical expression. These second-rate musicians, unfortunately, helped to obscure the initial stars so that they never received the benefits of fame or fortune. The industry, which developed behind closed doors through questionable deals, neglected them miserably, and those stars ended up amid the anonymity of the subways, creating and enjoying their own happy rumbas that never reached the greater public.

Between the Traditional and the Modern

In 1973 an orchestra entered the New York salsa world and, without any major fanfare or adulation, became one of the most important groups of the movement. This band was La Típica 73, a spin-off from Ray Barretto's orchestra. As its name (meaning "typical," that is, "traditional") indicates, this group focused primarily on the matancera style of salsa, although unlike what was happening to salsa globally, they always interpreted the son with considerable respect to its original forms. Perhaps because of this—that is, they did not accept the strict mandates of the commercial trend and its dominant styles—La Típica was relegated to a second tier, since the dancing public of the time did not understand adequately what they were trying to do. Since we have seen a number of examples of gifted musicians with great potential whose talents declined when they conformed to the pressures of the industry, it is good to highlight the situation of La Típica 73 as an orchestra that always put musical considerations first. This accounts for the steady improvement in the quality of their experiments during the years to come.

In its beginnings, La Típica followed the conventional format of a conjunto: a couple of trumpets (in addition to the inevitable salsa trombone) and a rhythm section of tumba and bongo, piano and bass. In this format, they recorded their first album, exhibiting what would become one of their chief characteristics: the collaboration of some of the best musicians from their community. That first year, the orchestra featured Johnny Rodríguez Jr. as leader and tumba player, Orestes Vilató on bongo and timbales, Dave Pérez on bass, René López on trumpet, and the always effective singing of Adalberto Santiago. All of them came from Barretto's disbanded orchestra. To this quintet, they later added Sonny Bravo, a very fine pianist of Cuban descent; Joseph Manozzi, the Italian American trumpet player whom I mentioned when discussing Patato's albums; and the Dominican Leopoldo Pineda, unanimously considered one of the best trombonists in all of salsa. The following year, after La Típica had resolved its initial difficulties and was ready to record its second album, Nelson González, the dynamic and diminutive tres player, joined the band.

This was the group that traveled to Caracas for that famous and frustrating Primer Festival Internacional de la Salsa. There, thanks to their unique version of the classic "Amalia Batista," the group received first prize. However, business matters intruded, and the producers, unaware of the jury's decision, awarded first prize to the Gran Combo de Puerto Rico, which was much better known and more easily understood by the audience. La Típica 73, then, began to experience the paradoxical consequences of making good music.

In 1975 the group released their third album, *La candela*, which maintained the traditional style but also progressively moved toward the experimental. This record introduced another element that would become a hallmark of the orchestra's development: the incorporation of themes from contemporary Cuban pop music. For example, next to an extraordinary version of the classic "Jamaiquino" by Fellove they included, first, "La escoba barrendera," originally recorded on the island by the charanga

155

group Estrellas Cubanas under Félix Reyna. Second, they added "La candela" by Juan Formell, the director of Los Van Van, a sort of sophisticated charanga orchestra cataloged as "modern" in Cuba itself. At the time when they interpreted these two songs, La Típica was trying to maintain the new spirit pushing forward the current music of Cuba while also molding it to the basic criteria of the mainstream salsa being produced outside the blockaded island. Our recent experiences and tastes, however, lead us to accept the versions of La Típica more readily. They feel closer to us and, thus, more effective. (The Cuban version of "La candela," of course, never aired on the commercial radio of our countries.) In the particular case of "La candela," the New York orchestra offered us not only excellent solos by González and Vilató but also a truly polished piece that began to suggest a different path. This new path was especially groundbreaking given the wider creative stagnation of the boom. Equally important was the musical integrity of the members of La Típica, who always acknowledged their natural and direct Cuban influences. At that time, partly out of political fear but partly as the result of a creative and brazen hypocrisy, many musicians and orchestras chose to hide their deep and legitimate indebtedness to Cuban music. La Típica, on the contrary, not only published Formell's name on the album label but also openly called their style a modern Cubanization of salsa. Furthermore, to this day, I do not know of one of them who has received the punishment that Cuban exiles fear most.

With their next album—*Rumba caliente* (1976)—La Típica suffered one of those apparently inevitable and necessary splits that happen to salsa bands. Santiago, González, Manozzi, and Vilató left the orchestra and immediately went on to form the group Los Kimbos. Rodríguez and Bravo, who still served as the leaders of the group, decided to capitalize on this division and substantially change the composition of the band. They shifted it from a traditional ensemble to a much larger orchestra more capable of dealing with the experimental approaches. They kept the trio of two trumpets and a trombone in the brass section, substituting the Cuban Lionel Sánchez for Manozzi. Now, however, they also broke with the rigid configuration of most New York salsa bands and added the saxophone, handled capably by the Cuban virtuoso Gonzalo Fernández, who proved more extraordinary for being able to play the traditional charanga-like flute as well. For the percussion section, José Grajales became the tumba player (Rodríguez switched to the bongos), while Nicky Marrero, months after the album was released, joined the group as its regular timbal player. As we can see, the restructured orchestra had very little that resembled a conjunto. Finally, they added the young Cuban Alfredo de la Fe, a virtuoso violinist, and Tito Allen, rightly considered one of the most technically adroit singers in all of salsa. This type of personnel allowed La Típica 73 to go from a charanga style to the jazzlike mambo, from the son ensemble to a conventional, salsa orchestra, interpreting a range of musical possibilities. This situation also meant that the group was positioned easily at the forefront of authentic avant-garde music. By 1977, La Típica was among the best of the best, and the album they released that year, *Los dos lados de la Típica 73*, is an excellent example of this. Without a doubt, it was one of the most interesting productions of all salsa music.

The idea, according to Sonny Bravo's notes on the album cover, was to embrace the entire gamut of salsa. On one hand, they offered music that audiences could dance to, and on the other hand, they conveyed the unlimited combinations of styles available at the time. This proved to be the ideal combination for salsa going forward: A focus on dancing remained intact (as I already indicated, in the Caribbean, if the music does not encourage dancing, it is not really music), but they also articulated the incredible cultural confluences embodied in the times. Once the boom and its fads had passed, only this oppositional music held any interest amid the continuous reinventions that took over the mediocre and complacent. The option chosen by Típica 73 was not theirs exclusively; on the contrary, it was only one indication of the limitless and fertile terrain that lay ahead. What a pity that so few were able to see this.

While La Típica—now contradicting its name—was aligning itself with modernity, Los Kimbos were reaffirming the ensemble style of the traditional son. In 1977, when they released their second album—*Los grandes Kimbos with Adalberto Santiago*—the group could have been considered the best band of the salsa son throughout the New York region. This claim was possible because of the group's repertoire—a smart selection of new compositions alternating with old Cuban songs. They also had a similar balance of young and veteran musicians who represented some of the best performers that the city could offer. The band's leader, Orestes Vilató, was still irreplaceable on the timbal. The percussion section was comprised of two young musicians who soon gained the respect of their demanding colleagues: Eduardo Montalvo on tumbas and, on bongos, Charlie Santiago, who continued to respect and master the ancestral techniques of the instrument. Manozzi was now the pianist, while González remained on the tres. The group also included Salvador Cuevas as bass player, a young man who, in just a few years, became widely acknowledged as the best bass player in all of New York salsa. Brass included Roberto Rodríguez, a Cuban who served for several years as the leader of that section in Barretto's orchestra; the Dominican trumpet player Pablo Domínguez; and the young Puerto Rican trombonist Reinaldo Jorge, already well known in the music world. Of course, these musicians were presented with good arrangements and an even better repertoire, which enabled them to produce a sound of indisputable quality. On both albums, Santiago continued to demonstrate his multiple talents for the soneo, making it very difficult to overlook his predominant role in the world of salsa.

Los Kimbos, however, did not stay together for long. In 1978, following some *mala maña* (bad business), they split up and launched two new orchestras: the Nelson González group and Los Nuevos Kimbos de Orestes Vilató. Neither group, comprised of less-gifted musicians, lived up to their successes of the past. Santiago, for his part, decided to remain a soloist, relying, like many of his colleagues, on the whims of the record producers. That year they each released an album: one by González and his orchestra, another by Santiago, and *Ayer y hoy* by what was left of Los Kimbos. The value of these albums was very mixed. Perhaps Vilató's album was the more complete, but his prior vitality was gone. The same was true for Santiago's, and González's luck was even worse. These three cases exemplify the precarious situation of musicians during this period who succumbed to the frenzy of an industry ravenous for a quick buck. For a conga player who for years had been relegated to a secondary position without being given sufficient credit or consideration, the dream of his own orchestra — through which he could earn what he really wanted! — was too much. This explains the exaggerated proliferation of bands, of tenuous groups that were marked with the sign of death from the moment they were conceived. Thus many musicians, blinded by an economic ideal that never arrived, threw themselves desperately into a lion's den that turned the musical world of Latinos in New York into something that resembled a zoo. Clearly this was a painful loss not only for the musicians but also for the music that they had to offer. In Venezuela, perhaps, some were fortunate not to have had the experience of the North, but I will show how this malaise spread elsewhere without prompting any reflection.

Despite these circumstances, La Típica 73 was able to continue its more ambitious musical ascent, bolstered as it was with enviably solid criteria. After changing singers — Allen was replaced by the Panamanian Camilo Azuquita, and he, in turn, by the Dominican José Alberto — and filling Pineda's vacancy with the remarkable sax player Mario Rivera, La Típica was prepared to do what every group in New York salsa dreamed of: travel to Cuba and record an album there. They achieved this in the final months of 1978 with the album *Intercambio cultural: La Típica 73 en Cuba*, which must be considered an absolute classic, one truly important for the salsa music that had been developing for more than a decade. On this album, La Típica enjoyed the participation of virtuoso Cuban masters such as Richard Egües, the inimitable flutist of Orquesta Aragón; El Niño Rivera, one of the best tres players who ever existed; Guillermo "Barretico" Barreto, the timbal player in Cachao's jam sessions and the one directly responsible for many of the technical innovations of the instrument; Félix Chapotín, for whom readers can please add their own epithets; Tata Güines, a well-known tumba player with hardly an equal among his colleagues; and Juan Pablo Torres, an expert trombonist considered one of the most effective promoters of the new Cuban sound. Thus, this album explicitly aroused a host of speculations: How would Chapotín function within a salsa orchestra? How would El Niño Rivera feel about the new style of the son? What would Cubans do with salsa? Indeed, such questions spurred long hours of debate among salsa fans.

The answer—to lessen your suspense—was incredibly simple: Since salsa was nurtured by the son, and this was primarily developed by Cubans, the distance between the two was not the abyss everyone supposed. On the contrary, the musicians built a bridge that extended the path of Caribbean music. The new sound did not upset Chapotín, El Niño, or Tata. They found in La Típica 73 an effective dish that exuded the old sabor that could be neither smothered nor diluted by innovation. In effect, one phase was coming to an end, for the musicians of yesterday finally joined those of today in an appropriate venue. Despite the many incessant critics, the collaboration with Cuba was far from representing the death or even the end of salsa. So went the myth, and it fell by the wayside under the weight of the actual, obvious reality. Salsa could continue freely down the paths it saw ahead, capitalizing on both the old and new Cuba. Here was evidence of the filial connections that the Caribbean and its music suggest, where fads and eras do not exist or, rather, do not amount to much. A shared spirit persisted, indefatigable, reaching out across generations. Salsa could go back to the Cuba of yesterday and onward to that of today; it could come and go and continue echoing the Caribbean that breathes life and liberty into it.

Once a series of salsa productions began streaming into the market, new fans became familiar with the names of those who had been well known among the dancing public since the 1960s. Thus, the Cotique label—another direct extension of the Fania monopoly—again produced albums for the Lebrón Brothers and Johnny Colón, New York figures who had developed a music much more in line with U.S. culture than with Caribbean sensibilities. In the initial chapters, I addressed those days of the boogaloo, of salsa in English, of blueslike chords transcribed awkwardly over the Latin clave. Halfway through the new decade, however, both Colón and the Lebrón Brothers realized that the predominant spirit was the most Caribbean one, so that singing in English and mixing the rhythms no longer made much sense. Colón, then, decided to pursue salsa directly, while the Lebrón Brothers, although intrigued by the trend of "funk" and conceding a bit to that mode, were able to produce a couple of noteworthy, distinctly salsalike songs.

Johnny Colón, who continued with his raucous and suggestive singing style and with his same sabor on the piano, released the album *Tierra va a temblar* long after his old *Hot Hot Hot*. In *Tierra*, all the compositions and arrangements were his own. The album deserves special recognition for the way it reflects the streetlike spirit of the salsa from the 1960s—a spontaneity that was getting lost in the coldness of the music business. By improvising sones in "Tierra va a temblar," "Cuero pelao," "El retorno del mambo," and the very flavorful "Entre compay y comay," Colón created a refreshing production in the midst of the dull and repetitive commercialized salsa. Regrettably, the pianist did not continue in that vein and, rather than reaffirming the son, retraced his steps. His last album with Cotique bears the pathetic title *Disco Hits* (clearly the new international pop sound was beginning to take over), and you can imagine the unfortunate music stamped on that vinyl.

A similar thing happened with the Lebrón Brothers, who, in some cases, used Americanizing influence to give a new feeling to their salsa arrangements. Thus, the albums *Distinto y diferente* and *Décimo aniversario*—from 1976 and 1977, respectively—do offer some quite effective songs even though they were altered with U.S. elements. Still, it is better to listen to versions produced by those who truly own the music. As far as I know, their last album was *Nuevo horizonte*, produced by Ralph Lew, and it exhibits the same confusion of sounds. Indeed, "disco fever" caused Fania a lot of problems that they awkwardly tried to overcome by producing haphazard albums that were supposedly salsa and disco at the same time. The Lebrón Brothers' albums were concrete examples of this tragic-comedy.

As if trying to find the proverbial needle in this haystack of mediocrity, we turn to the work of a gifted pianist who never garnered the prestige and recognition he deserved: Markolino Dimond. Dimond began the decade with his album *Brujerías*, and he contributed several classic solos to albums by a variety of other artists. In 1975, with the collaboration of excellent instrumentalists and the voices of Francisco "Chivirico" Dávila and Frankie Dante, Dimond released one of the best albums of salsa, *Beethoven's V*, which nevertheless continues to be ignored by most music lovers. Markolino's fame was divided between his musical talents and the persistent commentaries about his chaotic personal life. Many of his colleagues and all of the record companies viewed him as a "country bumpkin," a simple, odd little figure. That is why he was never taken seriously and why no one ever expected much from him. The Beethoven album—which included, among other cuts, the extraordinary son "Por qué adoré" by Curet Alonso—was passed over as a minor product when, in reality, it was a powerful illustration of the aggressive salsa, genuinely identified with the essential barrio spirit of salsa. Yet Dimond, with neither support nor incentives, ended up cut off from the studios and from the recognized world of salsa. I tried to find him when I was in New York, since I always thought he had a special talent that deserved to be known, but nobody—not even his old band members—knew anything about him. That is how New York is: Sometimes it is just like the jungle that we see in Hollywood movies, full of quicksand that musicians disappear into soundlessly and without any notice.

Frankie Dante and the Orquesta Flamboyan with Larry Harlow was not a very special album, but it gives us an idea of the singer's personality and style. Dante, who was one of the many victims of the famous "black lists" in the Latino world of New York, was always characterized by the rebellious and irreverent spirit closest to what salsa was all about: the desperate feeling of the marginalized subject who demands to be heard. Dante, however, did not make it very far, nor could he—not so much because of his rebellion and his being blacklisted but simply because he was too limited as a singer. None of his albums stand up to the demands of music lovers who are used to good, solid Caribbean singing. The same thing happened with Angel Canales, another child of the music world who, without any particular singing ability, was eager to show the street side of salsa. In contrast to the anonymity of Dante, however, Canales was applauded by an enthusiastic audience. This occurred also because his orchestra, Sabor, offered interesting arrangements that compensated for Angel's vocal deficiencies. In Caracas, trying to listen to these terrible albums, I could never understand how this bald singer acquired such fame, especially since Canales exhibited the opposite of so many fundamental musical qualities. In September 1978, during a salsa concert at Madison Square Garden, I finally pinpointed the source of his fame. Though not a real singer, Canales was more intelligent and novel than a great many of his peers who sacrificed their vocal abilities in order to conform. On that stage, dressed in shocking yellow, Canales knew how to say what the New York aficionado wanted to hear. There was variety in his spectacle, and his performance differed from those of the tedious salsa orchestras with musicians and singers much superior to Canales and his Sabor but who did nothing more than repeat the same, little montuno of old. After this experience, I understood his success, although I still cannot tolerate any of his recordings. This was the 161 beginning of the end for the boom (but not for salsa), and Angel Canales emerged just as it was fading. Bombarded by the exaggerated repetition of the same approaches, the audience preferred any novelty, without regard to its quality. If Canales had appeared before or after this point, he would not have been received as well, since he did not bring much individual talent with which to enhance the quality of the music.

Just as Dante and Canales represented a new generation, salsa also embraced veterans who, with varying degrees of success, were able to hold their own. This was the case of Chivirico Dávila, who, in addition to his excellent work on *Beethoven's V* by Dimond, had released four other albums for the Cotique label—*Chivirico, Desde ayer, Chivirico Dávila*, and *Brindando alegría*—all of which showcase his quality, experience, and veteran skill. None of these albums appealed to the greater public, but this was never the producers' or Chivirico's goal. A veteran Panamanian singer named Meñique also recorded for Cotique under the same conditions and with the same results (*Soy hijo de Changó*). Among these veterans, the most renowned was Roberto Torres, an authentic Cuban sonero who never succumbed to the influence of the Fania wave. In contrast to many singers in the New York world, Torres understood profoundly the most diverse nuances of Caribbean song, and he knew how to exploit the full potential of the montuno. Complementing those skills was his smooth and powerful voice. Like many others who had done their thing in Cuba, Torres never pretended to sing salsa, but only the son, the same one that had been developed on the island, and that is why he remained relatively unknown.

In 1976, Héctor Castro, considered one of the most assured pianists performing the traditional style in New York, decided to leave the Johnny Pacheco orchestra with which he had been a primary musician for many years. He was joined by Charlie Rodríguez, the Puerto Rican tres player, and Víctor Venegas, a well-known Mexican bass player. Together they formed the Conjunto Candela, along with such younger musicians as Papo Sierra on tumba, Chukie López on bongo, and the singers Carlos Santos and Néstor Sánchez. As expected, their music continued the matancera-style salsa, although they managed to slip in a couple of contemporary songs from Rubén Blades: "Amor pa' qué" and "María Mercé." With those, they put together their first album, which proved to be significant because of Sánchez's vocals. Ever since the days of Tony Pabón's La Protesta, which gave Sánchez his beginning, he had earned some fame for his technical skills and for the authenticity with which he improvised the sones. Santos was equally adept, and together they drew attention to an album that otherwise would have been ignored. After the public lost interest in Conjunto Candela, Rodríguez and Venegas decided to record with Pacheco again, and there was very little that Castro could achieve on his own, despite his indisputable merits. Furthermore, the singers, who were the real attraction of the group, soon left it in search of better possibilities for fame and fortune. Santos joined Vilató's Los Kimbos and then moved to Roena's Apollo Sound, while Sánchez landed a starring role with Harlow's orchestra.

Alongside the work of Conjunto Candela, we can consider the work of Saoco, a smaller band but one with greater aspirations, formed through the initiative of William Millán and singer-songwriter Henry Fiol. This group, made up of young and unknown musicians, emerged with an album that, despite its being produced in New York, intended to reflect the flavor of the Caribbean countryside with its *guajiros* and huts. The result, which clearly ran the risk of ending up as nonsense, actually scored some interesting points. Fiol, for instance, trying to imitate the old style of the Cuban singer Abelardo Barroso, was able to carve out for himself a particular niche among the other soneros of his generation. The musicians, with an average age of little more than eighteen, tried to reflect, with the utmost fidelity, a style that they imagined as pure. Thus, trying to evoke the Cuban countryside, the landscapes of Las Cillas that we know only through photographs and hearsay, these young musicians born and raised in New York committed themselves to the bizarre and contradictory task of ignoring their own reality in order to invent another—one that was hardly important given that they had the whole world of the barrio right in front of them. If we limit ourselves strictly to the music they recorded, we cannot honestly say that they failed, because there is sabor in their montunos and an evident freshness in their songs. But amid the demands of a new urban culture, this approach was nothing more than a youthful game, another of the many misuses of talent and time.

In this sense, there is more merit, for instance, in the production *El chino* by Cruz de Jesús, a bongo player who, despite his limitations, never stopped inventing. After having gone through many second-rate (and even some third-rate) New York orchestras, de Jesús decided to form his own band, El Conjunto Melao, which, in the midst of difficult times, managed to make a few recordings. While unexceptional and even musically marred in places, El Melao, unlike many groups who screamed senselessly, tended to perform a salsa that remained close to the small barrio that gave birth to it. They also avoided the trap of boisterous self-praise. De Jesús always tried to reflect the streets of his own life experience, and although he never completely achieved his intentions, his work remains invested with indisputable interest. This shows us how, in the midst of the excessive gimmickry, some honesty prevailed. Yet without the most basic resources, his honest representation of the barrio could not fulfill its intentions.

In 1976 the Vaya label released the song "Número 6," which almost immediately became a hit. For the first time since the salsa boom had faded, here was a completely New York salsa song, directly framed by the everyday life of urban Latinos. Composed by Rubén Blades, the song was recorded by a new orchestra with a fresh and original sound: Bobby Rodríguez and his Compañía. The modest band centered around Bobby's virtuosity on flute, tenor sax, and clarinet. In addition, their well-defined goal of making something new was clearly felt. One could hear the difference in the arrangements, the repertoire, and the approach to it. La Compañía quickly gained the attention of producers, secured regular performances at major ballrooms, and became a constant at the Club Corso. Obviously, this allowed the orchestra to move out of the sorry category of anonymous bands that, without any backing or luck, ended their musical lives playing in small dives. Bobby Rodríguez aimed high and was determined not to remain in second place for any reason. The public demonstrated its support for the band by attending its performances and filling the dance halls, and the orchestra, during this initial phase, never let them down.

The next year they took the risk of recording a live album—*Salsa at Woodstock*—that increased interest in the orchestra. Once more, the hook was a song by Rubén Blades, "What Happened," that tried to succeed in Spanglish, going from English to Spanish and vice versa. The song was purposefully not recorded live. It represented a return to the initial style of the 1960s, when Joe Cuba sang "Bang, Bang, Bang" and "Push, Push." Now, evidently, there was a different standard, for the English in "What Happened," far from being assumed as one's own language, was understood as only a variation of the random, everyday speech used by Boricuas in New York. This difference is important, because for Joe Cuba, using English was basically an attempt to reach the greater U.S. audience, whereas for Blades, English was just another element that reflected the reality of the New York barrio. I refer exclusively to Blades because Bobby Rodríguez radically undermined the meaning of "What Happened" with his recording "Latin from Manhattan," the old Hollywoodesque theme arranged in salsa style with the same quick fix in mind: to sell the North Americans a cardboard version of the Caribbean. The gap between these two songs is abysmally clear. By its third album, La Compañía had lost much of its initial appeal. For example, the hit song "Siete mujeres," by Ismael Miranda, ended up being nothing more than one of a series of songs that the monopoly produced. Meanwhile, in the dance venues, the orchestra came across as monotonous and exclusively dependent on the virtuosity of Rodríguez, since his flute-playing always stood out. The boom, then, continued to devour its own performers.

This innovative trend was also developed by Ricardo Marrero, but with less commercial luck. Marrero, a young and talented arranger, tried to approach salsa through the routes imposed by U.S. music. Marrero's first album, *Time*, was totally ignored by the public; he had no chance at success because he was swimming against the tide, relying on innovation for its own sake, which is never enough. His case, of course, was an example of the overwhelming confusion that affected many young musicians in New York. Trying to capitalize on the fame and fortunes that salsa offered and also trying to be original, to create sounds unlike any other sounds, they became desperate and encountered nearly constant failure.

In 1979, at the annual ceremony for the best New York salsa, hosted by the magazine *Latin NY*, a lanky young man from Puerto Rico received the most awards. He won for best arranger, best trumpet player, best orchestra (for the band he had recently created), and finally, for musician of the year. His name was Luis "Perico" Ortiz, a central figure in any account of the history of salsa. Ortiz, with a talent comparable to that of Louie Ramírez, can guide us through the spectrum of salsa during the boom, from the traditional to the modern and back again. The prizes that night were little more than a small recognition of his multiple contributions. These include not only Ortiz's virtuosity as a trumpet player but also his talent for arranging music in the diverse styles that helped to enrich it.

Perico began working professionally for the Mario Ortiz orchestra in San Juan and, at age seventeen, already had the role of first trumpet. After a brief period, he came in contact with Lito Peña from Puerto Rican television's Channel 4. Through him, Perico began to work as an arranger. He had the ability to write with efficiency and with remarkably good taste, and his talent was quickly recognized by veteran musicians. Ortiz then began to experiment with the most diverse kinds of music: U.S., commercial, ballads, jazz, and, of course, salsa and Caribbean cadences. In 1972, having turned twenty-three, Perico decided to travel to New York, since his ambitions had exhausted what was possible on the island, and the city would offer him the ultimate gathering of the musical styles that he was interested in. Unlike many of his colleagues, Ortiz always had good luck. The very first day he arrived in New York, not knowing anyone and without any idea of what to do, where to go, or how to get started, Ortiz happened to run into Izzi Feliú, the bass player for Tito Puente's orchestra. As it turned out, there was a dance performance that night and the fourth trumpet player could not make it. Without thinking twice, Ortiz accepted the challenge. Years later, after Ortiz's talent had been recognized by the New York music world, the master Puente came to him and said, "Well, Perico, I would love for you to play in my orchestra someday." To this, the young musician replied, with his signature smile, "But I already played in your band, the first day I arrived in New York, only you didn't notice." This kind of luck continued to follow the trumpeter. That first night, between the dance sets, he met Monguito Santamaría, Mongo's son, who invited him to interview with his father the next day. The Cuban conga player had no difficulty recognizing the talents of this young arrival and immediately offered him a spot in his jazz ensemble. It was there, according to Perico, that he developed professionally. Ortiz not only played the trumpet but also arranged a good part of Santamaría's repertoire; he also composed songs, recorded albums, played both the flute and percussion, and, as if this were not enough, traveled all over the world.

After this extraordinary stay, Perico returned to Puerto Rico. There he founded the experimental band known as Los Escogidos (The Chosen Ones), which was much more popular among musicians than among the larger, general audience. He then returned to New York, where he and his band had been promised a contract. That offer turned out to be nothing more than empty words, and the project failed as soon as they arrived. Perico, however, stayed in New York, since people already knew him, and he knew he could find other jobs. In 1976, Johnny Pacheco hired him as first trumpet in his band while also offering him the possibility of working as an arranger for Fania, and success was not long in coming. Perico completely adjusted to Pacheco's orchestra, and his arrangements for numerous artists soon became synonymous with a sure hit. In concrete ways, those arrangements brought together the traditional and the modern, as we noted earlier. With Pacheco, Perico had to deal with the traditional son, but he did so with his own fresh perspective that drew on his experiences outside salsa. He also did so with a respect for keeping clear the connection between the traditional sound and the Cuban son. Through his arrangements for the principal figures of the company—especially his work for Willie Colón, Apollo Sound, Héctor Lavoe, Cheo Feliciano, and the Fania All Stars—Perico molded a great part of what would become the new ways of arranging and imagining salsa. He fully mastered both trends, and, during the height of the boom, this was nothing short of mastering the totality of this expression.

In 1977, already having attained the status of a predominant figure in the New York salsa scene, Perico made a "star" recording with José Mangual, the veteran Puerto Rican bongo player. In some ways, this work allowed him to return to the styles that he had developed with Mongo Santamaría, and it became the impetus for the first album he directed, which was released the following year outside the commercial mainstream. Titled *Mi propia imagen*, the album was more or less a mix of salsa and jazz. The album has value mostly as a direct precursor to the truly significant work that Perico produced in the months that followed. In December 1978 at Manhattan's Club Corso, the Orquesta de Perico Ortiz had its debut. This salsa band represented an excellent compendium of the valuable experiences that the trumpet player had had. Making its appearance during New York's musical decline, this orchestra shined its own light and brought together, in a very thorough way, the whole spectrum of salsa, from the traditional to the modern, from the classical to the experimental and avantgarde. Their debut performance was imbued with special significance in those closing days of the decade because a new path was already being felt, and it made sense to draw on the best the salsa boom had offered in the 1970s. Perico Ortiz, with his characteristic intelligence and good taste, fully embraced the responsibility of this synthesis, and his first salsa album exemplified this. It created a short passageway, let us say, leading toward the new salsa that was knocking at the door.

As I suggested before, along with Perico Ortiz, Louie Ramírez proved to be the other figure able to represent, through his own talents, a range of salsa from the traditional to the modern. Unlike Ortiz, who virtually arrived at the last minute, Ramírez had been part of the New York scene all along. Ever since the old days, following the blockade of Cuba, when the city had taken over the role of representing Caribbean music, Ramírez had stood out as an arranger, as an effective band and recording leader, and as a talented pianist and vibraphone player. In many ways, Ramírez had been involved with all of the major successes of the time. Characterized by slow speech and a very introverted personality, Ramírez was hardly noticed by the wider public. For musicians, however, he was a natural leader, one of those people whose final word was always respected. In the midst of the boom, when he was hired by Fania as a producer, Ramírez was able to push forward a great deal of the truly important music that the monopoly published. It is to him that they owe, for example, two arrangements that by themselves would have been enough to shape the new paths and tendencies. As mentioned in the beginning pages of this chapter, these pieces were "Canta" and "Juan Pachanga." Louie Ramírez then became the unacknowledged brains behind the new salsa style. For Fania, he was a blessing of sorts, one of those very versatile musicians for whom popular music holds no secrets. This is why, in 1977, when the international style of disco began to make inroads through New York salsa, the company employed Ramírez to produce a hybrid album, one of those pathetic concoctions that the entrepreneurs dream up out of desperation. The album, called *A Different Shade of Black*, was a failure because such a hybrid was an obviously stupid mistake. Despite the commercial agenda of the album, however, the musical work of Ramírez cannot be so easily dismissed. He was obliged to make disco music—the so-called "hustle"—and he did so without any difficulty, since he had more than enough talent to pass any test.

Yet the Ramírez album of real interest—because it is a salsa album—is *Louie Ramírez and His Amigos*, released in 1978. Here the musician truly expanded his work, moving from the traditional to the modern, mingling the two extremes, and making, therefore, really good salsa. This album became a sales hit thanks to the song "Paula C," composed and sung by Rubén Blades. Furthermore, according to many musicians, this was one of the best productions of salsa at the end of the boom. The album also featured some recordings sung by another Panamanian, Camilo Azuquita ("El poeta lloró," "En un beso la vida," "Cuando llegaste tú"), and others sung by the Puerto Rican sonero Adalberto Santiago ("Borinquen me llama"). To complement the vocal numbers, Ramírez also included three instrumental cuts, two of them based on the Beatles' "Something" and "Because." The first was created in the traditional style of the jazzlike mambo, while the second, thanks to a precisely crafted arrangement, was converted into a danzón, an authentic danzón that respected all of that form's rhythmic rules. After this album, the company, further succumbing to the musical confusion in New York and the devastating disco trend, forced Ramírez to try another underhanded hybrid—this one called *Various States of Mind*—which, of course, was produced under the table. This led to Louie Ramírez's predicament: He became labeled as a studio musician, one who only records music and only as a tool of commercial interests. Ramírez's achievements need to be seen, therefore, in the context of Fania's mass production. While he was a musician of the first order, he was overly dependent on Fania's myopic vision and its commercial successes. So, while his salsa album deserves recognition, it must be considered as an exception to the rest of his work. It represented a moment of freedom that passed through his gray matter, which was otherwise confined to the cold anonymity of the recording studio.

Puerto Rico

For the island of Borinquen, during the mid-1950s to mid-1960s, popular music, which was authentically rooted in the bomba and the plena, found its fullest expression in the work of Rafael Cortijo and his Combo. In this modest environment, far from the sensationalism of their colleagues in New York, the orchestra from Santurce found a way to invade all of the Caribbean, including Cuba before the blockade. They did so with a long list of hits that have continued to appeal to the musical tastes of succeeding generations. Many of those songs were hits because of the presence of

Ismael Rivera, one of those irreplaceable figures able to single-handedly determine the new paths and tendencies of popular culture. In assessing Cortijo's success, some credit most the voice of Rivera, the "Ciudadano de la Calle Calma" (citizen of the peaceful street). The way things turned out seems to justify that assessment, since once Ismael was forced out of the musical world, Cortijo's group notably decreased in popularity. None of their subsequent hits matched the extreme heights of their earlier ones, and even while maintaining the same spirit and quality, the orchestra never received the acclaim or the following that it previously had known throughout the Caribbean.

Despite this evidence, I do not think that Ismael's retirement alone was enough to explain the quick demise of the Combo. Several obvious factors contributed, and I assign them the following order: first, Rivera's retirement; then, the departure of Rafael Ithier and other musicians who left to form El Gran Combo de Puerto Rico; and finally, the ostracism to which Cortijo was subjected by the new breed of Latin record producers. Cortijo was left on the sidelines to contend with humiliating contracts and weak albums produced without any feeling. He began living only for those who knew his former fame and was reduced to being an anonymous face amid the indifference of fans who did not know enough to appreciate and respect the overwhelming importance of this humble Puerto Rican timbal player.

In 1975 the Coco label—a new record company founded by Harvey Averne—decided to produce something worthy of the talents of Cortijo and his Combo. They put on a fabulous concert in San Juan's Coliseo Roberto Clemente, where for the first time ever and after so many years the old colleagues could get together and re-create the majestic glories of yesterday. All the major players showed up: Eddie Pérez on sax, Mario Cora Alvarez on trumpet, Rafael Ithier on piano, the conga rhythm of Martín Quiñones, Roberto Roena on bongo, and the very same Cortijo on timbales, topped off with the still full and flowing voice of Ismael Rivera. According to witnesses—Tite Curet among them—the concert was a real downhome fiesta, a tribute to the best of Puerto Rican music and to the best of its interpreters.

Days later, the entrepreneurs decided to reunite the band in order to record their old hits, and from this they produced a very significant album, *Juntos otra vez*. The album included new songs to celebrate the occasion, such as "Dios los cria," as well as some of their classic hits—for example, "El negro bembón," "Quítate de la vía, Perico," "Maquinolandera," "Oriza," "Severa," and "El bombón de Elena." Because the album included music that came before the salsa trend, it proved particularly influential for salsa itself. The new salsa fan, unfamiliar with that former freshness and spontaneity, encountered a strange document: a music less sophisticated than salsa but with as much or even more sabor. The lyrics, while not as aggressive as salsa, were still roguish and witty and exhibited a cleverness significantly missing from the lyrics of the salsa boom. The musical forms did not include the son but featured instead the bomba and plena. Finally, rather than speaking of New York and its angst, the references were to the Caribbean and a sense of pride, not stemming from any need to pose or brag, but naturally resulting from their connection with the popular. All of these elements, newly discovered by young fans thanks to the reunion of Cortijo and Ismael, influenced many of the eventual developments in contemporary salsa.

Curiously, from 1976 on, the bomba and the plena became firmly incorporated into the rhythmic repertoire of salsa—not only in Puerto Rico but also in New York and even in Venezuela. Equally curiously, during this same time, new ways of performing music, particularly in a "Cortijo-style," began to be used by the new arrangers, especially those from Puerto Rico. This mixture of tendencies—the old sabor from a new perspective, the old style with a contemporary twist—converted Puerto Rican orchestras (but not those of New York) into an authentic avant-garde. With this solid avant-garde collective, salsa triumphed over the decadence of the commercial boom. Thus, Rafael Cortijo and Ismael Rivera made very important contributions to the new music of the Caribbean, especially during a time of confusion when miscalculations and failures nearly overshadowed such genuine accomplishments.

This fabulous reunion in 1975 was a unique, onetime event. As soon as the concert and the recording sessions were over, each musician went his own way: Ithier with El Gran Combo, Roena with his Apollo Sound, Rivera with his Cachimbos, and Cortijo with his Combo, the new version of it that had very few successes during the period of hype. Although Cortijo had the unconditional support of Curet Alonso, who composed a good number of bombas for him, rich in quality and sabor; although he had the participation of masters such as Víctor Paz, the virtuoso Panamanian trumpeter who single-handedly doubled the trumpets in his arrangements; and although Fe Cortijo, his niece, would become one of the best female voices in this new musical generation, the master was not able to ride the crest of the new salsa wave. His albums did contain some really good songs, but they received no support from either the radio stations or the new fans who continued to be swayed by the tastes that the Fania empire dictated; and so those albums remain forgotten. Not even an album as interesting as *La máquina del tiempo*, for example, achieved much popularity in its time. On this album, Cortijo worked with young Puerto Rican musicians and veterans of the U.S. jazz-rock style in an attempt to develop a more progressive approach to the bomba, a form he already had mastered. Amid the disparagement of promoters and so-called experts who were full of themselves and beginning to dominate the music scene, however, the album did not stand a chance. Nevertheless, all that Cortijo had accomplished by 1975 did have an impact on musicians and the public. His influence was spreading across the music world, although very few realized that the individual directly responsible for those contributions was Rafael Cortijo, master of rhythm and an extremely modest musician who never demanded rewards or recognition.

While Cortijo's Combo had very few commercial successes during the heyday of salsa, it did achieve an unusual degree of prestige, and in Puerto Rico it became the group to dance to. Rafael Ithier had more commercial sense than his mentor and managed to secure two key singers, Pellín Rodríguez and, more importantly, Andy Montañez. Together, they adapted the trends and styles coming out of New York to Puerto Rican styles. In this way, El Gran Combo remained the best salsa orchestra outside the New York scene for a long time. They alone enjoyed sufficient popularity throughout the extremes of the Puerto Rican community.

El Gran Combo represented a needed variation in salsa: while the New York orchestras were increasingly conforming to unoriginal styles and excessively rigid commercial criteria, the Puerto Rican group represented a fresh and spontaneous alternative. Although its music never matched the quality arrangements or ambitiousness of the New York groups, it certainly excelled in conveying sabor and that essential Caribbean pluck so frequently missing in the salsa of the North. As would be evident years later when Dimensión Latina arrived from Venezuela, the presence of "an orchestra spectacular" that did more that just "play" the music proved to be a compelling attraction for New York audiences. No one disputes that New York was the home of innovation and the musical avant-garde, but freshness and a Caribbean notion of music were elements of equal or greater importance, and those elements continued to be housed in Puerto Rico. El Gran Combo, with Rafael Ithier in charge, knew how to capitalize on that fact.

In 1974, viewing themselves as the direct heirs of the musical foundations set by such figures as César Concepción and Rafael Cortijo, El Gran Combo added the singer Charlie Aponte, who, with the superb Andy Montañez, formed the ideal combination for increasing the group's successes. The orchestra was already the pride of the Caribbean. They had received many prizes and awards within the region, and they had garnered impressive sales figures, most importantly with their own label, EGC. This is an important detail to note during this period of greedy merchants and dominating record houses. They were, then, already fully immersed in the wave of salsa, although they had been performing long before it hit, and although they operated under criteria very different from those of salsa music proper.

Seen from this larger perspective, El Gran Combo's production was similar to that of a group such as Billo's Caracas Boys. Both orchestras began well before salsa, and although the Combo integrated itself into the boom, in the long run, they remained at its margins. However, that similarity is not of great interest to us here. More important is the musical criteria that both orchestras adhered to on their albums. For the most part, any group that releases albums doggedly year after year risks having them all sound the same, and any music lover can confirm that to hear one Gran Combo album is to have heard them all, since each one followed the same formula. For those all-important salsa figures, however, each album was meant to be distinct from the others, to establish a certain distance from its predecessors; yet El Gran Combo's sound remained constant, so that there is no major difference between *El barbero loco* and *Aquí no ha pasado nada*, to give just one example.

Of course, for the music lover who is strictly a salsa fan, who in the specific case of Venezuela is raised with a curious prejudice against any of the music of Billo Frómeta, El Gran Combo represented a much more acceptable "sameness." This was not only because of Ithier's ability to take on some of the most diverse tendencies but also because unlike Billo, El Gran Combo remained closer to that marginal feeling, profoundly inscribed in the barrio, which also did not change much during the new salsa wave. This explains why, even as late as 1978, when the creative decline of the boom was most pronounced, El Gran Combo was able to reinvigorate one of its old songs, "Falsaria," the tale of an unhappy man stubbornly in love with a prostitute who abandons him and ignores his misery:

> How false was your love
> You've betrayed me
> Your promise was a fiction.

At the beginning of 1977, El Gran Combo suffered the worst blow of its musical career: Andy Montañez, who had been the voice and image of the orchestra, left the group to take an offer from La Dimensión Latina in Venezuela. The contract they offered him was one of the most lucrative in the history of Caribbean music. He was replaced by the young singer Jerry Rivas, a sonero with a deep voice but without the power or creative range necessary for producing inspiring montunos. Faced with this diffi-cult situation, the orchestra put more pressure for their future success on Aponte, even though he had neither the prestige nor the background of his predecessor. El Gran Combo, however, did not fail as many expected it would. Unlike many performers in the music scene at the time, they en-joyed a solid following, because the public had long been familiar with them and was accustomed to their conventional sound. Furthermore, the crisis of the boom and the lack of stable orchestras made it possible for El Gran Combo to continue performing with their usual regularity. Overall, their music remained obstinately the same, and despite the loss of Monta-ñez, to listen to the new Gran Combo was pretty much the same as listen-ing to El Gran Combo of old. For the recording business, sometimes this is a good thing.

In 1969, having left El Gran Combo and having recorded a solo album for the Tico label with his short-lived Megatones, Roberto Roena decided to form his own band, the Apollo Sound. He chose this name because of the worldwide excitement over the first manned landing on the moon. In addition, this name was meant to suggest the adventurous spirit that char-acterized the band. From the very beginning, Roena broke with the struc-ture that had been traditional in every New York salsa band. Drawing on the influence of the previous bands he had been a part of—namely, Cor-tijo's Combo and El Gran Combo—Roena gave his Apollo Sound a brass section of two trumpets, one trombone, and the tenor sax that had never been allowed by "official" salsa in the North. Likewise, backed by young ar-rangers from the Island, Roena embraced a new approach that, after much insistence and patience, brought him a great deal of success with the ma-jority of music lovers.

Let us pause here to note that at this point, with the decade drawing to its close, New York was at the height of its creativity, and Fania was about to take off with *Nuestra cosa* and its explicit launch of the salsa boom. At this moment Puerto Rico and the rest of the Caribbean remained in the wings, considerably far from having any major influence and not yet capable of making itself strongly felt in the larger arena of the new expres-sion. At the outset, Roena had signed a contract with the recording mo-nopoly, which explains why, from 1971 on, he became an important figure with the Fania All Stars. However, his true contribution to salsa—that of the Apollo Sound—did not become evident until the boom was much fur-ther along, six or seven years later, when Puerto Rico and all of the Carib-bean had overcome the initial New York influence. The case of Roena and that of his companion in the All Stars, Bobby Valentín, thus offer a useful review of this shift.

Between 1970 and 1974, both orchestras released varied albums every year, but for one reason or another, they were not widely supported by the fans. Valentín, who composed nearly all of the arrangements for the "star" orchestra, used his own band to develop the harmonic experiments that, in a more superficial way, he had already begun with Fania. (His own band was almost a "big band" in the style of Puente, Rodríguez, and Machito, with the full combination of trombones, trumpets, and various saxophones.) The public, who still expected the basic sound of a pair of trombones, was not attracted by this "new" sonority that "came from the south." The company, worried about promoting local artists, neglected the true importance of the innovative work that Valentín proposed. A similar thing happened with the Apollo, except that, in this case, the experiments were much less radical, the orchestra did not have its own arrangers, and Roena's own aspirations were not as daring or ambitious as they would be later. For the music lover at that time, completely taken in by the fury over the New York sound, these Puerto Rican experiments sounded rather flat, weak, haphazard, and, in some cases, imported. Therefore, while Roena and Valentín continued to enjoy the prestige brought on by their association with the All Stars, they did not connect with the larger public on their own. This, as we have seen repeatedly, was not the result of any musical shortcoming but, rather, of the inability of the industry to manage and market all of the work of the artists it had under contract.

By the end of 1974, the situation had begun to change considerably. Roena released one of his best albums, *Apollo Sound 6*—a must for any salsa collection—while Valentín made an incredibly brash move that had to do with more than just musical issues. He decided to create a new arena for himself by starting his own company, Bronco Records, in which he could work as he wanted to, without the imposition of others' criteria. Roena's album offers us a good overview of what was happening on the island. This record included rising young arrangers, a repertoire that ranged from the old to the present Cuba and from the traditional to the new Boricua composers, and a style that was more encompassing and therefore more receptive to salsa. For example, *Apollo Sound 6* featured a new version of the classic "El que se fue" by Tito Rodríguez, with a smart debut arrangement by Julio "Gunda" Merced, the young and virtuoso trombone player of the orchestra. It also featured the as-yet-unrenowned Luis "Perico" Ortiz and his impeccable arrangement for "Traición." He mixed, for instance, the son "Yo te tuve en un altar, como a un dios yo te adoré, te quería tanto tanto, te tenía tanta fe" (I had you at the altar, I adored you like a god, I loved you so so much, I had so much faith in you) with phrasings from a traditional comparsa, using the old chorus that says, "Allá ya viene la Picarona, dice que tiene miedo, caramba, de dormir sola . . . ay ay ay" (Here comes a Pica-rona, she says she's afraid, caramba, of sleeping alone), capitalizing fully on all the melodic and rhythmic possibilities available to him. In ways such as these, he radically modified the patterns and schemes that char-acterized the conventional salsa from the North. Finally, the album also included arrangements by well-established musicians. Jorge Millet pre-sented the old son "Cucarachita cucarachón" and two of his own composi-tions, "En mis rosales" and "Herencia rumbera," with a spectacular timbal solo by Endel Dueño, while the singular Bobby Valentín offered "Que se sepa," a very popular song in the new Cuban music. Such an album, draw-ing on a plenitude of criteria and resources, would have been very difficult to produce in New York. There, only the leading musicians dared to pursue initiatives like these. The rest conformed to the expected repetitions of the same old styles and resigned themselves to following the criteria of the producer in charge.

Bobby Valentín, for his part, released his famous collection *Va a la cár-cel* in 1975. This two-volume set exhibited a marked independence far from the patterns and forms dictated by New York. At this time, Valentín had a certain advantage over Roena. Valentín not only led his own company where he had complete control over all the arrangements for his orchestra, but in that orchestra he also had one of the most spectacular singers that salsa ever produced, Marvin Santiago. Santiago was a rebellious and irrev-erent character with a surprising ability to play with the montuno as the mood struck him. The guaracha "Tú no haces nada" on the second volume of *Va a la cárcel* exemplifies the brilliant and inspired liberties that San-tiago took with the montuno. He makes his voice sound like a machine-gun as he sings,

Why did I ask you to stay
Don't you realize that in here you can't do anything?
Why did I ask you to stay?

Santiago's version of this guaracha provides the ideal evidence for feminist arguments that salsa (and, indeed, a good part of our continen-tal popular music) is sexist and demeans the dignity of the contemporary woman. Yes, probably. Perhaps the despised Latin American machismo that has been so vigorously attacked by intellectuals from all possible angles is intimately linked to the cultural essence of our peoples. Yes, per-haps. Perhaps this guaracha that I have praised for its musical virtues, for its merits as salsa, would be openly censured and censored from a feminist point of view. However, rather than confusing these two perspectives, I am interested in foregrounding something that has been obscured by these angry, intellectual discussions, something that has been neglected. In all of our popular music, there is a notable persistence of storylines in which the man (who is most often the one singing) reminds the woman of certain "natural" obligations. I am not, of course, going to deal with the legitimacy of those obligations. The tortilla, as we know, can always be flipped over, exposing the other side of the argument. I am simply pointing out the invariable repetition of this model: a man falls in love with a woman because he is here and she is there, and all of the dramas and stories unfold from the limits and extremes of that scenario.

Let us now consider the pros, cons, and validity of those limits, of that scenario. From the strict, salsa perspective of this book, this machismo varies considerably from the idyllic Mexican postures where the risks that men faced were those of the countryside and not of the city. It is within the urban setting that Santiago, fully employing the language of the marginalized, calls on his woman to keep the police from coming, to help him start the car when it doesn't work and he is desperate to escape, to soothe the tick-tock of the clock and the burnt milk in the coffee; in other words, to live in his house and his world and to accept his life and his buddies. Of course, from start to finish, the underlying sexual innuendo of his requests is also present. When none of them is realized, he demands a breakup and kicks her out. These demands—fair or not—were never articulated in such rude and direct language in the other "machista" lyrics of our popular music. The so-called macho belongs now to another era, and in this one he neither promises eternal love nor pursues beauty, heart and soul. For Santiago, and for the numerous Caribbean men that he represents in his song, the situation of women is not idyllic either. It is not about romantic dreams but about reality. The guaracha singers of this time no longer live in the placid world of the old bolero, either, or in the bucolic world of the Mexican ranchero. They have no need of expressing things in a delicate way; on the contrary, a distinctly new rhythm reflects the furious vertigo that swirls around them. The woman is no longer the "muñequita linda de cabellos de oro" (the pretty little doll with golden hair). She is now "my pal, my buddy," and when she fails (and here any discussion about the causes and consequences of machismo can come in), the salsa singer jumps to this argument: "Friend, why are you killing me?"

By the end of 1976, Marvin Santiago had left Valentín's orchestra. According to personal testimonies from his friends, the departure was Valentín's decision, not Santiago's, and it stemmed from Santiago's supposed drug addiction, which kept him from fulfilling his duties and meeting the deadlines that any orchestra would require. After this, Marvin virtually disappeared from the world of salsa. He produced no known recordings (except for occasional appearances with the Puerto Rico All Stars), and his audience, like his old friends, abandoned him to anonymity. In the summer of 1977, by pure chance, as I was walking down the streets of San Juan, a common friend introduced us. Santiago was one more unknown face in the crowd. We tried to ask him a couple of quick questions, but the singer offered only one-syllable answers or vague phrases such as "This salsa thing doesn't work any more. . . . People don't get it, I don't know, you know. . . . I don't know if I'll sing again or not." After three minutes of this we were already saying good-bye: "Venezuela is very pretty, I would love to go there." After that exchange, we felt the unpleasant letdown one often feels after meeting a popular musician. His art, which is rarely recognized or adequately valued (most of the time it is not even considered art), emerges from the daily misery that is part of living on the margins that receive only the minimal benefits of civilization. Drug abuse is common because it seems to help a little. The notion of a better life is, in many cases, an unattainable and murky ideal that leads to anger and desperation. Sometimes the same is true for the music. Salsa offers us this vast panorama: from Marvin Santiago to Rubén Blades, from frantic efforts and uncertainty, to more effective certitude and calculated intentions. Yet, salsa comes from the barrio, and there its figures assume their wholeness—some poorer than others, some more or less fortunate, some more conscious of or clearer about what is happening and what has happened. This range of experiences and of responses to those experiences gave rise to the immense diversity of variants within salsa, the strokes of genius and the blows of failure, the highest highs and the lowest lows. Salsa, then, reproduces the infinite richness that authentic popular music is about. It is a music whose values are eclectic, irregular, and even contradictory, like its musicians, like the reality that produces and nurtures it.

To replace Santiago, Valentín invited Luigi Texidor to join his band. Texidor was a black singer capable not only of representing the same popular roots that Marvin had but also of offering comparable skills as a singer and, in addition, as an effective sonero. Luigi came from La Sonora Ponceña, where he had been for many years. (La Sonora Ponceña was an orchestra of such special interest that I will devote a few paragraphs to it later.) Although Texidor's work was always of the highest quality, he was never fully recognized by the larger world of salsa. This happened with most of the stars who developed their music outside New York. Indeed, Luigi and Marvin are just two examples of what happened to the Dominican and Venezuelan orchestras that the New York music business world always saw as second or third rate. The music industry and the musical avant-garde were again following different paths; but only the former was able to determine who got to be stars and who did not, and this created a good number of false icons and disingenuous hype.

Texidor, however, never felt included in that disparagement, for his strong sense of modesty kept him from any sort of posturing or arrogance. When I interviewed him in 1977 for Radio Nacional of Venezuela, he barely responded to my questions. He preferred to let Papo Lucca, the director of La Sonora Ponceña, take charge of the interview. "I'm just another musician, don't bother, sir," he said. They were visiting Venezuela as a result of the success of "Pío pío," a song interpreted by Luigi and included on their album *Conquista musical* (1976). That song and other cuts allowed Texidor to showcase his many vocal talents. His rendition of the son "Nanaracai" was especially inspired:

> I started to see a blind man watching television
> And a cow crash against Pacheco
> And a mosquito dying of laughter
> Nanaracai, Nanaracai.

However, the song that truly allowed the audience to appreciate Luigi's virtuosity as a sonero was "Moreno soy," the first great success of Bobby Valentín's orchestra, released in early 1978:

> I was born dark
> Because it had to be
> Because of my color
> I'm easy to understand
> I go along singing
> Making the world happy.

In the middle of that same year, the Fania Company, which was still in a kind of crisis over which singers and artists could attract a greater audience, decided to sign Luigi Texidor as one of its stars. As a member of the already discredited Fania Stars, he released *El negrito del sabor* (1979), an album that reveals the misappropriation of his talents. Valentín, for his part, had distanced himself from all that the Fania monopoly stood for, musically and commercially. He, therefore, decided to replace Texidor with a young singer named Carlos "Cano" Estremera, who continued, more of less, the style of the aggressive soneo. Estremera was famous not only for his fine, pure voice but also for his albino features, unusual in a world of mulatto musicians. Estremera became noted for a song that had even greater commercial success than "Moreno soy," "La boda de ella." This gossipy and roguish tune told the story of a groom left at the altar:

"Si el cura sabe lo que tú y yo fuimos no bendecirá esa unión" (If the priest knew what you and I have done, he would not have blessed our union).

In 1979 the height of the boom was fading fast, and the music industry confronted an audience that was no longer swayed by its marketing. The industry was in no position to invent an idol, some fictitious star performing mediocre music. Finally, only those with sufficient talent to merit it stood out, and New York no longer dominated the scene. Puerto Rico, Venezuela, and the Dominican Republic operated on their own terms, disregarding the musical models imposed by the North. The avant-garde that Borinquen had quietly developed over the last few years began to be clearly recognized by a larger public. This explains the strong support that Bobby Valentín and his orchestra were now receiving. It was time to applaud quality music, good arrangements, and, primarily, the honesty and impact of this music, a music that previously had been stripped of its positive attributes by a desperate industry.

An example of the New York decline—and with it the salsa that produced the boom—was the push that the Fania Company finally gave to its Puerto Rican orchestras, principally the Apollo Sound and La Ponceña, which had been used previously only as fillers on Fania albums. The city of skyscrapers had no more to give (or at least the music that the Fania monopoly directed and produced there had nothing to offer). Now the vitality clearly came from the south. This explains Roberto Roena's transformation. At the beginning of the decade, his albums sold modestly; by 1978 he had become a bongo player with top-selling albums. I already noted that the beginning of this change was felt in 1974 with the album *Apollo Sound 6*. With his next album—*Séptimo sortario (Lucky Seven)*—Roena achieved his first hit of significant proportions: the song "Mi desengaño." Composed by Gunda Merced and Pucho Soufront, the trombone and bass players in the young band, this song illustrated the orchestra's polished style. It was a style with notable Brazilian influences and simple lyrics that expressed their discontent with the social situation (as in "Los demás," "Hora cero," and "El progreso"). It was also marked by arrangements quite unlike the customary ones in New York salsa and by increasingly experimental rhythms that went beyond the worn-out son of the boom era. With this style, the Apollo Sound became synonymous with innovation and the avant-garde, those very elements so in demand by music lovers tired of the matancera trend.

Still, for many, it remained puzzling how Roena—who, unlike Valentín, for instance, was neither an arranger nor a virtuoso instrumentalist nor a master of musical theory—was able to lead an orchestra that was always on the cutting edge. His case exemplifies that of numerous Caribbean orchestras that, under the baton of a musician who played by ear, were able to develop strong and captivating sounds. From an orthodox point of view, any real merit lies not in the bandleader but in the musicians who can read music and in the arrangers who produce the music that is being read. This orthodox view is, in some ways, partly accurate. However, significant voids do appear in the world of popular music, and they are only filled by those leaders who can go beyond mere conducting.

Let us recall what a salsa orchestra is really about—that is, the gathering of professional musicians who have had to try to make their living amid irregular performance schedules and shady deals. An orchestra in the Caribbean (or in the Caribbean barrios of New York) does not derive from the same social, cultural, or economic conditions that surround an orchestra from the United States or Europe. There the musical profession (including the popular musician) has a different status. It is never the marginal category, say, of the Saturday-night maraca player, as often defined in our latitudes. In the Caribbean, an orchestra has to fight not only the musical war but also the social, cultural, and economic wars imposed on it by the context of "underdevelopment" from which it emerges. This accounts for the erratic nature of the musicians and the bands they create. More than occupying himself with basic musical concerns, the director of a popular orchestra has to wear a number of hats. In Venezuela, Federico Betancourt (of Federico and his Combo), whose case is similar to Roena's, told me more than once about the thousands of nonmusical difficulties that are part of keeping a salsa orchestra afloat. Thus, in the world of popular music, the leader, even if he does not hold a doctorate in composition, is more than a figurehead.

This fact also helps us to understand the extreme dependency that an orchestra's members often feel for the musician who brought them together. This dependency is fostered not only by the music that they love but also by critical social and, even more so, economic circumstances. Tito Rodríguez once said that the most important thing a bandleader can do is to keep the musicians happy, to ensure that they feel well-paid and comfortable enough to develop their creativity freely. They should never feel that they are just cogs in a wheel, but authentic musicians capable of fully enjoying the work that they produce. Rodríguez's was the only band able to guarantee the kind of comfort that allows for authentic creativity on the part of the musicians, and his orchestra became the pinnacle of perfection, something rarely seen in the history of our popular music. His example, then, and his definition provide an even clearer idea of the real work of a bandleader. Likewise, Roberto Roena was one of many others who stood up for the integrity and independence of their musicians, even though they had not mastered the official intricacies of music. Instead, Roena fully understood his musicians and the nonmusical factors surrounding them, and that understanding eventually led his Apollo Sound to a primary position within salsa. Indeed, extra-musical circumstances ended up influencing the music itself and contributing to the unique style and unusual sound of Roena's orchestra, which set it apart from other bands on the market. His arrangers consistently went beyond the range of available influences and trends and followed an indescribable approach that became distinctly recognizable as the Apollo Sound. Roena himself never wrote a single arrangement, yet his band's very particular style of arranging salsa belongs legitimately to him. This shows, I have said repeatedly, that in the popular music of the Caribbean, cold notions of a particular theory are never the most significant thing.

By the end of 1976, the Apollo Sound released its eighth album (*La octava maravilla*), with experimentations that were far ahead of their time. The promoters and experts (who, as I have mentioned, sometimes have not the slightest idea what the new music is about) mistakenly discarded it before audiences could take notice. There were two extraordinary songs here by Merced, "Rico guaguancó" and "Tema del Apollo." This last song was developed as a sort of collage in which the singers alternated phrases from various hits of the orchestra. Likewise, they offered "Para ser rumbero" by Rubén Blades, with an aggressive arrangement by Perico Ortiz. The lyrics can be interpreted as a declaration of Roena's musical principles, which he performed for all of his peers: "To be a rumbero you must have cried / To be a rumbero you must have laughed."

Despite the commercial failure of this album, the band was already well established in the hearts of the fans. The last two albums that we know of (numbers nine and ten), with compositions by Curet and Blades, were readily grouped among the most distinguished salsa of the decade. By mid-1978, Gunda Merced, the singer Papo Sánchez, the saxophonist Miguel Rodríguez, the tumba player Papo Clemente, the bass player Polito Huerta, and the pianist José Lantigua had all left the band. Although the orchestra had split up, Roena drew on the support of Mario Cora, his longtime friend from their days with Cortijo, and re-formed the Apollo in record time. Without any gap in production, then, they were able to release the tenth album, titled *El progreso*. Unfortunately, it included a ridiculous song by Roberto Carlos that could not be redeemed even in its salsa version.

Among the many salsa musicians that I have known throughout the years, Roberto Roena is one of the few who inspires deep respect in me. In his way, he represents the best qualities of this music of ours, and this is why his orchestra, even after so many rejections and so many objections from orthodox critics, earned a place among the most important avant-garde expressions of salsa. Roena may not have had all of the necessary musical training, but there is no doubt that he had a healthy enough feel for salsa and a natural talent that made him successful while so many virtuoso musicians ended up unacknowledged.

In 1974, through the album *Celia y Johnny*, the larger public connected with another musician from Puerto Rico, the pianist from Ponce, Enrique Lucas Jr., better known in the world of salsa as Papo Lucca. On this album, just a few solos were enough to delight listeners with this petite virtuoso who had quick hands and exquisite taste. Of course, by 1974 Lucca was already a veteran, although the larger public who had followed the boom had not noticed. According to Lucca, from the time he was very young, he had been a member of his father's orchestra, La Sonora Ponceña. For many years the orchestra limited itself to the Ponce area, where they performed for weddings, school dances, and baptisms, as was customary. They had no ambition to go beyond this, and their sound was very similar to that of any other Caribbean orchestra, influenced by the institutionalized matancera sound. However, as soon as Papo, still an adolescent, went from being a mere pianist to an arranger, the orchestra extended its fame to every corner of the island. By the end of 1972, the Fania monopoly, which had recently started the Inca label, decided to sign La Ponceña and release their album *Desde Puerto Rico a Nueva York*. Blinded by the New York splendor of those days, neither the industry nor the public took any notice. The band, however, was not concerned about the reaction of big record companies or the larger public. For them, the recognition of Ponce and the entire southern end of the island was enough. Without much effort, they completed their end of the contract, and in the following years, they released the necessary albums as Fania required: *Sonora Ponceña*, *Sabor sureño*, a small collection titled *Lo mejor de la Sonora Ponceña*, and *Tiene pimienta*.

Thus without any of the foolish fanfare so often found in the New York music world, Lucca and his musicians quietly came and went with unpretentious, fresh, and flavorful music. The boom was already in the air, and record producers began to feel the need to find talent from far beyond the closed world of the New York barrio. It was during this time that Pacheco capitalized on his extraordinary commercial and musical vision. He was well aware of Papo's virtuosity as a pianist and arranger and invited him to record with Celia Cruz and his orchestra. This stroke of genius by the Dominican was obvious, and Lucca took off, quickly becoming one of the most important figures of salsa (and one of its most humble, as well). From

that moment on, not only were Lucca's arrangements highly solicited by
the New York orchestras, but his presence during recording sessions also
was constantly in demand, as evidenced by the profusion of albums that
Fania recorded with him at the piano. No longer could Borinquen keep
this virtuoso to itself.

With his talent revealed, Lucca took over the direction of La Ponceña,
but he still considered it his father's orchestra. Just as happened with
Roena's group, La Ponceña quickly took over the preeminent venues of
the salsa avant-garde. Lucca released such flawless albums as *La conquista
musical* (which featured Luigi Texidor's talents), *El gigante del sur*, *Explorando*, and *La orquesta de mi tierra*. All of them demonstrate a new conceptualization of salsa. The music continues to employ the Cuban son, but it
also goes way beyond it by drawing on the black folkloric tradition of the
island and the influences of jazz and modern Brazilian music. These elements allowed La Ponceña to present itself as an innovative force, and, unlike what happened to the avant-garde orchestras of New York, it never sacrificed that essential Caribbean sabor. La Ponceña produced hit after hit.
From a tonality that began with "Pío pío," it went on to salsa versions of
"Borandá" by Edú Lobo, "Suena el piano" by the Cuban Rubén González,
"Cantándole al amor," "Ahora yo me río," and a very successful "potpourri"
based on the old boleros "Todo y nada" and "Seguiré mi viaje," where Papo
himself sang alongside Miguel Ortiz and Yolanda Rivera. Once more this
confirms that the only way to avoid the decadence of the New York boom
was through the Caribbean, primarily Puerto Rico. To further document
this, I present the son "Lo que el viento se llevó," which was released by
La Ponceña and which uses the same principal tonality as Roena's "Para
ser rumbero" by Rubén Blades. With some already established differences,
the rumba in each clearly exhibited a force that was now emanating from
spaces other than those of New York.

I'm sorry for you
But you can see now
Your mandate was not followed
Your legislations failed
Your rumba has gone with the wind.

However, as one can surmise from what I mentioned earlier, Papo
Lucca's achievements did not come from his work with La Sonora Ponceña alone. He went above and beyond that, paradoxically, in the pieces
he developed for the New York orchestras. In 1976, for instance, recognizing the importance of Lucca's piano work within salsa, the Fania All Stars
decided to add him, as an individual musician, to their team, replacing

Larry Harlow, who until then had been one of its principal leaders. Lucca participated in all of the unfortunate "crossover" albums that the company released with CBS International. In the small bits of salsa that he recorded on those albums (in "Picadillo," "Juan Pachanga," "Sin tu cariño," and "Prepara"), Papo demonstrated both his ability to adapt to the most diverse styles as well as his own indisputable virtuosity. For the benefit· of fans unable to attend their concerts, the *Fania All Stars Live* album, released in early 1979, offered two explosive solos by Lucca: "El nazareno," the classic by Ismael Rivera, and "Público oyente," a very mediocre son composed and sung by the other Ismael, Ismael Miranda. If this were not enough to demonstrate the contributions of the diminutive black man from Ponce, albums by Cheo Feliciano, by Papo's buddy Roberto Roena, by Pacheco (with Casanova and with Celia), by Ismael Quintana, and by many others, marshal more than enough convincing evidence.

In September 1978, at a concert in Madison Square Garden, I was able to witness one of Papo Lucca's riveting performances. I sat with the rest of La Ponceña waiting as his solo went on for more than ten minutes, casting a spell over an immense audience. Based on my experiences, I can say that not even Eddie Palmieri could have achieved such a feat: imagine being in an audience of more than twenty thousand spectators, expecting to hear "hard-core" salsa and its loud drums, only to become totally absorbed and hushed by the solitary piano. Yes, Papo, on that still, warm evening, was singularly possessed. Unfortunately, nobody had a tape recorder handy, and the phenomenon remains lost to the whims of memory. In his recording of "Sin tu cariño," Rubén Blades pronounces Papo, "O melhor piano do mundo" (Portuguese for "the best pianist in the world"). It is possible that this is an exaggeration arising from the euphoria of the moment, but, with respect to salsa, such a claim is not far from the truth.

This Puerto Rican avant-garde, primarily represented by the orchestras of Bobby Valentín, Roberto Roena, and La Sonora Ponceña of Papo Lucca, was immediately carried on by the work of such veterans as Willie Rosario, Tommy Olivencia, and Johnny El Bravo. To them, the boom of New York salsa seemed like a strange explosion, since they had been performing that kind of music all along. In fact, the names of these three figures were already familiar in Caribbean circles. Rosario, for instance, was a top performer among those legendary stars of Cesta, while Bravo and Olivencia had a substantial following in the Puerto Rican dance scene. Despite their renown, however, none of them was able to take back the leadership from the new stylistic values emerging on the island. Olivencia, for example, had the effective voices of Simón Pérez for his guarachas and the warlike Paquito Guzmán for the boleros. Under the direction of Perico

Ortiz, they produced albums worthy of mention, but none of them allowed Olivencia to create a distinctive imprint. For his part, Rosario, who had Junior Toledo as a singer, also produced some interesting records full of sabor and expertise, but in the larger salsa context, they became relegated to the second tier. Not even Johnny El Bravo, leader of one of those orchestras that was capable of playing anything, could dominate. Still, whether recording with new singers or older ones, like Chuíto el de Bayamón—a veritable "institution" in Puerto Rican folkloric music—Johnny El Bravo was able to zigzag in and out of the various modes and tendencies of salsa. We owe to him, in fact, one of the most representative salsa cuts of all time, "La corte." This song portrayed in salsa a recalcitrant pedophile who is eventually caught by the justice system and who has to face the universal consequence of society's collective reproach.

On the fringes of those leading groups just mentioned, the younger generation of Puerto Rico made its presence felt through a range of other orchestras, each offering its own attraction and its own degree of talent. For example, we have the excellent Latin Tempo, led by the talented arranger and trombonist Luis García; the orchestra Impacto Crea; Salsa Fever, formed by Gunda Merced after he left the Apollo Sound; and the Orquesta Revolución. Also deserving mention, among so many others, was the orchestra La Terrífica, a small-town band that modestly offered its quota of sabor with an awareness of its musical roots. So, after the demise of the boom in New York, with all of its annoying arrogance and its strutting fanfare, it was primarily the youth of Borinquen who filled the musical void.

The Charangas

In the first chapters of this book we saw how part of the euphoria that would later develop into salsa had its direct origin, at least, in New York, in the early enthusiasm for charanga music. Therefore, salsa, though now a famous millionaire and towering presence, would have to, in some way, render tribute to that immediate antecedent. The traditional Cuban orchestras, known on the island for their gentle and melodious cadences, became a direct extension of the vigorous salsa of trombones and aggressive montunos. Seen from Cuba, this step must have appeared quite abrupt, but in New York, it was viewed as natural and automatic. Even though Charlie Palmieri had abandoned his Duboney and Pacheco now lived off of a son ensemble and Barretto could not care less about his Charanga Moderna, the memory of the charanga remained very close at hand and ever within reach.

In the chapter dedicated to the evolution of salsa during the period 185 prior to the boom, I pointed out how important Larry Harlow's *Salsa* album was for the contemporary rebirth of the charanga style. For the majority of audiences who knew about Caribbean cadences only through the salsa boom, Harlow's *La cartera* was their first experience with the world of flutes and violins. However, this initial experience would not have been as important if the local scene in 1974 had not included any particular charanga ensemble able to nurture that new euphoria. So, to elaborate on the real history of charanga in salsa, *La cartera* by Harlow is an insufficient example. The actual protagonist of this new spin-off was none other than the Orquesta Broadway, rightfully considered the dean of the charangas within the salsa context.

Orquesta Broadway was formed by the three Zervigón brothers and was the only charanga ensemble able to maintain a bridge between the first fever of the 1960s and the later one of the 1970s. Although the Broadway remained in the second or third tier of performers, it never disappeared from the scene. While most charanga musicians gradually migrated to the dominant forms, the Zervigón brothers insisted on performing traditional charangas even when nobody seemed interested in their type of group. In any real assessment of salsa, however, their resolve must be recognized as truly significant.

When the boom took off—and with it the commercial possibilities of having a hit album—the Orquesta Broadway was the only ensemble ready to follow through on what Harlow's *La cartera* had initiated. Under the Coco label, they gradually began to abandon the Cuban criteria (under which they had always worked) and move toward more New York and salsa forms. Their first album to be embraced by salsa audiences was *Salvaje*, released in early 1976. Here Eddie Zervigón, the flutist and bandleader, worked a wide repertoire, which even included charanga songs from the new Cuba. Somehow they intuited that the modernity in demand could well emerge from spaces outside salsa, and the best of these spaces were offered by the contemporary Cuban charangas. Thus, the Broadway performed "Sin clave y bongó," a dense son by Pedro Aranzola that had been recently recorded by the Orquesta Aragón. This new Cuban influence increased considerably in later years, but in fact the Cuban charanga had never lost power, since it was constantly moving forward and making essential innovations. This new Cuban charanga—from the Aragón to Los Van Van, from traditional to electric pop combinations, from classical percussion to the inclusion of *batá* drums and even the U.S. trap drum set—came to represent a surprising reinvigoration of the salsa boom. Indeed many of the avant-garde orchestras played this repertoire. Obvious examples include Barretto, Roena, Lucca, La Típica 73, and even Harlow himself, who continued to sustain himself through both yesterday's and today's Aragón.

In 1977, under the extraordinary production of Barry Rogers, Orquesta Broadway released an album that not only fully represented the style of the salsalike charanga but also became a key recording for the overall development of the boom. With the songs on this album, *Pasaporte*, the Broadway went from uniquely New York lyrics with explicit reference to drugs ("El material") to a beautiful son, "Isla del encanto" that expressed the ever-present nostalgia of Nuyoricans for the island of Puerto Rico. "Isla" became one of the most spectacularly successful charangas of the salsa boom. With this son, the Broadway asserted a fundamental trait of the charanga music recorded from and for salsa: the idea of the montuno. In the traditional, Cuban charanga, the percussive elements were always secondary, as is evident from any of the early albums recorded. Now, however, with salsa, a form characterized by aggression and vigor, the charanga had to overcome that old approach to percussion: the skins, rather, had to be as prominent as the characteristic sharpshooting of the *tercerola* flute had been. This was not just a simple matter of redistributing instrumental roles in the final mix of an album; it meant transforming the conga player into a *pailero*, a salsa percussionist. "Isla del encanto" is a good example of this new percussive style. Yes, they added new musical layers to the mix, but they also had the conga player take on the son as if he were doing so in a conventional salsa orchestra. Meanwhile, when the montuno enters, the pailero joins in fully with the handbell, the principal nuance found in salsa montunos.

The value of *Pasaporte*, however, is not limited to these changes. It also offered a wider view of all that Latino life in New York entailed. The listener feels this in a son such as "Presentimiento," which offers an immediate view of life strongly rooted in the Caribbean feeling:

I have a hunch
It's something I feel
That everything will be over soon

. . . .

Enjoy life, enjoy life as I do, enjoy it.

For its part, the guaguancó, "Fiesta en el barrio," featured a quintet that is dressed up with street noises—buses, crowds, sirens, horns, scandals, and so on. It is a figurative sample of a rumba amid the turbulence of the city. With this, the Broadway presented a rumba markedly far from the original and placid guaguancó that was played in old Havana. The combination of these types of elements clearly allowed Orquesta Broadway to gain a privileged place, not only within the limited category of charanga groups, but also within the larger framework of New York salsa.

In any discussion of this Orquesta, one must include, in addition to the Zervigón brothers and the noted virtuosity of Eddie on flute, two veteran musicians who contributed a great deal to the look of this ensemble. One is Rafael Felo Barrio, the guiro player, singer, and songwriter, who conveyed a special sabor in his montuno improvisations. The other is Roberto Rodríguez, the Cuban trumpet player who came from Los Kimbos and from Barretto's band. He not only bolstered the Broadway's chorus, but he also contributed his traditional trumpet playing, the "stepchild" from old Cuba that had been adopted by the new charanga.

By 1976, with the boom at its height and with charanga music comfortably playing everywhere, New York City witnessed the birth (or rebirth) of various "traditional" orchestras that, with varying degrees of luck, shared in the euphoria. The first one that stands out is Típica Novel, under the direction of the Cuban pianist Willie Ellis. Like the pioneering Orquesta Broadway, the Novel had its share of "pre-charanga" misfortunes. Now it was able to achieve local fame, thanks to the appeal of its live performances. Unlike the Broadway, however, the Novel made use of the Cuban and Caribbean notion of music as spectacle. A dance in New York with the Novel of those days was a force to be reckoned with. The orchestra created such enthusiasm that the audience quickly became worked up, not only because of the inherent quality of the music, but also because of the innovative ways in which they performed it. The Novel was one of those orchestras whose live shows were more appealing than their albums. (In salsa, after the New York record industry began producing "miracles," many groups experienced the opposite fate: fabulous albums but disappointing concerts.) This explains why the Novel had a difficult time extending its popularity beyond New York. The release of their first album, *Salsamania*, went unnoticed, as happened to all of the albums produced by the TR label. In 1978, however, when they recorded their second album under Fania, the Novel was able to reassert Caribbean songs, such as "Salud, dinero y amor," an old classic now offered in an unusual and complex version.

From its very beginning, the Novel was considered the most modern charanga ensemble in the world of salsa. They were, for instance, the first to incorporate a trombone section, following that old initiative of Barretto's Charanga Moderna. Likewise, they were the first to break free from the all-powerful influence of the Cuban repertoire (both past and present). Willie Ellis, the Novel's director and arranger, once told me that his charanga was, in fact and in all aspects, quite different from everything else in

188

the Cuban tradition. The musician, Cuban to the end, took great pride in his judgment.

Although with less power or particularity than the Novel, other orchestras arose during the New York boom, and, in some cases, they borrowed the names of famous charanga groups from the old Cuba. As a result, audiences became familiar with the Charanga América, the Orquesta Sublime, and the Orquesta Novedades, under the direction of Gene Hernández. During this same time, the veteran flutist Lou Pérez recorded two very interesting albums for the Tico label, now under the control of the Fania monopoly. The first, *Nuestra herencia* (1977), took its title from a sort of charanga suite composed and arranged by Pérez himself. Here he was able to show off his view of the evolution of Caribbean music, from the beginning of the world to contemporary times. Though it ran the obvious risks of getting mired in the ridiculous and losing its effectiveness, the suite managed to pass its own test. The rest of the album, to be honest, ignored any contemporary references to salsa in order to throw itself entirely into the old, Cuban spirit. Still it benefited from the participation of many important musicians, including Adalberto Santiago, in what appears to be his only charanga recording; Rolando Valdez and his legendary guiro; Cándido Camero, the famous tumba player; Rafael Carrillo, the most Cuban of all timbalists; the Colombian Eddie Martínez as pianist and arranger for the album; and Maestro Cachao, don Israel López, whose uncontested bass playing gave the music an added "umph."

On the second album, *De todo un poco* (1978), Pérez inaugurated his very own creation, the rhythm of "bom bom." This album somewhat maintained the quality of the earlier recording, but now, evidently desperate that it was not selling, Pérez recorded two songs using the "hustle" beat that, as expected, ended up making the whole album a waste. Even so, if not judged solely on the scant interest in the new bom bom rhythm, that same album did offer the son montuno "Para comer, para bailar," itself worthy of being included in any anthology of charanga music from the salsa boom.

Nevertheless, the euphoria triggered by this charanga renaissance never really made it beyond New York. A group of young musicians in Puerto Rico created the Orquesta Criolla and, in Venezuela, Elio Pacheco, having left La Dimensión Latina, formed La Magnífica. Even then, the Caribbean public, with the obvious exception of Cubans, continued to prefer the (salsa) albums and dances of orchestras based on the trombone and trumpet. Not even the spectacle of the Festival of Charangas, celebrated in Caracas in 1978 and featuring nearly all of the New York groups as well as Cuba's prestigious Orquesta Aragón, could capture the attention of the public as much as the promoters expected. A solo recital by bassist Oscar D'León, by contrast, easily could have drawn three times as many fans as attended the festival.

Like a reveille, the song "Cuca la loca. Eh! Eh!" introduced salsa—through its new charanga trend—to one of the old Cuban leaders, Félix "Pupi" Legarreta, who was considered one of the best violinists in the charanga tradition. In commenting on Legarreta's participation in salsa, I once again have to mention Johnny Pacheco's famous business savvy. Indeed, even before Orquesta Broadway's phenomenal success with *Pasaporte*, and even before the Novel's albums, which, known only to pockets of the charanga world, were seen as a whim in the larger world of salsa, Pacheco decided to produce an album that became a commercial hit just ahead of the charanga renaissance. Furthermore, instead of going with a new and unknown orchestra, Pacheco produced the album for Legarreta himself, and to capitalize on that famous name, he titled the album *Pupi and His Charanga*. The album, however, did not go much beyond its title. While Pupi certainly brought all of his talent and experience with him, he never properly established his own orchestra for recordings but, rather, relied on gatherings of other legendary musicians. Except for the money it made, *Pupi and His Charanga* was nothing more than a name. Pacheco and Legarreta never saw this as a problem, though, since what mattered most to them was making the album and the fact that it also made money.

In the studios, Pupi and Pacheco brought together a string section that added to Legarreta, as first violin, the young virtuosos Alfredo de la Fe and Eddie Drennon, star of the Novel. The cellist was Patricia Dixon, who drew on her earlier Cuban experiences to give the sound more essential body and density. The rhythm section was comprised of Pacheco on guiro, Johnny Rodríguez Jr. on tumba, and master of both the Cuban and salsa styles, Vilató, on timbal. At the piano they had Oscar Hernández, another young virtuoso who, though raised in New York, was attracted to the classic sonorities of the Cuban music. On bass was the Mexican Víctor Venegas, and to perform on the traditional flute—still the most important instrument in any respectful charanga—the producers asked Gonzalo Fernández, an authentic Cuban master who had recently ventured into the New York world after a very enriching experience with jazz in Paris. Such a team, of course, offered a music that, from all points of view, both represented and refigured the best of the Cuban charanga. Given the trends of the indefatigable matancera style and the predominant commercial criteria of salsa, this was especially important for the producers.

Under these circumstances, Legarreta was able to release two albums.

The first, *Pupi and His Charanga* (as discussed above), came at the end of 1975 and showcased a photo of Pacheco, Fernández, and Pupi himself on the cover. Later, in mid-1977, he released *Los dos mosqueteros*, which oddly gave no credit to Fernández as the flutist. This latter album did very well on Broadway and also produced a couple of hits in the Caribbean, particularly in Venezuela, where the album was promoted on the radio as Pacheco's exclusive product, again blatantly ignoring the contributions of the Cuban Fernández. The album included two songs of great interest, both compositions by veteran Cuban percussionists: "Lo saen," by Virgilio Martí, and "El penado," by Patato Valdez. The first, which lauded the Santería *babalaos*, evinced a style that attacked the music in a profoundly rich and mature way rarely achieved by New York ensembles. The second song, sung by Martí himself, went from the guaguancó to the pachanga, from lament to ecstasy. Its major merit is perhaps its lyrics that tell another of those cruel and bloody stories. Despite criticism that it was clichéd, it has, as such songs tend to do, incredible mass appeal.

> You've stained the bars with your tears
> Dry them up, for a prisoner could poison himself by touching them
> With the poison of your tears, you woman of the streets.

Alongside the charanga groups mentioned above, the New York boom fostered two very special bands that represent the extremes of salsa styles. At one end of the spectrum, there was the Típica Ideal, an aggressive ensemble full of musical ambition, and at the other end, the Charanga 76, a sort of pop orchestra rich in melodic nuances and delicate lyrics. The Ideal, which like many other groups took its name from the Cuban tradition, was formed through the initiative of pianist Gilberto Suárez. He was joined by the excellent tumba player Tomás López, violinist José Chombo Silva, and flutist George Castro. These four had significant status as veterans throughout the Latino sectors of the city. The Charanga 76, on the contrary, was made up of unknowns, most of them young musicians who were just starting out. These differences account for their distinct approaches and fates. The Ideal was already in a position to launch a bold and ambitious music, while the 76 had to count on originality and a search for new forms and styles to keep from perishing amid so many other talented groups.

Ideal's first album, *Vámonos pa' Senegal*, was produced by the master Gonzalo Fernández. It established a number of extraordinary characteristics and clearly showed the range of possibilities and reach this type of ensemble could have. From the danzón to the jam session, from the cha cha chá to both the traditional and salsalike son, the Ideal offered a truly quality album. We already saw how well Orquesta Broadway represented the "new" New York charanga and how Pupi Legarreta, capitalizing on the salsa boom, returned to the traditional Cuban charanga. This album by Típica Ideal created the definitive bridge from one style to the other, producing a music as worthy of salsa as of Cuba. The Ideal accomplished this because at that time—in 1976—they were able to bring together not just a diversity of musical elements but also those elements that were most influential. First, they drew on the virtuosity and experience of their musicians. Second, they were free from the pressures of the new "millions-focused" industry. (In fact, this album was released by Artol, the fading record label of the otherwise powerful Pancho Cristal.) Third, this initial album distinguished itself by the clarity of its objectives: the Ideal was not concerned with producing either salsa or Cuban music per se. Their only goal was to develop the charanga style freely so that it could reach its full potential and empower other related expressions and styles. For these reasons, this album easily transcends conventional categories, from the old "Bim bam bum," by Noro Morales, to Suárez's Chopin-inspired danzón, and from the sax of Fernández in "Vámonos pa' Senegal" to the overflowing power of "Ritmo changüí."

In that same year, the TR label released the first album by Charanga 76. It was produced by the Cuban Félix Pipo Martínez, who brought in the singers Raúl Alfonso and Hansel Martínez in order to lend some name recognition. The other interesting aspect that caused commotion among the orthodox followers of the charanga was the presence of the North American Andrea Brachfeld as flutist. This choice was doubly irreverent, not only because it was the first time a woman had full responsibility for the charanga flute, but also because this woman was a "gringa." (It ought to be noted, however, that Brachfeld always played the conventional flute and not the typical wooden tercerola.) Thus, even before a note was played, the Charanga 76 had achieved the small success of calling attention to itself. Then, as soon as the phonograph needle touched the record's grooves, the voices of the singers undulated, with great skill and sophistication, between a range of styles from rock to the Spanish ballad, from advertising jingles to the traditional harmonies of the serenade. The lyrics took care of the rest. The 76 did not have the musical virtuosity of the Ideal or of most of the important charangas in the city, but it was quite evident that they had more than enough intelligence and creativity to give it their best shot. Possessing a style and a sound all their own, the 76 achieved their first hit with "Soy," by Willie Chirinos. This song's lyrics were typical pop, the kind that bounce around between naïveté and good intentions, from one lucky hit to another:

I am the smallest village in a distant land
I am the noise and the tide of the vast ocean
I am not chains or bars
I am sugar and I am salt
I don't care if you want me or leave me.

The following year the Charanga 76 released their second album, *Encore*, which surpassed the quality of the first, with a much more polished version of the pop style. Despite her "limitations," Brachfeld sounded more charanga-like, and the combination of Martínez and Alfonso continued to attract an audience long tired of the mediocre soneros of the boom. Their lyrics remained full of adolescent romanticism, but the band had become more aggressive and salsalike in their handling of the rhythms. The boom was at its height, and so was the new charanga trend. The 76, keenly aware of what was happening in the market, capitalized on this with their own contributions. Despite the indisputable virtues of Pipo Martínez, two of the most effective singer-composers, and all of the young musicians who were part of the band, the Charanga 76 was one of those ensembles whose viability was determined by the popularity of certain trends. Once that moment passed, their demise was inevitable. This in no way discredits the group. One has to understand that in addition to the musical intentions and virtues of salsa, it was a commercial trend, and some musicians will do whatever is necessary to meet those commercial demands. As we have seen, some struggled and failed, while others, without aspiring to go beyond the trends, found themselves in the right place at the right time. Such was the case with Charanga 76, an enjoyable and reasonably successful orchestra. Therefore, though it was not one likely to become part of the ultimate history of the *ritmo bravo* (hard beat), it will be remembered.

One night in the fall of 1978, I talked with timbalist Orestes Vilató. Without hesitation, he offered an extraordinary description of the difference between the Ideal and the 76: "It's like we used to say in Cuba, there are masculine orchestras and there are feminine ones. It's not that one is better than the other, it's just that they are different, and each has its own style. The Ideal is a masculine orchestra, very, very traditional. The Charanga 76 is a feminine one, very fine and delicate . . . part of another style . . . and, well, to each their own." Vilató's opinion was shared almost unanimously by musicians throughout the Latin music world, especially the Cuban veterans. They cared very little about trendy styles or the preferences of the general audience, and so, for them, the Ideal was always much more interesting than the 76. Clearly, the talent and ambition of the 76 were not viewed from a strictly musical perspective. Meanwhile, the Ideal, which never enjoyed the popularity of the 76, concerned itself only with the best rhythms and the most powerful montunos.

By the end of 1978, the Ideal had released a second album for the Artol label. Although it barely matched the quality of their first, they quickly released yet another, the considerably ambitious *Fuera de este mundo*, which was fully imbued with the elements of salsa. Produced by Perico Ortiz, the album boasted a rich repertoire composed mostly by Gilberto Suárez, who smartly used a brilliant trumpet team. This album must be considered among the best albums of the entire salsa period. Appearing during the last stages of the commercial boom, it integrated not only the fundamental characteristics of the charanga that had been embraced by salsa but also many of the salsa characteristics that had led to the boom.

Before closing this chapter on the role of the charanga orchestras in salsa, I have to give special mention to Gonzalo Fernández, the virtuoso Cuban flute player justifiably addressed by all of his colleagues as "maestro." Fernández was a fundamental contributor to the first Ideal album as well as to the two albums by Pupi Legarreta. He also was extensively involved in most of the various flute and violin orchestras known throughout New York. In 1977, Fernández fully assumed his role as leader of this expression and took on the most ambitious project in salsa charanga: a reunion of all the virtuosos in this field, known as the Supertípica de las Estrellas. Fernández took advantage of the achievements of the Ideal—and their synthesis of Cuban and New York sounds—and then went even further. Not only did he call on the best musicians in the Latin music world, but he also possessed a mature understanding of the music's concepts and intentions and of the richness and plentitude that the charanga could offer. The repertoire repeated the formula of interweaving compositions of the past and present; for example, the beautiful "Potpurrit criollo de música antigua" was developed with the schemes of the danzón and a base of classic Cuban sones from thirty or forty years earlier. The arrangements— all under the direction of Fernández—respected the traditional patterns while adding a radically contemporary spin. For these reasons, it is difficult to catalog the album only as salsa, and this achievement helped lead to the Caribbean music of that day—a music that, whether viewed within or outside the criteria of salsa, represented both a blend of what had happened and a valid idea of what could happen. Even taking into account the twenty-year gap in Cuban charanga production, this album of the Supertípica de las Estrellas is a charanga document of the first order. As the one directly responsible for this production, Gonzalo Fernández deserves significant credit.

In the winter of 1978, however, I noticed that don Gonzalo was no longer working or recording regularly and that he was rarely seen in the world of Latin music. I asked René López if my fears were true: Was this the result of another backhanded decision made by the industry? I was well aware of numerous cases in which some decision from on high virtually erased a musician from the scene, and I suspected that perhaps don Gonzalo was such a victim. López shared with me a more terrible truth, worse than anything I had suspected because it was irreparable: Don Gonzalo had developed a rare illness in his mouth muscles, and he would never again play the flute. How horrible, I kept repeating to myself. How horrible that an illness that could attack anyone else without affecting their livelihood had taken over a flutist, and so, overnight, the musician sees his profession, the fundamental basis of his existence, totally lost to him. Some say it was black magic; others simply believe it was bad luck, but we are left with no way of knowing. The only sure thing was that don Gonzalo would never again play the flute, and that is cause for great anger and sorrow.

Earlier, in May 1977, in a Caracas hotel, I witnessed a more pleasant event, a uniquely significant encounter. After twenty years, by mere coincidence, the two biggest flute players known in Cuba ran into each other: Richard Egües, the director of Orquesta Aragón, and José Fajardo, bandleader of the Stars, who had taken over the charanga. For the first time after the Cuban revolution, the Aragón was visiting Venezuela, and Fajardo was also there, capitalizing on the popularity of salsa. The orchestras, however, never got together, since the two musicians felt that it was better to leave nostalgia alone. Fajardo, who, like most Cubans is quite effusive, screamed, "Baca . . . Bacallao," and extended himself to firmly embrace the singer of the Aragón who, for many years, had been a singer and dancer in Fajardo's old orchestra. The flutist, after declaring to the newspaper *El Nacional de Caracas* that the Aragón was the best of all traditional orchestras, the best charanga of Cuba and, indeed, of the world, related with great emotion the details of this encounter:

> I was in the lobby and when I found out that the Aragones were there, forget it, immediately I ran to a phone. . . . "Hello," I said, changing my voice, "Is this Maestro Egües?" And he said, "Yes sir, this is he." "Listen, maestro," I said, "could you give me a few lessons, since I'm just starting out? . . ." But Richard did not understand, so he said yes, he would, but then, no he couldn't, because he was very busy and tired, and the tour was very hard. Then I became a bit impertinent, and I said to him, "Hey, maestro, but don't get like this, you have to give me a lesson, and that's it, forget it. . . ." Then Richard got out of control and started asking, "What is this, some kind of a joke," and "Who is this, and what's

going on," you know. . . . And I started laughing, and I said, "No, man, don't worry, it's me, Fajardo." And Richard was quiet for a long time; then he came to the lobby and screamed: "Fajardo, damn it, Fajardo, how are you doing?" And I was so moved. We embraced each other very passionately, given all that had happened, and, because more than anything else, I'm a musician, a Cuban musician, and as a Cuban musician I have to be moved by such a meeting, unbelievable, what a great thing!

The tragedy of what was lost because of the Cuban situation became clear to many of us during those days in Caracas. While the Aragón, truly at the height of its power, bathed in the glow of popularity and filled up dance clubs alongside Oscar D'León and La Dimensión Latina, José Fajardo's orchestra was frail and faded, without any of the grandeur of its old Star days. It played without pomp or pity in the lesser dance clubs of La Guaira. Fajardo's mastery and virtuosity remained untarnished, but clearly the years of bitter musical times had affected him. The Aragones, on the contrary, were all over the radio and television programs—including political programs—and they performed everywhere for the Venezuelan public, both then and now, with all the dignity worthy of their legendary status. The distance between these groups was simply enormous.

After that and after his trip to Japan and his old "Sayonara," Fajardo never returned to Cuba. He remained in the United States, making his home in Miami, like many of his old compatriots. Amid the difficulties of that environment, the maestro continued to live off his music. Of course, his extraordinary orchestra with its numerous violinists, trumpet players, and even dancers was reduced to a paltry group of eight or ten musicians, many without the talent of the Stars group of old. Many people commented on Fajardo's performances in Miami in a tone of nostalgia and disappointment. Larry Harlow, in fact, once told me, "The place was empty, only four or five couples. . . . And here is the King of the Flute, man, the best, and there was nobody there, as if it wasn't important." For those who had experienced Fajardo's old glory in Havana or the sharp stylish sabor of his albums, these new days in Miami were like a bad joke, something one wishes to forget quickly.

While Fajardo's work in the 1960s is not well known, in the 1970s, living on the fringes of the salsa championed in New York, the master once again began to perform his music. He released various albums with the Coco label, easily moving between the old quality styles and the new trends, proving again that his flute defied categorization. In September 1978, I met up with him at a salsa club. Fajardo, sipping a brandy, was as effusive as ever: "Now here I am, in New York, unbelievable, back in Miami, it's impossible, it's no good at all, people don't get it, they don't know anything, oh well." That night the master went onstage with his new orchestra and tooted those fabulous high sounds that are his alone. I remembered when Fajardo came to Caracas, the band had played a song that said something to the effect of "Here's Fajardo, with a terrific son and a terrific message." And this was the message: "I am a musician, and I'm a Cuban musician." It was a message that still has meaning, especially after all those years of putting up with an unpleasant rumba.

To recap, the other side of the story was represented by the Orquesta Aragón, a group that embodied all of the myths of Cuban music. For New York salsa, Cuba was the definitive frame of reference, and the Aragón was an important figure within that frame. At the end of 1978, these Cuban musicians finally came to the United States, and their arrival signaled the fulfillment of many long-awaited opportunities. Not only did they confirm the perception about the famous son that had left Cuba, but they also confirmed, for all of the young musicians who had grown up in the exclusive air of salsa, numerous stories that had been told by the veterans of those older times. In addition—and perhaps this was even more important than the music itself—the fact that the Orquesta Aragón was playing in New York was in some way a political victory. The period of boycotts and insults had passed, making way for the days of the rumba and pride. Rarely has the New York world known the burst of emotion that took over that evening of December 28, 1978, on the stage of the Avery Fisher Hall in Lincoln Center. Before the concert, the outpouring of fans of all ages— from middle-class Cubans to Nuyoricans of little means—made clear how much excitement surrounded this event. As the audience filled the theater, most of the salsa musicians, without regard to style or school, talked animatedly with one another, sharing a range of speculations and commentaries and a little rum, waiting for the moment when they would come face-to-face with the legend. Finally, at eight o'clock on the dot, the lights went down and the musicians appeared onstage in their sharp, white suits. Rafael Lay, the orchestra's director, approached the microphone to make his standard introduction, but that evening the phrase was historical: "Ladies and gentlemen, with you now, from Cuba, the Orquesta Aragón."

Aragón, Aragón
If you feel a richly flavored son
Put your stamp on it:
"It's the Aragón."

That night, in effect, history was made into sound, and the fullness of the Caribbean overflowed with sabor.

As the reader may well know, the Aragón and Fajardo have very little to do with salsa. However, in this chapter where I have discussed the charanga ensembles that developed thanks to the euphoria for salsa, it seemed only fitting to comment on the Cubans, for, on the whole, with or without salsa, all of those flutes and violins came from Cuba.

A Singer and Songwriter

Catalino Curet Alonso, "El Tite," was a very black Puerto Rican journalist and a singer with a timid voice who made his living from neither his journalism nor his music but from the post office where he worked all his life, starting out as a mail carrier. The first time that Curet's name appeared on an album cover was when Joe Quijano recorded his song "Efectivamente." Then came La Lupe, who, from a radically different perspective, connected his name with a new type of Caribbean song: the salsa song. The first three of his boleros to be recorded were "Carcajada final," "La tirana," and "Puro teatro." They were all in a style that abandoned the melancholic and whining tone that had characterized the Cuban bolero in the times of "feeling" and that had been cultivated over time with a kind of sugary sensibility by the most important Cuban composers. Curet never dwelled in the melodious and sweet; instead of making a request; he asserted a claim. That is why his songs were closer to Alvaro Carrillo's than to Rafael Hernández's, more in the style of the Mexican ranchero's revenge and repudiation than in the idyllic and flowery tone of the Caribbean bolero of the 1930s. This same warlike style, once it was articulated in the voice of a woman, started to take on very special meanings and to have powerful effects, as in the former years of the good, strong love ballad: "According to your point of view / I'm the evil one."

After "La tirana," Curet Alonso became the most extraordinary singer of love songs in the world of salsa. Going beyond the bolero, truly capitalizing on the bomba and the guaracha, Curet was credited with a very significant production that made him the first reference point for defining the traits of the salsa song, one deeply rooted in the most contradictory themes but foremost and forever imbued with the love song.

In 1977, when I first met Tite, I immediately asked him about that song and how it avoided the usual focus on happiness in order to re-create itself in disavowal and rejection. Curet's answer, his theory, was as follows:

People live happily, more or less, but they don't realize it . . . so that joy has to be nurtured by bad or unhappy things. That's the way it is. . . .

People are in love with the idea of love, but love, contrary to what most people think, is a confrontation, a fruitful and dramatic confrontation that always leads to drama. . . . When a relationship is stable, let's say, when it's normal, it loses that edge. . . . Nobody ever talks about the "so-and-so" family who live happily, how the Mr. woke up happy and ate his breakfast, how he loves his wife and kisses her. . . . When that happens, nobody comments on it, or, if it is mentioned, it's because it's a lie, and just the opposite is happening. . . . When people speak about love, they do so because it's over, and they want it back. This is where the bolero comes in. . . . The bolero is an act of aggression and treachery, a challenge to what happened and a challenge to what will come. . . . That's how I see it, and I feel honored when I'm walking down the street, and I hear people singing my songs. That must be evidence that I'm not too far off. . . . For me the bolero is like steaming food, a languid conversation, something warm and sweaty; it recounts a love affair, and that love affair, if it's worth anything, is always hot and sweaty. . . .

As on a stage
You pretend your cheap pain
Your drama is not needed
I already know this theater.

I leave it to the reader to reflect on Curet's theory and lyrics. The certain fragility of this kind of love song, the unbreakable intimacy that it implies, and the modes and habits that are imposed on it, both limiting and exaggerating it, always result in postures where the indifferent and imaginary accusation of its being ridiculous serves, momentarily, to hide any particular or definite position. This book's objectives are far from untangling that confusion of posturing and passion. The love song, and the Caribbean bolero in particular, requires other erudite books free from intellectual prejudices, those books considered "cultured, but pretentious" and published in the name of "culture." For the moment, I am interested only in pointing out the unwavering persistence of a certain kind of love song, one perhaps more authentic and enduring than the disguised or disingenuous ones. The line of the former extends solidly from Curet Alonso's contemporary boleros to the first expressions of that urban love song that emerged on our continent at the beginning of the twentieth century. These songs easily transcend the passing of generations, the rise of sophistication, and the development of new trends. This resurgence of popular taste over Gardel, for instance, is too important to be undermined by claiming that it is ridiculous or just melodrama. With varying degrees of intensity and pronouncement, this same resurgence can be found in other singers and composers of popular music, who, skirting the goals of the industry's pitiful marketing ploys, perpetuated a uniquely Caribbean way of being.

Pedro Flores and Daniel Santos; Rafael Hernández and José Alfredo Jiménez; and Augustín Lara, Alvaro Carrillo, and Portillo de la Luz together formed a sort of indestructible bastion for this kind of love song. Felipe Pirela, a small man from Maracay who with his very intimate voice created a massive following who bought (and continue to buy) millions of his albums, also belonged to this group. This bastion offered common ground across the continent, enlivening the quotidian coming into its own, destroying some myths and creating others, persisting in a secret alliance with time and cultural habits.

The opposite of this traditional love song was the accommodating one, the one drawn from artifice and passing trends. Many of us have seen singers disappear and reappear as balladeers representing the image of a different love relationship, that of a blonde couple running in slow motion through flowering fields toward a romantic embrace, as if they were selling soap or shampoo. This song and its image, inherited from the mass market clichés produced by industries in the United States and Europe, were repeated in the Caribbean like secondhand copies, copies that remained lifeless. As another example, in Venezuela, the Festival of Saint Remus was translated into a banal type of love song that, despite all the efforts of radio and television publicity, never took root among the masses. Likewise, we received from Argentina (where even the tango was prohibited because of its rebellious roots) a pop singer called Sandro, a sort of Spanish Tom Jones, even more spastic than the original, who briefly made the teenaged girls go crazy. In these ways, trying desperately to ignore the traditional love song, the music industry kept producing divas who imitated poses learned from U.S. television and sang songs translated from English in an effort to enforce fleeting trends and, thereby, transform popular taste.

Of course, all of this was clearly inflected with dishonesty and danger. To continue with the Venezuelan case as an example, I remember how, in the middle of the 1970s, our radio stations became divided into those that were called "youth and modern stations" and those that were referred to as "popular stations." In the former, U.S. music was the order of the day; it imposed a new way of life, expecting us to translate attitudes and gestures that were uncomfortable and absurd for us. The latter played the same music as always—guarachas, boleros, and also the new salsa—without any seeming paradox or confusion. We knew that the criteria behind this division was spurred on by exclusive class interests. The youth stations addressed the upper and upper-middle classes, the only ones able to pay for the desired sophistication, while the popular stations addressed the rest of the population, one that was considered, based on the new image that publicity had produced, as *balurdo*, *chabacano*, *niche* (stupid, styleless, delinquent), and its music, therefore, was likewise scorned as poor and pathetic. This repudiation reached such a point that when salsa began to be heard widely in Venezuela, the disc jockeys of the youth stations—frequently seen as the embodiment of the frustration with "backward nationalism"—went so far as to characterize salsa as "the music of monkeys and for monkeys."

As a result, the so-called sophisticated love song, which emerged from the musical hodgepodge of the U.S. pop ballad, garnered limited participation only from the Venezuelan youth stations, while the other music, the bastion, remained housed in the popular stations. The "sophisticated" song, of course, gave up the most important characteristics of the traditional song. Paraphrasing Curet, we can say that instead of viewing the love relationship as vitalized through confrontation, with all the dramatic weight that that implies, the new ballad was the banal song of love as exalted in certain U.S. films so favored by teenaged girls and spinsters. Those songs had no edge, no grittiness; rather, they were "prettified." They sang of a northerly spring that does not exist in the tropics, of the longing for prince charming as depicted in Disney movies, and of the redemption that, as in soap operas, oversimplifies love and life in this world as nothing more than a platonic kiss that inevitably comes at the end.

However, just as the music of the youth stations was easily categorized as following only one style and criteria, the programming of the popular stations requires some examination: not all of the music aired was part of the bastion. If a good number of paragraphs in this book have accused the Venezuelan radio programming of terrible mediocrity, one of the elements that contributed most to that mediocrity was, precisely, a lack of musical criteria. The music that did air was chosen either by the preference for a certain tendency, the trend of the moment, or by the always persuasive lubricant of plugging. Beyond these guidelines, there was little reflection on criteria, and thus mediocrity took over. For that reason, the popular stations, as a block, did not serve as an effective model for defining the popular love song of the moment, though that love song was able to survive the foibles of radio and publicity. Equally involved in mass record productions that were grounded neither in live concerts nor in common sense, salsa itself turned to that kind of love song a good number of times. Instead of being dressed in the formulas of the bolero and the traditional song, many salsa tunes ended up closer to the idyllic song of the shampoo commercial and the romantic movie. Yet, in order not to go beyond the limited intentions of this book, let us return to Curet Alonso and his music as a valid model for the traditional type of the indestructible love song. Going beyond the bolero to include the guaracha, the guaguancó, and the bomba as well, his vast production offers us a balanced overview of that other expression, the one that matters most to us.

Just as La Lupe owed a good part of her rootedness and initial popularity to Curet Alonso and his boleros, so did José "Cheo" Feliciano, who, returning to the recording studio and dance club after his forced retirement, gained new popularity from the support that he received from Curet and his music. In fact, with Cheo the Curet connection was even more critical, since Tite was his producer and adviser, the mentor who showed him the steps and options available. When I wrote about the reunion of the Fania All Stars in 1971, I noted the extreme popularity of Feliciano, a popularity that was rooted in his first solo album, *José "Cheo" Feliciano*, on which some of Curet's canonical work was first recorded. That album included, for instance, what might be his most famous bolero, "Mi triste problema."

> To live next to you
> With my thoughts out of place
> To continue in anguish
> Seeing how all happiness is lost.

Along with "Mi triste problema," Cheo also recorded a song that became the first great hit or success of the salsa explosion, "Anacaona." In this song Curet explored the old Caribbean myth of the Taina princess who seemingly had been treated in past musics from all possible vantage points (even the Cubans, by the nineteenth century, had worked this topic into their high cultural expressions). Curet, making the theme into salsa, displayed it in bits—"Anacaona, India de raza cautiva . . . Anacaona, de la región primitiva" (Anacaona, captive Indian maiden . . . Anacaona, from the primitive)—while developing a long montuno based on the legendary phrase of "Areíto de Anacaona."

Well into 1974, all of the important records produced by Fania and its monopoly featured at least one song by Curet Alonso. Thus, the initial debts that La Lupe and Feliciano owed to Tite expanded to include many others. El Tite, then, began to mold his music based on the demands and characteristics of diverse interpreters, developing three basic thematic lines: (1) the festive song, full of roguish and playful phrases, where the music itself (its world, its musicians, its singers), served as the principal source of inspiration; (2) the song that he himself defined as socially engaged, chronicles about the marginalized barrios, portraying characters in their everyday dramas and sufferings and also delving into political themes that had to do with Puerto Rico's current situation; and (3) Tite's core theme, the one that makes up the highest percentage of his songs, the love song, which, in the long run, privileged the guaracha over the bolero as its frame.

Examples of the first theme can be found in Roberto Roena's "Tú loco loco y yo tranquilo" and "El traqueteo," from the first albums of the Apollo Sound; "Tiburón," included on Larry Harlow's album *Abran paso*; "La oportunidad" and "Sonerito," both sung by Ismael Miranda; "Guaguancó ta' moderno," "Como lo canto yo," "Camarón," "Presencia," and "De mí para Puerto Rico," featured on a number of albums by Justo Betancourt; "Reunión en la cima," which became a classic on the first album of the Puerto Rican All Stars; the extraordinary bomba "De la verdegué," performed by Celia Cruz and Johnny Pacheco on his 1975 album; and likewise, most of the bombas and plenas produced by Rafael Cortijo and his new combo in the 1980s. It is important to emphasize to the reader that this brief list is only a representative selection of all that Curet Alonso produced in this thematic line that I have called "festive."

Later I will discuss the socially engaged theme; for now I will jump to that other music that essentially identifies not only Curet but also a great part of the salsa expression: the love song. In the boleros, for instance, Tite was able to develop his theory about love and boleros as "steamed food" more emphatically. He produced extraordinary boleros such as "Asesinas" and "Temes," both recorded by Vitín Avilés; "Las cosas de tu mente," recorded by Monguito; and "Nervios de acero," included on the album titled *Ismael Miranda en fa menor*. However, while the salsa fever was heating up, Curet's boleros became increasingly sidelined. This was a direct result of salsa's proliferation during the commercial boom. The bolero was sacrificed for the guaracha, and a fundamental form of Caribbean expression was neglected in an act of shortsightedness on the part of the record executives. This happened because they did not understand the most elementary characteristics of our music (most of them were U.S. natives who hardly spoke or understood Spanish). They made the mistake of thinking that the guaracha, due to its festive and happy tone, would be more accessible and popular than the bolero, which they found too slow and dramatic. Curet, therefore, had no other choice than to shelve his boleros.

In the same vein, once salsa tried to penetrate the upscale markets, these entrepreneurs pushed forward a melodious song saturated with fragile and feminized violins. Therefore, during the few times that the bolero was brought in, it was presented in a form that directly negated the authentic bolero. The effective, melodramatic, and heart-wrenching song of the bolero was neglected in favor of a shallower and simpler ballad. Unlike those truly salsalike boleros, rich in musical and literary possibilities, like the ones developed by Palmieri, for instance, we now had a sterile, plodding love song trying to be "pretty," which inevitably languished before the indifference of most audiences. Thus, we sadly see how extraordinary bolero singers such as Vicentico Valdez and La Lupe were reduced to singing the most miserable love songs that, from the first chords, cut them off from more angelic choruses and from any violins worthy of a Corín Tellado and the romantic philosophy of Delia Fiallo. The bolero, then, was not properly integrated into salsa.

Therefore, for salsa, the love music of Curet Alonso gets expressed through the bomba, the guaracha, and the guaguancó, forms that, handled intelligently, bolstered and balanced the arbitrary dictates of the entrepreneurs. In some cases, Curet sharpened his aggressive style, offering confessional guarachas full of irony and black humor; in other cases, he drew on the common but effective alternative of including satire, the advice of a third party, or the dramatic rejection that sacrificed humor. Markolino Dimond—as I highlighted in previous chapters—recorded Tite's "Por qué adoré," an extraordinary son with the refrain, "Por qué adoré tu cuerpo de carretera que tiene más curvas que la vuelta de la culebra" (How come I adored your body slithering in its many curves like a serpent). Likewise, Willie Colón recorded the bomba "Pena de amor" on his album with Mon Rivera: "Aprende bien corazón, máquina de la ilusión que es alegría y dolor, esa cuestión de amor" (Heart, machine of illusion, learn well that love is a question of both joy and pain). El Conde Rodríguez, for his part, recorded Curet's "Guaguancó del amor": "Para cantar desde aquí a la que yo tanto amé al cielo yo alcé la voz, cantando por guaguancó" (In order to sing from here to the woman I adore, I raise my voice to heaven, singing a guaguancó). Justo Betancourt featured "El pedregal": "Pasé por tu pedregal . . . un pedregal fue tu amor, de mi divina ilusión" (I went by your pile of rocks, your love was a pile of rocks, a divine illusion). Roberto Roena, on two of his most recent albums, was fortunate to record two of Curet's most polished compositions. One was "Marejada Feliz":

> Marejada feliz
> Vuelve y pasa por mí
> Aún yo digo que sí
> Que todavía pienso en ti.
> [Happy tide come through me again, I still say yes, still think about you]

204 The other was "Guaguancó del adiós":

Sí, yo sé quién eres tú
Tú no sabes quién soy yo.
[Yes, I know who you are, but you don't know who I am]

Ironically, Willie Colón, the salsa artist who has, proportionately speaking, recorded the smallest amount of Curet Alonso's music, is himself known for three of Curet's love guarachas. First, "Barrunto," included on the album *La gran fuga*, released at the end of the 1970s: "I have a feeling in my heart, a presentiment / That soon we will part."

Later, in 1973, on the album *Lo mato*, Willie recorded "La María," which shows the profound influence and attraction that Curet had for Brazilian music:

La María
Dreams the dreams of a woman
Where so much can be lost
In one of her kisses.

Lastly, the album *El juicio* featured a guaracha that is already considered a classic, not only in Curet Alonso's total repertoire, but in the final assessment of salsa expression. It is titled "Piraña" and includes the lyrics,

See how I found you
Turned into a bad thing
I don't know why
They call you piranha.

In 1975, Ray Barretto, who, like Willie Colón, had recorded very little of Curet's music, brought out a song that, in addition to its intrinsic musical values, took on even more importance. With "Vale más un guaguancó," salsa musicians reclaimed the old spirit that, from the rumba of old, had characterized the love song. This spirit recognizes the rumba and love as the same thing, as the unique factor that nurtures and spices up human existence in our part of the world. One aids the other, complements it, balances it, or, in the worst case scenario, replaces it. For example, when the infidelity of a woman inundates the spirit, a vigorous drum emerges to assuage the pain through the indomitable optimism of the festive, the guaracha. This guaguancó by Tite, therefore, served as a powerful reminder of this situation and assured the prolongation of that spirit. True salsa, the best salsa, the salsa most able to survive the hassling and stubbornness of the industry, was now felt as the continuation of an expression and a music that belonged to the Caribbean, as indelibly as its coasts and its 205 people. Its montuno says, "A guaguancó is worth much more than a bad love."

Finally, let me mention another one of Curet Alonso's themes that also represented the authentic feeling of salsa music in terms of its love songs, "De todas maneras rosas." In 1977, Ismael Rivera recorded this song, and in just a few months it became a classic with the montuno, "Roses anyway / For the one who forgot me."

Now I will conclude with the third thematic line of Curet Alonso's salsa production: that of social themes. As with the previous thematic lines, here his purposes and approaches are diverse, displaying a range of powerful messages. In his early period, Tite felt that by singing to the "original race," to the old slaves who had been brought to the region, he was singing to his people, to the communities that populate the barrios of the great cities, whom he understood as direct descendants of that first group of slaves. Under this tonic, for instance, we have to include the song "Babaila," recorded by Pete "El Conde" Rodríguez on his 1974 album. Likewise, in "Primoroso cantar," recorded by Pacheco in 1973, Tite speaks about the origins of salsa in that first slave song that was heard in the slave houses of the plantations. A similar theme infused "Plantación adentro," a song that Willie Colón and Rubén Blades recorded in 1977 and one that also became a top-selling salsa hit.

> People are like shadows
> Inside the plantation
> Brother.

Tite also experimented with social themes that went beyond slavery. This was a way of sidestepping the censorship of the producers and distributors of salsa, which was, in a number of cases, more stringent and arbitrary than the official censorship of the government. For example, Roberto Roena's son "Con los pobres estoy," released in 1972, included the lyrics,

> Agüita de ajonjolí, para los pobres soy . . .
> Para mí en esos lugares no no hay felicidad . . .
> Cada pobre un amigo, a ese la mano le doy
> Agüita de ajonjolí.
> [Juice of the ajonjolí, I am here for the poor. . . . In those places where
>   there is no joy. . . . To each poor friend, I offer my hand]

By 1977, songs that directly addressed social issues without any beating around the bush had become a new tendency within salsa. With singer-songwriter Rubén Blades boldly producing and promoting such songs,

Curet Alonso felt freer to publish his own lyrics dealing with these themes. Most of those songs had been shelved for years. Now, within a matter of months, some of these compositions, chiefly sung by Rivera, became instant classics. In this way, the guaguancó "La perla," a musical portrait of one of the oldest and most miserable neighborhoods in San Juan, also made it big:

> La Perla,
> La Perla mutes its paint
> It is a watercolor of poverty.

Building on those successes, Curet Alonso inscribed the old salutes to the black race in one of his most complete and powerful compositions: "Las caras lindas" ("Beautiful Faces"), again sung by Ismael Rivera on an album released in 1978. "The beautiful faces of my black people / Are a parade of candles in bloom."

Throughout all of this production, Curet Alonso remained very clear about not falling prey to unpleasantness or posturing. As a result of the forced movement of the protest song, everyone realized that when popular songs try to address social problems—whether offering solutions or issuing denouncements—there was always the risk of their ending up as clichés and stereotypes and, thus, of becoming ineffective. They also risked getting categorized in a sterile formula that never went beyond certain university spaces. Rivera's response to these risks came in the song, "Mi música." Here Tite's lyrics, with a characteristic economy of words, wholly defined his sense of music, of good salsa, of all the authentic Caribbean music that transcends times and changing social habits: "Mi música no queda ni a la derecha ni a la izquierda. . . . Mi música queda en el centro de un tambor bien legal" (My music is of neither the Left nor the Right. . . . It stands at the center of a very lawful drum). When this album was first released, many listeners saw it as a kind of betrayal on the part of Curet. They alleged that it exaggerated the realities, and that his music was succumbing to the apparently irrevocable division between the Left and the Right. I do not intend here to enter that debate or to offer analysis of the political spectrum, since our focus is on the *musical* circumstances involved. Nevertheless, I do want to emphasize that authentic popular music always has been a mirror of the social, economic, cultural, and political sufferings pulsing within the people who want that suffering to be confronted and/or denounced. In some cases, the confrontation is premeditated and direct; in other cases, it serves only as a reference. The collective nature of this music determines what meanings and effects to give to such a song, because the message of that song comes from the collective, the people. Because, for the most part, the Right has governed our region and, therefore, has been directly accountable for our difficulties, while the forces of the Left most often have been opposed to those governments, many of our songs have been labeled automatically as "left wing." The audience that lives on the margins of these political poles sees clearly how a music that rightly belongs to them is reduced to categories that are arbitrary and awkward. Ironically those positions that avoid being defined as Left or Right have been associated with conformity, acquiescence, and an empty apolitical attitude. In this context, Curet Alonso, as just one example of the many popular composers of the Caribbean and Latin American tradition, far from "exaggerating the realities," offered a fairly direct confrontation. Furthermore, his confrontation was much more significant and powerful, because it remained on the margins of the binaries and created a true "north" that reflected the authentic feelings of the people, and the people are the ones who interest us in the long term. Therefore, although authentic popular music that sings about the sufferings of daily life could be understood as an expression of the Left, against the Right—since it can and usually does become shaped by the demands and needs of a determined political party—that same music goes well beyond those limits. In the reach of its real meanings, its actual content, this music transcends the circumstances of any particular argument or political interests. Thus, songs such as "Preciosa" and "Lamento borincano" by Rafael Hernández remain authentic hymns of the Puerto Rican people. Likewise, Curet's social music went beyond momentary concerns in order to convey the lasting. This, of course, always happens with popular music: rather than disappearing, it endures, generation after generation. If Curet avoided the Left and the Right in order to locate his music "at the center of a very lawful drum," that same drum, then, represented many, many things and the many life experiences that are preferable alternatives to the political rant of the moment.

Since I have mentioned Rafael Hernández's songs for Puerto Rico, it is only fitting that I close this section about Curet Alonso's social songs with another one of his canonical compositions, "Profesión esperanza," which again was transformed into a hymn by the voice of Ismael Rivera:

Puerto Rico will always be beautiful,
It will always remain lovely, lovely
I am Puerto Rican
And my profession is hope.

Salsa will forever be imbued with the presence of Curet Alonso, a figure who, while not directly engaged in the salsa world, enabled salsa to represent a large part of the roots, image, and transcendent qualities of the larger Caribbean community. He did this primarily through the voice of Ismael Rivera, who, for many and very good reasons, has been hailed as "The Greatest Sonero." At this point, it is pertinent to transcribe some of the interview, "Quiebre de quintos," that I recorded with Ismael for the National Radio of Venezuela in March 1977:

Ismael, how did you enter the world of salsa, the world of music?
Speaking humbly, I did not enter the world of salsa, I was born
   into it. As it happens, I come from a town called Santurce in the
   metropolitan area in Puerto Rico, on the north coast. I lived in
   Calma Street, and every morning I woke to the clock in that street.
   It sounded like this: pum qui pum . . . pum qui pum. That clock
   got inside my blood. It felt like I was carrying something within
   me, and before I knew any better, I was already at the beach with
   the drums, with a man named Rafael Cortijo, whom you know very
   well, and, well, he's the one responsible for me being part of this
   whole mess. . . .

When did this relationship with Cortijo begin?
Well, we were together in middle school in Santurce. And, Cortijo,
   naturally, had always played the drum. . . . You know, there are
   pleneros, those pure drummers, and Cortijo was one of those. . . .
   So, after school we'd go to the beach, about a five minute walk, and
   we'd play. . . .

You said you were in school, how old were you then?
Rafael was fifteen and I was fourteen. . . . And it was around that time
   that we started to get together and jam. He was the one who began
   to help me to raise my consciousness, he kept saying that I was a
   singer, a special vocalist, and I thought that he was exaggerating,
   but he went on and on. . . . And later, he came looking for me at
   the construction site, because by then I'd become a bricklayer,
   and a good one. . . . I was working for my grandpa, a contractor,
   and he'd give me a couple of bucks a week, but I always spent it
   on the movies on Saturdays. . . . But, you know, we had to sweat
   and break our backs. Then there'd be Rafael, waiting for me with
   his drums, and my grandpa would see him coming and say, "Here
   comes that black guy with the drums again. I'm going to throw
   him out, and I'm going to throw you out, too, so he won't come
   around anymore. . . ." And that's how it all started. Rafael was the
   one who got me out of bricklaying . . . and that's how this accident

happened: Cortijo and his Combo . . . Ismael Rivera . . . "El bombón de Elena," and so on, and here we are. . . .

What do you mean by "this accident"?
Well, what happened was that we used to do a big show on the weekends, and people would come to see us, and they liked us. . . . I don't know, but they used to say that we played differently. I think it was the hunger. . . .

What do you mean, "the hunger"?
Well, the group had an anger about it, a forcefulness, we were crazy to get out of the slum, unconsciously, you understand? This was the time of the revolution for blacks in Puerto Rico—Roberto Clemente, Peruchín Cepeda, Romaní—blacks began to be admitted to the university—and poof—Cortijo and his Combo come along with that hunger, as a part of that movement. . . . But let me say this, it wasn't a planned thing, you know, sometimes these things just happen, and this is what was happening in Puerto Rico then. . . . It was something that came from the people, from blacks and for blacks, like a classroom opened up for us, and there was anger, and Clemente began to distribute sticks, and we got in, you know, with our music. . . . And it seems that that same wish of ours, to get out of the slums, made us want to do more. It was all because there was a hunger, César, there was hunger. . . .

This hunger influenced everything that I have emphasized and elaborated on since the opening chapters of this book. Ismael's style really caught people's attention, because it was a style that broke with all the previous musical patterns and brought new forms and phrasings to the Caribbean song. His principal virtue was in his way of approaching the montuno: Ismael brashly elided the traditional structure of the four lines and instead improvised numerous phrases and melodies between the refrains. These four lines were one of the most profound legacies of the Cuban son. Traditionally, once the montuno arrived, the singer would limit himself to inspiring phrases that complemented the idea exposed in the son. Thus, between one refrain and the next, there was a free space of about four measures that could be filled with the inspired riffs of the improviser. Generally, they used four verses or phrases that corresponded to each of the four measures. Most of the time, the singer limited the alternating themes and words to two or three standard melodic variants, ones that squared perfectly with the measures that were already set out. These improvisers, known as "soneros," always respected the melodic possibilities and made up brief phrases that would support the thematic ideas introduced in the rest of the song. Thus, a sonero's virtue was limited to the peculiarity and the strength with which he confronted the son, and the intelligence with which he could toss diverse ideas into the montuno. In more recent times, this situation has changed considerably, especially with the presence of two exceptional Cuban improvisers: Miguelito Cuní and, of course, Benny Moré. The value of their contributions extends beyond what they did with the montuno. They knew how to transcend the tradition of a singer limited to the same melodic pattern. In this way, they became authentic creators of another music that shrewdly distinguished itself through the refrains of the montunos; they developed, that is, the style that would become salsa singing. This explains why, from the perspective of the Cuban tradition, Benny Moré has been deemed the clear and direct antecedent of the salsa vocalist.

With Ismael Rivera, however, something different happened. Guided by motivations and influences beyond those of Benny's, Ismael not only committed himself to inventing melodies over the montuno, but he also was irreverent enough to break with the particular demands of each song. He would reduce to two lines all of the measures intended for him, or he would extend them to eight or ten verses that he would spew out, breathlessly, like a machine gun. For these reasons, in his early years, Ismael was ignored, often purposefully, by the experts and the musically orthodox. To them, Ismael sung so many things that he ended up saying nothing, and he played with so many melodic possibilities that, to them, the result sounded jumbled. It did not take Rivera long, however, to demonstrate the validity of his style. Just as Moré's innovations both shaped and represented the characteristic spirit of the son in the 1950s, so Ismael's improvisational style represented the texture of salsa that would take over the region from the 1960s on. From this perspective, salsa improvisation cannot define itself without acknowledging its relation to Ismael, since it was he who gave it a face and anticipated its greatest possibilities. This is not to fall into the simplistic assertion that the best salsa singers are only those who resemble Ismael. I simply suggest that those singers who endured the test of time inevitably possessed a number of traits developed by Rivera. For example, Oscar D'León and Rubén Blades—each with their own unique style—approached salsa singing from a perspective very similar to that of Ismael, one requiring the boldness to confront the montuno and a freshness and freedom to improvise over it. Above all, they exhibited the requisite sabor of the people and of the barrio. Each one had his own style, of course, but they had one thing in common: They both made the salsa song unique.

Now let us continue with Ismael's career. For the purposes of this book, the period that interests us most is the one that begins during the final years of the 1960s. Before the end of the first half of the decade, while enjoying all of the fame and prestige that came from being part of Cortijo's Combo, Ismael was forced to give up that world when Puerto Rican Customs discovered a large amount of drugs in his possession and he was sentenced to five years in prison. This event radically modified the spirit and purpose of all of his work afterward. When he was released, he recorded a final album with Cortijo, but it had none of the strength and vitality of his previous work. It did include, however, his famous bolero (one of the very few of his known compositions) "Mi libertad eres tú," which, together with the theme from "Las tumbas" by Bobby Capó, gives us an idea of what happened during his prison years:

> I want to leave the tombs
> I don't know when that will be
> The tombs are for the dead
> And I'm not dead at all.

Trying to regain his lost footing, Ismael recorded two albums with the timbal player Kako and the Panamerican Orchestra (*De colores* and *Lo último en la avenida*). Here Rivera began to perfect the nuances that would characterize his singing on future albums. Finally, in 1971, when New York began to experience the next wave of the boom, Ismael was able to create his own orchestra, which he named Los Cachimbos. Rivera confessed that this period was very, very difficult for him. After what had happened, he could not go back to Puerto Rico, so he had to accept New York as his new home, though he always thought of it as an adopted one. Furthermore, any hope of a rebirth with Cortijo failed, since Cortijo was never attracted to the life and tumult of the United States and returned a few months later to his plenas in Santurce. Ismael, then, took off on his own. With Los Cachimbos he abandoned the Puerto Rican rhythms—basically, the bomba and plena—to pursue the son that was capturing all of the salsa sound. The first album of his orchestra, *Controversia*, became an immediate hit. The band was small, with just a trumpet, alto sax, and trombone combo and a complete rhythm section. This allowed him to cultivate a much more intimate and direct style. The next year Ismael released a song that instantly became a classic, "Incomprendido." It, too, was expressly composed for him by Bobby Capó:

I, I, I think that when I die
I will be alone
I've been the misunderstood one.

This type of song turned Ismael Rivera into an icon, one able to embody, all on his own, all of the sadness and vicissitudes of daily life. People began to see in him something more than a singer. They justified his excesses and demanded from him only an almost absolute identification with themselves. Rivera fully understood what this phenomenon meant. He kept himself on the margins of the recording hype and produced slim records full of the kinds of life experiences that intensified that identification. On his albums we see the absence of fillers. Since he produced his own albums, he alone decided what went into them. He rediscovered composers of the past and discovered new ones of the present, thus developing a repertoire that was consistently successful both in popularity and in sales. He took composers such as Pedro Flores and Bobby Capó and, to a lesser degree, Rafael Hernández and made them the primary composers of his repertoire. Thus Ismael recorded again "El cumbanchero," in one of the most extraordinary versions ever known; "El pañuelito"; "Mi negrita me espera"; and the classic "Jaragual" by Felipe Goyco, known as don Felo. Likewise, and revolving around the love theme that shaped his style, Ismael turned "Dime por qué" into a widely known hit, singing, "Tell me why, tell me / Why did you leave me."

In 1974, after having recorded the album *Vengo por la maceta* with Los Cachimbos, Ismael offered the market a one-of-a-kind production, an album that became fundamental for any understanding of salsa. That album, *Traigo de todo*, again brought together compositions by Flores and Capó and also incorporated new songwriters, such as the Panamanian Williams, who gave Ismael the very significant "El nazareno." The origins of this song began with Rivera's trip to Panama, where he visited the town of Portobello during the month of October, just as the residents were celebrating the feast of the Black Christ. Ismael confessed to me later that this was the most important moment of his life, and he said the same thing on my program for Radio Nacional:

Look, César, I admit it, I'm a delinquent and I've always been one, and I pray to God that your program doesn't get damaged from this. . . . But when I saw that in Panama, when I saw that man who stared very fixedly at me, as if he already knew me, I felt a bit weird, as if somebody was shaking me from the inside. . . . And I don't know, I changed, in my own way, you know, but I changed. . . . And I don't care if people believe me or not, but sometimes things like this happen to people in their lives and well . . . that's why I sang to the Nazarene, who is a Christ, black like me. I sang that song, and now it's famous, but it was nothing more than a song about friendship, about solidarity with my people, my race and my nation, because I can't sing about anything except the things that I feel and experience.

> Do good to your friends
> Offer them your friendship
> And you'll see that bad things
> Will never come
> Everything good
> Will always be with you . . .
> (montuno)
> The Nazarene told me to take care of my friends.

On all of these albums, the presence of Javier Vásquez, then musical director of Los Cachimbos, stood out. Vásquez was a veteran Cuban pianist who took on the responsibility of all of the arrangements sung by Ismael. Vásquez's style on the piano, with a slow and solid montuno in the best Cuban tradition, gave the orchestra a definite vitality, so common in salsa but one rarely achieved by more than a dozen musicians. Thus credit is due Vásquez for being the ideal vehicle to convey, in the precise language of music, the unbridled spontaneity of Ismael's talent.

That same album of 1974 also included other songs that, like "El nazareno," soon became classics. This was the case with "Qué te pasa a ti" and "El niche" by Boby Capó, "Traigo de todo" and "Orgullosa" by Pedro Flores, "Satélite y witinila" by Javier Vásquez, and "Yo no quiero piedras" by Enrique Boné. After this album, however, the production of Ismael and his Cachimbos came to a standstill. This resulted mostly from nonmusical circumstances, particularly Fania's sale of the Tico label—the label for which Ismael had recorded once he had left Cortijo's group. Rivera, who in various ways had opposed the musical criteria imposed by the management of Fania, found himself under the control of new bosses who made him perform in ways counter to his traditional style. Thus in 1975 the album *Soy feliz* appeared under the Vaya label with only a few redeeming songs, namely, "Las tumbas" and "Soy feliz." Meanwhile, Ismael kept playing with the idea of an alternative, hoping that Fania would decide it could do without his contract and set him free. But Fania, which had by now become the most powerful company in the Latin music world, would never release Ismael. Given the murky situation of the industry, Fania must have felt it was better to keep him under their wing—even if he did not produce much or produced badly—than to let him create potential profits for strangers, that is, the enemy hands of other music companies.

So the year 1976 came and went, and the company, in order not to lose its hold on the public, decided to release an extraordinary "greatest hits" album called *Total Eclipse*. Ismael, however, remained on the sidelines with only "Traigo de todo," produced two years earlier, to represent his work. Around this same time, to satisfy the minimal demands of his contract, Ismael issued a Christmas album—*Feliz navidad*—but it again conveyed none of his former passion or vitality. From a larger point of view, however, this album deserves special mention because it included one of the best bombas that Ismael had ever recorded: "Seis de borinquen," a composition of the young Ramón Muñiz with such lyrics as "I bring the flavor of the beach in my own body / And the taste of coconut that burns within."

By this time it was already clear and often noted that Ismael's career was in decline. People spoke about his loss of vitality and effectiveness and of the supposed chaos of his private life. But above all, people commented on the loss of power in his voice. Ismael, perhaps moved by pride and also because he was aware of the rumors spread by his enemies, insisted on denying them. "I am a singer and it is not by chance that I have this voice," he once declared to a Venezuelan magazine. However, despite his protestations, it was obvious in his performances that his voice was going. The situation gradually worsened, and it was painful to watch this legendary figure struggle in his live performances, trying to save face.

But the old contract with Tico, now under the rigid control of Fania, which refused to make excuses for him, continued to force him to produce records. They released his last two known productions (at least they were the last known when I was typing these pages in the early 1980s): *De todas maneras rosas* from 1977 and *Esto sí es lo mío* the next year. This was evidence of Ismael's popularity and the powerful hold he had on the public ever since he began recording. That popularity allowed the albums to succeed without much difficulty even though they were recorded at half voice, almost in a whisper. On these albums, in addition to the arrangements by Flores and Capó, there were some by Tite Curet, and that combination led to the important songs I have commented on throughout this chapter. Aided in no small way by modern recording techniques, Ismael was able to shine in these albums. He demonstrated his understanding of the songs and conveyed their connection to Caribbean music, so they could not be ignored despite the weakness of his voice. For example, his inspired rendition of the guaracha "De todas maneras . . ." is certainly incontestable, and the same can be said of "Si te cojo" by Boby Capó, where Ismael, silencing the critics, enunciated every note of the quinto, translating the sounds from the drums to his own words. What his voice could not offer him, his intuition did, and this, of course, is also a gift.

For example, Roberto Roena once told me this anecdote about the recording of "Las caras lindas." As is usual, modern recordings are done part by part; that is, each section—the rhythm, brass, percussion, and chorus—is recorded separately, and, once all of that is complete, the voice of the improviser is incorporated. It was said that when Ismael went to record his voice track, he spent a while listening carefully to the tres solo that Mario Hernández had recorded. Ismael then asked the staff to repeat just that tres part a couple of times. Then he turned to Javier Vásquez and said, "Hey, I think Mario is telling me something, I feel it, I know what he is saying." And immediately, he ordered the technician to record something new, a new instrument, his own voice, as a parallel track to that of the tres. It is also said that Ismael did this in one sitting, without rehearsal or retakes, without fearing mistakes. He just took off singing, repeating some ideas that he had not even written down, phrases that sound in unison with the Hernández tres in the final recording, phrases and nuances that are eloquent examples of all that is true and best in Caribbean singing. Yes, Ismael no longer had a voice, but he did not need it; in this type of music, in the music sung in this part of the world, the throat only has meaning if it is used as a bridge between the brain and the heart.

To conclude these paragraphs on Ismael Rivera, it may be fitting to share some of the lyrics of an old guaracha by Plácido Acevedo, "Comedia," recorded in 1978 and chosen by the singer as the personal summary of his last stage:

> On the great stage of life
> I'm the villain in your final scene
> I have to play the part, it's my destiny.

The Venezuelan Situation

Unfortunately, after the old days of Los Dementes, Federico and his Combo, the Sexteto Juventud, and other salsa groups in the 1960s, Venezuela had been unable to cultivate new groups for the avant-garde beat emerging in the Caracas music scene. The same fans who, as before, rarely changed their taste despite the international trends were now well aware of all that was happening in New York. These were the same fans who, in 1974, without any major inducement from marketing, filled up the Nuevo Circo of Caracas to see the country's first performance of the Fania Stars. But the country lacked its own expression, and the fans lacked a native group that could give a local flavor to the new salsa sound. That same night of the Nuevo Circo, for instance, the Venezuelan counterpart to Fania was a "superband" of the same old top musicians brought together just for that occasion under the direction of Porfi Jiménez. Their music, while undoubtedly skillful, only verged on the new trend. With the mambos "a la Machito" and arrangements from bygone decades, it still sounded old-fashioned, and despite its potential, it faded away once the concert was over. Buying all of their albums from New York, without any opportunity to take refuge, even for the moment, in their own national production, Venezuelan fans remained musical orphans. Therefore, even if that visit of Fania in 1974 indicated the birth of the salsa boom, the boom did not really take off for Venezuelans until they themselves contributed their own sound through an orchestra able to compete in popularity with those from the North. This happened one year later, in 1975.

The band that I refer to emerged in the first years of the 1970s through the initiative of two veteran trombonists, César Monge and José Antonio Rojas, "Rojita," who, like others, had gained experience in military bands and in one or another of those occasional dance bands with a repertoire that was little more than a pastiche of the current trends. Joining their initiative was Oscar D'León, a bass player who had also performed in some of those unknown bands and who liked to sing. One day they decided to form their own orchestra to play at beer halls and festivals, in private clubs and at parties, and wherever they could in the limited Caracas music scene. They got together in La Guaira at the home of pianist Enrique "Culebra" Iriarte, and their rehearsals began. In one way or another, all of the musicians already knew one another, except for José Rodríguez, the timbal player, who was a newcomer to the world of professional music and who was introduced to the group by D'León.

José himself has said that his friendship with Oscar D'León was purely coincidental. At the time, D'León used to drive a car for hire down the Antímano road, the same road that Rodríguez took to work each day, so they hooked up quite often. Oscar, said José, always had recordings with him, of old and new hits, and he sang along with them in his own style while he picked up and dropped off passengers. The topic of conversation was inevitable—music—since José confessed that he was also a musician. While Oscar raised his voice above the recorded versions, José would tap out the rhythm on the upholstery, on his knees, or on the seats. After a couple of trips like this, they were friends. José confessed that his specialty was the Zulian gaita, but that he would have no problems adapting to the salsa style, and he thus accepted Oscar's invitation to form a new band that "I tell you, brother, will take over the world."

217

After two months of rehearsals, the orchestra signed a contract to play in the beer hall La Distinción. At this time they finally decided to name the band, and, to a man, they all agreed on La Dimensión Latina. At the time this name meant very little, but later it took on a special significance. Using the word "Latina" suggested a response to the New York influence: only in the United States did the expression "Latino" have any meaning, since it is how Anglos there distinguish themselves from those born in Mexico and other places south of the border. Even the Puerto Ricans in New York, for various additional reasons, have never been able to escape this modifier, and so they call themselves Latinos, and Latino, then, applies to everything they do. From the point of view of Venezuela, however, the term "Latino" does not hold that kind of meaning. Here we are all the same, and we belong to the same culture: the whites and the blacks, the mulattos and the blondes are all equally Venezuelan, without major distinctions. Furthermore, salsa music, before being Latino, had been basically Caribbean, and it is always important to reiterate this point. Nevertheless, salsa, which did not emerge as an industry in Venezuela or in any other part of the Caribbean, had to take on New York styles, even when many of them were absurd or countersignificant. By that point, too, the term *música latina* (Latin music) had come to refer to contemporary salsa. La Dimensión, then, was called "Latina," to reaffirm that they were a contemporary orchestra doing something new and with a distinct style.

The group they inaugurated in the beer hall was a sextet comprised of Monge and Rojita on trombones, Rodríguez and Elio Pacheco on percussion, Oscar D'León as both singer and bass player, and Culebra, initially on the piano. Later Tony Monserrat, a virtuoso who eventually became famous for playing the merengue in scandalous costumes, took over the keyboard, and finally Jesús "Chuito" Narváez served as the group's permanent pianist. From the start, La Dimensión reflected everything that was happening in the local music scene. They brought together all the trends coming from New York, the particular phrasings that characterized Venezuelan music, and whatever musical fashion was deemed necessary by disc jockeys on the midnight shift. For example, that La Dimensión molded its music to the sonority of a pair of trombones gave evidence of its New York influence, and its rhythm followed a very simple scheme in order not to strain the ear of the Venezuelan dancer, accustomed, after so many years of Billo's dominance, to undemanding rhythms. Finally, La Dimensión kept to a neutral repertoire of nonchallenging lyrics in order not to rob the habitual drunkard of the sweet little song on the radio he needed to help him in the middle of the night. The convergence of these three elements smoothed the way for La Dimensión, so that when they made their grand appearance before the Venezuelan public, the public had to accept the group as its own. Indeed, there was something imperceptible at the bottom of their music that sounded like Caracas, something that became a source of automatic identification for all those music lovers who now, finally, had a musical home of their own.

At Maracaibo, during the Carnival season of 1973, the orchestra was on fire. That same year they recorded their first album, *La Dimensión Latina and El Clan de Víctor*. The way the album was conceptualized and the limited criteria that, in general, had long characterized the Venezuelan record industry kept this first recording from offering much of musical value or creating popular interest, however. Still, La Dimensión was able to distribute one of the recorded songs, "Pensando en ti," to smaller, regional radio stations and to some of the popular stations of the capital and its suburbs. This allowed them to produce a new album, all of their own, but it was riddled with poor music in mediocre styles in order to please the producers, who saw an exaggerated and erroneous opportunity in the Andean, and particularly Colombian, markets. La Dimensión, however, considered itself an established band. They maintained an average of eight monthly performances (basically for dances), and the musicians were comfortable with that. In 1974 they recorded a third album, along the same lines as the previous ones but with much clearer quality. Radio Rumbos promoted them (and in Venezuela, radio stations are still distinguished as either Rumbos or the rest), and they were able to create their first real hit: "Que bailen todos." They also went back to other carnivals in Maracaibo, and this return to the western regions signaled the incorporation of a musician who was very important for the later popularity of the orchestra: the bolero singer Wladimir Lozano.

Wladimir was already a frequent member of La Dimensión rehearsals, but he had not integrated himself fully because he was under contract with La Cueva del Oso, another modest venue in the capital, which guaranteed him a budget of sixty bolivares a day. However, due to La Dimensión's success in Zulia, Wladimir decided to give up his "economic security" to devote himself to the challenging opportunity that La Dimensión represented. The combination was perfect: Oscar, an exceptional guaracha singer, focused his talents on improvising over the montunos, now that Wladimir was taking care of the boleros. As a result, Wladimir eventually inherited much of the old popularity of Felipe Pirela. In addition, the combination of the two voices allowed the group to develop a new approach that became a major attraction of the orchestra: the boleros that began in Wladimir's voice were taken up in Oscar's festive montunos, setting the stage for sure success.

In 1975 the Venezuelans, who were gradually being seduced by the new salsa sonorities coming from New York, totally surrendered to a home-grown album: *Dimensión Latina 75*, the second record produced with the voices of Oscar and Wladimir and the first one to make it big. The album opened with "Llorarás," a guaracha composed by Oscar D'León with lyrics that revolved around the classic theme of the love revenge:

> I know that you don't want me to love you
> You always avoid me in some way
> When I come looking for you, you go the other way.

"Llorarás" truly exemplified the style of the band, a style that was primarily characterized by the way they conceived of and developed the rhythm. La Dimensión, for example, for a long time had been considered a foreign band by fans who preferred the aggressive and innovative spirit of New York salsa. This label was based on the neutral beat that the orchestra relied on, one that was exaggeratedly elementary and supported by the timbal and the guiro performed without much force, very much in the style of Billo's orchestra. However, this way of handling the rhythm—perfectly palpable in "Llorarás"—turned out to be, as I mentioned earlier, their gateway for reaching the largest number of Venezuelans. Actually, La Dimensión did nothing more than reshape the old rhythmic patterns of the traditional dance crowd into the modern sounds coming from New York. This is why many music lovers defined La Dimensión as the "Billo of salsa"; indeed, La Dimensión was the only orchestra able to break with the old dancing empire of the Dominican musician Luis María "Billo" Frómeta, who had dominated Venezuela.

With this 1975 album, La Dimensión became part of the trend that soon took over the salsa boom: the indiscriminate exploitation of the themes of the old Cuban guarachas. "Llorarás," of course, proved to be one of the few themes composed by La Dimensión to become a hit. This occurred not because the Venezuelan musicians lacked creativity but because, once the market was glutted, it was easier to return to old models. In fact, the philosophy of many record producers has always been "If something's a hit, there's no reason to change it; if something's been successful, there's no need to run an unnecessary risk and try anything new." Thus, as happened with a great number of salsa orchestras, La Dimensión preferred to sacrifice creativity for commerce, despite all the terrible consequences that that could entail.

Along with "Llorarás," La Dimensión also made the old "Parampapam" and "Taboga" by Ricardo Fábregas into successes by dressing them up with slight variations in the style inaugurated by the Casino de la Playa in the days of Miguelito Valdez. They repeated this formula the following year with a new album that sold very well thanks to their update of "Dolor cobarde," also by Miguelito. In contrast to the many orchestras that used classic themes with less success, La Dimensión chose songs with undisputed relevance to the times at hand. They searched for old unrequited love songs whose absurd tragedy had a rich history of melodrama. An example of this is "Mi adorada," a bolero by Bobby Capó that was also included on the 1975 album:

> I went to serenade my love
> I sang the most exquisite song
> I behaved like a true Juan Tenorio
> What for? She wasn't at the window.

The album *Dimensión Latina 75* affirmed that the salsa boom had fully made its way into Venezuela. Fania productions were being heard regularly on the local radio, and record sales were progressively exceeding estimated figures. The orchestras that served as the star attractions for run-of-the-mill Saturday television shows began to come from New York, and those orchestras also made appearances at the riotous dances in La Guaira's Passenger Terminal and other low-income venues in the capital. Little by little, however, the concerts became more polished, a strange phenomenon, considering our society at the time, and one that indicated the importance of this new euphoria for Caribbean music. In 1975, for instance, Antón, a salsa entrepreneur who was very adventurous and irresponsible, decided to stage a supposed International Festival of Salsa in the new Poliedro de Caracas. The festival, in which Ismael Rivera, El Gran Combo, Cheo Feliciano, and La Típica 73 participated, was an unprecedented display of what was happening: after years of being marginalized by international pop trends and by radio programs in Venezuela that catered to the industry's publicity, Caribbean popular music was experiencing a tremendous renaissance. Our one and only, enduring music had transcended exclusive national barriers to become an outstanding global manifestation of an entire region of the continent.

I remember, for instance, one night of the festival—nearly early morning—when Daniel Santos, a character who was cloaked in the popular mythology that goes beyond generational differences, was onstage. The audience listened to him in a kind of ritualistic silence. I had never seen a human mass of such great number entranced in such a way by the figure of an old, gray-haired man who barely moved while he sang his boleros. Ibsen Martínez, who was with me at the time, mentioned this very detail: "When would we have imagined that Daniel Santos would be singing in a concert, a concert of boleros and in front of such a crowd?" In effect, the era of inferiority complexes and forced imitations had come to an end. The youth, who years before had tried to translate the aura of Woodstock into an ill-fated rock concert in Playa de los Cocos, now found itself in awe before an authentic local Woodstock, as immense and ostentatious as the other, but instead of reflecting unfamiliar experiences, it was imbued with those that colored their own lives and the lives of their parents. Unsurprisingly, then, Venezuelans discovered that they did not have to resort to imitations; they discovered that "our music" was better than that of others, or, undoubtedly, just as worthy.

This, more or less, was the tone that would be developed in all of the future discussions about the cultural identity, uprootedness, and cultural unity of the Caribbean and of Latin America. The salsa boom gave rise to a theoretical discussion, a fruitful and significant conversation that pervaded universities and high schools, youth groups, and even the parties where the dance began to take on a new importance. However, let us momentarily leave aside all of the consequences of the boom and the phenomenon of the salsa industry, since later pages in this book will address the considerations that lent a special value to salsa beyond its commercial circumstances. Let us now continue with La Dimensión and the emergence of the salsa fever in Venezuela.

In 1976 La Dimensión Latina released the album *Salsa brava*, which was less polished than its previous album but which had caught the fever. Having found its sales formula, La Dimensión could not be expected to abandon it. Thus, while all of their future albums were progressively less interesting, more repetitive, and dull, their sales, rather than decreasing, increased substantially. With the album of 1976, La Dimensión popularized "Si tú supieras" in addition to "Dolor cobarde" and, most noticeably, "El frutero," an old Cuban classic written by a very special individual, Félix B. Caignet, none other than the author of *El derecho de nacer*, the super radio and television hit that had brought tears to the eyes of more than one generation across the continent.

By this time, La Dimensión was the most important thing to have happened in Venezuelan popular music. They hardly had time to satisfy all of their dance contracts, television presentations, El Poliedro concerts, and even bullfight performances. For a long time, they had been the opening act for the Sunday amateur bullfights in the new Circus of Caracas. This was the best indicator of the renaissance of Caribbean music, summarized now under the generalized term of "salsa," a Caribbean music that was beginning to recover the old terrain it had lost in the times of pop music and silly ballads sung in English. The hype that arose now was of such magnitude that before the end of the year, La Dimensión had released yet another new album: *Dimensión Latina en Nueva York*. This was a truly important album because it was the last one that Oscar D'León recorded with the orchestra. Its title, a tacit recognition of the New York avant-garde, also implied an interesting shift: not only had Venezuela cultivated its own salsa expression, but it was now in a position to export that expression to audiences elsewhere in the Caribbean and even to New York, which was still considered the capital of salsa.

La Dimensión Latina's first visit to New York was a total success. The public of the north, accustomed to full and aggressive rhythms, overlooked the weak beat of the Venezuelan orchestra, applauding them, rather, for those details and variations that were not present in New York salsa: crafted and resonant voices, choruses rich in harmony and color, and a stage spectacle that was never developed by the New York bands. (Although, granted, the albums of New York salsa employ their own rich and effective choruses, none of those included the full participation of members of the orchestra: the voice of the singer, in these cases, was accompanied only by the weak and intermittent voices of one of the musicians of the orchestra, and this, obviously, resulted in less quality.) By contrast to those groups that limited their stage presentation to the simple performance of the music, without enhancing that presentation with any dancing or color, La Dimensión appeared as a wonderfully fresh, new orchestra. Not only did their costumes draw attention, but the musicians also used choreography to illustrate the phrases of the music. La Dimensión put onstage a large array of musicians: the three trombone players (at this point Carlos Guerra had joined the band as first trombone), Wladimir on the guiro, and Oscar D'León, who attracted special attention by using his bass as if it were his dancing partner, stroking it and moving it around during his singing and montunos. In the back row, besides Chuito at the piano, was Pacheco on the tumbadora, and Rodríguez played the timbales, the small timbales, and the bells. These three musicians also performed, whenever possible, the same steps of the orchestra's choreography. La Dimensión, therefore, presented a total spectacle when they performed, and this surprised and captivated New York audiences who had been used to sedentary bands who offered nothing visually to mirror the emotions that their music triggered aurally.

Any reader, however, could argue that the use of choreography, far from being an exclusive feature of La Dimensión, had been a standard part of most Caribbean orchestras. For instance, we all remember those old big bands that limited the choreography to movements of each section (saxophones, trombones, and trumpets), once the mambo and the montuno 223 sections came along. This is precisely the interesting difference between the New York and Caribbean orchestras. The former, despite their clear Latin or Caribbean essence, were not able to give up certain forms and habits of U.S. music. Since jazz musicians, who attracted the greatest audiences, performed their music without any visual elements—without the spectacle—the salsa musicians of New York, then, did not feel obliged to complement their music with dancing. This, however, was never the case in the Caribbean, even with the Puerto Rican orchestras who recorded for Fania. For example, Roberto Roena added a sparkling flair to his concerts by moving from his bongo to dancing and back again. Rather than being merely anecdotal or superficial, this difference between New York and Caribbean orchestras began to take on a very special significance.

This difference had to do with the conceptualization behind the music and the meaning that the music acquired. While U.S. musicians had to invent diverse musical styles in response to the dominating influence of jazz, the trends in Caribbean music acquired their popularity to the degree that the music invited dancing. (To a certain extent, popularity is intimately intertwined with the commercial aspect of music, and this tends to favor music that is accessible, that is, less sophisticated or less complex and less demanding music.) Speaking from the U.S. point of view, then, music that is intrinsically of good quality must gradually avoid the kinds of performances designed to meet the demands of the dancing audience. This is what happened with rock and roll. Once it started to become the image and symbol of a whole generation and culture (rock as counterculture was the mantra used by the majority), it abandoned its role as dance music that had characterized it from its beginnings in the 1950s. Similarly, therefore, salsa musicians in New York, who started to imbue the music with a range of values that are not necessarily linked to dancing, did not feel compelled to augment their live performances with any element that was extraneous to the music itself.

The problem, however, as I have already mentioned, was with the conceptualization of the music. From the Caribbean perspective, the quality of the music did not come from sacrificing its support of dancing; rather, it grew out of that very role. This does not suggest a mediocre category of "music to dance to," either; instead it emphasizes that the music, in addition to its own quality, innovations, and variations as music, also carries within itself the condition of the dance. In our part of the world, making music that cannot be danced to simply makes no sense. This approach to the music is quite different from the very exclusionist thinking in the United States. There the assumed conflict between quality music and dance music is so pronounced that one ends up denying the other. Here,

224

on the contrary, both categories of music are fused, mutually supportive, and inevitably complementary. Obviously, in the New York salsa scene, the U.S. view of popular music never eradicated the Caribbean idea, which continued to guide the development of salsa, despite the "majestic" construction of North American culture. Even if they seldom used any visual enhancements, New York Latin orchestras always performed music that inevitably encouraged their audiences to dance.

By performing live, La Dimensión Latina located themselves within the tradition of the Caribbean orchestra. In their case, the tradition was updated with new variants and styles. The primary attraction of the orchestra, however, was much more than their fabulous stage presentations. Old boleros intertwined with montunos sung by the exceptional singer Oscar D'León captivated audiences and set new standards for the singers who followed. By 1976, when the salsa world was so full of singers forced into stardom, Oscar D'León was developing into a truly special sonero with his own unique style that showed little influence from any of his peers or predecessors. D'León's talent came from his ability to fulfill the fundamental, age-old requirements of singers of the son: first, the clarity and strength to sing the "lyrical" part, or the son itself, and secondly, the creativity to invent, through both the music and the words, the development of the montuno. Given the proliferation of singers that the salsa boom induced, good soneros were few and far between. Most of the singers exhibited hardly any interest in the son, not to mention the montuno, where these singers generally resorted to phrases and melodic turns long established by the great, old soneros. Oscar D'León rose above this mountain of mediocrity. He added a touch of novelty to the old sones, and he made the montuno his specialty, playing a continuous and clever game with the melodies while having at hand the perfect phrase to extend the sense and spirit of the songs that he interpreted. Audiences, therefore, paid special attention to La Dimensión Latina because of the energy and style of D'León. When he left the band, it quickly went down hill.

Before the end of 1976, when radio stations were still playing hits from *La Dimensión Latina in New York*, such as "Don Casimiro," "Mi sufrimiento," and "Divina niña," the salsa world in Venezuela was shaken by upsetting news: La Dimensión had split up, and Oscar had left. The orchestra tried to recover from this loss with Argenis Carrullo, a veteran singer of the Zulian gaita who knew how to adapt to the salsa style. To replace D'León as a bass player, the orchestra added Gustavo Carmona, a young expert in the nightclub bands of the city and one who demanded from his fellow musicians the capacity to "play everything, absolutely everything." With these two new musicians, plus the special place that the hype from their previous albums had secured for them among the local dancing audience, La Dimensión was able to survive the blow. Despite the poor quality of the album they released in 1977, they dominated the market with "Flores para tu altar" and "Dame tu querer," two old Cuban songs that clearly revealed the inexcusable thematic limitations not only of La Dimensión but of all Venezuelan salsa and, really, of the majority of Caribbean and New York musical production. Carrullo stayed with the group for only a few months. When he decided to leave, La Dimensión executed a brilliant stroke: They hired Andy Montañez, one of the idols of Puerto Rican salsa, and the pillar of El Gran Combo de Puerto Rico.

Montañez's hiring illustrated a fact that shaped much of the salsa boom: Venezuela is where the money is. In Venezuela, musicians charge the most and albums sell the most. Montañez signed for an incredibly high salary in the salsa world, an amount that turned Venezuela into a sort of flea market where the most mediocre items could be bought and sold easily. In the Caribbean, but mostly in New York, Venezuela began to be seen as a bazaar, an "Ali Baba's cave," where any price could be justified and where fraud ran rampant. Venezuelan oil paid for the decadence of the salsa boom, for a salsa that, lacking any real musical value or creativity, was inundated with repetition, imitation, and ego. Had Venezuela not opened up to salsa, the boom would not have lasted as long as it did: Just at the right time, our country emerged as the right place, uniquely situated to provide the maximum support. However, once times changed and new directions arose, the role of Venezuela also proved very important for preserving other styles and trends. This happened after the boom had died down, and so I will come back to it later.

In 1977, despite the fact that Andy Montañez was a resourceful and experienced singer, he never fully became a part of La Dimensión. Many fans felt disappointed, since there had been talk of "El Gran Combo de Venezuela," an evident irony, given that this group was far from achieving the expected innovations such a title implied. Instead, they limited themselves to the comforts of what was already established, producing music that was increasingly repetitive and sterile. Thus, when the local audience began to demand an expression that somehow would represent Venezuela specifically, La Dimensión responded with the poorly chosen "Por el camino," a joropo arranged in the salsa clave rhythm and with a rather condescending montuno that sang to the farmer, the rancher, and the valet, mixing the three, in a forced and awkward way, into one entity. La Dimensión's "Por el camino" serves, then, as a good illustration of what was going on with salsa at this time.

La Dimensión now realized that they had to make their music much more Venezuelan; they realized that their fame and easy sales had distanced them from the appeal they first held for local audiences. However, instead of confronting the problem head-on, they decided to attack it from the periphery. Thus, instead of singing about the urban experience of the Caracas resident (after all, salsa will always be an exclusively urban phenomenon), they sang about the countryside. Here they committed two errors. First, they ignored the real theme of salsa, and second, they approached a strange world—the Venezuelan plains—from the false and stereotypical perspective of city dwellers who cannot possibly convey, let alone embody, the rural life of the rancher. In addition, in a strictly musical context, the "Venezuela-izing" that La Dimensión experimented with included something even more dangerous: the joropo. At this point, we need to dedicate some discussion to a very important, related theme: Venezuelan popular music of *today*.

On one hand, as a consequence of awkward and self-enclosed cultural politics, Venezuelans who grew up under democracy have been given only a limited understanding of our national music. They understand that, par excellence, the music of Venezuela is the joropo, and, mistakenly, by extension, they think it represents all of the rustic folklore. Given its preeminence, by virtue of a bureaucratic decree, Venezuela lacks a contemporary expression. Yet, a country that was now predominantly urban could hardly be sung to with a rural perspective. Resorting to folklore, it seems, and only to it, censored or cut off any contemporary *popular* expression that could emerge spontaneously from the lived reality that colored the experiences of contemporary Venezuelans. This, of course, leads to a discussion about cultural identity, because, in the long run, it reveals the shameful disenfranchisement of large numbers of young people. Having been subjected to the vertigo of contemporary urban life, even when they got the chance to sing something of their own (*our own*, the authentic?), they were forced to sing the bucolic songs of a placid countryside far removed from them, and of a sweet cow whom they never, not even by mistake, had to milk.

La Dimensión bought into this flawed idea of custom, took on the joropo as the only means of making Venezuelan music, and ignored the variants that were actually relevant. For instance, the gaita is the only *Venezuelan* form able to draw in the majority of our audiences by stirring up in them a spontaneous and profuse sense of rootedness. Likewise, the old *merengue caraqueño* (or the *guasa* that always accompanied it), another important musical form, was grossly overlooked due to the indifference or ignorance of the planners of our cultural and political development, being too bogged down, as they were, in bureaucracy and conformity. I could continue to name any number of rhythmic variants characteristic of the central coast that also could have reflected the spirit of the urban life of our times. But no, for Venezuelans, Venezuelan music officially begins and ends in the prairie, and nothing else matters. The alternative for La Dimensión, then, seemed obvious: True Venezuelan salsa could be nothing else but a salsa-joropo, complete with harp, cuatro, and even maracas.

The intentions to make a specifically Venezuelan salsa resulted in a musical pastiche. It is necessary to emphasize this desired specificity because, in effect, salsa was already a legitimately Venezuelan phenomenon to the degree that it represented the urban feeling of all Caribbean communities and, therefore, Venezuelan urban residents as well. Any attempt to make a particularly "Venezuelan" salsa needed to start from there: in the urban, not the rural, reality. Clearly, the protagonists of urban everyday life did not see themselves mirrored directly in the lyrics and forms of the salsa produced in Venezuela, because the local musicians felt an exaggerated dependency on New York and Puerto Rican expressions. The intent of "Por el camino," for example, had its direct antecedent in the "Cunaviche adentro" of Alí Primera, arranged into a salsa version by El Gran Combo de Puerto Rico. The starting point, then, was not even Venezuelan. However, before I mention all of the Venezuelan orchestras who threw themselves into the frenzy for salsa without making any major contributions or innovations, let us focus on the figure who, with or without La Dimensión, continued to represent the avant-garde and to offer a viable model for national fans: Oscar D'León.

In the early months of 1977, Oscar started his own orchestra, characterized by its combination of trumpets and trombones, an orchestra that he somewhat arrogantly called La Salsa Mayor (The Principal Salsa). Fans swarmed to buy their first album, which initiated a series of albums of varying quality but of steadily increasing sales. With this first album, Oscar abandoned the simplistic approaches that he had performed with La Dimensión and launched into a salsa much more in line with the innovative and forward-looking elements of Caribbean (and especially Puerto Rican) music. Almost inevitably, in keeping with the general tendency, this album revisited a good deal of the repertoire from the Cuban guaracha, sometimes without any fresh ambition or showiness. Nevertheless, it also showed enough of the musicians' own intelligence and flair, as in "Tú no sabes na," the first big hit of this new orchestra. However, the really interesting song on this initial album was the son that Oscar D'León composed himself, a son in the best tradition of the cadence, strikingly effective and full of sabor: "Oscar D'León has come back without hurting anyone / The world belongs to everyone, and that's why I want to sing to all."

The rest of the lyrics once again affirmed how much Caribbean orchestras enjoyed new challenges, although this was perhaps a more personal than professional inclination among the musicians. This son also fed into the continuous rumors about the breakup of La Dimensión. The general impression was that the orchestra had split up over money. It seems that the great sums that they were charging had become insufficient for satisfying the individual greed that arose among the group's members. Oscar, who in most of the rumors appeared to be the bad guy, decided to fight back with this son.

His second album, also released in 1977, revealed a more ambitious Oscar with a more pronounced sonero role, even though the general quality of the music he interpreted was rather static. The arrangements seemed particularly uninspired, and except for the virtues of Oscar's voice, the montunos were also unremarkable. Still, the album set unheard-of sales records, given the limited, local recording industry, and it included a few hits, such as "Huele a quemao," written by Oscar himself. The song that became most important, however, was "Mata siguaraya," the old son by Lino Frías that Benny Moré had made a classic. This, precisely, was the challenge: to take a song made famous by another voice and remake it so well that it would not be ridiculed. Oscar did just that and became great. I mention this, however, not to be impertinent or to make a value judgment between the two versions, since each has to be seen in its own context. In the case of the original "Siguaraya," Benny worked with the musical patterns of his times, that is, with the son preeminent over the montuno, with brief mambos, and without a single solo by any of the other musicians. Oscar's version represented a clear counterschema. He had the montuno convey all of the power of the theme, and he added considerably longer mambos and a couple of solos by other orchestra members. Thus, even though the four improvisations done by Benny in the montuno are considered classics, the greater coup of his version lies in the son itself, while in Oscar's rendition the opposite is true. To judge them side by side, then, makes no sense. The interesting thing, for a change, is to see how Oscar dealt with the challenge of reshaping a canonical piece, without taking away anything from the original or from its salsa version. In this way, he extended the life of the song itself and also paid homage to the memory of Benny, the sonero par excellence, as he has been lauded so many times throughout the musical world.

By this time Oscar was already a star in Venezuela. In the dance clubs where he performed, he drew the largest crowds who, in most cases, refrained from dancing in order to line up along the front of the stage where Oscar made his bass playing and his singing into a spectacular performance. Likewise, every time he held a concert, as soon as he was announced, the audience went wild with applause, professing almost hysterical adulation that reminded me of those famous human throngs so common during the pop concerts in the 1960s. His third album, released at the beginning of 1978, sold more than 100,000 copies in the first weeks (a top figure and an incredible one for the national market). The album "open-fired" with the merengue "Juanita Morel" by Luis Kalaff, and the whole album represented all that was happening in the larger world of salsa at the height of the boom. At this point, the music had become inbred, producing little more than repetitions and imitations and saved, in a few cases, only by the talent and charisma of a special performer. Of course, Oscar, being one of those performers, was able to produce albums, such as this one from 1978, *El Oscar de la salsa*, that, despite some remakes and other vestiges of conformity, did present clear and stimulating options for the development of the salsa expression. As we have seen, Oscar's albums always had at least one or two songs that deserve special mention, and those cuts validate all of his albums. In this 1978 production, Oscar D'León fell back on traditional cuts that had been repeated ad nauseam by others. For example, he recorded "Suavecito" and "El que siembra su maíz," both by the easygoing Matamoros; however, he also delivered a new son, one imbued with personal and mysterious lyrics that immediately and totally capture the listener: "Siéntate ahí." This theme blended the peculiarity of its lyrics with a powerful musical arrangement. The lyrics are straightforward and tell a story that everyone can relate to while hinting at the melodramatic and almost blurring the two. The arrangement—perhaps Oscar's best ever—likewise conveys sounds of everyday life in Caracas infused with a slow and weighed-down spirit, all without letting the showy harmonics undercut either the melodic theme or the rhythms. The third attraction was none other than Oscar himself and his unique ability to bring the drama to life:

> Sit there
> And wait for me to pass by
> So that you will see the fruit of our desire.

Around this same time, however, money problems and personal ambitions threatened the relationship between Oscar and his musicians. One day the entertainment press woke up to the news that all of La Salsa Mayor had left Oscar D'León, except for Enrique "Culebra" Iriarte, who stayed on as pianist and arranger. After a dispute that was resolved by legal means, the new band decided to call itself Nuestra Orquesta: La Salsa Mayor, with Alfredo Padilla, the veteran timbalist, as its director. The group was built, basically, around Oscar's old musicians. Among them, the best known were Leo Pacheco, the singer who was used simply to support the choruses, William Puchi on trombone, and Henry Camba on trumpet. Initially, this new orchestra received backing from the Velvet label, which was beginning to make its way into the larger world of salsa. Following the precedent set by La Dimensión, they filled out their vocals with the addition of Pellín Rodríguez, the Puerto Rican veteran and another mainstay on the early albums of El Gran Combo de Puerto Rico, and Carlos El Grande, a young Panamanian who had been discovered by the musicians on one of the many tours that they had made to Panama with D'León.

When La Salsa Mayor entered the local scene, Venezuela was already the principal market for international salsa; sales there doubled and even tripled the totals made in New York and in the Caribbean. This was why Caracas became not just an alternative for many musicians but also often their only hope. With the boom nearly exhausted by mismanagement and stagnant development, the money to be made from Venezuelan fans enabled the survival of a good number of artists who, however, had hardly any importance for the salsa style as a whole. The Venezuelan world was caught up in a frenzy that confused the good with the bad and was incapable of distinguishing between authenticity and gimmicks, but it had enough money to pay for any fad. It began to spotlight many orchestras and artists that are no longer even worth mentioning. Furthermore, homegrown bands, desperate for the easy money to be made, apparently, on any corner, found themselves thrown into the middle of this economic free-for-all, only to end up as its first and most exploited victims. They forfeited all of their creative potential, were reduced not just to imitations but to imitations of bad music, and wound up completely out of luck.

The first album of La Salsa Mayor, for instance, reveals a band with good musicians and interesting arrangements. Nevertheless, this album sticks out for being at least ten years behind: Its material was identical to what had been produced before and too similar to the work being done by a majority of the bands that survived only by inhaling the artificial oxygen exhaled by the boom. I mention La Salsa Mayor because it was one of the *best* Venezuelan orchestras, one with highly talented musicians capable of performing the boldest and most diverse repertoire of music from throughout the Caribbean. But the band, far from taking advantage of those alternatives, limited itself to the old Cuban store from which it selected whatever would satisfy the hunger of the industry. In light of this overview, we easily could end up scolding only the musicians when, in fact, despite their best intentions and their indisputable talents as interpreters, they were merely pawns in the complex game of the recording industry.

As I have mentioned before, far from creating victims, they were victims themselves.

The case of La Salsa Mayor was repeated in almost all of the bands of the period. Some were luckier than others, but all remained second rate, contributing nothing special or of lasting importance. Most of the groups that emerged after the initial takeoff of La Dimensión Latina began to work with the trombone formulas, imitating the same patterns without adding any interesting variants. Also, thanks to the boom, two of the orchestras that were key to the popularity of salsa in Venezuela in the prior decade reappeared: Los Dementes and Federico and his Combo. The former re-emerged under the initiative of Ray Pérez, who previously had tried to take advantage of the salsa fever with a band called Casabe, only to have it totally ignored by local audiences. In this second attempt, Los Dementes tried again by emphasizing the sounds of the trombone combined, here and there, with the violins; still, they had none of the sparkle or spunk of the original group. Their vocalist, Teo Hernández, was young and talented but lacked the essential reach needed during this period inundated with salsa. The new Dementes, though now recording for the almost omnipotent Fania label, died with their second album, the musicians scattering before the strong indifference of the public.

Federico and his Combo were more fortunate. Although none of their albums made it big, the band did record with certain regularity, and they maintained the minimal average of dance gigs that ensured the livelihood of the musicians. This was due to the considerable influence of Federico Betancourt, whose sizzling energy "took charge" of the Combo. Betancourt was able to come up with engaging arrangements that met the expectations of both the dancers and those salsa fans accustomed to the aggressive styles determined by the first wave of New York innovations. Federico returned to the songs by Dimas Pedroza, an unpretentious and capable sonero. Occasionally he also called on Orlando Watusi, a long-standing and talented professional musician. The most interesting addition to Federico's reformulated Combo was Canelita Medina, an old guarachera from the Caracas scene who, for whatever reason, had never become famous or garnered the prestige that she more than deserved. Even with its reputation, however, Federico and his Combo never became more than a footnote in the salsa boom that had rewritten the former values and views of quality music. The Combo played its role without any fanfare, and much better than others.

Another Venezuelan orchestra that was able to acquire some success during the salsa boom was Los Satélites, a band that preceded La Dimensión Latina but that had to follow Dimensión's lead in order to distribute its records. Of all the bands during this period, Los Satélites most closely followed the New York styles, something that led to a very shaky situation for them. To Venezuelans, they sounded like a foreign band; to outsiders, they seemed to be just another band without any uniqueness or major achievements. The song that brought them the most success was the old bolero "Maybá," which introduced a young singer who later became famous: Rodrigo Mendoza. With a sharp timbre to his powerful voice, Mendoza was able to create his own style. After Los Satélites, Mendoza moved on to D'León's original La Salsa Mayor; later he joined La Dimensión Latina, but despite having some hits with the group, he did not remain with them for long.

This kind of desertion caused one of the most common and deadly problems of the Venezuelan orchestras: the inability to maintain stable groups who could then focus on the development and production of equally reliable music. The problem was too much easy money. For so many years musicians had learned to follow the "tiger"—to live constantly on the move, without any economic security, and depend completely on the whims of a disorganized record industry. They had nothing to count on but luck and the generosity of some entrepreneur. The surprising arrival of the recording boom, of a crazy fever for salsa, turned out to be, in a sorry sort of paradox, a destructive phenomenon. Since the boom did not require high quality or any specialization from the musicians or orchestras, musicians felt they had the right to multiply their opportunities as they desired, spawning copycat orchestras regardless of talent or purpose. It was as if they were desperately and frantically trying to absorb the lucrative waters of this oasis after so many years of poverty and drought.

Attempting to win dance contracts and get their names out to the public through the mediocre Venezuelan radio stations, the musicians took to the streets with records they had produced overnight, albums that, from the cover to the very grooves of the vinyl, were of exceptionally poor quality. The only worthwhile thing to come of this is this anecdote, and that is very unfortunate. Having known so many of these musicians, having listened to them talk about their passion for music and for the musical profession, and having seen them perform amazing and unexpected marvels in many of the nightclubs around the city, I came to the inevitable conclusion that they were good musicians, that some were excellent artists, and that all were worthy representatives of this popular genre. Those same virtues, however, rarely translated onto their albums or into their television, radio, and stage performances. Such a realization makes this situation even more unfortunate.

To borrow a metaphor from Joselo—the fabulous Venezuelan comic who created, among many other characters, the famous old man of the *marabunta*, a type of terrible plague, a disease that consumes a person from the inside out—we could call this period of the boom "the marabunta of salsa." Far from benefiting musicians, it devoured them. I assert this because in the long run, even if we ended up with a few extra bolivares, we have nothing left of the music, and the music, finally, was always our concern. Even when we pose the problem in strict economic terms, it is essential to realize that only the things of quality, only those things that are interesting and innovative, receive the support of capital in any concrete and meaningful way. Thus, despite all the bolivares so plentiful in the middle of the boom, once the hype ended and the marabunta was over, those gains ultimately proved insufficient and incidental, like the fortunes of our boxers who, overnight, become nothing more than a sad memory.

In the midst of the marabunta, there were some orchestras that the boom sustained. Radio distribution, however, was erratic, with some groups receiving exaggerated airtime, thanks to paid plugging, and others getting virtually no airtime at all. Similarly, these groups had varying degrees of fortune: some had weeklong lineups of dance gigs; others, one or two bimonthly performances. Their music, too, varied in quality. Here I refer to such orchestras as La Banda and his Salsa Joven, Grupo Tres, La Crítica, Sexteto Juventud (another reinvented veteran band from the old times), Tabaco and his Sexteto, Orquesta Palladium, Orquesta La Sociedad, Orquesta la Selección, Ideal 78, Rebelión 75, Yacambú, Don Filemón y su Banda, Noraida y los Moré, Explosión Latina, Los Compadres, Los Pacheco, and Grupo Clave. In addition, these groups incorporated, in one "salsa" way or another, veterans of the traditional Caribbean expressions: Porfi Jiménez, Johnny Cedes, Nelson and his Estrellas, Supercombo Los Tropicales, Los Blanco, Los Solistas (a band derived from the Los Melódicos), and finally, the same Melódicos, Renato Capriles, and the Billo Caracas Boys—orchestras that were strongly established in the dance traditions of Venezuela.

Lastly, before ending this section on the Venezuelan salsa orchestras, I must mention two groups that even without major backing from the industry were able to develop projects of great interest. One of them was Grupo Mango, which emerged in 1975, and the second was La Descarga de los Barrios, an initiative that began in 1978. The former, Grupo Mango, arose from the regular jamming sessions staged by some of the nightclub musicians in the city. After satisfying the bland tastes of their regular audiences, when it was already deep into the night, when only those music lovers avid for the real thing remained in the club, these musicians experimented with their personal music. The group had no fixed structure;

anybody could jam with them. Gradually, however, they became more organized. I remember meeting them when they had just named themselves Ajoporro and his Legumbres, after the pianist Moisés Daubeterre, more commonly known as "Ajoporro." Ajoporro, the principal singer of the group, soon became its focal point. One fine day, however, the record producer Orlando Montiel gave them the opportunity to make a recording. They then decided to change their name, since the former one was a rather irreverent slang idiom. Hence, Grupo Mango and their first album, which remains one of the most complete productions ever done in the whole of salsa. The group, once organized into an official orchestra, was reduced to a sextet: Freddy Roldán on vibraphone; Moisés "Ajoporro" Daubeterre, piano and voice; Argenis Carmona, bass; Cheo Navarro, timbal; Gustavo Quinto, congas; and Luis Gamboa, bongos and bells. This structure was clearly the same as the one used by Joe Cuba ten years earlier, and this was the group's principal weakness: a forced association with the New York precedent. Connected with this weakness, the group even said that it was a second Joe Cuba Sextet, but they did so without recognizing the evident distance between the two bands, regardless of their having a similar structure. However, the real difficulty that the group faced was in the type of music that they chose to develop: a music that did not conform to the styles and tendencies imposed by the boom, a music that tried to move into new, more meaningful, and interesting directions. The recording industry, of course, could not accept this. The industry, at least in Venezuela, had erased from its vocabulary the terms "creativity," "innovation," and "originality." Grupo Mango, then, was left to be applauded by those isolated music lovers who could not be bought.

Analyzing all of this from a distance, we could make the mistake of considering Mango as just another group; they began as a simple gathering of friends, of musicians who periodically escaped the tiger in order to set free the good music they wanted to make. Perhaps the real loss of Grupo Mango came with that inevitable and probably necessary step—from being a group that occasionally jammed together to a stable one with regular sessions. However, even once Mango became an official sextet, they welcomed as their own some of the best musicians in the local scene. To give just one example, Mango brought in Joe Ruiz, a veteran singer of salsa with years of experience serving the tiger and endowed with the most outstanding abilities characteristic of the best Caribbean singers. But for various reasons (and not always musical ones), Ruiz never distinguished himself with the propriety required of the industry. The huge public, prey to the gimmicks and goals of radio and recording magnates, ended up applauding singers, national and foreign, who should have been overshadowed by this black singer; instead, he was ignored for the remainder of the boom. The reader must realize that Ruiz's case is not an isolated one but representative of what happened once salsa had become a million-dollar industry. There were many good singers, excellent ones like Ruiz, who were lost in the anonymity of a solitary club or of an independent album produced outside the big monopolies. In the long run, the industry created and accrued a list of stars while unfairly ignoring other soneros who were equally or potentially more important but were unfortunate victims of deceptions and dark deals. The reader must realize also that this happened not only in Venezuela but in Puerto Rico, Santo Domingo, Panama, and New York, where many individuals lost ground to the public relations machinery devoted to other singers.

As a final example of the uneven situation created by the Venezuelan salsa boom, I will mention the album *Alfredito and His Stars*. It was produced on a shoestring budget by Alfredo Linares, an excellent Peruvian pianist and veteran of the same club music. Grupo Mango and some of Linares's old friends contributed to the recording, with the vocals performed by Joe Ruiz. This lone album, produced with little interest by a record company of little means, received hardly any airtime and really no reviews, favorable or otherwise, by the music critics, yet it remains a striking example of good salsa. Despite the pressures of the marabunta, it continues to linger in the air, hinting—more shyly than we would like—at a quality that never really disappears. At the time, though, things were so hard that, except for the musicians who participated on the album, I think I was one of the few aficionados who ended up with a copy. The last I heard, Alfredo Linares was in Billo's orchestra, repeating the same canned routines in one of those abominable Saturday shows staged by our new television personality Amador Bendayán.

La Descarga de los Barrios, on the other hand, never had the opportunity to record anything, let alone to appear on radio or television. An initiative of the percussionist Pedro Villoria, La Descarga suggested the occasional gathering of random musicians who met in various barrios in Caracas in order to, as its name indicates, jam in the open air. Thus, in a very spontaneous way, the more humble sectors of the capital were given the pleasure of a music that belonged to them and that they could enjoy in a straightforward and immediate way, not in the limited forms and absurd styles pushed on them by the salsa industry. These jam sessions provided an authentic source of pride and a healthy, musical passion. Without any commercial backing, they allowed the same talented musicians to get together who otherwise regularly had to compromise their abilities on albums and in orchestras of poor quality and little significance. Of course,

I have already discussed how popular music, if it occurs only in isolated, anonymous, or expected spaces, can no longer ensure its permanence or its authentic connection to the people, especially once the culture of our time becomes defined and disseminated according to industry standards. La Descarga, for example, never went beyond its good intentions of being the laid-back and happenstance gatherings of good musicians who wanted to make good music. Its very essence made it unacceptable to the industry and also limited the innovations and experiments that it could have achieved. The situation was so drastic that if La Descarga had adapted to the great salsa industry, it would have lost what made it authentic, valuable, and unique. Thus, even as I typed these words, La Descarga de los Barrios was only a memory—nothing more than a simple anecdote of a friendly little group.

As I close this chapter, it seems appropriate to highlight an important fact: the innovative musical virtues of Grupo Mango and the gathering of diverse musicians by La Descarga arose freely and independently in another project. This project also was attracted to the musical avant-gardes that have embraced infinite musicians with different backgrounds but who perform with the same quality and share the same passion. This project exceeded and extended the experiments that Mango had imagined and only tentatively begun. In contrast to what happened to La Descarga, this project was also able to document its achievements on the album, since it was conceived *as* an album. The project that I refer to is El Trabuco Venezolano. More than an orchestra, it was an authentic Venezuelan salsa movement, created through the direct initiative of Orlando Montiel and Alberto Naranjo, who, surprisingly, decided to make music and not business matters their priority. I will discuss El Trabuco more fully in the next chapter because how the group was formed and the music it recorded take us beyond the sense and spirit of this present chapter.

EIGHT : ANOTHER THING

In 1974, a group of young musicians in the Bronx formed a band that came to be called Conjunto Anabacoa. Amid the regular work that salsa required, their idea was to do nothing but get together and jam, to develop freely the music that they were most excited about. They had no pretensions to record, not even to have an audience, given how small the crowds were that turned out to listen to them. This was a private project, one of those groups that arose from the exclusive pleasure of the musicians themselves.

Eventually, however, they were invited by Wesleyan University to give a series of recitals to illustrate, in a purer and fresher way, the characteristics of Latin music in New York. It was then that the González brothers, Andy and Jerry, having prompted this gathering of colleagues and friends, decided to give a name to the improvised group. They named it Anabacoa after an old son by Arsenio Rodríguez, a son that the group interpreted with special feeling. For the recitals, Andy and Jerry were joined by Nelson González on the tres, Frankie Rodríguez on the tumba, and Chocolate Armenteros, the veteran Cuban trumpet player and their former colleague in the Eddie Palmieri orchestra. Drawing on the enthusiasm triggered by the university recitals, the original group of friends began to expand considerably. René López, the musicologist who also performed as a singer, gradually emerged as the group's leader. Already by 1975, interest in the group carried beyond their occasional Saturday jam sessions, and López took the initiative of recording the group in a serious way. He also coined the name by which the group would hereafter be known: Grupo Folklórico y Experimental Nuevayorkino. Indeed, the group had been working with traditional folklore, combining it with experiments and contemporary innovations, and all with the shaping influence offered by the New York scene. The group took that approach into the recording studio, and what they produced surprisingly received unconditional applause from the entire Caribbean community.

Before the end of 1975, the group had released its first album, a double one smartly titled *Conceptos en unidad* (*Concepts in Unity*). The cover showed a long line of congas alternating the old ones with the skin nailed on with the new ones that have the skin attached by keys. This image made clear the complete synthesis that the Folklórico implied: the music of the past with the vision of today *and* the music of today with the vision of the past. In other words, folklore and experimentation were combined solidly into one music. In addition, the New York position was not taken on exclusively as a Boricua or Nuyorican characteristic that had radically nurtured the salsa boom but, rather, as a rich blend of all of the Latino communities in the city. Thus, conceptually and musically speaking, the Folklórico adroitly transcended the perspectives of the commercial music of the moment.

Recognizing that one of the principal virtues of this group was its spontaneity, López kept the musicians, once in the recording studio, from giving in to the modern technique of having the sections record separately, since this usually made the music sound sterile or cold. The Folklórico did its best work as a jam session, so when the time came to record, they would invariably have to go on jamming. López called in Fred Weinberg, a veteran Colombian musician and producer who, according to many, was the best recording engineer in the city. Weinberg immediately understood the nature of the group and their music, and he facilitated a collective recording method that allowed them to jam freely without getting in one another's way. They used the immense Plaza Sound studio—the same studio that had been designed for Toscanini—and filled it with percussion instruments strategically distributed so that they could jam with the necessary freedom.

The group's large percussion section really stood out on this first album, and it challenged the usual structure of salsa orchestras that relied on a maximum of two drummers (on conga and bongo) and the occasional addition of a timbal player. The Folklórico, by contrast, included an average of six percussionists for each song. This clearly made for a music that not only was innovative but also had a much fuller, more complete and substantive sound. The group's most prominent percussionist was Manny Oquendo, the timbalist for the original Conjunto La Perfecta led by Eddie Palmieri. Oquendo, who was born and raised in New York, never really bought into the salsa boom. Like many other musicians who developed under Palmieri's wing, he maintained a rebellious streak, and under no circumstances would Oquendo sacrifice his music for any secondary, commercial interest. As far as the local music scene was concerned, Oquendo was a master on the timbal, and despite his origin, he was also considered the most traditional of all the timbalists outside Cuba. Unlike many others who used the timbal as a mere extension of the U.S. drum set (giving up its melodic qualities for *repiques* or up-tempo redoubles), Oquendo was satisfied to work with a deeper timbal (where proper tuning made a radical difference). Rather than adopting any jazzlike or U.S. style, he remained committed to the old role that had been assigned to the timbal in the Cuban tradition: to be a bridge between the main rhythm carried by the tumbadora and the melody carried by the other instruments, especially

239

the brass. Indeed, far from being one of those drums that are limited, like the isolated snare, or like the bell that supports the montuno or the cymbals that announce the mambo, Oquendo's timbal was a drum in the fullest sense and sound, never the awkward filler that the timbal had been in salsa. Apart from the very important Cuban context, the Caribbean also had its share of bold timbalists who were influenced by Tito Puente. These include a range of stylists from the speedy Endel Dueño to the versatile and modern Nicky Marrero, passing through older (more experienced) musicians such as Vilató, Sabater, and the Venezuelan Frank Hernández and reaching toward newcomers like Jimmy Delgado, Cheo Navarro, and Cuqui Santos, for instance. However, even within this ample diversity of styles, it is very difficult to place Manny Oquendo. He clearly represents the final frontier: the most traditional of all timbalists and the one most able to handle and to master the latest avant-garde. Here you have, ladies and gentlemen, the one and only leader of the percussion section of the Grupo Folklórico and Experimental.

The rest of the Folklórico's percussion section was made up of young tumba players. They moved from the "tres" (a triple tumba, essential for playing the Cuban rumba properly) to the quinto and from the street-like redoblante (the same drum that traditionally is found enlivening small gatherings and Sunday processions) to the Brazilian *cuica*, all without ignoring the important presence of the batá drums. During the early period, the musicians who performed all these percussive feats included the following: First, there was Jerry González, the youngest of the brothers and an extraordinary trumpeter but a better tumba player, who had experience not only with salsa but also with diverse rock and jazz ensembles. Then, Frankie Rodríguez, a conga player who came from the Orquesta Harlow and who in 1973—after Ismael Miranda had left the group—went on to form part of the new Orquesta la Revelación. Milton Cardona had been the tumba player for many years in Willie Colón's band and, when that band dissolved, in Héctor Lavoe's new group. The virtuoso Jamaican conga player Gene Golden, who frequently performed on jazz recordings and was a regular in the salsa orchestra La Conspiración led by Ernie Agosto, was also in this group. The final tumba player was also later a star singer for the Folklórico, Virgilio Martí, an irreverent jammer from the legendary barrio of Cayo Hueso in Havana. Martí was directly responsible for importing many of the characteristics of the authentic Cuban rumba that were later developed in the United States.

Along with these percussionists, the second album also featured Julito Collazo. Collazo was an expert in Afro-Cuban religious music, and all of the Latino drummers in New York had long considered him *the* authority on Caribbean rhythms. The U.S. soneros Chef Bay and Bess Taylor also joined the group, and the Brazilian percussionists Porthinho and Guillermi Franco were brought in when the Folklórico needed to perform sambas from the south. Oscar Hernández, Nelson González, and Andy González completed the rhythm section. Hernández was a young pianist who had been strongly influenced by Palmieri and who began his salsa career with La Revelación. He had the ability to move easily between the traditional and the avant-garde styles. Nelson González also came from La Revelación, and Andy González, the older brother, not only played bass but also became the natural leader of the newly expanded and renamed Anabacoa.

The brass section was comprised of two trombones (because New York required it), a trumpet, and a sax. The two trombonists were José Rodríguez, the Brazilian master, and Reinaldo Jorge, the young but experienced Puerto Rican. On trumpet was Alfredo "Chocolate" Armenteros, the most Cuban and, at the same time, the most innovative of all trumpeters one could find in New York. On sax was the equally masterful Gonzalo Fernández, who, in addition to the tenor saxophone, contributed his virtuosity on the traditional wooden flute. Lastly, the "cast" of singers included, in the paradoxical case of the Folklórico, no more than two vocalists: the old Boricua Heny Alvarez, who had participated in Larry Harlow's opera, *Hommy*, and the young Cuban Willie García, whom I discussed in the section on Joe Cuba. Together with Virgilio Martí, who alternated between the tumbadora and vocals, these were the rest of the musicians who, under the production of René López, presented the first *Conceptos en unidad*.

The album opened with a nostalgic salute to the land left behind, a guaguancó titled "Cuba linda" ("Beautiful Cuba"), composed and sung by Martí. In the first part—the traditional narrative that begins every guaguancó—Martí capitalized on various traditional verses of the "Vueltabajera" by Ignacio Piñeiro in order to deliver his message: "Tan solo pido armonía entre los buenos cubanos, igual queridos hermanos, salven a la patria mía" (I only ask for harmony among the good Cubans, and also, dear brothers, please save my country). Here, what had originally been composed to attack the Machado dictatorship was now being used to question the Castro regime. It mattered little that the author of these verses, Maestro Piñeiro, had stayed in Cuba firmly supporting that same revolution that was now being attacked with his own music. However, the Folklórico, informed by an avant-garde and rebellious spirit, was far from getting caught up in the anticommunist pamphleteering pushed for by the Miami Cubans during the 1960s. René López, while known for his leftist inclinations, explained this apparent contradiction:

The group represents the Latino community in New York, a community that has strong Caribbean, Cuban, Dominican, and obviously Puerto Rican roots. We, who have been born here and have lived here, felt obligated to address, with the utmost objectivity, the whole of our world today, the world of New York. If "Cuba Linda" seems a critique, that's because it's a summary of what the city offers. Here we are, Puerto Ricans struggling to get our rights recognized by a city that is theoretically ours, but, in reality, isn't. And here are the Cubans, too, especially the poor Cubans, the workers, not the middle-class professionals, also struggling to make a decent living. They live here because they rejected Cuba's new regime, and it's not a question of whether the majority of Puerto Ricans also rejects that government. It's only that the Cubans live with us and, well, more or less, we're all in the same situation. Besides, all of the music that's made in New York, whether it's salsa or not, has very strong Cuban roots, and this, from an artistic perspective, unites us even more to the Cubans who live here now. "Cuba Linda," for us, in the Grupo, is not a song opposing what happened in Cuba, but the representation of a facet of our Latino world in New York, since, you know, everything is here.

The rest of the album developed around "La guajira de Chocolate," a traditional guajira designed to show off the Cuban trumpet player; "Carmen La Ronca," a festive and flavorful guaracha composed and sung by Heny Alvarez; and their rendition of "Anabacoa" by Arsenio Rodríguez. In each number, the Folklórico structured itself to the specific requirements of the various styles. Thus, for the guaracha, the Folklórico became a traditional conjunto (ensemble) of tumba and bongo, while for the guaguancó, the percussion section expanded to include the whole spectrum of tumbas and the quinto. In addition, reflecting on López's commentary, the Folklórico recorded a Canto Asoyin ("Arara Babaluayé") and a Canto Ebioso ("Arara Changó"), themes imbued with *santero* elements (in this case, the percussion went from the "profanity" of the tumbadoras to the "religiosity" of the batá drums). Their initial repertoire also included a Puerto Rican plena and a mazurka from Boricua folklore. Here, the traditional tambourine and the harmonica took center stage, highlighting the streetlike voice of Víctor Montañez alongside the solidly salsa-styled tres of Nelson González. The lyrics, finally, completed the portrayal of the popular culture of yesterday and today:

> If I win at pool,
> Adelaida,
> I'm going to marry you.

The last side of this double album was filled with two of the most interesting songs of their *Conceptos en unidad*: "Iya modupué" ("Thanks, Mom") and "A papá y a mamá" ("To Mom and Dad"). The first, conceived as a multiple jamming session where all the percussionists in particular took on a different Caribbean rhythm, became a signature piece of the group. It was not only the favorite among the musicians, but it also reflected the entire folkloric and experimental character that defined their project. The jamming kept to no specific beat. Instead of following the convention of jamming in montuno or in guaguancó or in mambo, the musicians threw themselves into mixing up and recombining all of the various rhythms into one musical form. The amazing thing is that at no moment are the individual rhythms marred in any way. The drummer assigned to the guaguancó indeed performed a guaguancó, and the one who had the bomba clearly played the bomba. If it had been otherwise, then the experiment would have been pointless. The other song that represented something special—amid so much that was special about this album—was "A papá . . . ," defined by its author, Heny Alvarez, as a "street guaguancó." While the song faithfully mirrors the type of guaguancó that was developed by salsa, it shows us the other side and the way out of this style. Salsa played the guaguancó with an exaggeratedly rigid rhythm to show off, instead, the harmonic flourishes. The Folklórico did exactly the opposite. They gave the rhythm absolute freedom under the encouragement of the harmonic line. That is, while the tumbadora players were developing the guaguancó in proper Cuban style, Manny Oquendo's timbal was freely coloring other riffs in dialogue with the voice of Alvarez. Of course, this is the basic pattern of the quinto in the Cuban guaguancó, but now, and in the contemporary context of salsa, the roles of these instruments were reformulated into a new standard. This came about because this guaguancó—in addition to its streetlike character and despite its deep respect for the Cuban style—was basically a salsa number, a song saturated with the world of salsa. The beautiful lyrics that Heny wrote also deserve attention. They function as a majestic and poetic salute to how everyday people explain some key things about life:

Alalalalá . . .
Brother, live your life
And share what you have
Anananá Nanaynananá.

These lyrics, however, could be discarded easily for the apparent simplicity of their Oedipal connotations, when, in reality, they go much deeper. Let us analyze them, part by part. In the first place, after the "alalalá . . ."

243

that creates the musical background and mood, we encounter the reference to the friend. The singer has a doubt about something, and he asks his companion, "Si todo lo que nace sin nada de engaño viene y deja algo y luego desaparece?" (Does everything that is born without any deceit come and go, leaving something behind, later to disappear?). This question invites many interpretations; however, the most recurrent and significant one suggests a loved one or beloved. In this interpretation, the core of the song is about the pain of loving. What is born "without any deceit," leaves "something behind, and later disappears" is the same female figure whose supposed insignificance has made her the most prominent and abiding protagonist in all of popular music. The singer's dilemma, then, is how to know whether that loss is not only necessary but also reparable. The loyal friend responds with the typical aphorism, "Esa es la vida, ni más ni menos, así es siempre" (That's life, more or less, that's the way it always is), and then offers the following advice: "Seguro, monina, muchacho vive tu vida y reparte lo que traes" (Absolutely, brother [in Santería, *monina* means brother], live your life and share what you have). With these words, the singer is advised that many losses will come to him in the future, losses that inevitably come with being loved (and, inevitably as well, being unloved). From here, the lyrics conclude with an emotional appeal to life and its cycle of losses and gains: "Dale gracias a Dios, que tu inspiración te inspira y vamos a cantarle un viva a la madre que nos parió" (Thank God that your inspiration inspires you, and let us sing praise to the mother who gave us life). The reference here is not to a literal mother but to the life force itself, and to the small privilege of being able to see life from that other side of things. All of this pathos was supported by the powerful music that the Folklórico created, and that music raised the theme to a unique and extraordinary level.

Grupo Folklórico's second album, released at the end of 1976, demonstrated a richer and more mature development of their overall and ongoing project. The spirit of the Latino community in New York was expanded to include the Brazilian presence ("A meu lugar voltar"), innovations on the harmonic level were much better developed ("Corta el bonche"), the Santería elements that remained very much part of the musicians were reaffirmed ("La mama" and "Agüemimó"), the tradition of the Cuban son and guaguancó were reiterated with total respect for folklore ("Dime la verdad" and "Trompeta en cuero"), and the rhythmic blending already evident in "Iya modupué" perfectly culminated in their new song "Cinco en uno callejero." The Grupo Folklórico, then, honored all of this with the title of their second album: *Lo dice todo* (*It Says It All*).

244   Let us begin with the song "Cinco en uno" ("Five in One"). The theme,

composed by Heny Alvarez, as its name indicates, brought the five rhythms together into one clave. The Puerto Rican bomba was used as the center-piece in order to blend into it the Mozambique of the new Cuba, the Trini-dadian calypso, the Brazilian *batucada*, and the rumba, which, with its ties to many Caribbean traditions, goes well beyond its roots in Cuba. While the chorus was happily chanting,

> Your way of loving, Your way of looking
> Your way of having fun
> Crying if you want to cry

the solo voice of Heny Alvarez told the story of music,

> Open, rumba, conga, and son
> Mozambique opening up the path
> Bomba and the batucada
> Hey, let's go to the carnival.

In order to flesh out the other sides of the theme, René López recorded street noises over which the musicians came together. As López said, "This is the whole Latino community of New York, the whole diverse commu-nity becoming one single group because the music unites us all under one rhythm and one song. It is as if we were one great, big family, and the music is the blood that makes us all brothers and sisters."

For the song "Corta el bonche"—the first number that the group re-corded from written scores—the band used the conventional structure of the charanga ensemble, so violinists Alfredo de la Fe, Noel de Costa, and Gail Dixon and cellist Ron Libscomb joined the band. The theme, an old guaracha by Alberto Ruiz, had become a traditional New York salsa num-ber. Grupo Folklórico used an arrangement by Bobby Paunetto, a talented vibraphone musician of Hispano-Italian descent. Taking advantage of the creative potential that these musicians offered, Paunetto departed from the rhythmic combinations that the group had mastered already and pro-posed harmonic schemes that were totally foreign to conventional salsa arrangements. Félix Cortés accurately described the finished product in his blurb for the album cover:

> Arranged and directed by Paunetto, this song expands the combina-tion of a very prominent jazz feeling with the heavy Latino avant-garde trend. . . . The rhythm here seems even freer than the previous version recorded by Paunetto (Pathfinder PLP, 1775). . . . Again, this song has a solid hold over the diverse sources of its tradition. The chorus develops the first part of the harmony (just as in the conjuntos), while in the

245

mambo they work in unison (as in a charanga); the tumba players perform guaguancó throughout all of the introductory bars, while Manny Oquendo keeps bringing on the traditional danzón cadence, carrying it into the rest of the song.

The other song that was also "read" by the musicians was "A meu lugar voltar," a nostalgic samba that turned out to be the only composition by the veteran trombonist José Rodríguez. Initially, the lyrics were going to be sung by Rubén Blades, famous for his affinity for Brazilian music and his facility with both the Portuguese language and the characteristic phrasings and turns of the samba song. However, Fania, who had the strictest and most exclusionary policies, would not allow Blades to record with a different company, much less with the group that had so aggressively undercut the pompous image of its All Stars. In the end, Blades had to settle for contributing to the choruses, while Ubatan Do Nascimento—described to us as the "happy clockmaker from Queens"—sang the solo parts.

The two *santero* songs were composed by Cuban veterans: "Agüemimó," by Julito Collazo, was recorded with an extraordinary flute solo by Fernández, and "La mama," a guaguancó by Justi Barreto, "represented the union of the religious with the profane," just as Cortés said. The lyrics convey a certain humorous irreverence by suggesting that the *santero* religion has taken over Europe:

Mother, the child loves its mother
Arrivederci, Rome, in Italy there's a guaguancó
And he who doesn't love his mother alaguatacoicó
Because I am the son of Changó.

Also for this second album, the Grupo Folklórico added two musicians who were very important figures in the history of the Caribbean son. The first was Marcelino Guerra, the legendary "Rapindey," composer of an extensive and valuable repertoire. Rapindey also had been the singer on some of the most renowned performances of the son, including Piñeiro's "El nacional" and the last works that Arsenio Rodríguez completed in New York. The second figure was Félix Rodríguez, "Corozo," a major promoter of the son in Puerto Rico, thanks to his extensive tenure with the very famous Cuarteto Mayarí of Plácido Acevedo. Both of these individuals came together to sing the son "Dime la verdad," composed by Rapindey himself. For this son, the Grupo Folklórico comfortably transformed itself into a traditional septet (tres, guitar, bass, bongos, trumpet, maracas, clave, and the vocalists). They believed that if the fundamental base that inspired contemporary salsa was the original Cuban son, then to interpret this son ("Dime") with a respectful exactitude to its historical form was a valid way of presenting the true origins of salsa. And they were right. The Grupo Folklórico, temporarily converted into a septet, was automatically understood by the average music lover as a conjunto of old salsa, but salsa nonetheless. In Venezuela we saw this same phenomenon when the Sonero Clásico del Caribe performed the old son and thereby became one of the favorite bands of the local salsa scene.

Finally, I need to mention the song that opened the doors to an even larger audience for the Grupo Folklórico: "Se me olvidó," another old tearjerker of a bolero, composed by Lolita de la Colina. This song was selected by Virgilio Martí, who, as I have already mentioned, felt a particular affinity for these types of subjects. On principle, the theme should have been sidelined by the musicians, but Martí sang it not as a bolero but as a guaguancó, and one with a very special cadence, tenuous and recursive, quite removed from the conventional way of treating that beat. Although it was a piece outside the usual purview of the group, the musicians recognized that Martí's restyling of the song offered an added attraction by conveying the ultimately irresistible appeal intrinsic in the lyrics of a good Caribbean bolero. As the producer, René López had the final word: the song would be included; it did not matter that the guaguancó had a weak rhythm. Just as they had developed the rest of their repertoire, the musicians became collectively and fully engaged in the song. In order to mask the apparent weakness of the cadence, they decided to do a different montuno, one with the shadings both of a redoblante (performed against the grain by Jerry González) and of a Mexican marimba as a counterpoint to the bass. The rest of the drums (tumbas and the quinto) followed the usual conventions, while de La Fe, on violin, the only melodic instrument in the whole arrangement, riffed freely in open dialogue with the singer. The rest, of course, was in the hands of Martí and his uniquely effective style of articulating the bolero, confessing the pain of love in a joyful and honest way, since, after all, the bottom line is always about confession and pain:

I remember you, dear
You were too much for me
I always called you my dream
I always called you my life.

In the spring of 1977, when the Grupo Folklórico and Experimental Nuevayorkino was consistently solicited from all corners of the Caribbean, the musicians decided to split up, putting an end to a project whose import went well beyond the music. Once again, it seemed, the temptations of unlimited fame and the fortune that was just coming in were enough to destroy the fraternal character of this group, which began as a simple gathering of musicians who simply wanted to enjoy their excitement for the rumba without ego or excess and without glory or commercialism. That same year, when Channel 2 in Venezuela hired them as a result of the extraordinary success of "Se me olvidó," the musicians got together again in a modest Latino television studio in New York. There, albeit reluctantly, they once again played their music, and the results transcended any sense of falseness or remorse. Already, the salsa boom had indirectly affected the group, poisoning its folk music and its experimentation. The musicians gave in to the inevitable temptation and went their own ways, weaker and less effective, leaving the music lover, once more, to hold on to the albums while ignoring the personal details behind the music, details that sometimes are more harsh than happy, even when the album covers show a smiling black man trying to say the opposite.

The Traditional and the Avant-Garde

Once the Grupo Folklórico dissolved, the two González brothers, who in no way would concede to the commodified salsa, decided to continue with their jam sessions. In 1977, still energized by the fame of the Folklórico, the González brothers put into action a recording project that they had been concocting for a number of years: El Conjunto Libre (The Free Ensemble), which, as its name suggests, operated outside any impositions or restrictions, whether commercial or conceptual. In a certain sense, their first album featured the same cadre of musicians that had distinguished the Folklórico. The music they offered was as purely folkloric as before; but it was much more experimental, and it more clearly carried the banner of good salsa (not all of the Folklórico's work, as I have pointed out, could be considered true salsa music).

Andy González and Manny Oquendo led the conjunto of Jerry on tumbadoras, Oscar Hernández on piano, and the first reunion of trombonists Barry Rogers and José Rodríguez, who had not worked together since the old glory days of the original La Perfecta. For vocals, they had a pair of young singers, Héctor "Tempo" Alomar (the former timbalist for Agosto's La Conspiración) and Tony "Puppy" Torres. Guest artists on the album included former musicians from the Folklórico: Cardona, Golden, and Nelson González. To complete the conjunto, they brought in the talented trombonist Angel "Papo" Vásquez, who was still a teenager, and the flutist David Valentín, who, though more interested in jazz than in salsa, still performed very much in the Caribbean style.

In addition to an effective salsa version of the classic "Lamento borincano" by Rafael Hernández, the album included such cuts as "Saoco" by

Rosendo Ruiz, a danzón rendition of Charlie Parker's "Donna Lee," and
the bolero "Risque" by the Brazilian Ary Barroso, which conveyed the same
edge so characteristic of effective boleros during the initial stages of salsa.
For fans who had followed Latin music long before the boom emerged,
this material marked a return to the styles and standards of an Eddie Palmieri of the 1960s. Not only was the instrumentation identical to that of
La Perfecta—a pair of trombones, a flute, and a full rhythm section—but
almost all of the musicians had been influenced by the Palmierian experience, especially the two González brothers, the aforementioned trombone
pair of Rogers and Rodríguez, and Manny Oquendo himself. Beyond this
similarity in the sound, Conjunto Libre also took care to reproduce one of
the most basic characteristics of salsa: the pulse of a powerful beat always
in conjunction with a furious montuno. After the salsa boom had made
complacent rhythms, weak mambos, and repetitive montunos the norm
and seemed incapable of getting beyond this malaise, Conjunto Libre
represented not only a healthy change but also the return to the beginnings of what would signal the end of a cycle. Without a doubt, this was
one of the principal virtues of the group: they brought closure to this final
period of the salsa boom by connecting salsa not so much to its long tradition but to its most immediate past.

Commercially speaking, it is true that 1977 was perhaps the best year
of salsa. In those days, almost everything that was recorded sold easily to
a new mass of fans who wanted to satisfy their fever in any way possible.
However, if we look carefully at the whole of that same production, we find
that the quality of the music was consistently low. While the boom was
at its height, this did not represent a major problem: the records sold as
much as ever. But as soon as the boom faded, it was clear that only high
quality music would last, and by 1977 that music was already rather scarce.
The problem, then, was in the hands of the industry, not of salsa. Knowing
this, the best music lovers easily predicted that the development of this
expression was coming to an end. Despite its millions and despite all of
the fads and frenzies it created, the industry could not keep itself going for
much longer if it lacked the essential fuel of good salsa music. In the next
two years, the decline became obvious. By 1979, only the good musicians
received the praise and support of audiences, while thousands of mass-
produced recordings sat in warehouses. This explains why 1977 became
such an important year in the history of salsa, not because of any gains
made by the industry, but because the salsa that would outlast the boom
began to emerge at that time. The Conjunto Libre of New York fits in here
perfectly.

As previously mentioned, salsa developed its principal characteristics in New York in the second half of the 1960s when new leaders and new influences emerged. The first source of inspiration was the turbulent and marginalized barrio, and the music, therefore, was equally turbulent, even desperate. When that first salsa had become the mature expression of the Cuban son, it also became able to channel fully all of its own characteristics. Then the new decade began, and with it came that extraordinary salsa that powered the next waves of the salsa craze. The rest is history, and more than half of this book has tried to tell that story—a story, now disappointing, now inspiring, of everything that followed. Now we are left with the aftermath, the inevitable confusion after the storm. The leaders— that is, the vanguard—were already two years ahead of the game. This was when Conjunto Libre recognized the need to get back to the good salsa, the vital salsa of the preboom era, the salsa that surely could survive the destruction to come. Seeing an obvious option, they decided to retrace Eddie Palmieri and La Perfecta's old path, and while it was not the only path, it would lead them to a safe place.

Of course, this does not mean that Conjunto Libre simply refashioned La Perfecta—not at all. There had been an intervening decade between these two bands, during which all of the styles and standards of Caribbean popular music had been mixed up and shuffled around, and this clearly (and fortunately) had its effect on the Conjunto. More pertinent is the result of that combination of the Palmierian origins of salsa and the salsa of the next ten years. The result, evident in the two albums that the Conjunto recorded, was more than satisfactory.

According to Fred Weinberg, the recording engineer and author of the first album's liner notes, "after so many cold, mechanical and lifeless albums, it is a pleasure to listen to music like this." Weinberg clearly points us in the right direction: instead of the cold and rigidly planned music produced to fulfill commercial interests, we were now given a salsa that had no other objective but its own free expression. The repertoire on the album went from Cuba to jazz, passing through the real Latino barrio on the way, and all in salsa arrangements. And when I use the term "salsa" here, I am using it with all of its musical significance. For example, they included "Tune Up" by Miles Davis, now rooted in the rhythms of the batá drums, as well as a respectful update of the classic "Suavecito" by Piñeiro, with its refrain, "dance, Carola, the salsa of today," and they performed all of this so thoroughly as to satisfy the requirements of both the authentic son and the true salsa.

I remember the first time I saw the Conjunto Libre perform. It was in July 1977 when they played at a modest venue known as Nuyorican Village, a sort of refuge for Puerto Rican poets, musicians, and actors, obviously intent on reaffirming a cultural identity that they felt was threatened. That evening I witnessed an extraordinary musical manifesto. On the margins of the commercialized "salsa," already as clearly packaged and nondescript as ketchup, these musicians showed what was possible. Despite their modest resources, they performed, with pride, the enduring and daring salsa that remains an authentic musical testament to the contemporary barrio. I remember how pleasantly surprised I was with the guaguancó, "Imágenes latinas," later recorded with one of salsa's best trombone solos ever, performed by Barry Rogers. The lyrics were adapted by Andy González from a poem by Colombian Bernardo Palomo. They show the unifying character of salsa, a musical expression that, though primarily born in the New York barrio, brought together all urban Caribbean communities:

Indians, Hispanics, Blacks,
Let's all come together
With our roots and our blood,
To form one successful future.

In September 1977, the Venezuelan audience began to rave about a rare song that had the mustiness of a museum piece. This song aired on radio salsa programs, announced, without any explanation, as "'Carmelina' . . . by the Sonero Clásico del Caribe," but it had nothing to do with salsa. It was a son performed without trombones or conga and without the characteristic mambos of the montuno. Instead, the instrumental stars were the tres and a solitary trumpet with a mute. The singer also performed not in the style of salsa but in a voice that had a sharp and festive timbre that sounded completely odd, given the usual styles that salsa vocalists used. In addition, this singer, who was clearly past his youth, articulated the son as if he were partying with friends, conveying a strange sort of impudence that clashed with the conventional professionalism of the musicians, so much so that this man seemed to assert a pleasure in the montuno: "When I see you on the corner / I know what you're up to."

This son, with its verses and its voice and its familiar, party spirit, quickly became one of the great hits of Venezuelan salsa. Of course, as I already cautioned, this was not a salsa number, but a son; even so, it became fully identified as the kind of salsa that dominated during the imperial era of the boom. Despite all of its nonsalsa elements, the Sonero Clásico del Caribe behind this son played a very important role in adjusting the balance of salsa. In the final years of the decade, the Sonero Clásico presented an example of the authentic song that had served as a foundation for the development of salsa, and it did so with orthodox exactitude. I foreshadowed this phenomenon when I wrote about El Grupo Folklórico and

Experimental Nuevayorkino. Once the excess of the boom had exhausted itself, salsa entered an intense period of confusion. While the Conjunto Libre, for instance, was reclaiming the immediate predecessors of salsa, this same period was an extremely healthy time to explore the true son of the first decades of the century. The Sonero Clásico del Caribe performed this role for salsa quite successfully.

The Sonero albums presented a radically distinct standard from the one manipulated by the powerful New York industry, and they offered an important additional feature: texts that illustrated the rationale and principles behind the music. According to Domingo Alvarez, the idea was to publish these textual guides with the albums. In addition, the entire production, from the album cover to the actual grooves on the vinyl, showed an absolute respect for the artists and their music, a respect that, as we have already seen, was so often lacking in the New York world. In this way the Sonero advanced their project with absolute clarity and carefully thought-out planning to ensure they would achieve what they had set out to do. An example of this was the following excerpt of a text that was written by Domingo Alvarez, the soul and founder of the group, and published with the first album:

> Throughout all of the recordings, from the studio to the myriad conjunto performances [here he refers to the primary son ensembles] presented throughout the Caribbean, a type of cult has arisen: the son has transcended its original borders and, in practice, it has become *the* definitive musical form, par excellence, for dancing everywhere in the Caribbean. Its histories are in its poems, because in the communities that began that history, people did not write it down, they sang it.
>
> In Venezuela, on the south-eastern coastline of the Caribbean, the cult was initiated through the recordings that were coming in, basically the ones by the Sexteto Habanero by Guillermo Castillo, the Cuarteto Caney with its first singer, Panchito Riset, and later, Johnny López, Davilita and the Quinteto La Plata of Machín, the Trío Matamoros with Siro, Cueto, and Miguel, etc. etc. Venezuela offered its fruits, diverse groups and ensembles developed, and they cultivated the son.
>
> With these cultivators, who then learned the son in its purest and most genuine form, we improvised a sextet that moved toward those in the 1920s in Santiago de Cuba, and the reason for this was the recital-conference that we gave on Friday, December 3, 1976, in the Auditorium of the School of Architecture of the Central University of Venezuela, which we entitled, "Son Montuno y Guaguancó." In it the group had to demonstrate the son in its most classic form. Carlos Landaeta,

also known as "Pan con Queso," had the task of finding performers and bringing them in. For many years he and I had shared this admiration and cult-status for our marvelous, extraordinary, and one-of-a-kind Caribbean music.

Pan con Queso, a bongo player, brought in José Rosario Soto to be the primary vocalist because he already knew and agreed with what we wanted to do. Then he added Pedro Aranda on guitar, Juan Johnny Pérez on clave, José El Cumanés on marímbula, and, as a second voice, Santiago Tovar on tres—all of them had known each other since they were kids.

The sextet was complete, and one night of rehearsals was enough, since they were all experienced musicians.

This first group was the forerunner of the later Sonero Clásico, which made it big in the recording world when Alvarez and Montiel decided to record their work before it became part of the industry and lost its original flavor and purpose. Alvarez also wrote about this in the same text referenced above: "The group was comprised of natural musicians, none of them was a 'virtuoso'; they were simply interpreters of the music who shared a common goal: to revive the son for those who had once lived it and to teach the next generations how the son ought to sound and how it is danced it its purest and most classical form, the son that they had learned when they were young, the son that they have cultivated all of their lives." With this in mind, the Sonero Clásico del Caribe recorded two albums of son music that have a central place in the complete canon of salsa.

For the Venezuelan public, who financially supported all of the inventions of the international boom, the Sonero was a pleasant and more than worthwhile surprise. Unlike the local orchestras who felt they had to misuse their talents reproducing the hits and misses that came down from the north, the musicians of the Sonero experienced a success that led to continuous television spots, dance gigs for every night of the week, and even university recitals where the group continued to exercise its "didactic function" as defined by "skinny man," Alvarez. The second album, recorded at the end of 1978, exceeded the expectations that the group had stirred up. Conceived in homage to three of the greatest composers of the son—Miguel Matamoros, Ignacio Piñeiro, and Bienvenido Julián Gutiérrez—this album brought back the original versions of many songs that fans had enjoyed previously in their salsa forms. Subsequent fans who felt betrayed by the shenanigans of the boom were now in a position to recognize the gulf it had created: not only could they see how, in desperation, the industry had fomented a salsa that destroyed all of the richness of the original son, but now they could also observe the logical evolution of the expression and how the son was appropriately and perfectly expanded into the new world of salsa.

They recorded "Reclamo místico," "Camarones y mamoncillos," and "Mamá, son de la loma," by Miguel Matamoros; "Qué extraño es eso" and "Convergencia," by Bienvenido Julián Gutiérrez; and three sones by Ignacio Piñeiro that, thanks to their evident salsa feel, became fabulous sales hits: "Sobre una tumba, una rumba," the classic "Suavecito," and "Dónde estabas anoche," which, based on that old version by Tito Rodríguez, had been recorded in salsa by changing the lyrics and renaming it "Avísame a mi contrario." The Sonero, of course, offered the original lyrics:

> Tell my neighbor
> That I'm here
> Tell her to come so that she can enjoy
> The sweet singing.

Finally, it is worth noting that what ultimately attracted audiences to the Sonero was the down-to-earth character of the music and the musicians. Amid a boom that made "divas" out of most of the popular stars, the Sonero retained the same humble spirit that had characterized them all along. Just as the biographies on the second album made clear, the musicians of the Sonero came from the working class and continued to make their livings doing a combination of odd jobs, as is common among musicians in developing countries. They have been bricklayers, bus drivers, carpenters, and even traffic cops. Even Pan con Queso, the only one who was a professional musician from the start (thus, the extraordinary fame that he had not only in Venezuela but in the whole world of Caribbean music), never stopped depending on this first career with the post office. After all, as is well known among musicians, music often pays you back only with hunger and often rejects most of your efforts.

One night I had the opportunity to go to Las Lomas de Urdaneta, a sector of the populous neighborhood of Catia in Caracas. They were having a birthday party in honor of José Rosario Soto. The house was modest, and friends of the family came and went through the open front door. José Rosario offered everyone rum, as was the custom, a succulent *chivo coreano* (Korean goat), and the fresh, flavorful music that he himself sang from living room and kitchen. All of his fellow musicians from the Sonero were there, armed with their guitars and an impressive collection of anecdotes. With them were their children and grandchildren, young people who had grown up with the salsa craze. In one way or another, they all shared the old son that the musicians were singing and that was later supplemented with the salsa that came from the stereo. The focus continued to be the barrio and the music, intensely nurtured by all generations, who shared the same purpose and the same goals. The rich evolution from the son of yesterday to the salsa of today was palpable in the emotion and ambience of this Saturday night party. I am convinced that their ability to maintain that same spirit through all of their future professional appearances was one of the fundamental keys to the Sonero's success. After so many bad rumberos who had violently distanced themselves from the very barrio that had fed their music in order to deck themselves out as millionaires dripping with arrogance and posing as stars, the presence of these humble and happy soneros was something more than a wake-up call: it was a primary lesson in the truest possibilities and musicality of the Caribbean.

In 1977 and outside the boom, from the Conjunto Libre of New York to the Sonero Clásico del Caribe from Venezuela, from the avant-garde to the traditional, we saw the start of a multifaceted and open musical expression that ended up reinvigorating the salsa that was closing out the decade. That same year, Puerto Rico, as I have also mentioned, likewise began pursuing a more solid and far-reaching avant-garde than that of New York. It did so through a group that made its own contributions in charting new pathways: the Puerto Rico All Stars (PRAS).

Up to now, I have commented on a number of stars who, backed by specific recording houses, found themselves straddling two dangerous extremes: settling for banality, as was the case of the Fania Stars in this last period, or pursuing exclusionary and difficult forms that were not very accessible to the majority of fans who did not study music, as was the case of the energetic Tico Stars of the 1960s. Now, under the sagging weight of the salsa boom, anyone's formulation of an All Star group had to keep in mind some new factors: first, the obvious disaster of Fania as a stellar orchestra; second, that a return to the old jazzlike influences at this point would be supreme nonsense; and third, that the conventional salsa (son-mambo-montuno) had to be avoided in any project that wanted to be successful. The Puerto Rican musicians understood all of this and produced an exceptional first album. They had in their favor the fact that they were not working for any recording consortium, and, therefore, the musicians themselves had the last word.

In order to meet, the stars took time away from the orchestras to which they belonged, and they ignored the styles that each musician had been associated with previously. The only things that mattered were the quality of the instrumentalists, the level of virtuosity with which they performed, the clarity and precision of the arrangements, and the sabor, the fluidity and resonance, of the singers; in short, only the music mattered, and this accounted for their notable difference from other groups. For the rhythm section, the PRAS called on Tony Sánchez as a trap drummer (previously only Tito Puente had used this instrument to its fullest extent in experimenting beyond salsa), the virtuoso Manolín González on bongo, Eladio Pérez on congas, and the quick-handed Endel Dueño on the timbales. On piano they had Papo Lucca, who despite his constant presence in New York music—especially the music produced by Fania—was considered to be from the Puerto Rican music world, *never* an "import" from New York. Completing this rhythm sextet was Polito Huerta on bass. The rest of the orchestra was made up of a powerful brass section structured in a very salsalike way with the combination of trombones and trumpets. Here, in no particular order, were the best of the island: Juancito Torres, Elías López, Augie Antomatei, and Mario Ortiz on trumpet, with Rafi Torres, Gunda Merced, and Aldo Torres on trombone. The singers were none other than Marvin Santiago, Luigi Texidor, Paquito Guzmán, and Andy Montañez. This ensemble, performing the arrangements of Jorge Millet, Elías López, Ray Cohen, and Papo Lucca, produced, as their first album, one of the best documents of salsa.

Six years after the Fania All Stars had performed at the Cheetah, the standard was once again the music of intricate and exhilarating arrangements. The overall theme that PRAS used for this album was a potpourri conceived in homage to Rafael Hernández. This repertoire takes us not only through the classical melodies of the island but also through an effective sampling of the myriad rhythmic variants from Puerto Rican folk music to salsa itself, all dressed up in the incredible virtuosity of the musicians. The rest of the album kept up with a quality repertoire and presentational style that went on to offer, of course, a salsalike defiance—one that brought the real salsa face-to-face with its imposters. In other words, the salsa stars of the island confronted, head-on, the stars of fame and money who had been responsible for the scam. For example, the PRAS defined themselves through the son "Reunión en la cima," composed by Curet Alonso expressly for the orchestra and for the voice of Andy Montañez:

> I speak from the heart
> There's a meeting at the summit
>
> . . . .
>
> We're all for one
> Without boss or bombast or money
> Tell it to them, Andy . . .
> We're simply singing and playing music
> for whoever can enjoy it.

In addition, as if the suggestions here were not enough, in the middle of the song's mambo, there was a direct accusation made by Montañez against Masucci. Clearly, the musicians felt the need to say *something* that, for various reasons, went beyond what they were saying through the (instrumental) music itself. Throughout this book, the reader perhaps has come to understand the motivations, inflected with anger and frustration, that led to these charges against the recording monopoly of New York. In any case, a good number of the albums produced outside that powerful industry, whether in or outside New York, constituted a constant rebellion, and the first album of the Puerto Rico All Stars is another such example.

Also in 1977, in a fashion parallel to that of the Puerto Rican example, *all* of the Venezuelan musicians decided to formulate an "all stars group," and in a very Venezuelan way, they baptized it with the name Trabuco. The idea was engineered by Alberto Naranjo, a veteran drummer and arranger whose musical career spanned the range of styles and schools of Caribbean popular music. Naranjo had spent years considering the real possibilities of this project; now he relied on the direct collaboration of Orlando Montiel in order to translate into a record what he had so far only imagined. As with the PRAS, the music was recorded outside the purview of the big recording consortiums, which meant Naranjo and Montiel would have the invaluable freedom to create their music. (Montiel had already founded the YVKCT seal, Conmusi C.A., more out of cultural than commercial interests, in order to disseminate the truly important groups in Caribbean music.) By July they were able to gather the necessary musicians in the studios of Ricardo Landaeta (the sound engineer) to record what came to be considered one of the most mature expressions of Venezuelan salsa. At Naranjo and Montiel's invitation, I witnessed the recording process of that first album from the very beginning, and afterward I was in charge of writing the text for the album cover. I would like to share with you some of those paragraphs:

> I don't think I run any risk when I state that most of you who read this are baseball fans, and going to a game between Caracas and Magallanes, for instance, is just something that you do, with the same group that gets together on Saturday nights at our buddy José So-and-So's house, where you play salsa and dance the night away. Well, those of you who understand the importance of batting and running can easily understand what "Trabuco" means: it's that powerful coming together of the best of the best, pros or "maestros," to say it in the language of salsa. Musically speaking, then, we're bringing together the best to form a Trabuco, and here you have it, because that's precisely what happened

on those rainy nights of June and July, when in the studios of Flaco Landaeta, Alberto Naranjo and Montiel got their friends together—these musicians—to make the salsa that *we* like. . . .

Today the whole world talks about salsa, and, more than ever, everybody dances it. This is why salsa is overproduced, *ad nauseam*, without taking care of the details and the small tricks of the trade. The mass produced salsa, then, inundates and exhausts those of you who really know it, who for years have tried to ignore the foreign invasions in order to take pleasure in our true rhythms. For you, the tireless *good* dancers, this album is the first to offer an alternative. More than anyone, you know what this project means, you know what is contained in the grooves of these eight cuts. The others, those who are just now being initiated into the world of the "ritmo bravo" [the hard beat], have here a true document of the feisty and dynamic music which is, simply, what we today know as salsa.

Sometimes music gets made because of a formal agreement, because it has to be made. Other times music is loved and needed. When this happens, the music reaches beyond expectations, and it starts to sound different; it drops down to the very depths, where it has to plunge. This is the case with this album, a project among friends, of "maestros" who wanted to do what they loved.

In August of that same year, in a conference-recital that we offered with Domingo Alvarez in the Museum of Contemporary Art in Caracas, El Trabuco Venezolano made its debut. That Sunday the idea was to give a brief demonstration of the evolution of Caribbean music from the son to the true salsa. For the former, Alvarez had the cooperation of the Sonero Clásico del Caribe, who illustrated the son in its original form. Then, when it was time to present salsa—the modern expression—the Trabuco musicians eloquently performed a complete array of salsa's characteristics and possibilities. The recital, which took place just as the Fania All Stars were visiting the country, served as an extraordinary counterpoint, and the people of Caracas had the opportunity to experience the extremes of the expression: a salsa in name only, reduced to splashy spectacle and stage smoke, and a much more consequential and effective continuation of the true salsa line identified with the urban Caribbean. This shows again how, by 1977, the boom was singing its swan song while, without posturing or bravado, another music was beginning to chart the new paths.

El Trabuco, however, was a direct victim of the dark pressures very much present in the world of salsa and was drastically cut off from primary media exposure. Still, the musicians, far from being disappointed, continued with their project, offering extraordinary recitals at the city's universities and in some barrios, and always for free, paid only with the applause and support of their consistently large audiences. In any case, the musicians did not make their livings from El Trabuco; all of them were highly recognized professionals, performing with *this* orchestra as the ideal way to jump in and have fun with the music that satisfied them the most. Thus, their goal remained intact, despite other difficulties. By March 1979, El Trabuco had its second album ready, and it was far superior to the first, which is saying a great deal. Their salsa here exhibited what was beginning to be a favorable constant in the new, avant-garde expressions: a salsa that contributed to the larger Caribbean tradition with music that was perfectly crafted and self-aware. What began in the confines of the barrio now went further, taking complete control of the host of meanings, implications, and consequences that salsa represented as the mouthpiece of the Caribbean people. El Trabuco reaffirmed the unifying nature of salsa that the Cojunto Libre had proposed. They offered, for example, an updated version of the "Imágenes latinas" with a new vision of Bolívar as presented in a curious cumbia composed by Víctor Gutiérrez:

There was a man who won a thousand battles
Who freed the people . . .
Who believed that this region could be reborn with dignity

. . . .

Simón, Don Simón.

By the time this album was recorded, El Trabuco Venezolano had stopped being just an orchestra and had become part of a larger movement in the local salsa scene. More than fifty musicians had participated in it, and all were recognized as among the best in the Venezuelan world. Of course, many musicians remained on the sidelines, because the recording companies' simple stinginess did not allow them to contribute to El Trabuco. However, once the long wake of blunders and empty boasts made the demise of the boom obvious, the situation showed signs of improving. Already Wladimir Lozano, the most famous of all the salsa bolero singers in the country, had recorded with El Trabuco, lending hope to the possibility of bringing together, in one immense celebration, *all* of the good musicians from the southern coast of the Caribbean who had been making valuable contributions to the world of salsa. Indeed, at this point, the musicians had taken off; what would follow remained to be seen.

Before closing this chapter about the musicians whose "alternative salsa" represented the traditional and the avant-garde, I must highlight a young Puerto Rican musician who, for various reasons, especially political ones, never received the benefits of large media exposure. Frank Ferrer was a singer and songwriter who aligned himself with the nationalist movement that defended Puerto Rican identity against the traumas and cultural complexes created by its sad situation as a free associated state.

All too easily, Ferrer became characterized as a "protest singer," for lack of a better term, a modifier that he himself never bothered to deny. Yet Ferrer, to be sure, was much more than what is commonly understood by that title: the university character that moves from supposed folk music to supposed political rant precariously oblivious to the consequences. Even at the beginning of the decade, when the first group Ferrer formed, the Puerto Rico 2010, explicitly identified itself with the leftist platform (asking for independence, attacking the *gusanos* who had left Cuba, questioning imperialism), the music of this young composer always had clear popular objectives: to encourage dancing, to make albums that would reach the masses, and to compete, then, with all music, good or bad, that the industry produced. Those objectives invite us to consider Ferrer's music from a perspective other than that of conventional protest music. The music of Frank Ferrer, far from screening out salsa (the majority of protest singers accused him of being "just another commercial product"), tried to include salsa on its own terms. Of course, I never sensed he would have the same impact that I later saw in Rubén Blades, for instance, and this was because Ferrer preferred the more open-ended and somewhat disorderly experimental styles that Blades skillfully avoided. Yet, because he dedicated himself to those innovations that shut out some of the purists among salsa fans, Ferrer served as a rallying figure for many of the best musicians and arrangers from the younger generation. We could say that Ferrer rushed the process by ignoring some steps or stages that still needed to complete themselves. While Rubén Blades understood how to shape and preserve the best features of the salsa that came out of the boom, Frank Ferrer threw himself into a new style where folk music and the avant-garde were comfortably coupled.

A concrete example of this initiative is a beautiful album released in 1976 with the title *Yerbabruja*. Here Ferrer adapted poems by Juan Antonio Corretjer, an extraordinary Puerto Rican poet who had dedicated himself to working through the indigenous ancestry of the island, to the search for identity, where all sources, all avenues were valid, as seen in the words of "Caminando por el monte" and "Guanín," respectively:

. . . I kept walking, kept walking
Without knowing the path or the way. . . .

... I have to walk, hatchet in my hand,
With death in front of me. ...

In his lyrics, Ferrer elaborated on the indigenous world of the poems, using words that specifically referenced the actual lives of contemporary Puerto Ricans as seen in "Jayuya/Jayuya":

The warriors of Coabey
Descended the mountain and hills
Like cascading water
The voice of the Batey arose.

Furthermore, the illustrations on the album cover honored paintings by young Puerto Rican artists and included a necessary glossary:

Guanín: a lower quality of gold, of an almost purplish color that
   the indigenous recognized by its smell, and which they highly
   esteemed.
Cemí: Idols of the Taíno Indians that represented the spirit of the
   good.
Seboruco: Forest.
Manicato: During Taíno nuptial ceremonies, the bride would resist
   a simulated attempted rape performed by members of the tribe.
   At the end of this farce, the bride would scream triumphantly:
   Manicato! Manicato! (I am courageous and pure), indicating her
   worth and her worthiness.
Coabey: Valley of the dead. A sort of paradise, the Taíno nirvana; also
   a barrio in Jayuya with a very beautiful landscape, center of the
   nationalist insurrection of October 30, 1950.

Clearly, Frank Ferrer, like many other Puerto Rican musicians, was moving into an area that had very little to do with the commercial salsa that was being produced in New York. After the boom, Caribbean musicians had to work to raise salsa to a new level. The avant-garde examples that I have documented in this chapter became the new alternatives, but the wide range of Caribbean culture cautions us against reducing those alternatives to one single solution. On the contrary, the future wealth of salsa was already guaranteed by the extensive possibilities that existed. And Frank Ferrer, from his humble Boricua corner, offered guidelines for creating meaningful options with *Yerbabruja*, including the cut "Fin de fiesta" and featuring Corretjer's poems and Ferrer's music, as an excellent starting point:

In life everything is a process
Which time undoes
Man knows where he is born
But not where he will die.

Quisqueya

On the morning of April 24, 1965, the Dominican people watched, with surprise, anxiety, and a certain joy, as the city streets were invaded by cars full of rebel soldiers. The new government, now in control of certain sectors of Santo Domingo, began broadcasting radio and television messages, and each was preceded by a new anthem inevitably in the form of a merengue: "Let's do battle, valiant soldiers, / because the revolution has begun."

This merengue had been composed by Aníbal de Peña, and with the tambora and the guiro, it extended this new fervor of the people. The republic was living through a decisive moment, one that does not accept anything middle of the road. The people could support the rebels or fight against them, but they could not remain indifferent. Similarly, the musicians, who as popular artists reflect the collective feeling, also had to make a choice because the merengue was in the streets. Johnny Ventura went down to the lower parts of the city, the principal bastion of the rebels, and there he played his music in order to raise their spirits. But four days later, on April 28, the U.S. marines landed on the Dominican coast despite the indignation of all of Latin America. The Cuban experience was too fresh in their memories and, more importantly, too nearby in the Caribbean. The rebels were accused of being communists, and the United States did not hesitate to order an attack by their famed—and always cursed—military forces. Uncertainty, fear, and anger overwhelmed Quisqueya, and the merengue resounded with the popular suffering. Cuco Valoy, a completely bald black man who approached his role as a singer with a curious and dignified solemnity, composed a song titled "Páginas gloriosas" that took on the role of an anthem: "As long as there are still men, brave men and patriots, / There will always be a motherland."

We know the rest of that history: Joaquín Balaguer set up a mock democracy and governed from 1966 until 1978, when, after fears and threats, he passed his power over to Antonio Guzmán, the undisputed winner in the national elections. During those twelve years, the Dominican people lived lives of anger and irony, but always with the persistent optimism of the Quisqueyan merengue. In those last years, while the Caribbean was conveyed through the fullness of salsa, Dominican music reemerged with unexpected strength and made an essential contribution of the first order. Let us review how this came to pass.

For salsa that continued to locate its commercial center in New York, Quisqueya began to make its presence felt through the great flow of Dominican immigrants. (By the end of 1978, it was estimated that more than 400,000 Dominicans were living in metropolitan New York.) This sector liked salsa and became one of its principal economic supporters, although they never stopped demanding the cadences of their traditional merengues. By 1976, therefore, a good number of the principal salsa orchestras of the city began to include merengues in their repertoires—a tendency that would be virtually required by all bands (inside and outside the city) within the next two years. Johnny Pacheco, who as a Dominican felt particularly connected to the community of his compatriots, was the first musician to incorporate the merengue into salsa. In his 1973 album, *Tres de café y dos de azúcar*, he showcased the start of this trend in "Los diablitos," a well-polished merengue that he himself had composed, drawing on traditional and folk elements. That same year Ismael Miranda and his Orquesta Revelación recorded "Ahora que estoy sabroso," a merengue that pointed directly to the new approach that salsa would take in regard to the Dominican genre. Meanwhile, Primitivo Santos, considered the pioneer of the New York merengue, continually performed such works with his orchestra, although his merengue relied on overly conventional forms that limited its effects on salsa tendencies and audiences.

Thematically, conceptually, and musically speaking, however, the merengue made in the United States had very little to do with the merengue produced and enjoyed in the Dominican Republic. On the island, where a particular sense of humor and an understanding of social events as communal and quotidian were the constants, the sources of inspiration were radically different. None of their lyrics was arbitrary, and neither was any arrangement. With years of experience and an extraordinary maturity, the musicians from the island performed a merengue rich in quality that easily synthesized the most diverse elements into a unique musical form, perfectly achieved. In New York, on the contrary, the merengue continued to be felt as a mere ornament of the salsa industry. The arrangements, far from being intentionally crafted, were empty platforms for the beat, and, in the majority of cases, the lyrics reproduced superficial themes that were pointless and expendable.

In Santo Domingo, Johnny Ventura had already created a school of music, and although he was not an exceptional singer, he had garnered so much public support that music lovers held him up as the one most responsible for the modern merengue. Even so, the new style that came to take over not just Quisqueya but all of the salsa-inflected Caribbean was the style developed by a young trumpet player, Wilfrido Vargas, the leader of an orchestra that was quickly on its way to becoming immensely popular, Los Beduinos.

In 1977 I listened for the first time to one of this band's albums and found that they played an intelligent merengue, full of humor and political references, presented in very interesting arrangements. At this point, salsa had already lent some importance to the merengue, and the New York musicians had found the Dominican form an intriguing alternative. Those musicians introduced me to the music of Vargas. Some praised his group's arrangements, others applauded the power and quality of the beat, and all noted that the lyrics were "que están en algo"—"really something," "hot," "cool," "in style." Now, in the context of "Páginas gloriosas" by Cuco Valoy and "Himno de los rebeldes" by Aníbal de Peña, a listener might have expected that this new merengue came wrapped up in the banner of protest. Granted, for some critics, the quality of the message is determined by the clarity of its social or political awareness. But as far as authentic popular music is concerned (as I emphasized in my discussion of Curet Alonso), the quality of the lyrics can be measured only by the degree to which they relate to the language and vision of the everyday, collective lives of the people. Since salsa now lived so far from the life in Cuba described by lyrics sung more than thirty years ago, lyrics with popular and distinctly contemporary messages must have been a truly pleasant surprise. In his 1977 album, Vargas included a merengue in which two Dominicans, one from the capital (city) and the other from El Cibao (the country) debate the pros and cons of each locale. With a touch of humor and roguishness, both protagonists defend their respective places of origin. At the end, by way of a moral, a chorus throws the winning punch, representing the collective national argument:

> From time immemorial
> There has been this controversy . . .
> Let's have no more debate between city and country
> It's our unity that brings peace
> And with peace, justice.

Further along in the album, a merengue titled "El calor" references a return trip by a Dominican who had immigrated to New York. Playing with an arrangement that alludes to the United States through certain phrasings and harmonies typical of jazz from the swing era, the lyrics speak of how the Dominican—who has put all of his earnings in the bank and become acclimated to the cold of the north—finds himself instantly suffocated by the heat of the Caribbean. There was irony here and also humor, a special knack for saying things that attacked the commonplaces in such a way that all of the Dominicans (whether residents of the republic or in the north) could identify fully with the song. Seen superficially, the lyrics of this merengue could have alienated non-Dominican audiences unaware of the controversy between El Cibao and the capital and unaffected by the Dominican migration to New York, but they did not. The merengue continued to attract audiences because, after all, the particularity of those problems and situations are universal and applicable to all, especially if popular art, in this case music, serves as the conducting wand. Amid the tired lyrics of commercial salsa, the reference to Quisqueya was almost a blessing: the young Dominicans, in their own way, were giving back to salsa that poetic touch that had been eroded by the ignorance and desperation of the music business. As "El calor" has it,

The merengue San Antonio
Is an offer of love
A beautiful legacy
Of our folklore.

With the interest generated by Wilfrido Vargas and his Beduinos, salsa audiences began to embrace the new orchestras that exhibited a similar level of energy. Los Kenton and Los Hijos del Rey were the groups that took off next. Their chief feature was a choreographic display that bordered on the acrobatic. Also capitalizing on this renaissance, musicians of the past again began making appearances on radio programs and onstage. Examples include Joseíto Mateo, the singer par excellence of the Dominican merengue, and El Cieguito de Nagua (The Blindman of Nagua), an extraordinary proponent of the traditional merengue who performed with a trio of tambora, guiro, and accordion. Salsa, then, opened itself to the whole of Dominican music, both the traditional and the avant-garde, in a fusion of styles that had relevance for all of the Caribbean.

Following the Dominican lead, New York, Puerto Rico, and Venezuela began to present their own salsa versions of past and present-day merengues: Roena recorded "La mala maña"; Lucca, "Perico sin pico"; Olivencia, "Madame Chuchú"; El Trabuco Venezolano, an extraordinary "Compadre Pedro Juan," the classic of Luis Alberty. Oscar D'León performed "Juanita Morel," a hit that filled the airwaves of every radio station in the region. Pacheco, for his part, without losing his role as the leader in salsa (a role that was so characteristically his), also began to compose merengues that were recorded by various New York bands, numbers such as "Pun pun catalú," released by Celia Cruz with Willie Colón, which netted the highest level of sales. Furthermore, on his orchestra's album featuring Héctor Casanova, Pacheco demonstrated his deft handling of the humor and roguishness that were now staples in the "salsa-merengue" form, with the incredibly well-done "Me llevaron la cartera":

> I didn't see the hand
> That snuck close to my body
> I never saw it coming.

Still the dominant voice came from the south, from Quisqueya itself, and Wilfrido Vargas, without a doubt, was at the helm. In 1978 his song "El barbarazo" opened everyone's eyes to the new leading role of Dominican music; audiences that had resisted the merengue were finally won over by this composition. However, things happen. "El barbarazo" is now perhaps the least representative song of the larger spirit that the new merengue initiated. The same album, *Punto y aparte*, that included that song offered merengues of much better quality and importance than the famed "Barbarazo." For example, "Enrique Blanco," composed by Ramón Díaz and Wilfrido himself, offered a biting narrative of an actual figure in Dominican history:

> Some day Dominican history will recall
> A man who fought for freedom,
> Body and soul,
> A simple country man
> An expert marksman
> His name was Enrique Blanco.

In the same camp, I would include "Desiderio Arias" ("It was in La Barranquita where they fought the first battle in which the yanqui surrendered"), composed by Julio Alberto Hernández and released by Los Beduinos on the same *Punto y aparte* album. I would point out also that the lyrics of merengues are noticeably much longer than those of conventional salsa because the role of narrative is a fundamental part of Dominican music. While salsa was characterized by lyrics that did not go beyond identifying a problem, encountering or rejecting a lover, or conveying the defiant attitude of the music or the singer, merengue favors telling a story narrated in its totality through the inflections and with the emphasis of the music. This narrative style was quite common in the guaguancó that primarily came out of the barrios of Matanzas and Havana. As it developed at the beginning of the century, the son also attended to narrative, but already by the 1940s it had lost this characteristic. Therefore, since salsa derived from this latter son, it (salsa) was less influenced by storytelling. Only Rubén Blades (about whom I will write later and at more length) began to explore this approach that had been an essential aspect of popular music throughout the continent. Meanwhile, overflowing its own borders with exceptional quality, the merengue became the narrative music par excellence in the salsa world.

On February 25, 1979, at New York's Radio City Music Hall, there was a concert to commemorate the 135th anniversary of the independence of the Dominican Republic. The theater was packed, and there was a feeling in the air unlike that of any ordinary salsa concert. The audience exuded a certain solemnity, a patriotic spirit that was contagious. Anyone without previous experience of this type of event would have expected nothing more than a political show. However, what was scheduled was a recital of popular music, a simple merengue concert. The performance began with the national anthem as a huge national flag was displayed across the backdrop of the stage. At that point, the unprepared spectator might still be wary, but any doubts were quickly swept away when, from above and below a moving platform, Los Kenton orchestra appeared performing their incredible acrobatics and their excellent music. Then it was Primitivo Santos's turn, a group that added pure tradition to the New York elements. Primitivo remained onstage to accompany Joseíto Mateo ("I am such a merenguero, I am the tambora"). He was introduced as "the Frank Sinatra of the Dominican song," even though he was black and only smiled shyly, suggesting a more dignified demeanor. This was not a political event; but the flag did remain in the background, and the national pride that was triggered by the merengue spread effusively throughout the hall. Later, when Cuco Valoy was announced, he received an emotional standing ovation. Cuco was one of the best vocal performers in the Caribbean music world. He brought a freshness and simplicity to his music, and that is why his band, costarring Ramón Orlando and Henry García, had the somewhat pretentious name of Los Virtuosos (The Experts). He started with the humorous song that includes the lyrics, "From an attack of the nerves, Marcos Matías collapsed / And worn out with living Marcos Matías died."

After another ovation, more uproarious than the first, Cuco sang his "Páginas gloriosas," and all of Radio City shook with an outpouring of collective tears, hugs, and shouts that swelled what had been purely Dominican pride to a passion fully shared by anyone who was Caribbean. Later, when Cuco performed the hit song of the moment—"Juliana, qué mala eres, qué mala eres, Juliana" (Juliana, you are so bad, you are so bad, Juliana)— Johnny Pacheco joined in the festivities with his flute, because that flag-waving event was also a true community celebration. At the end of the son, in which Cuco had demonstrated his own amazing talent, the fans nearly would not stop applauding. The musicians had achieved their most complete role as popular artists. To cap off the euphoria, the closing act was Wilfrido Vargas. There had been a rumor circulating about the split-up of his orchestra, because three key musicians had left the original band—the virtuosos Quilvio Fernández (trumpet) and Sonny Ovalle (piano and first-rate arranger) along with the excellent singer Vicente Pacheco, who had formed a new orchestra, Los Genuinos. But Vargas, with an orchestra of mostly twenty-year-olds, took the stage and once more made his leadership clear. After playing his recent merengues—"El gallo," "Wilfrido," and "Dame un consejo"—the Dominican debuted a merengue that reaffirmed, with all of the urgency and energy of the occasion, the nationalistic and political feeling that had been coursing through the evening. The audience listened to phrases that gave them goose bumps: "Venga un policía, vengan dos, el pueblo siempre es más. Y digo la verdad porque para eso es el merengue y mi canción" (Come on, policeman; come on, with even two of you; the people will always outnumber you. And I speak the truth because that's what merengue and my song are for). All the while, the cold New York winter was being forcefully displaced by the extraordinary expression of a Dominican and, moreover, Caribbean fervor. The concert, which for some reason had been billed as a "Salsa Show," became one of the most spectacular Latino events that New York has ever witnessed. Actually, then, it *was* salsa, because salsa, understood as the totalizing manifestation of the Caribbean of our times, was in a position to absorb and express the best virtues of popular music. And the merengue, with its intrinsic exuberance, fed directly into that largesse. All that remains is for me to confess the wonderful fortune of having been there at that celebration, one of the most emotional concerts I have ever witnessed and one that any music fan would have appreciated with, of course, the greatest pride.

The Leaders

The fall of 1978 saw the release of an album that was preceded by hype and speculation: Eddie Palmieri's first production since "Un día bonito." (Here it is prudent to note that *Obra maestra inconclusa*, released by the Coco label in 1976, was openly protested by its very own artist, who considered it simply a draft of his later works and never a definite project in its own right. According to Palmieri, his last real album had been his 1975 *El sol de la música latina*, which included the song mentioned above). With obvious reason, then, music lovers had the greatest expectations for this new release. Furthermore, this new album, titled *Lucumí, Macumba, Vodoo*, on the Epic label, extended the reach of the international empire of Columbia Records. This was the first time that salsa had been produced and distributed by that premier international label, and Palmieri was ecstatic that CBS had signed him to a fabulous contract—the best yet awarded to a Latin American artist working in Caribbean styles. More importantly, he had been guaranteed absolute freedom to record his music as he saw fit.

However, all of these expectations were dashed by an onslaught of frustrations. *Lucumí, Macumba, Vodoo* was a bitter disappointment, and the anticipated millions-plus came in at conventional sales figures that did not at all justify the initial investment. Why did Eddie Palmieri, who was without a doubt the salsa musician in the best position to break into the international avant-garde scene, fail, when, on the surface, he had all the elements in his favor? Why was this leap to the "other music" cut short, when the industry had used the best athlete of all, the only one capable of jumping so high? The answer, once more, escapes us if we look within the strict confines of music. Instead it points to the other end of the spectrum, to the producer or entrepreneur who sits behind a desk and has the audacity to decide what audiences will like while ignoring the wisdom and experience of the artist who, in the end, is the one who really matters. Palmieri, regrettably, did not have the "absolute freedom" he had been promised. His goals were compromised to accommodate those of the producer, and the result was an album that straddled two distinct and diametrically opposed poles.

In terms of the industry, the album was defined as a "crossover," an album that began in one mode and finished in another. The problem with this was that the industry did not really think in terms of modes, but of markets, and the confusion of these terms led, irrevocably, to a blooper. For the musicians, the true creators, formal limits are not that important, because to develop music sincerely, they must include whatever qualities, diverse forms, trends, and influences are necessary. For example, a composer of danzones could, at any given time, based on the needs of the work being composed, make use of certain harmonic conceptions of the blues. In other words, music is the "true north," the guiding direction that enables the composer to bridge one side of the musical world with another without any real difficulties. An entrepreneur, however, would see the hypothetical danzón in our example only as a product that needs to be sold to every audience that has any interest in either the danzón or the blues. Thus, the so-called crossover is a commercial term, not a musical one, and when producers decide that an album is a crossover, they make the musicians mix, a priori, styles and criteria without taking into account their relative compatibility with the music being developed. The general result, then, is an awkwardly forced and ineffective product. I noted earlier the glaring failure of the Fania All Stars' crossover attempts, and the same, inevitably, happened with the master, Palmieri. Music should never be treated as the arbitrary mix of musical elements and audience tastes that an entrepreneur invents from the sterility of a desk, with the sole aim of *invading* markets and increasing sales. Music is intrinsically a spontaneous and free-flowing process that must in no way be disrupted by any secondary interests, even when those interests promise all the millions in the world.

Palmieri's album represented two distinct musics tightly wedded and offering very few benefits. On one hand, there was salsa, the true music of the pianist, and on the other, the so-called Latin rock that was brought in to satisfy the crossover label. The first flowed smoothly with freshness and impact, but the second was rather pointless, making no impression on either rock fans or the lovers of "the Latin thing," which in this case was nothing more than a little salsa. Unfortunately, not even the quality of two individual songs was enough to save the album. "Colombia te canto" began with a most beautiful danzón that featured, in its montuno, an exquisite dialogue between the pianos of Eddie and his brother Charlie, and "Mi congo" expertly brought together the wide range of experiments from "Vámonos pa'l monte" to "Un día bonito." While these two numbers are among the best of salsa, as a whole the album *Lucumí, Macumba, Vodoo* rang false because it failed to deliver on the excessive expectations set up for it. Music lovers were left only with the pleasure of the nostalgia and imagination that had fueled their hopes for all that Palmieri could have done had he truly been permitted to work freely. "What a pity" was, once more, the only response available to the fan.

A similar thing happened to Ray Barretto who, beginning in 1976, decided to stop doing salsa for Fania in order to join the jazzlike experiments of the very powerful Atlantic label. Barretto also prompted high hopes, as I noted regarding his last salsa album, *Barretto*, released by Fania in 1975. This album had become the most successful of his recording career. His debut with the new label—*Tomorrow* (1976)—also reproduced an excellent live performance of his "new band," in which he effectively combined jazz and salsa. At this point, the future could not have seemed any brighter. However, to the dismay of fans everywhere, the later albums by the conga player—*Eye of the Beholder* (1977) and *Can You Feel It?* (1978)—had almost nothing to do with his earlier work. The music of these albums was neutralized and numbing, totally in the style of "commercial jazz" that had very little resemblance to jazz and, in the unfortunate case of Barretto, even less evidence of being commercial. Nor did even an experience as interesting as *The Other Road* (1973), where Barretto displayed his ability to exploit the overlap between salsa and jazz with intelligence and flair, have any bearing on these last two albums.

During this transition period from good salsa to what was expected to be good jazz, I had the opportunity to speak with Barretto. I saw in him a desperate desire to leave the insular environment that he had been a part of for so many years. He was not tired of the music but of the oppressive world that he worked in professionally in New York. He was not tired of salsa, but of the same salaries, the same lies, the same sabotaging criteria with which the Latino musician of that city was exploited miserably. Barretto was a name, inside and outside salsa; he was a performer of the first rank, one with enough right to demand a future that would be more open and also more just. But at Atlantic they were far from properly valuing his talents and prestige, and he was reduced to producing those types of albums whose shelf life is limited to two or three months. Once again, with an annoying regularity, the fans were moved to pity.

In 1979 a shortsighted and irresponsible industry accused Barretto and Palmieri of being the sole causes for the failure of major recording projects and immediately dismissed them. The U.S. companies no longer wanted anything to do with them. Rejected and feeling offended, the musicians returned to the world that shared their values and that received them with open arms. In June 1979, at the height of the Newport Festival, Palmieri and his orchestra performed in the Avery Fisher Hall. There he again showed the vigor and rootedness of quality salsa. Without giving excuses or appearing disingenuous, Palmieri surprised both jazz critics and salsa fans with the majestic power of his montuno, the Caribbean cadence that he should never have abandoned. With the support of fifteen instrumentalists and the voice of his old pal Ismael Quintana, Palmieri loudly announced in that cathedral of jazz,

> What I hear is
> A quinto calling
> My guaguancó . . .
> A rich bongo
>
> I bring it to you
> Listen well . . .
> Tambo, tambo, tambo, tambo.

Larry Harlow, another one of the leaders who had contributed to the beginnings of salsa since early in the decade, also went through a period of crisis and decline, although his impulse for modes outside salsa never passed muster. In Harlow's music, the salsa itself seemed worn out because he had not had a hand in it since 1975. Other factors began to cause him constant problems, and this took a toll on him. His disagreements with the industry, especially with the directors of Fania, soon led to his being blacklisted, and like many others, he became relegated to the sidelines.

Harlow's pinnacle was, as I mentioned in previous chapters, in 1974, when he recorded his best album, *Salsa*. From then on, his production felt uneven, incomplete, and rather halfhearted, and the quality of his albums gradually declined. In 1975 he released *El judío maravilloso*, an album recorded, for the most part, during the same sessions that had produced *Salsa* the year before. Then, in 1976, in an attempt to boost sales for the tenth anniversary of the orchestra, Harlow again recorded with Ismael Miranda on an album titled *Con mi viejo amigo*. Despite all of the promise that such a venture would suggest, the album had little impact. By 1977, having lost his former leadership role in the New York salsa scene, Harlow once more recorded with Junior González, but again, despite some very accomplished songs, the album (*El jardinero del amor*) failed to attract larger audiences. By this time Harlow felt frankly at a disadvantage in comparison with his colleagues. He had only his name and a fading prestige, so it was imperative that he throw himself into a bigger, more ambitious project. He changed singers and hired Néstor Sánchez, a sonero whom experts lauded for his impeccable technique.

As happened to González five years earlier, Sánchez was introduced through a "monster work," in this case a "suite of salsa" titled *La raza latina*, which purported to tell the entire "history of salsa," from Africa to New York. This was, more or less, the same terrible blunder that Geraldo Rivera had made with the film of the Fania All Stars. Harlow fell back on the mambo, the guajira, the son, and the guaguancó in order to narrate a story that barely reflected the actual development of the music. Nevertheless, ignoring this first and fundamental mistake, *La raza latina* did one thing worthy of applause: it included not only extraordinary arrangements, but it also sincerely sought out something beyond the limited and repetitive salsa that had inundated the boom era. Sánchez, despite his supposed debut, sang only one number on the album; the rest were performed by Rubén Blades, who sang the actual history in English. The fans, however, were neither enthused nor enraged by the album. Despite its ambitions, the project proved insubstantial. Harlow was not able to recover his position as a leader, and from this point on he slipped even lower within the hierarchies of salsa. In the spring of 1979, faced with difficulties from the industry and the perhaps unjustified rejection of fans, Harlow had to dissolve his band. It seemed that there was no longer a place for the grand

and showy orchestra of old, and so, like many of his colleagues, the Jewish musician retreated to a country house in Pennsylvania, with only his disappointment for company.

In many ways, Harlow's situation was repeated with another pianist who was also fundamental to the initial development of salsa. Ricardo Ray, who in the 1960s had the devoted support of fans, little by little felt them pulling away. Although he lived in Puerto Rico during the 1970s, Ray was never able to participate actively in the salsa avant-garde that began on the island. He made a respectable living from his former fame and virtuosity on the piano, but he never exercised again his previous role as a leader. The first factor that contributed to his decline was the shaky salsa that the pianist turned to after moving back to Puerto Rico. Ray kept exploring sophisticated forms, but now, far from evincing the fierceness that had previously aligned him with the avant-garde, he became carried away by trends and styles that, to be honest, had very little to do with salsa. The pianist reveled in a pop style that was totally extemporaneous and bordered on the pointless and even silly, especially when seen from the radical perspectives of the new decade. While the new salsa was being performed and offered in and for *la candela* (the fire), Ray's music was limited, characterized by sterility and the stereotypical. Of course, the combination of Richie Ray and Bobby Cruz always suggested an inevitable level of quality, and this, in the long run, saved the albums they recorded in that period from total disregard. Still, the musicians lagged behind the times, muddling along among the many performers of the retro-guard.

In 1975 Ray succeeded in setting the music of Bach to the rhythms of the mambo. The following year, when his orchestra celebrated its tenth anniversary, the pianist had a few more hits by putting some of his old songs into new arrangements. These, however, were isolated hits, nothing that amounted to much influence or innovation. After this, Ray and Cruz converted to an evangelical religion and began to use their music to preach. This resulted in rather vapid songs that spoke of universal love and a magnanimous generosity that would solve all the problems of everyday life. This was the final straw that led to their disaster. It is not that salsa is incompatible with religion, but simply that popular music does not take to these types of messages more appropriate for greeting cards or expressions of corporate sentiments at the holidays. The ideal dream where we are all one happy family was forced into the music, making for a very pathetic salsa without rhythm or power, vigor or passion. Moreover, the larger audience, which is never as malleable or gullible as is usually believed, began to suspect that all of this was posturing and just one more peculiar and pointless prank of the entertainment industry. At one point there was a concert billed as Salsa con Evangelio presented in Caracas's Poliedro. The headliners were Ray and Cruz, and they were joined by José Luis Rodríguez and Lila Morillo, both Creole singers equally involved in that religion. At the concert people were drinking beer and dancing in the aisles, making it seem like some sort of ecclesiastical orgy. The skimpy attendance was easily made fun of, and the failure was absolute. To any reasonable observer, this was a mockery not only of salsa but of religion itself, and the audience had every justification to ignore this new Richie Ray and stick with his old music, like those fabulous classics, "Jala, jala," and the coded "el niche que facha rumba . . . lo atara la Araché."

We have seen how, one by one, the former leaders lost their avant-garde standing within the salsa world. There was, however, one exception: Willie Colón. "The minor musician," the youngest and the least expert of all, Colón began performing with a band that was easily criticized only to become the most excellent representative of salsa. He exemplified all of salsa's weaknesses and all of its strengths—the best of the fancy salsa of the boom and the restlessness of that other salsa emerging on the outskirts and braving new paths and possibilities. Colón was fortunate to have been born into salsa and, therefore, to remain one of its leaders from beginning to end. Unlike many of his colleagues, Colón, who turned twenty-seven in 1979, was able to keep his avant-garde nature intact and still capitalize on the benefits of the industry and the boom that it had invented.

In previous chapters we observed how, in contrast to Eddie Palmieri, for example, Colón was able to count on the unconditional support of the recording companies; he consistently developed his music within the industry and for the industry. On the surface, this could lead to the mistaken idea that Colón was successful only because he was commercial and kept up with the latest trends and, thus, that he contributed very little to salsa. This common argument that more accurately applies to many other salsa figures has no relevance in Colón's case. Yes, he was commercial—perhaps the most commercial of all—but his virtues radiated authentically from salsa, not from the industry, and this difference determined his status as a true member of the avant-garde.

In 1975, having been out of the music scene for two years, Colón released a particularly unusual album, titled *El bueno, el malo, y el feo* (*The Good, the Bad, and the Ugly*). Here he worked through a wide gamut of musical experiments: from the danzón to rock, from salsa to Puerto Rican folk music, from the Spanish *pasodoble* to the Brazilian bossa nova. Colón was aided by the talents of Marty Sheller as arranger and by those of Yomo Toro on guitar. For vocals he asked Héctor Lavoe (who sang only two songs) and the then-unknown Rubén Blades, but Colón himself sang most of the repertoire, using that famous nasal tone of his for the first time. The album appeared at a time when the matancera trend was still fresh and interesting, when the boom had not yet exhausted all of its resources, and when the old style of Willie Colón—magnificently developed in *El juicio* and *Lo mato*—was still considered among the best in all of salsa. A change of similar magnitude was seen as totally unnecessary and inappropriate. But Colón made it anyway; he kept taking risks, and he kept himself in the avant-garde.

In parallel ways, before the end of 1975 Willie released another album that was particularly important: *Se chavó el vecindario*, in which he rescued for salsa the prominence and musicality of Mon Rivera. In this production, Colón's band of trombones also paid deserving homage to a figure that many considered directly responsible for the trombones in salsa: the already legendary Ramón Rivera Alers. Featuring the bomba and the plena, Colón emphasized the thread of continuity not only from the Puerto Rican tradition to salsa but also through the diverse sonorities in that line, from the trombones of yesterday to those of today. Likewise, Mon Rivera brought to bear a distinct focus rooted in the popular, with roguish and festive sensibilities and attention to the social issues that so often appeared in Colón's productions. This led to an extraordinary potpourri, including the classic tongue twisters that he revived for the new salsa:

Mangandinga talai trangandando contopitam
Y que tam con den tombe
Cachi cantandom.

Despite their interesting and expert qualities, these two albums from 1975 did not match the sales figures that Colón had achieved two years earlier. The musician, however, did not change the nature of his experiments. Far from going along with the conventional standards of the recording industry, he continued working on unique and innovative projects. For example, he played with the idea of a ballet, "a Latin ballet," based on the poem "Angelitos Negros" by Andrés Eloy Blanco. With a little artistic luck, it was produced for television and later recorded as the album *El baquiné de Angelitos Negros*, a sort of sampling of salsa music. This album sold even less than previous ones (it seems that salsa audiences were not readily attracted to albums without lyrics, and this one obviously featured only instrumental music from beginning to end). Furthermore, despite its great arrangements and interpretations, the music seemed less bold and less relevant. Colón, however, far from giving up, pursued his quest to find new possibilities. Regardless of the protestations and pleading of the entrepreneurs, he refused to return to the music that had made him famous at the beginning of the decade. For him, the experiments had to go on.

In 1977 those experiments finally came together on an album that became crucial for all of the salsa that followed, and that album was *Metiendo mano*. While Rubén Blades was already considered the most influential of all salsa composers, here, on a grand scale, Colón featured him as a singer. Colón also reaffirmed all of salsa's characteristics, and, with the trombones, he presented music full of social, even political content, a move that began a new style called "salsa with a conscience." This same trend was firmly established two years later when Colón and Blades released *Siembra*, an album that even amid the decline of the boom became the best-selling record in the history of Caribbean music. Before this feat, Colón had dominated the market with his album featuring the voice of Celia Cruz, the 1977 release, *Sólo ellos pudieron hacer este album*. As if this were not enough, *Comedia*, an album that Colón produced for Héctor Lavoe a year later, also reached maximum sales figures. All of this indicates how, in the closing days of the 1970s, with disco music taking over and with the New York salsa industry in a tailspin, Colón was able to reassert his avant-garde stance and become not only one of the leading figures of the salsa expression but also a consistently best-selling one.

Already by 1979, when the grooves of *Siembra* were spinning across the region, Colón released yet another new album characteristic of his constant questing and never conforming: *Willie Colón solo*. For this album, he replaced the usual trombones with a large band full of saxophones, violins, and complete percussion. This production was marked by clear and extraordinary achievements as well as clear and impressive failings. Searching for the ever-dangerous sophistication, Colón made the unpardonable mistake of "smoothing out" the music, making it fragile, even breakable, with delicate montunos that in no way could produce the fierceness so essential to salsa. Using a very poor female chorus, Colón recorded equally poor numbers such as "Sin poderte hablar" (although the practice of paid plugging turned this into a partial hit), "Tú eres tú, señora," and the instrumental "Julia," with a salsa that seemed like background music for a soap opera or for a television commercial trying to sell soap products to the average housewife. That same album, however, included great arrangements by Marty Sheller, Tom Malone, Héctor Garrido, Perico Ortiz, and Colón himself and quality songs such as "Juancito," "Chinacubana," and "Nueva York," a sort of final homage from the Latino to that ostentatious city, simultaneously cruel and generous, that had been the stage for a community to develop the salsa expression that eventually defined and represented every barrio in the Caribbean.

The song, advertised as one of Perico's best arrangements, was full of "figures," street noises that seeped into the mambo and montuno, elevating everyday life to a sphere where it seemed only music could go. All of this was spelled out in Colón's explanation of how he had come full circle: "El malo de aquí soy yo porque tengo corazón" (I am the bad one here because I have heart). That was where he began, only fifteen years old and full of defiance. Then came his second posture of "Mete la mano en el bolsillo saca y abre tu cuchillo y ten cuidado" (Shove your hand into the pocket of your suitcoat, pull out your knife, and watch out), where the violence of the barrio continued to dominate. The third posture, influenced by Blades's fuller involvement, revealed a more planned and thoughtful public consciousness: "Pablo Pueblo, Pablo Hermano . . . , siembra, siembra con amor y el futuro te dará" (Village Pablo, Brother Pablo . . . , sow, sow with love and the future will be yours). Now came this final posture in which the singer looked back in order to come to terms with it all, a complete and distinct summary of the "Latino turbulence" of the city still considered the capital of the world:

New York . . . when I am with you
I feel restless to get away
When I am far from you,
I'm crazy to see you . . .
Magical city of golden dreams
Capital of disillusionment.

A Singer-Songwriter

In 1970, Pete Rodríguez, still riding the fame of his "Micaela" and his boogaloo, recorded a special album, *De Panamá a Nueva York, Pete Rodríguez presenta a Rubén Blades*. This was the introduction to a new singer, Blades, who had composed all his own repertoire, an unusual occurrence in the salsa world. The album cover showed Rodríguez's orchestra sitting in a convertible—a typical scene of the times—and about to pick up a blonde hitchhiker who looked like one of those middle-class teenagers devoted to the insufferable subpar rock and roll. The young man, however, was into salsa, not rock; in fact, he was into a very particular kind of salsa noted not only for its evident rebellion but also for its clear political stance, as in the number "Juan González," about a slain guerrilla fighter: "The mountain is in mourning / Because they've killed Juan González." This album, released by the Alegre label, did not draw any major reaction from audiences. In New York, the Latino community had very little connection with the stories of guerrillas or those killed in the mountains, and in some Caribbean countries this album was preemptively banned for being subversive. Blades had no choice but to return to Panama, where he decided to give up his musical activity and enroll in the university to continue his study of law. Four years later, in 1974, Rubén returned to New York. With its politics of signing everyone to a contract (since, according to the greedy values of the industry, it was better to contain the competition in-house, even if they were ignored there and left to rot), Fania offered him an unfair agreement, and the Panamanian, eager for success, signed it without a second thought. Fania was beginning to enjoy the fruits of the boom and did not want to invest much in a virtually unknown singer who, besides, already had failed in his first big attempt. Because of this situation, aided by Ricardo Ray and armed with his law degree from the National University of Panama, Blades also negotiated for an office job with the company. He was assigned to the Office of Correspondence, a glorified mailroom. Stuck there licking stamps, the singer grew increasingly frustrated.

Blades, however, kept writing songs, although the producers discarded them for "having too many words" and for being too odd or too sophisticated. Even so, Ray had recorded Blades's "Guaguancó raro" back in 1971, and Ismael Miranda, who had gotten to know Blades on one of his many Fania tours to Panama, had acquired some of his songs. In fact, Miranda was the one who introduced the larger public to Blades's unique talents. That same year, 1974, Miranda recorded "Las esquinas son," a festive pachanga that portrayed the everyday incidents that happen on any street corner in any barrio. The song had wide appeal, even though it was nothing out of this world. The following year, though, when Miranda released *Este es Ismael Miranda*, the audience became acquainted with a new kind of salsa telling the story of a Panamanian bandit from 1806. This song, "Cipriano Armenteros," penned by Blades, inaugurated the all-important style of "narrative salsa" and became an extraordinary hit. Here was a new way of saying things with an intelligent irony that seeped into and revealed secondary meanings in the anecdote:

> The earth is trembling
> Armenteros has escaped
> The windows are closed
> And they won't open, not even for cash.

Two years later, when Miranda released his lesser album *No voy al festival*, the audience, which had been held in suspense, finally got the second part of Cipriano's story in the cut, "Vuelve Cipriano":

The second time, even the rooster was quiet
And the drunken voice of the bandit hummed
"I am a brave man, a male, one of the good ones,
And if I took off once, I can take off again."

In 1975 Ray Barretto decided to incorporate Blades into his orchestra as a singer, along with the Boricua vocalist Tito Gómez, and together they recorded and released a fabulous album. Months later, for his experimental album *El bueno, el malo, y el feo*, Willie Colón invited Blades to record "El cazanguero," a song Blades had written during his university days. Already, then, by 1976 the salsa world had found in Rubén Blades not only a songwriter with the exquisite ability to turn everything he wrote into a hit but also a singer who, with sophisticated phrasings, offered all of the spontaneity and rootedness that was expected of the soneros of popular salsa. The Panamanian, who was in some cases criticized for having a timbre similar to Cheo Feliciano's, was still able to create a personal style that quickly proved influential. For these reasons, the Fania All Stars, who had a closed-door policy when it came to letting new singers perform with the larger group, decided to break their own rules and invite Blades to participate on the album *Tributo a Tito Rodríguez*. Thereafter, when the orchestra was assigned the unfortunate duty of becoming a crossover in the U.S. market, Blades was the only singer to be contracted on a regular basis. In 1977 he recorded the extraordinary "Juan Pachanga"; the following year, "Sin tu cariño"; and by 1979, his last creation for the Stars, "Prepara," an intelligent son-montuno that showed off his ability to apply folk traditions to a strictly urban situation.

Blades achieved his greatest hit, however, when he was able to record his former music of social chronicle. This happened in 1977 with the album *Metiendo mano*, which I mentioned earlier in the discussion of Willie Colón. On this album, Blades returned to the work he had composed during his university days ("Pablo Pueblo"), augmenting his treatment of the initial event ("Pueblo") with irony and wit to sing about the conditions of the many "illegal" Caribbeans living in New York ("La maleta" ["The Suitcase"]). More remarkably, he made use of the full range of salsa styles that had been developed by the boom up to that point. For example, the album included the classic bolero "Me recordarás" (by Frank Domínguez, recorded with an impressive guitar solo by Yomo Toro); an obligatory classic of the best Cuban music (in this case "La mora" by Eliseo Grenet, smartly arranged by Willie Colón); a representative of folk music in its new urban adaptation ("Según el color"); and two intensely salsalike songs ("Lluvia de tu cielo," by the one-of-a-kind Johnny Ortiz, and "Plantación adentro," by

279

the essential Curet Alonso). This album became the most important model for the future development of salsa, a salsa that had been suggested from the beginning of the boom and that would be essential after the boom. At a time when the matancera trend was arbitrarily limiting salsa to an exclusively Cuban context, when the New York salsa was beginning to grow stale and wearily accommodating, the appearance of "Pablo Pueblo" was more than a surprise—it was a signal of real consequence. Again it is fitting to note that, despite the boom and its millions and the crazes created by the industry, salsa was a popular music created to give voice to the lived realities of the barrio where it was born, and it would have to continue to do just that:

> A man returns in silence
> Weary from his work. . . .
> To the street corner
> With its streetlights, its garbage, its noisy cantinas . . .
> Pablo Pueblo, son of the cry and the street,
> Son of the misery and the hunger,
> Son of the alley and the pain.

Because of this song, many critics began to speak about "the ruined salsa," the salsa "turned into protest," as if salsa, by some mysterious design, were condemned to speak only of topics that the matancera trend had made popular, those with exclusive reference to the "mulattas who dance in the fields" and to the betrayals by lovers who leave once the passion fades. These critics did not understand that popular music, as a true mirror of the social and cultural circumstances that give rise to it, can do nothing less than sing the stories that have accrued in those circumstances. Furthermore—and it is good to repeat this as much as is necessary—despite the industrial boom that created the trend for the matancera style, salsa was at its core only and wholly popular music. That core was explicitly affirmed by Blades himself in an interview that I did with him for the Caracas newspaper, *El Nacional* (May 13, 1979):

> I understand the strong reactions [to my music], but that, in fact, was my intention. Still, things aren't the way they've been painted, you know. I'm not the one who invented tap water or anything like that; music, like people, like love, has always been political, it's a simple thing. The composers of old, if you notice, wrote about love but also about politics and social issues, and it's like that, if you know what I mean. You can't separate yourself from the world you live in, from the reality that

surrounds you. If I make the kind of music that's considered popular, well then, I have no other choice but to work with and perform songs that connect to the people, and César, you understand this, the people know about parties and about love, but they also know about the other stuff, they know a lot.

Unlike other composers who were popular at the time, especially those who sprang up around salsa, Blades did not see the social theme as something tangential, as a simple attribute. On the contrary, the themes that concerned the daily lives of the collective were the focal point of his work and were treated with a specific political criteria rather than being left to arise by coincidence or chance. Therefore Blades provoked what he himself defined as a strong reaction. Some considered him a protest singer, and others, who continued to think of salsa as a minor art form barely good enough for a Saturday dance party, did not waver in their judgment of him as a demagogue, a trickster, and a showoff. But Blades rose above the criticism, the chatter, and the extreme labels they tried to pin him down with; he became an icon, an unusual personality who not only sold an impressive number of albums but who also *said* things and, more importantly, said them in the best ways that salsa has ever known. Without a doubt, by 1979 Rubén Blades had become the most important figure in salsa, and he sealed this achievement with *Siembra*, the second album he recorded with Willie Colón's orchestra. The album opens with the song "Plástico," "She was a plastic girl like many that we see; / Like those who when agitated sweat Chanel No. 3."

In this number Blades questioned the social position of "plastic people" (artificial, superficial people). Here his inspiration took a radical turn. The song begins by referring to other Latin Americans as "la gente de carne y hueso que no se vendió" (people of flesh and bones who do not sell themselves out). Then, while the chorus repeats only the first part of the phrase, "se ven las caras, se ven las caras" (we can see the faces, we can see the faces), Blades calls for unity and concludes with a majestic salsa-style roll call of Latin America:

A esa raza unida como Bolívar soñó [To that united race that Bolívar
    dreamed about]
Panamá: presente
Puerto Rico: presente
Venezuela: presente
Cuba: presente
República Dominicana: presente.

Finally, Blades recognizes that other presence: "la esquina, los estudian-tes, el barrio" (the street corner, the students, the barrio).

The rest of the album honors the popular as defined fully in Blades's interview. This definition includes love songs ("Buscando guayaba" and "Dime"), other affirmations of the social theme ("Ojos" by Johnny Ortiz, the only song not composed by Blades), "Siembra," and a portrait of two incredibly significant figures from popular culture. "María Lionza" repre-sents the deeply religious tradition in Venezuela, and "Pedro Navaja," de-picts the classic hoodlum of salsa, a threatening figure who is both the cause and effect of a world of drugs, knives, and violence: "I saw him pass by the corner of the old barrio / With that swing that the tough guys have when they walk."

"Pedro Navaja" became a hit of astounding proportion. Throughout the Caribbean, and especially in Venezuela, the lyrics gave rise to a host of interpretations and wild speculations, while the music inundated the airwaves and the figure of "Pedro" was parodied on television and in im-provised theater. All these media cashed in on the unbridled popularity of the song and enjoyed their share of its commercial success. Blades, how-ever, despite the deluge of commentary, critique, and praise, described his music from an exceptionally simple and humble perspective. In the inter-view cited previously, the singer also confessed,

> I think this is just my style, you know, I sing what I see, a whole line of characters that are all the same, all over Latin America. Since I know some of them, because, pretty much, I've been close to them my whole life, I know what they think, what pains them, what they long for, you know. If I am a popular singer, I have to sing about them, for them, whether it's the good stuff or the bad, they are part of the world that we know. And this isn't to praise them or make them heroes, no, it's just to try to say what they are all about, you know.

This approach secured Rubén Blades's position of privilege among the larger community of music lovers. He alone had the luxury of determining the new paths that salsa would branch into in the 1980s. This was not be-cause music now had to address social issues to have any value, but simply because a new spirit—deliberate and conscientious—had begun to mark salsa definitively in this way. The matancera trend of the boom—that ster-ile salsa of ineffective repetitions and exhausted harmonies—had petered out completely and was now left by the wayside.

NINE : ALL OF THE SALSAS

In 1979 another salsa album by a singer without any special talent or connections was produced in New York. I did not buy the album but looked at the cover. There was the singer, dressed elegantly in the style of a model advertising men's cologne, getting out of a luxurious Rolls Royce as a chauffeur in an impeccable uniform held the door open for him. A friend of mine who knew this singer laughed with a mixture of pity and dismay, saying, "But this guy is dirt poor, and now he wants us to think that he's a millionaire. . . . Look, the car is a private car, owned by the company, and the chauffeur is the driver for the company's owner." So we left the album on top of a huge mountain of albums, all forgotten and meaningless, also displaying that millionaire fantasy. Meanwhile, the store was playing Donna Summers's latest hit, more of the disco music that was dominating the market. Out on the street, a group of kids had a radio going full blast with an old song by Eddie Palmieri: "Vámonos pa'l monte, pa'l monte pa' guarachar, vámonos pa'l monte que el monte me gusta más" (Let's go to the mountain, to the mountain, to have fun, let's go to the mountain, it's better there). That song was recorded years ago, and still it had a mysterious force, full of power and *sabor*, with all of its feeling intact. After this song, there had been numerous trends, and the montuno, as if nothing had happened, went happily on. In those days, the entrepreneurs of salsa in New York, the same ones who had created and promoted the boom, were living their worst nightmare: the majority of their productions had gone cold, and the albums, instead of selling, were piling up in the warehouses. Disco music was creating a stir now, and the salsa boom, it seemed, had slipped into a coma.

In Venezuela, however, salsa albums were selling like hotcakes. Oscar D'León was a sort of mythic figure, and the best interpreters of salsa were received as true heroes of the real, enduring music. One journalist was upset about this, since he preferred English and any music in that language. But the most fabulous venue for popular music ever known in the Caribbean, the Poliedro, was sold out every time a musician from the barrio came to perform. Everyone was saying that salsa was dead, and it seemed that the pangs of the boom proved it. Those singers who impersonated Frank Sinatra were no competition for the Bee Gees. The others, however, those who continued to dress up as any neighbor of El Valle, maintained a rootedness and popularity that could not die. Something strange was happening when, in the midst of the decline of the salsa industry, a salsa album sold more than any other in the history of Caribbean music. At the height of a new international trend, when particular singers—authentic popular artists—were firmly ranked number one, something strange was happening indeed. The salsa industry was losing ground and sliding downhill, but the music, lifted by some unseen and indefinable force, was gaining strength and ascending the hill. In Caracas a small group of the exquisite and "cultured" argued over a mediocre show by Gloria Gaynor, while at the same time in Maracaibo, Rubén Blades performed live to a diverse crowd of people, singing his salsa with the gaita from the ensemble Guaco. This happened despite the fact that salsa "was not popular anymore," and despite that "fact," the venues, even the largest ones, were always full. We were now at the dawn of a new decade, and the inferiority complexes, it seems, were locked away. Two distinct levels were now apparent—perhaps the same ones as always. On one hand, at a supposedly refined and delicate height, there was the foreign music that requires deference to the world and that has never had anything to do with us. On the other hand, at the so-called low level of the everyday and the common, there was the other music, that roguish and piercing expression that brings together all of us who share the same culture, and this "low" level has always been more valuable than the high level. The salsa boom, which as a trend was able to move easily between both levels, was now dying under the weight of its own ridiculous arrogance, its gimmicks, and its fanfare. It is possible that the boom, which brought to light and imposed the term "salsa," may have taken the term down with it in its demise. However, and I have stated this already, the term is the least important thing. Instead of speaking of "salsa," from now on it would be better to speak of "salsas," for the Caribbean is vast and rich, and that richness suggests a magnificent synthesis. After all, before the term was introduced, the music already existed, and after the term disappears, the music will carry on. The barrio is in the Caribbean, and it is the ultimate owner of this song.

Twenty-five Years Later

In 1980, when *El Libro de la Salsa* was published, the so-called New York boom was already passing away. In the final chapter, I wrote about that death as an opening to a possible future, a future that would come through figures who have proved to be more than secondary. I insisted in my closing observation that "it is possible that the boom, which brought to light and imposed the term 'salsa,' may have taken the term down with it in its demise. However, and I have stated this already, the term is the least important thing. Instead of speaking of 'salsa,' from now on it would be better to speak of 'salsas,' for the Caribbean is vast and rich, and that richness suggests a magnificent synthesis." Twenty-five years later, the debate has not changed much. When the book's original editors and distributors referred to it as "the book of salsa" long before any title had been decided on, it seemed logical and natural to call it that—after all, that's what it was, a book about salsa. And they, Venezuelan to the core, had no major difficulty understanding the music in question. The same could be said about the Colombians or the Puerto Ricans, whether on the island or in New York. But something different happened with musicians of other generations, especially the Cubans, who read the term as an affront and an appropriation. The vigorous and inevitable return of Cuban music to the international scene in the last few years has done nothing more than exacerbate the debate: if the music making a comeback was the old son, then why call it "salsa"?

During the 1970s, however, it was already easy to gauge the distance that separated the traditional Cuban son from that other, disturbing and aggressive music being distilled in New York, Caracas, or San Juan. How much clearer, then, must the situation be today when the son is no longer the exclusive and fundamental source? (Why deny the gap—to quote one example—between the model that Pacheco made of the Sonora Matancera and the irreverence, from inside the barrio, of the duo of Colón and Lavoe?) Given the past two decades of satellite television, the Internet, the profusion of rock and its "Latino" derivatives, more jazz and also, of course, more "traditional" music, the question, de rigueur, must be "What is *salsa* today?" Or, better said, "What is *salsa* as distinguished from all the sounds created in the last decade?"

Let us return to the death of the boom in the 1980s. Among the many causes that precipitated this premature finale there were two distinct blows. First was the managerial chaos of the Fania Company, whose production drastically fell off and that featured, anyway, very little of interest, since its "Stars" had abandoned it to seek their fortunes with other labels. With a diminished catalog, therefore, Fania had no wind to fill its sails and carry on its wonderful initiatives of the past. The second blow came from the vigorous growth of the Dominican enclave in New York. A dynamic community, it consisted mostly of undocumented individuals who were highly motivated to make money fast and send it back home. Unlike the Boricuas, the Quisqueyanos had everything against them, and, despite the fact that they had been in the north for many years, with second and third generations born there, they continued to see themselves as migratory birds in a sort of temporary exile. They were very hard-working, and as their numbers increased, they began to make demands: the merengue, then, became the Latin music with the most volume and power in the city.

In the section titled "Quisqueya," I take into account how, in the mid-1970s, the salsa orchestras, given the push of the Dominicans in New York, began to incorporate merengues into their repertoire. Without repeating the precise details, I had assumed that the merengue would be considered part of salsa: "Actually, then, it *was* salsa [as I asserted in reference to a merengue concert in Radio City Music Hall in February 1979], because salsa, understood as the totalizing manifestation of the Caribbean of our times, was in a position to absorb and express the best virtues of popular music. And the merengue, with its intrinsic exuberance, fed directly into that largesse." But in those years of minimal salsa production, the increasing presence of merengue crowded out everything else and left other forms behind. The merengue was so pervasive that nobody chose to call it salsa. And, indeed, between the two expressions, a rift was beginning to grow.

In the two decades that followed, we encountered singers and orchestras of all types. The merengue diversified in such a way that the musical spectrum became more diffuse, with orchestras of all colors, sizes, qualities, and leadership, from the traditional ripiao to that computerized and scandalous version known as technomerengue. To the list of distinguished Dominicans such as Cuco Valoy, Rubby Pérez, Sergio Vargas, Fernandito Villalona, Chicha Peralta, Wilfrido Vargas, and Johnny Ventura, other names were added, those who were born outside Quisqueya but who had great success with the Dominican beat, as was the case with the Boricuas. For example, Elvis Crespo and, even more so, Olga Tañón, seemed unrivaled when it came to the merengue expression.

However, of all those responsible for this singular explosion of the merengue, there is one name that stands out as especially influential: Juan Luis Guerra and his 4:40. In fact, if there is a bridge that can be built between merengue and salsa, Guerra was its best and most important architect. In 1990, when everyone had spent a decade becoming accustomed to a merengue full of elegant and unusual harmonies marked by good taste and intelligence, Guerra presented the music world with an album full of humor and roguishness. That album quickly exceeded the sales records set by the already legendary *Siembra*. I am referring to his *Bachata rosa* (considered by many scholars and journalists, without exaggeration, as the most popular album of all times). Guerra surprised everyone by employing the bachata, a popular form in the Dominican Republic (Víctor Víctor was one of its main interpreters) but virtually unknown in the rest of the Caribbean. The bachata (to be scrupulously accurate, the term is Cuban) is very similar to the son and characterized by soft montunos and stylized harmonies that sing only the supplications of love. In addition to "consecrating" the bachata with such numbers as "Burbujas de amor," "Estrellitas y duendes," and the eponymous "Bachata rosa," Guerra's album included songs that were closer to salsa (such as "Abeja al panal" and "Carta de amor") and some merengues worthy of becoming classics ("La bilirubina," "Rosalía," and "A pedir su mano"). Two years later Guerra released *Areíto*, also of very high quality but without the sublime heights of its predecessor.

That *Bachata rosa* displaced *Siembra* from its place of honor in record sales is no passing detail, no minor feat. It is not unreasonable to argue that the name of Juan Luis Guerra refers us directly to that of Rubén Blades. In fact, for many critics, the work of the Dominican can be understood as a continuation of what the Panamanian had begun. Using other phrasings, in his own rhythms and styles, Guerra extended Blades's experiments with more than enough intelligence and success. I wrote earlier that Rubén Blades had a secure "position of privilege among the larger community of music lovers. He alone had the luxury of determining the new paths that salsa would branch into in the 1980s. This was not because music now had to address social issues to have any value, but simply because a new spirit—deliberate and conscientious—had begun to mark salsa definitively in this way." There the book ends, with *Siembra*, but what came later proved to be much more significant and enduring.

Blades inaugurated the 1990s with what would be seen as his most ambitious work, *Maestra vida*, a kind of immense mural across which he narrated the saga of three generations of a modest Panamanian family. A great orchestra, singers, actors, and narrators all converged to create an immeasurably unique, inimitable work that today is still listened to with awe. At the time, however, it was a commercial failure of historic proportions, 180 degrees from the sales success of *Siembra*. Later, with Willie Colón, Blades returned with his last album of importance, *Canciones del solar de los aburridos*, only to take off immediately with his group Seis del Solar to record interesting albums informed by more of his personal experiences but of very uneven quality. The so-called poet of salsa continued to foreground the political tone of his lyrics ("Desaparecidos," "El padre Antonio y el monaguillo Andrés," "Buscando América," "Patria," and "Prohibido olvidar" are all excellent examples) and to experiment freely with music that was far from the conventional patterns of the salsa son. Few of these experiments, however, were well received by the usual listeners to and dancers of salsa. For them, the figure of Blades became more and more difficult to decipher (was he a film actor in Hollywood, presidential candidate in Panama, graduate student at Harvard, or . . . ?). Nevertheless, he was unquestionably one of the most important innovators to determine and influence all of the music known throughout the Caribbean in the second half of the twentieth century.

Yet, how do we define Blades's music now that a new century has begun? Is his music still considered salsa, or are we facing a wider panorama without thematic or formal limits? Two of Blades's last productions—*La rosa de los vientos* from 1996 and *Mundo* from 2002, without a doubt among the most beautiful in his long discography—can help us in reaching an answer. The former is an album that solidly represents Panama because he used only musicians from that country. He reached out to interpreters and composers of all generations and schools in order to present a music that represented the full and profuse spectrum of Caribbean sounds, where, from the cumbia to the son, everything fits. The latter album displayed Blades's growing ambition. Under the banner of "fusion" and supported by his new group, the very talented and versatile Costa Rican Ensemble Editus, Blades experimented with the Irish gaita in guaguancó; with the tango, flamenco, and Brazilian rhythms; and using a great deal of jest, anger, and joy, with salsa . . . always with salsa.

Blades was associated with the specific group Guaco. This was not an arbitrary connection. In the late 1970s, there were various opportunities for the Panamanian to perform sones with the Venezuelan band, and this was a tempting and interesting way to deal with the salsa that was struggling to find new paths, to chart its new destinies. Guaco, initially an ensemble of gaita zuliana, became a fuller ensemble with complete percussion and brass sections, an electronic keyboard, and choruses attempting risky harmonies. It did not take long, then, for this ensemble to develop a style and a rhythmic attack that was unique in the region. For them, the traditional definition of salsa was not enough. The Venezuelan critic and scholar Alejandro Calzadilla, in his much-needed book *La salsa en Venezuela*, identified the inventive Guaco with groups such as Guayacán in Colombia and Batacumbelé in Puerto Rico.

When we speak about musical expressions, we often point out that they arise from the most dissimilar origins and go through salsa on their way to defining their own path. In the process, they may adopt or ignore the term, but this detail is not that important. In the case of Venezuela, for instance, groups that were initially more closely defined as rock and its numerous "Latino" derivatives in reality took us further away. Amigos Invisibles, Bacalao Men, Desorden Público, and King Changó, among others, form part of this list, to which we have to add Vagos y Maleantes, in the hip-hop style, and unclassifiable musicians, such as the virtuoso flutist Huáscar Barradcas, who freely experiment with jazz, the gaita, and folk music.

True salsa, however, was never abandoned in Venezuela. Even in the 1990s when the field was being described as *salsa vieja* (old salsa) or, more relevantly, *salsa brava* (hard salsa), we had groups such as El Cadáver Exquisito; Team Malín; El Guajeo, led by Alfredo Naranjo; the legendary Moisés Daubeterre, who never stopped singing sones from his own repertoire; La Banda Sigilosa; and, as I prepare these final pages, the interesting and energetic Bailatino and Timba Loca, led by Gonzalo Grau. Among female performers, it is impossible to overlook the contributions of Canelita and her daughter, Trina Medina, each with her own distinct yet connected style, as well as the legendary Soledad Bravo, whose beat came steadily and durably through the Caribbean openings. In the commercial scene, the band called Los Adolescentes stands out for its extreme popularity among young audiences. Finally, in the traditional style, it is important to note the legendary Dimensión Latina, who despite all their ups and downs never completely abandoned the stage. Similarly, there are those other, almost eternal, orchestras whom the informed music lover would never call "salsa": Los Melódicos, led by Renato Capriles; the Billo's (now under the leadership of Luis María Jr., who replaced his father, the maestro Frómeta); and Porfi Jiménez. Of all these orchestras, however, there are two that merit special mention as we near the terrain that interests us now. One is Saxomanía, which, under the leadership of the sax player Rodolfo Reyes, released two outstanding albums: *Homenaje a Héctor Lavoe* (where they had the guts to do without a singer, a risk in a salsa orchestra) and *Homenaje a Ismael Rivera* (featuring the Boricua singer Andy Montañez and the Venezuelan Francisco Pacheco on a couple of songs and soneos). The other orchestra, under the baton of the distinguished arranger Andy Durán, has been able to offer the most demanding listener worthwhile productions full of sabor that energetically go against the current standards of the recording industry. Instead their music moves between salsa and jazz to present a sound in sync with the golden age of the legendary big bands.

A separate section should be devoted to Alberto Naranjo, drum player, arranger, composer, and orchestra director. He has assumed leadership of the Venezuelan musical expression of the last few years. His leadership ability developed during his days with El Trabuco Venezolano and was later confirmed through his numerous conference lectures and business articles and, of course, his music. Some of his productions from that time are worthy of being collector's items. For example, *Imagen latina* features a reunited El Trabuco, joined by performers of the caliber of Aldemaro Romero, Simón Díaz, Serenata Guayanesa, María Rivas, Otmaro Ruiz, and

Saúl Vera, among others. *Swing con son* showcased its Latin Jazz Big Band in a very important homage to Billo Frómeta, while *Dulce y picante* presented a New World Jazz Band interpretation of the music of Luis Alfonzo Larrain, and the palpably emotional production, *Cosas del alma*, was produced with the singer Delia.

But when speaking of salsa and of the Venezuelan contribution to this expression, the name that truly takes on a central role is that of Oscar D'León, as I discussed earlier: He was one of those exceptional singers who inevitably created unique models, always able to add a touch of novelty to the old sones. Just as he made the montuno the center of his specialty, attacking it with intelligence, making a continuous game of the melodies that he shaped according to his desire and whim, he always had the catchy phrase at hand, one that completed and added to the spirit and meaning of the songs that he sang. What was evident by the end of the 1970s was accentuated in the following decade so that, by the mid-1980s, Oscar D'León was known as "El Sonero del Mundo" (The World's Sonero). Even though this was just a fancy marketing label, it was not divorced from reality. Not only was Oscar the most complete of the great soneros (his name was a central one at every New York concert), but he also had been able to secure the dream that so often slipped through the hands of the Fania entrepreneurs: to take salsa to all the corners of the world. It was not long before he had taken over Europe, from the coldest point of the north to the warmest spot on the Mediterranean, and he became a regular presence in the Far East, just to mention two geographical extremes. The reason behind such a success story is to be found, obviously, in the quality of the interpreter. D'León, armed with an ironlike discipline, managed to have his orchestra function consistently like a precision machine. A veteran from the oldest and most intractable slum, he found a way to create a repertoire that met with applause and brought him a loyal following among dancers of all generations. Now I must add a couple dozen albums to those that I previously reviewed in this book, albums that, without major discrepancies or exceptions, maintain the quality and sabor of his work with the drive of a battering ram. After so many years, dances, rumbas, and concerts, lovers of good music acknowledged D'León's as the best-sounding band of a lifetime.

Of the many places to which Oscar D'León took his music, only one would seem faraway and impossible: Cuba, the very birthplace of the son, and only a few hours' flight from his beloved Caracas. For someone who grew up humming "Mata siguaraya" as Benny Moré sang it with Mariano Mercerón's orchestra, to step on Cuban soil was almost like stepping into paradise. Only there could he find the essential consecration of his work (the one he was truly interested in after having been around the world).

That was the only place and the only audience that he thought could give it to him. Although he went to Cuba during the 1980s, it was still a very risky enterprise, perhaps prohibited, for a singer with such commercial success in the United States. In fact, with the notable exception of his performance in Colombia in 1979 (including an isolated recording with La Típica 73), D'León was one of the few Spanish interpreters and Latin American sympathizers of the regime ever received on the island as an "international star." But, as a musician and grateful sonero first and foremost, D'León took the risks and arrived in Havana in November 1983 with his orchestra and excessive luggage. The rest is history.

It took even more for D'León to repair the damage of his courageous trip. It was years before the recording industry and the U.S. public, especially those in Miami, forgave his "sin." (For a long time, for example, Celia Cruz refused to sing with him onstage). D'León was not a man of politics, and he felt very uncomfortable having to explain his trip. Those of us who have known him well since the prehistoric days of La Dimensión can testify that this honest Caracas musician was far from sharing in or applauding what occurred politically on the island of Cuba, and for many in the Caribbean, the music is much more important than politics. It was for music, after all—and it is important to reiterate this—that Oscar traveled to Cuba. He owed a hug full of tears to Benny's mother, and he owed the "Suavecito a Santiago" and "Los tamalitos de Olga"—among so many other pleasures and flavors—to Havana. The chroniclers of the island (all of their stories corrected or deleted once D'León confessed that he did not like the Cuban regime) wrote tirelessly about the most important visit of this foreign musician, and they reviewed the virtual musical earthquake that represented each of the Venezuelan's performances. The euphoric multitudes quickly filled and exceeded the capacity of the theaters, spilling into the plazas, streets, and avenues, coming simply to dance and enjoy the Cuban music. And what was most remarkable was that this was a unique experience for most of them, especially the young people. Many years later, in a documentary by Mundo Olé, the Cuban singer Albita Rodríguez made this amazing remark: "It was Oscar D'León who made us know Cuban music, who taught us to love it and to enjoy it."

For the reader of this book, this phrase from Albita could be misread as a refusal to see another side of reality, for certainly there are extraordinary Cuban interpreters on the streets of Europe and the United States or crowned as successful musicians in New York. The Chan Chan of Compay Segundo, for example, will sound until the end of time in all corners of the earth. The issue, however, is not that simple. What we have, in fact, is a large black stain that has spread across too many years of the Cuban "silence." The questions accumulate: Why wasn't a pianist of Rubén González's stature able to record his first album as a soloist until he was nearly eighty years old and then only for a foreign company? Why was there no great explosion of Cuban music on a global level until the 1990s? What happened in the 1970s and 1980s? Was the blockade responsible for all of these omissions? And, if so, why did the music of Los Van Van never get silenced? Why didn't Chucho Valdez and his Irakere, for instance, stop touring the world, as happened with La Aragón or Los Papines? What was the difference? What distance really separated one Cuban musician from another? The answers to these and other questions may help to explain Albita's statement.

I first traveled to Havana in January 1978. I was there as a member of the production crew for an album that was going to be recorded with the singer Alfredo Sadel. This was a coproduction by a small Venezuelan company (YVKCT con Música) and the powerful Egrem Company owned by the Cuban government. Sadel, who was very excited about reuniting with an audience that had given him the most applause and showered him with gifts during his golden age, wanted to record a bit of everything: old classics and new music with both veteran and emerging musicians. The Cubans, however, insisted on accentuating the "modern," calling the rest "disposable." On the first night of our arrival we were treated to a presentation in one of the rooms of the Hotel Riviera by the great group, "the best that Cuba has to offer to the world," Irakere. This was the original band, with Valdez, D'Rivera, Sandoval, Averhoff, Del Puerto, Morales, and Plá. Everything was great: the music was wonderful, an extraordinary combination of Cuban music with a bit of rock and jazz, but . . . where was the son? Tony Tano, the musician who coproduced the album and who served as our liaison with Egrem, dissuaded us from looking for the old music and its interpreters. The Cuban revolution is set on looking to the future, he insisted, and the young people now are different—they have a different mindset and seek out other alternatives. As a result, he further explained, the pillars of past music—such as Chapotín, Cuní, or Celeste Mendoza—recorded very little or nothing at all.

Almost two decades later, however, the veteran U.S. rock musician Ry Cooder decided to bet against these odds and went to Cuba to look for and record the old music, only the old music. The concerts and recordings that came of that quickly became one of the most significant phenomena of popular music at the end of the century (*The Buena Vista Social Club*). Nominations for international awards were numerous—including the prestigious Grammy—and yet the multimillion sales of those albums were met with the shortsighted and absurd attitudes of many former Cuban producers and planners. Now, however, after musical lives marked in great part by the imposed silence, Compay Segundo, a spry man of nearly ninety, successfully flirted with younger women across the continents; Rubén González recorded a magnificent solo album before his death; and the soneros Manuel "Puntillita" Licea, Ibrahim Ferrer, Pio Leyva, and Raúl Planas, among others, finally received the long-overdue and well-deserved ovation of audiences on the most important stages of the world.

Following this genuine Cuban boom, a number of musicians from various generations who were devoted to the definitive, timeless, and controversial son also came to the fore. Chief among these were the bass player Orlando "Cachaito" López (who, as son of Orestes and nephew of the great Cachao, was a direct descendant of that dynasty); the tres player, arranger, and composer Juan de Marco González, to whom much of the sound of the Buena Vista Social Club and of the Afro-Cuban All Stars is indebted; the virtuoso trumpet player Jesús Alemany, who, with a band of his own, decided to rescue the unique sonority of Arsenio Rodríguez; and Sierra Maestra, an aggressive son ensemble that conveyed much of the new spirit through the brilliant and finely tuned voice of José Antonio "Maceo" Rodríguez. And these are only a few of the musicians who were part of the more "traditional" side of things. Others engaged in the timba, a musical variant of the last few years that is a modern, up-tempo, and somewhat strident way of attacking the son. Ironically, given that years before such a classification would have been considered an anathema, many of these musicians were now presented as performers of salsa. For example, the singer Manolín was called "the Doctor of Salsa," and the sonero Isaac Delgado was designated "El Chévere de la Salsa." In this vein, I also have to mention NG La Banda, the virtuoso flutist José Luis Cortés, and another flute player, Orlando "Maraca" Valle, who made key contributions with his own orchestra. Other interesting emerging groups include Vocal Samplín, which uses six a capella voices, and Asere, a sextet in the most traditional structure of the sonero ensemble that brings a truly fresh and youthful approach to the son. Likewise, Adalberto Alvarez and his band, Son 14, well known outside the island during the 1980s, have continued creating their own music, as has another group with so many decades behind them, Los Van Van, under the steady leadership of bass player, arranger, and composer Juan Formell. This is a very brief and paltry excerpt from what is actually an endless list, because (with some obvious and sad exceptions) just like the Cuba of old, the island today is still completely inhabited by musicians.

After the demise of the Soviet Union and in those times of the "special period," much of this Cuban reemergence resulted, as I already said, from the involvement of U.S. production companies. However, Spain was the country that truly guaranteed this whole display. It is not worthwhile to explain now the commercial ties that remained fairly intact during the long years of the embargo and of communism, nor the solid historical and cultural bonds that make Cuba the first (or, to be more exact, the last) of the Spanish outposts on this side of the world. More noteworthy, Spain enthusiastically embraced the salsa expression from the early 1980s on, and much of the best flamenco of that time—from Martirio to the Barbería del Sur, to mention two emblematic examples—fits very happily in this terrain. From audiences to recording companies and from television channels to theaters, all Spaniards adopted Cubans and other Caribbean musicians as their own, and this translated into albums, concerts, and even documentaries of a superlative quality. Special mention goes to the filmmaker Fernando Trueba, author of the beautiful film *Calle 54*. Among its many merits, the film preserved some of the last performances by musicians of the stature of Tito Puente and Chico O'Farrill. It "rescued" Jerry González and his Fort Apache Band and presented two classic duets—*Cachao and Bebo Valdez*—by the very Bebo and his son "Chucho," an event that had been considered impossible for many decades (although their first collaboration, of course, appeared on an album by Paquito D'Rivera). Trueba had become a kind of mentor to the old Bebo and later produced an album whose first chords announced its interests quite clearly. On that album, *Lágrimas negras: Bebo y Cigala*, the eighty-year-old Cuban pianist performed in a way that allowed the Andalusian thirty-year-old to sing, in his own dramatic style, the claims of love most deeply rooted in Caribbean despair. Listening to them brings to mind the saying, "We never get old in the music." In other words, it is senseless to speak about generations in a context where time, like the failure of love, stands still.

On the other side of the world, New York was the city that held absolute power over salsa music for almost thirty years. In the 1980s, for the first time, however, it fell under the influence of the music coming out of Puerto Rico. Young singers, originally trained in the traditional orchestras of the island, began to take over as soloists, and they imposed an easygoing and sweet style that was 180 degrees from what was called salsa brava. Their *salsa erótica* was characterized by an accommodating and bland style, a flat rhythm in the voices and orchestrations, and most of all, lyrics that tried to mask a lack of talent with a posture of sexual daring. This was the salsa of Frankie Ruiz, Eddie Santiago, Toni Vega, Ray Ruiz, and the youngest among them, Jerry Rivera. On another level, somewhat above those performers but within that overall style, I would put the Nicaraguan Luis Enrique, the sophisticated Marc Anthony, La India, and Tito Nieves.

Meanwhile, the orchestras that had been considered traditional, the same ones that promoted styles and sounds characteristic of the early boom days before the 1970s, persisted in a never-ending contest for dance gigs and for survival. While fans encountered album after album of varying quality, of hits and misses, this ongoing production was still very important. One tends to approach those albums with the same confidence, appreciation, and pleasure with which one visits an old friend. Willie Rosario (now known as "The Master of Rhythm and Swing"), celebrated forty years on the timbal, and the bandleader Tommy Olivencia was not far behind that milestone. Bobby Valentín, in a flawless album called *Vuelve a la cárcel* (recorded live), celebrated thirty-five years in the industry, and also nearing that mark, Ricardo Ray and Bobby Cruz put on a fabulous celebratory concert of their own. Visiting the island from New York, the "Dean" Ray Barretto (introduced as "The Giant of Salsa"), celebrated nothing less than a half-century on the congas; El Gran Combo, led by Rafael Ithier, seemed to challenge immortality; and the legendary Roberto Roena, already bald and stooped, went on dancing and playing his bongo with a delighted, devilish gleam in his eye. Meanwhile, the pianists in Borinquen opened up a place of honor for the master of all: Papo Lucca, accompanied, as ever, by his Sonora Ponceña.

We can add to this roster a newer orchestra, Puerto Rican Power, that, despite its youth, had totally absorbed the old spirit as well as some of the voices that helped to build the grand palace of the original salsa. Those voices included Ismael Miranda, Andy Montañez, Tito Allen, Luigi Texidor, Justo Betancourt, Henry Fiol, Adalberto Santiago, and Marvin Santiago (who, despite his retirement in 1979, was able to make a comeback, and what a comeback it was!). Most especially, I include Cheo Feliciano, who, after twenty five years, remains the most loved and respected of all. Feliciano maintained his unique timbre so emblematic of the Caribbean song (from the wildest salsa to the most passionate bolero), and his repertoire—with all that we experience and listen to on his albums—remains the most genuine and defining. The mere evocation of his name, today as yesterday, is a great cause for the celebration of this music.

Looking to the future, none other than Gilberto Santa Rosa has become one of Feliciano's clear descendants. Originally from Rosario's band, Santa Rosa began to carve out his own niche at the end of the 1980s with a style that was tuneful, intelligent, and elegant, one that quickly won him the nickname "The Gentleman of Salsa." In a musical field where taunts and trouble are more frequently valued, this gentlemanly quality seems synonymous with a complacent and cowardly song, as we can well imagine after so many earlier sappy soneos and erotic styles. Santa Rosa, however, struck the fierce tone that salsa demands: his music was fast, assertive, and full of sabor, as in the most aggressive salsa, and with the perfect mixture of revenge and acquiescence that makes for a great singer in the tradition of the love-song. He was directly influenced by Feliciano, it has been said, but even more so by Tito Rodríguez. Bolstered by arrangers such as Ramón Sánchez, Tommy Villarini, and the distinguished Cuco Peña, and by truly talented composers such as Omar Alfaro and Jorge Luis Piloto, Santa Rosa made an impact from his very first recordings: *Punto de vista* (1990) and *Perspectiva* (1991). This impact could make him the best-selling artist of the decade, equally applauded by old and new salsa fans. In Gilberto Santa Rosa, the term "commercial," which was generally used to disparage someone's music, acquires the completely opposite connotation, and in an ideal world, he would be the pinnacle of this expression, in any era and regardless of any current fashion in Caribbean music.

On another shore, without the privilege of mass marketing (because in reality they did not see this as a goal), other musicians, the rebels or the wild ones, navigated the waters of music intrigued only by innovation and the avant-garde. At the beginning of the 1980s, when the New York boom was still unwilling to recognize it was on its deathbed, many of the musicians who served to fuel it took refuge in Puerto Rico, looking for new beats and original sounds. The virtuoso percussionist Angel Cachete Maldonado stands out here, and he soon became the leader of a fundamental group called Batacumbelé. Their first album, recorded between January and March 1981, is a classic: *Batacumbelé con un poco de songo*. The bass player Eddi "Guagua" Rivera, the pianist Erick Figueroa, the Cuban percussionist Ignacio Berroa, the bongo player Pablito Rosario, the trumpet player and singer Jerry Medina, the trombone player Papo Vásquez, and the colossal conga player Giovanni Hidalgo all formed part of this initial takeover under the direction of veteran producer Frank Ferrer. A few years later, they offered an equally rich second album, *En aquellos tiempos*. Batacumbelé soon became the first plank of the bridge that would connect the avant-gardes in Puerto Rico, Cuba, Panama, Colombia, and Venezuela. Many of those musicians later did solo work that was characterized by the same sense of adventure and experimentation. The results were uneven but truly positive: their efforts were sincere and therefore respected. Before discussing other ensembles, let me mention Descarga Boricua, also produced by Ferrer, whose record creations, especially the second one, cannot be ignored. The big names of the good salsa of the 1970s now merged with those of younger talents who in the 1990s were just reaching adulthood. The music they produced together gives the sense of an open and limitless party, going from Tito Rodríguez to Maná and from Heny Alvarez to Aaron Copland in a unique display of inventiveness, bravery, and sabor.

South of the Caribbean, Colombia created its own unique displays. Somehow, without exporting anything during the boom, by the 1980s this country began to foster bands with their own particular and brilliant sound, most of them characterized by frankness, ingenuity, a fierce beat, and aggressive melodies. Besides Arauca, the first orchestra that I became familiar with was Fruko and his Tesos. Totally popular in Barranquilla and throughout the Caribbean coast, this group had plenty of attributes that even the foreign ear could identify as legitimately *Colombian salsa*. Two attributes especially stood out: the use of rhythms and melodies from coastal folk music (although, to be honest, these were never very pronounced or consistent) and an explosive sonero, Joe Arroyo, who was responsible for some of the most interesting songs in their repertoire. Considering that he had released his first albums more than twenty years earlier and that his later works as a soloist and bandleader emphasized more than ever his inclination for native rhythms, we can easily assign the whole weight and significance of Colombian salsa to this singular singer.

The other band that best illustrates the Colombian sound is Grupo Niche, under the leadership of the *jairo* Varela. For many music lovers, Varela was the first to internationalize Colombian salsa, and he established this beginning with his first album, *Al pasito* in 1979. As its title clearly indicates, the song to blackness was the banner and raison d'être of this band, a way of correcting the bland and "white" danceable music that other orchestras played. Embracing the so-called social song, which Blades and Curet Alonso, among others, had developed in a systematic way, Niche added the nuances of Colombian tones and circumstances in their first pieces from the 1980s. However, at the end of the decade, Varela made a slight but significant shift in the tone of his repertoire. The love song, treated with roguishness and simplicity, became his signature style. In some of his most recent productions (from the mid-1990s until the present), his repertoire is again accented with a full range of autochthonous rhythms.

Yet, in going against the current, the Caribbean coast was not the principal producer of the most important Colombian salsa. On the other side of the country, the city of Cali took on that privileged role. Site of legendary festivals throughout the region, it became the obligatory stage for all of the important orchestras of the Caribbean and New York. Many consider the Richie Ray and Bobby Cruz band that took off in the 1960s as the orchestra that was chiefly responsible for sowing the seed of salsa in Colombian soil. (It is no coincidence that much of the Puerto Rican repertoire was inspired by the themes, people, and cities of their neighboring country.) The leading orchestra and, according to general consensus, the one most representative of the Colombian sound also came from Cali: Guayacán. From its first moment, following the vision of Alexis Lozano and Nino Caicedo, this band pursued a new approach to the rhythm and the melody. They drew directly on all of the percussion instruments and on the beats of the black communities in Colombia, especially those along the Pacific. This was not an avant-garde group that cloistered itself inside a studio and produced only for the musicologist. Guayacán was, first and foremost, a popular orchestra, and an extremely commercial one, capable of transforming every recording into a hit, and not just in Colombia. After a hiatus of about five years, when people feared that they had disappeared for good, they released *Otra cosa*, perhaps one of their most polished works, and the musicians insist that Guayacán will be around for a long time to come.

Certainly, there are many Colombian orchestras that have come and gone, performed and pleased audiences, triumphed and disappeared over the past twenty-five years. For now, I will limit myself to three of the most representative and to the bandleaders that founded them. However, I do not want to close this section without mentioning some of the other musicians who, with or without their own orchestras, made significant contributions to the best salsa music. Almost all of them, curiously, came from outside Colombia. The list begins with the talented Kike Santander, pianist Héctor Martignon, trumpet player Eduardo Maya, percussionist Memo Acevedo, and saxophonist Justo Almario, and it includes, in a very special way, the pianist Eddie Martínez. Martínez, who had been chiefly responsible for the vigor and sonority of the best Barretto orchestra during the golden era of the boom, spent many tireless years straddling the avant-garde and the traditional. Many audiences in the United States and in Europe are acquainted with his bold experiments, his talent and inventiveness. For instance, Cubop City, the Dutch orchestra led by the Dutch timbal player Lucas van Merwijk (yes, you read correctly: they are all from Holland!) featured a song specifically arranged by Martínez in homage to Benny Moré. Martínez also led the band's performance of that number and, without a doubt, was the one who made those fair-skinned musicians use their obvious and incredible talents to sweat blackness so effectively they had no reason to envy the best bands of the Caribbean. I also want to make special mention of another of my compatriots, the forceful Venezuelan sonera Yma América. Like many others—including two great percussionists from my homeland, Gerardo Rosales and Orlando Poleo (a

legitimate member of the Mount Olympus of percussionists from his generation and a leader of the Caribbean rumba in Paris)—América is now on the other side of the world. These musicians took very seriously the adage that one should take one's music to the far reaches of the planet.

Nevertheless, let us return to the United States, to the west coast, where the weight of the Mexican community is so dominant that there is little space for other Latino communities, especially those from the Caribbean. This also may explain why salsa did not develop extensively or take root and spread throughout this region. Still, from Los Angeles and San Francisco, as was expected, interesting manifestations of salsa emerged in line with the sounds that Cal Tjader, Mongo Santamaría, and Willie Bobo had cultivated in the 1960s. They entered the scene through the side door of jazz, although some of the so-called Latin rock also played a part. From branches as diverse as Santamaría and Carlos Santana—especially in San Francisco—an audience began to develop and little by little to demand and cultivate its own musical groups. The Mexican conga player Poncho Sánchez, a direct descendant of Tjader, started a band that recorded regularly. (Though their repertoire did not contribute anything significant, they performed well enough and with sufficient sabor to remain solvent and develop a devoted following.) The pianist Rebeca Mauleón offers more eclectic recordings, along with other daring feats, and the timbal player Bobby Matos leads an orchestra that ceaselessly tries to promote Afro-Cuban jazz head-on.

That is also the territory of Pete Escovedo and his dynasty, as well as of the Cuban timbal player Orestes Vilató—a master among masters. In the last quarter-century, after having left New York, Vilató has been with a wide variety of bands, from Santana's to Mauleón's. Along the way he worked with a very special group, Cuba L.A., where he shared leadership responsibilities with the flute player Danilo Lozano. Together they made recordings of Cuban classics with a temporary ensemble that dared to be particularly irreverent: they used no vocals (only on his second album do we hear a pair of songs actually sung). Finally, San Francisco was the scene that gave birth to Conjunto Céspedes, a group with a repertoire strongly marked by the Cuban tradition and the Yoruba musical legacy. This exceptional ensemble was formed under the leadership of Gladis Bobi Céspedes, a sonera and songwriter of the band's original songs, and her nephew, Guillermo Céspedes, who also served as pianist, tres player, and musical director. Through all of these musicians the profile of Latino music in California radically changed.

On the other side of the continent, on the Atlantic coast, the city of New York moved to another beat when it came to salsa. No longer was this city the great mecca that until the beginning of the 1980s everybody had flocked to, anxiously searching for success. As a Latino market, New York continues to be very important, but it is no longer the place that dictates what is key: simply put, one *can* live without it. In fact, in terms of an exclusive site for salsa, there are very few orchestras or soloists who currently impose, from New York, their trends or approaches on the communities of music lovers and dancers in the Caribbean.

Thus, no longer under the guiding star of the salsa world, New York musicians watched as the old orchestras were dissolved or as they reformed themselves into less than innovative bands that, under the same or different names, spent more time on the streets than in the recording studios. The Orquesta Broadway had aged. In its place, a charanga ensemble with a very eclectic style more in tune with the new musical trends of the city emerged. Under the direction of the timbalist Johnny Almendra, they called themselves Los Jóvenes del Barrio. Elsewhere, the pianist Oscar Hernández, already a veteran among veterans, abandoned his experiments in order to concentrate on a band that renewed the best sounds of the old salsa, the Spanish Harlem Orchestra. As if diving into the tunnel of time, the label Caimán made up its own group of "All Stars," and under the leadership of Alfredo Valdés Jr. began jam sessions to stave off the sad state of things. (A number of old figures returned here in an attempt to revive the old spirit: Zervigón, Mangual, Cardona, Montalvo, Papaíto, Bobby Rodríguez, Casanova, Sabater, and so on and so on, ad infinitum it seems.) On other corners I witnessed performances by Harlow and Pacheco that, without the support of their former, iconic orchestras, suggested a sort of orphanhood from the glories of the boom. Willie Colón was one of the few in this lot able to maintain a regular recording schedule, but he had to do a little bit of everything, even soap operas, and for a long time took refuge in Mexico City. As for the Dominican sonero José Alberto, "El Canario," steadfast and persevering, he held on to an important place in the salsa scene, but his extraordinary colleague, the Cuban Miguelito Quintana, was not as fortunate. I mention only a few meaningful examples here because the whole list would be too long and painful. During the years of Marc Anthony and La India, there was just not enough space for these sonorities.

With this new tide against them, the enduring presence of Manny Oquendo and his Conjunto Libre is of double merit. With the unwavering solidarity of his bass player Andy González, the old master was able to keep the sound of his band youthful and pertinent, a band that for three decades had been fundamental to fans of the authentic salsa brava. While their record production was sporadic and in some cases carried by unknown labels that required their fans to take on the role of detectives, there was no doubt about their value. In the final balance there will be ample room at the top reserved for Oquendo, his heavy timbal, and his very particular way of embodying and performing this music.

But the city did open up another avenue for these Caribbean beats, the same one, curiously, that welcomed Chano Pozo when he put the first conga onto a New York stage: jazz. From the early days of be-bop with Dizzie Gillespie and Charlie Parker to the new millennium, the empire that made giants of Machito and his Afro-Cubans, Chico O'Farrill, and Tito Puente, among others, remained basically unchanged. From this perspective, the Caribbean music produced in the city already emits a different glow. Until the day that death took the drumsticks from his hands, Puente had dedicated himself to exploring this border with jazz, usually with small ensembles, and that was where he had put his best efforts for the last twenty-five years of his life. When he died in May 2000, The King left as his legacy a prolific output and an unequalled musical career marked by more than 100 albums and with a repertoire as extraordinary as it was extensive. This, of course, garnered him awards and accolades not given to any other salsa musician.

In 1992, thanks to the initiative of the German Gotz A. Worner (from the Messidor label), Mario Bauzá was able to regain his privileged place in New York; that is, he once again had a big enough "big band" to show off the full richness of his arrangements. Worner also released the first of Bauzá's three albums of remakes with his Afro-Cuban Jazz Orchestra (in reality, they were the old Afro-Cubans of Machito). During these recordings, Rudy Calzado again took over the microphone and, poking fun at the passage of time and its toll, he sang with his clean and powerful voice from the highest range possible. After Bauzá died, Calzado kept the band together for a while, continuing with their work.

In these last decades, at another extreme and from other generations and schools, the Latin jazz of New York has embraced such talented musicians as the trumpet and conga player Jerry González and his Fort Apache Band, the virtuoso Dominican pianist Michel Camino, the young timbalist Ralph Irizarry, the trombonist and seashellist Steve Turré, the Panamanian pianist Danilo Pérez, and the Puerto Rican saxophonist David Sánchez. Jazz was also the venue for trumpet player Charlie Sepúlveda and for the Venezuelan pianist Edgard Simon, and it was in this space that trombonist Conrad Hewitt carried on the legacy of Barry Rogers. Here, too, we witnessed the premature departure of two extraordinary pianists: Don Grolnik of the United States and Jorge Dalto of Argentina. Old Cuban conga players, such as Patato Valdez and Francisco Aguabella, also entered the jazz arena, as did younger ones such as Daniel Ponce and Richie Flores, drummers Ignacio Berroa and Horacio "El Negro" Hernández, and trombonists Papo Vásquez and Jimmy Bosch. For those who fled Cuba—Paquito D'Rivera, Arturo Sandoval, and Gonzalo Rubalcaba among them—this became the musical style where they found shelter. Even Chucho Valdez, who pretended that he had never left the island, recorded frequently in New York for the already legendary producer René López. Beyond passing tastes and trends, therefore, there remains a Caribbean sound that forms an indelible part of the musical foundation of New York, and, at this point and for as long as people have ears to listen, the two are inseparable and interdependent.

Now the time has come to acknowledge the fundamental leader of salsa, the one who marked the beginning and end of many cycles, the true keeper of the keys of the Caribbean music that beats in New York: Eddie Palmieri. Palmieri's music seems to flow steadily through only one channel, without any detours or blockages. It forever flows cleanly and vigorously, transcending time, styles, and generational tastes.

For the past twenty-five years, the Piano-Man has never stopped experimenting and innovating. As would be expected, not all of his attempts have hit their mark, but neither has he fallen too far from the bull's-eye. When he worked on his instrumental albums (*Palmas*, *Areté*, and *Vórtex*), many of the pieces left us with the sensation of something unfinished, as if the band were waiting for a sonero and chorus. But what a band and what solos and montunos! Other recordings such as *El rumbero del piano*, too "commercial" for the tastes of the most orthodox, or *Eddie Palmieri & Friends, Live*, too free and laid-back for those who like something more conventional, or *Masterpiece*, recorded in collaboration with Tito Puente (the Master's last and unfinished album), make evident the immense range Palmieri was capable of and the genuine richness of talent he had at his disposal. More recently, when he decided to update the sounds of his original Perfecta, he found a way to respect the nearly forty-year-old arrangements with an almost cloisterlike fidelity and yet to combine them with the purest of his jazz experiments of these last decades. He found again the perfect synthesis, the exact yoke that would bring together and balance all of the elements that converged into this music that we call salsa. For those individuals who even now still deny the existence of salsa, Eddie Palmieri is its most powerful and lasting proof.

The Endless Rumba

Over the last quarter-century there have been numerous musicians on the salsa scene. Singers, soloists, interpreters, composers, arrangers, and bandleaders all have enjoyed their dose of fame and applause. In most cases, obviously, that fame has been limited and brief, but in others the consecration of glory seems to have reached the next level. I hope more of this happens soon. Meanwhile, across the street, as it were, we find those who have left the spotlight, and among them are those who, despite their no longer being here, have attained a privileged passport to immortality. I thus honor the memory of Tito Puente, Arturo Chico O'Farrill, Ray Barretto, Mario Bauzá, La Lupe, Celeste Mendoza, and Daniel Santos; Rolando La Serie, Bobby Capó, Charlie Palmieri, Mongo Santamaría, Julito Collazo, Dámaso Pérez Prado, José Fajardo, Frank Grillo, Machito, Carlos Emilio Landaeta, Pan con Queso, Rafael Cortijo, and Luis María Frómeta Billo; Louie Ramírez and Juancito Torres; Jorge Dato, Barry Rogers, Don Grolnik, and José Rodríguez; Pete "El Conde" Rodríguez, Néstor Sánchez, Chivirico Dávila, Yayo El Indio, and Santos Colón; Ernie Agosto, Carlos Tabaco Quintana and Joe Ruiz; Virgilio Martí, Roberto Rodríguez, Rubén González, Manuel Licea, Puntillita, Francisco Repilado, and Compay Segundo; together with Catalino Curet "El Tite" Alonso, without a doubt the greatest composer that salsa has ever known.

More fully, we must add to the list three unique voices, now absent, without whom this music would have rung out with less volume, less joy, and less truth.

On a sleepy May afternoon (May 13, 1987) in Santurce, Puerto Rico, while watching cartoons on television with his mother, Doña Margarita, Ismael Rivera passed away. He was only fifty-six years old. They said that all he had left was his mother and that his last days had been marked by suffering and solitude. After his last meaningful albums from the 1970s, Rivera recorded little that was noteworthy. Failure and rejection began to be constants in his everyday life, and convinced that the world had turned its back on him, he chose that condition of abandonment in which death found him. The next day, when the news had spread like wildfire throughout the island, a crowd of unanticipated proportions filled the streets of Santurce. They carried him in their arms all the way to the cemetery in the longest, best attended, and most deeply felt procession that Puerto Rico has ever known. The mourning was expressed through song and dance with the rhythm of the bomba and plena. Choruses sang, amid shouts of "Ecuaje!" the best-loved melodies of the most beloved "Maelo." Rivera was buried in Villa Palmeras, but not next to his colleague Rafael Cortijo, as had been his desire.

A year later, on June 25, 1988, tragedy once again cruelly struck the Puerto Rican people. That day, Héctor Lavoe returned to San Juan after a concert in the Coliseum Rubén Rodríguez in Bayamón, a concert that the critics had labeled a failure. Lavoe went up to his room on the eighth floor of the Hotel Regency and jumped out the window. Conjectures about this attempted suicide soon followed: it was because of an excess of drugs or, perhaps, excessive sadness or the accidental death of his teenaged son, a terrible trauma that Lavoe was never able to overcome. In any case, Lavoe himself viewed his circumstances with a certain distance: he chose indifference and silence rather than offering any explanation or detail about his attempt at death. For the five years that followed that horrible afternoon when they carried him from the street bleeding and destroyed, nothing was ever the same for Héctor. It is preferable to erase any reference to this decade in which the singer stopped being a singer. His actual physical death—which was not necessarily the real one—occurred in New York in 1993, also in June. In contrast to Ismael Rivera, no crowds gathered for Lavoe's funeral procession. But the pain of his death was perhaps more profound and searing. The parade that said good-bye to him in the Bronx was so chaotic and loud that, according to rumors, Héctor was late for his own funeral, as a newspaper in San Juan wrote. If in life he epitomized the salsa singer, after his death he became its best legend and an eternal symbol through which salsa is exalted. So, even if people do not dance to Héctor Lavoe's music, they listen to it standing up.

Two posthumous albums are of very special interest. They both sound as if they were recorded live in a grand dance hall. In one, however, the ballroom was only a virtual one, a dramatic representation of the theater known as El Corso, that emblematic venue of New York salsa during the 1970s. El Corso was also the site for the performance of the musical titled *Who Killed Héctor Lavoe?* which was staged at the end of the 1990s; it was based on a script by the director Pablo Cabrera, and Domingo Quiñones played the role of Lavoe. In addition to its other merits and its real transcendence, this musical remains meaningful because during a time when salsa was leaping into other territories, like the ultimate New York–style Broadway musical, this one performed salsa in accord with the impulses of one of its most defining and tragic heroes.

The other album, which was actually recorded in a dance hall, is *Héctor Lavoe Live*, released in 1997 on the unusual Jerry Masucci Music label, a subsidiary of Sony. I want to emphasize that this album contains the best of Héctor Lavoe, the intimate singer, the true friend and brother, which rarely comes across in his other albums. I also want to point out that in the recording studios, in which he left so many samples of his talent and sabor, Héctor rarely was able to open up and fully share his magic and genius. His jam-packed concerts were not the most comfortable venues for him, either. He usually limited himself to repeating the soneros, the phrasings, and styles that had become popular first through the records.

Most of the time—whether in Caracas, San Juan, or New York—it was obvious that he rushed to get out of the trance of the live performance, as if
the dark masses that applauded him were nothing more than ghosts or a
fleeting illusion. In the dance clubs, however, especially in those small and
enclosed places where he could see the faces of the dancers and they could
feed off one another's emotions—where he could have fun with the music
and the band without time limitations, without feeling rushed—Héctor
Lavoe was something else. He was unleashed, joyful, and irreverent, as if
in a caravan with no brakes and no holds barred, where everyone fit comfortably together, just as "El Timbalero" once sang: "cincuenta parados,
cincuenta de pie" (fifty standing up, fifty on their feet).

At the time of Lavoe's death, Willie Colón, his close friend in the early
years and companion to his fame, was touring Spain. Profoundly affected
by the terrible news, he could not help but write a sad obituary that the
Puerto Rican newspapers circulated widely:

> He graduated from the University of Refrains with high honors. Member
> of the Great Circle of Soneros, A Poet of the Street, honorary delinquent,
> hero and martyr of the Wars of Fried Offal where he courageously fought
> for many, many years. The "Captains of the Have-Nots" respected him.
> This is why they baptized him as "The Singer of all Singers." The be-
> ginners were afraid of him. When it came to "sweet-talk" Héctor Lavoe
> was a brave man. In business matters, friendship, and love, he was not.
> The people were complicit in this tragedy. Héctor could swear on your
> mother and everybody would laugh. They indulged him.
>
> The history of Héctor Lavoe was full of betrayals and disillusionment.
> The good looking jibarito [country boy] who drove all the women crazy,
> also wanted to be a "bad boy" of the barrio. With time the "small gifts"
> of his "friends" who were dealing became chains weighing him down,
> snares entangling him, and this led to a series of fatal repercussions
> that finally took hold of this young man who once sang to God Almighty
> with all of his heart. He was also betrayed by the business world: record-
> ing executives continued to live like oil barons, first selling his albums
> and then reselling them as CDs without paying royalties, while Lavoe
> languished in poverty; promoters enticed him with crumbs in order to
> sell tickets to the spectacles that were the concerts of "The Singer of
> all Singers" but that really only exhibited his agony; impostors tried to
> claim rights to the career and memory of Héctor Lavoe; the Latino legal
> community also ignored him when he appealed for protection from
> being exploited; and I, I also betrayed him by not having the courage to
> visit him in that condition.

But the death that truly shook the world—and in this case, the name goes beyond the confines of salsa—was that of Celia Cruz. In funeral ceremonies worthy of the feverish imagination of Gabriel García Márquez, the coffin of "La Reina de la Salsa" (the Queen of Salsa) was paraded through the major thoroughfares of Miami and New York before tireless multitudes who offered her all manner of tribute in a homage that lasted an entire week. As was usually reserved for heads of state or legitimate royalty, the highest civil and ecclesiastical authorities officiated. Every moment of silence was magnificently counterpoised with hours and more and more hours of salsa. Never—and it would be impossible to exaggerate this—never did a human being born in the Caribbean have such a farewell.

On the afternoon of July 16, 2003, the news spread rapidly. Even though we all expected her death, it was difficult to accept. We always need some time to process the loss of those whom we love, but how can one react to a radio announcer's solemn pronouncement—"Celia Cruz has died"—when it is followed by Celia singing, "Ah, ah, ah, no hay que llorar / la vida es un carnavaaaaaal!" (There's no need to cry, life is a carnival)? Death had never been so false.

Another anecdote comes to mind. The Fania All Stars were rehearsing for a fabulous concert in Madison Square Garden. There were numerous musicians, many stars among them, each making demands based on his or her stardom. The hours passed very slowly. Some yawned and others complained more than usual, but Celia was the exception. She remained serene without showing any exhaustion on her face; she did not even yawn. "What is she made of?" Rubén Blades asked himself as he observed her. When they all took the stage, they sang at half-strength. It was, after all, a rehearsal, and they did not want to exert too much effort. When it was her turn, Celia also modulated her effort, but her voice still came out fresh and so powerful that it rebounded through every corner, so that the sound engineers had to adjust their equipment. "What is she made of?" Blades repeated. And this leads us to the obligatory and recurrent question that always came up in those contexts: "How old *is* she"? This was the great mystery. Celia, a most flirtatious woman, would never reveal the best-kept secret in the Caribbean. Only the most recent obituaries have allowed us to discover that she was seventy-eight when she died. So she must have been about fifty-five at the time of the anecdote above. If she had had children, she could well have been the mother, perhaps even the grandmother, of many of us who were there. But no one among us doubted it: She was the youngest. "Does she have her portrait hidden in the basement?" I asked Blades. He replied, very assured and with a smile, "No, of course not, that wouldn't be necessary, she never gets old; she's always the same. She is timeless." And it was true: While all of us aged inexorably, Celia remained the same, recording every year with the same flowing voice and the same flowing spirit.

That was why Fania's disaster did not affect her greatly, as it did many of the great figures of the 1970s. As I wrote earlier, for salsa, "she was a gift . . . the best guarachera ever known, both before and possibly after salsa." And when I say "before and after," I mean to say "outside of it all," I mean "beyond." She had nothing to do with passing trends and changing styles. Celia Cruz was herself, a unique, eternal style, a unique, inimitable style. While all the other stars had to adapt to changes (of status, fee projections, and budgets), Celia continued recording—and selling—as if worldly things had nothing to do with her or, to put it better, as if she revolved within the orbit of her own rhythm and desire. She exceeded our imaginations. One Internet biography reads,

> Her numerous prizes and recognitions include an honorary doctorate from Yale University, another from Florida International University, and another from the University of Miami; nominations and Grammy awards; a star on the Walk of Fame in Hollywood; a statue in the wax museum in Hollywood; and a major avenue in Miami named Celia Cruz Way in her honor. One of her dresses is part of the permanent collection of the Smithsonian, a testimony of her high distinction and her unconventional sense of style. In addition, she also received the Lifetime Achievement Award of the Smithsonian Institution. In 1994, Celia was awarded the National Endowment of the Arts' National Medal of Arts by President Bill Clinton, the highest honor given to artists in the United States. . . . In 1999, ASCAP also honored Celia with one of the most prestigious awards of their society, the Award of Herencia Latina, for her enormous contribution to Latino music and her tremendous triumph of introducing her marvelous music to millions of listeners all over the world.

This is why there is very little that helps to explain what Celia meant to her followers. In the last interview that I had with her (for the Venezuelan television program *30 Minutes* on Channel 10), when her agelessness seemed a spectacular victory, even though rumors about her illness were beginning to emerge, I asked her about death. And Celia Cruz, in an unusual moment of immodesty, announced, "I will never die. . . . I am sure that every household has at least one of my albums. . . . And wherever there is an album of mine, I will always be there."

And she has been.

The last day of her funeral celebrations in New York, the mayor ordered the closing of Manhattan's prestigious Fifth Avenue—a gesture reserved for war heroes, presidents, and generals in their moments of apotheosis; for athletes of tremendous accomplishment; for astronauts back from the moon. Now, for the first time, the avenue was being closed for a singer, for a guarachera born in the Caribbean, on the island of Cuba, in a humble Havana barrio. Saint Patrick's Cathedral opened its doors for the solemn rituals performed by cardinals, and more than one future candidate for the presidency of the United States allowed his mourning to be photographed amid the throngs. Did this woman really represent so much power? What did she do in life to merit such homage? What was her great deed? One that was very simple yet, indeed, quite difficult: She offered unlimited joy and happiness to the millions of individuals who knew her in this world. All we needed to hear was her battle cry, "Azúcar!!!" (sugar) even before the music began to play, and we all responded, our spirits suddenly soothed and sweetened by her sustained and appreciative smile. Thus, when Celia Cruz returned to the avenue, the crowds that waited to say good-bye to her offered a strange and unusual tribute: They threw handful after handful of sugar (which mysteriously appeared in everybody's hands) onto the carriage as it passed. Manhattan's farewell to her was all sweetness.

Do you have one of Celia's albums at home?

To summarize a quarter-century of salsa in these brief pages is an impossible task, to say the least. Therefore, please accept this brief chronicle as an invitation that remains open, a sort of coda where all who were there are here—well, no, obviously, not all of them. Or see it as a map, an itinerary for a trip that we might take together sometime in the near future.

BASIC DISCOGRAPHY

Afro-Cuban All Stars. *A toda Cuba le gusta*. Wea/Atlantic/Nonesuch, 1997.

Apollo Sound. *Roberto Roena y su Apollo Sound 6*. International Records, SLP-00473.

———. *Roberto Roena y su Apollo Sound 9*. International Records, JMINT-924.

Asere. *Cuban Soul*. Indigo, 1998.

Bailatino. *Llegó . . . con todo Bailatino*. Faisan Music, 2003.

Barretto, Ray. *Que viva la música*. Fania Records, SLP-00427.

———. *Tomorrow*. Atlantic Records (double album).

———. *Barretto 50th Anniversary*. Sony, 2001.

Batacumbelé. *Con un poco de songo*. Chez Tierrazo Records, 1981.

Bauzá, Mario. *Tanga (12/91)*. Messidor, 1992.

Bebo y Cigala. *Lágrimas negras*. BMG/Arbola, 2003.

Betancourt, Justo. *Lo mejor de Justo Betancourt*. JM-00513.

Betancourt, Justo, and Mongo Santamaría. *Ubané*. Vaya Records, JMVS-44.

Blades, Rubén. *Maestra vida*. Vols. 1–2. Fania, 1980.

———. *Buscando América*. Elektra, 1984.

Blades, Rubén, and Willie Colón. *Canciones del solar de los aburridos*. Fania, 1981.

Bravo, Soledad. *Caribe*. Top Hits/Polygram, 1982.

Buena Vista Social Club. *Buena Vista Social Club*. World Circuit, 1997.

Charanga 76. *Encore*. TR Records.

Colón, Johnny. *Tierra va a temblar*. Cotique Records, CS-1082.

Colón, Willie. *El crimen paga*. Fania Records, SLP-00406.

———. *El juicio*. Fania Records, SLP-00424.

———. *Lo mato*. Fania Records, SLP-00444.

———. *Fantasma*. Fania, 1981.

Colón, Willie, and Rubén Blades. *Metiendo mano*. Fania Records, JM-00500.

———. *Siembra*. Fania Records.

Colón, Willie, and Celia Cruz. *Sólo ellos pudieron hacer este álbum*. Vaya Records, JMVS-66.

Colón, Willie, and Héctor Lavoe. *Vigilante*. Fania (USA), 1983.

Conjunto Libre. *Conjunto Libre*. Vols. 1–2. Salsoul Records.

Conjunto Céspedes. *Una sola casa*. Green Linnet, 1993.

La Conspiración, Orquesta. *La Conspiración de Ernie*. Vaya Records, VS-9.

Cuba, Joe. *Bang Bang Push Push*. Tico Records, SLP-1152.

————. *Lo mejor de Joe Cuba*. Tico Records, SLP-1197.

Descarga Boricua. *Descarga #2 a gozar*. RMM, 1996.

Dimensión Latina. *Dimensión Latina 75*. TH.

Dimond, Markolino. *Beethoven's V*. Cotique Records, CS-1075.

D'León, Oscar. *El Oscar de la salsa*. TH.

————. *El más grande*. TH.

————. *El sonero del mundo*. RMM, 1997.

Fania All Stars. *Nuestra cosa latina*. Fania Records, SLP-00431 (double album).

Feliciano, Cheo. *José "Cheo" Feliciano*. Vaya Records, VS-5.

————. *El arco iris de "Cheo."* Vaya Records, VS-55.

————. *Una voz . . . mil recuerdos*. RMM, 1999.

Ferrer, Frank. *Yerbabruja*. Guanin Records.

Ferrer, Pedro Luis. *Natural*. Escondida, 2006.

Grupo Folklórico y Experimental Nuevayorkino. *Conceptos en unidad*. Salsoul Records (double album).

————. *Lo dice todo*. Salsoul Records.

Grupo Niche. *Antología del Grupo Niche*. Sony Discos Inc., 2000.

Guaco. *Como era y como es*. Latin World, 1999.

Guayacán. *14 éxitos duros como Guayacán*. Universal Music, 1997.

Guerra, Juan Luis, and 4:40. *Bachata rosa*. Karen Records, 1990.

Harlow, Larry. *Abran paso*. Fania Records, SLP-396.

————. *Tributo a Arsenio Rodríguez*. Fania Records, SLP-00404.

————. *Salsa*. Fania Records, SLP-00460.

Kimbos. *Los grandes Kimbos con Adalberto Santiago*. Corique Records, JMCS-1091.

Lavoe, Héctor. *De ti depende*. Fania Records, JM-00492.

————. *Comedia*. Fania Records, JM-00522.

————. *Lavoe Strikes Back*. Fania, 1988.

————. *Héctor Lavoe Live*. Jerry Masucci Music, 1997.

López, Israel "Cachao." *Masters Sessions*. Vols. 1–2. Messidor, 1992.

Los Van Van. *Llegó . . . Van Van*. Havana Caliente Corp, 1999.

Mango. *Mango*. CBS.

Miranda, Ismael. *Así se compone un son*. Fania Records, SLP-00437.

Naranjo, Alberto, and El Trabuco. *Imagen latina*. León, 1989.

Naranjo, Alberto, and Latin Jazz Big Band. *Swing con son*. Obeso/Pacanins, 1996.

Naranjo, Alfredo, y el Guajeo. *Alfredo Naranjo y el Guajeo*. Latin World, 2000.

NG La Banda. *Salseando con Malena Burke y NG La Banda*. EGREM, 1988.

Olivencia, Tommy. *Tommy Olivencia 1977*. Inca Records, JMIS-1055.

Oquendo, Manny, and Conjunto Libre. *Increíble*. Salsoul Records, 1982.

———. *Mejor que nunca*. Milestone Records, 1994.

———. *On the Move*. Milestone Records, 1996.

Orquesta Broadway. *Pasaporte*. Coco Records.

Ortiz, Luis "Perico." *Super Salsa*. New Generation Records.

Pacheco, Johnny. *Diez grandes años*. Fania Records, SLP-00409.

———. *El maestro*. Fania Records, JM-00485.

Pacheco, Johnny, and Celia Cruz. *Celia y Johnny*. Vaya Records, VS-31.

Palmieri, Eddie. *La perfecta*. Alegre, SLPA-8170.

———. *Champagne*. Tico Records, SLP-1165.

———. *Lo mejor de Eddie Palmieri*. Tico Records, CLP-1317.

———. *La historia de Eddie Palmieri*. Tico Records, TSLP-1403.

———. *Sentido*. Coco Records.

———. *El sol de la música latina*. Coro Records.

———. *El rumbero del piano*. RMM, 1998.

———. *La perfecta II*. Concord Records, 2002.

Palmieri, Eddie, and Tito Puente. *Obra maestra*. RMM, 2000.

Poleo, Orlando. *Lo bueno de la vida*. Sony, 2001.

Puente, Tito. *Tito Puente toca y la excitante Lupe canta*. Tico Records, SLP-1121.

———. *Tito Puente y su orquesta de concierto*. Tico Records, CLP-1308.

———. *Tributo a Beny Moré*. Tico Records, JMTS-1425.

Puerto Rico All Stars. *Puerto Rico All Stars*. PRAS.

Quintana, Ismael. *Lo que estoy viviendo*. Vaya Records, JMVS-41.

Ramírez, Louie. *Louie Ramírez y sus amigos*. Cotique Records, JMCS-1096.

Ray, Richie. *Jala jala y boogaloo*. Vols. 1–2. Alegre, SLPA-8570/SLPA-8630.

Rivera, Ismael. *Traigo de todo*. Tico Records, CLP-1319.

———. *Eclipse total*. Tito Records, TSLP-1400.

———. *De todas maneras rosas*. Tico Records, JMTS-1415.

———. *Esto sí es lo mío*. Tico Records, JMTS-1424.

Rodríguez, Pete. *Lo mejor de Pete Rodríguez*. Alegre, SLPA-8780.

Rosario, Willie. *Live in Puerto Rico*. TV Discos, 2002.

Santa Rosa, Gilberto. *A dos tiempos de un tiempo*. Sony Discos, 1992.

———. *En vivo desde el Carnegie Hall*. Sony Discos, 1995.

Saxomanía. *El nazareno*. Carijazz Records, 2000.

Sonero Clásico del Caribe. Vols. 1–2. YVKCT Conmúsica, 001/004.

Sonora Ponceña. *Explorando*. Inca Records, JMIS-1060.

Spanish Harlem Orchestra. *Across 110 Street*. Libertad Records, 2004.

Super Típica de Estrellas. *Super Típica de Estrellas*.

Típica Ideal. *Vámonos pa' Senegal*. Artol.

———. *Fuera de este mundo*. Coco Records.

Típica Novel. *Lo mejor de la Típica Novel*. TR Records.

Típica 73. *Los dos lados de la Típica 73*. Inca Records, JMIS-1053.

———. *Intercambio cultural*. Fania Records.

Trabuco Venezolano. Vols. 1–2. YVKCT Conmúsica, 002/005.

Valentín, Bobby. *Bobby Valentín va a la cárcel*. Vols. 1–2. Bronco Records.

———. *Vuelve a la cárcel, 35 años después*. Bronco, 2002.

Valle, Orlando "Maraca." *Descarga total*. Warner Music France, 2000 (Europe), Ahí-Nama Records, 2000 (rest of the world).

Valoy, Cuco. *Salsa con Coco*.

Vargas, Wilfrido. *Punto y aparte*. Karem Records.

———. *En el Madison Square Garden*. Karem Records.

INDEX